OXFORD CONSTITUTIONAL THEORY

Series editors:
Martin Loughlin, John P. McCormick, and Neil Walker

Constitutional Referendums

OXFORD CONSTITUTIONAL THEORY

Series editors:
Martin Loughlin, John P. McCormick, and Neil Walker

One consequence of the increase in interest in constitutions and constitutional law in recent years is a growing innovative literature in constitutional theory. The aim of *Oxford Constitutional Theory* is to provide a showcase for the best of these theoretical reflections and a forum for further innovation in the field.

The new series will seek to establish itself as the primary point of reference for scholarly work in the subject by commissioning different types of study. The majority of the works published in the series will be monographs that advance new understandings of the subject. Well-conceived edited collections that bring a variety of perspectives and disciplinary approaches to bear on specific themes in constitutional thought will also be included. Further, in recognition of the fact that there is a great deal of pioneering literature originally written in languages other than English and with regard to non-Anglophone constitutional traditions, the series will also seek to publish English language translations of leading monographs in constitutional theory.

ALSO AVAILABLE IN THE SERIES

The Twilight of Constitutionalism?
Edited by Petra Dobner and Martin Loughlin

Beyond Constitutionalism
The Pluralist Structure of Postnational Law
Nico Krisch

The Constitutional State
N W Barber

Sovereignty's Promise
The State as Fiduciary
Evan Fox-Decent

Constitutional Fragments
Societal Constitutionalism and Globalization
Gunther Teubner

Constitutional Referendums

*The Theory and Practice of
Republican Deliberation*

Stephen Tierney

OXFORD
UNIVERSITY PRESS

Great Clarendon Street, Oxford, OX2 6DP,
United Kingdom

Oxford University Press is a department of the University of Oxford.
It furthers the University's objective of excellence in research, scholarship,
and education by publishing worldwide. Oxford is a registered trade mark of
Oxford University Press in the UK and in certain other countries

© S. Tierney 2012

The moral rights of the author have been asserted

First Edition published in 2012

Impression: 1

All rights reserved. No part of this publication may be reproduced, stored in
a retrieval system, or transmitted, in any form or by any means, without the
prior permission in writing of Oxford University Press, or as expressly permitted
by law, by licence or under terms agreed with the appropriate reprographics
rights organization. Enquiries concerning reproduction outside the scope of the
above should be sent to the Rights Department, Oxford University Press, at the
address above

You must not circulate this work in any other form
and you must impose this same condition on any acquirer

Crown copyright material is reproduced under Class Licence
Number C01P0000148 with the permission of OPSI
and the Queen's Printer for Scotland

British Library Cataloguing in Publication Data
Data available

Library of Congress Cataloging in Publication Data
Library of Congress Control Number 2012932662

ISBN 978-0-19-959279-1

Printed and bound by
CPI Group (UK) Ltd, Croydon, CR0 4YY

Links to third party websites are provided by Oxford in good faith and
for information only. Oxford disclaims any responsibility for the materials
contained in any third party website referenced in this work.

For Ailsa

Acknowledgements

Early work on this book was greatly assisted by a British Academy/Leverhulme Senior Research Fellowship awarded in 2008, which supported one year's research leave. It was with the grant of this award, and in particular the supportive comments of the Fellowship's referees, that I became more certain that the theoretical issues surrounding constitutional referendums were both important and neglected, and that the time was right for a monograph exploring how the proliferation of referendums offers important insights into the relationship between constitutionalism and democracy today.

Edinburgh Law School has been extremely supportive of the project, in particular my Dean at the time, Douglas Brodie, and his successor Lesley McAra, who encouraged my application for research leave and my application for research assistance to complete editorial work on the manuscript respectively. David Massaro provided assistance in the early stages of the project, and latterly the work of Dr Kasey McCall Smith has been invaluable in editing the footnotes in line with OUP style guidelines and for a range of other editorial comments.

A number of colleagues have helped me develop my ideas, beginning with participants in a workshop, 'Constitutional Referendums and Deliberative Democracy', which I organized at Edinburgh with Navraj Ghaleigh and Ailsa Henderson in 2008. I subsequently presented papers on themes from the book in seminars at the University of Quebec in Montreal, the International Institute for the Sociology of Law (IISL) in Oñati, and the Universities of Kent, Edinburgh, Lancaster, Hull, Westminster, Pompeu Fabra, and Oxford. Again, numerous participants in these events offered very helpful comments on my work in progress. Anonymous referees both for OUP and for the Modern Law Review, to which I submitted an early outline of some of my ideas, engaged positively and encouragingly with the key aims of the project. I am particularly indebted to Keith Ewing and Michael Keating who acted as referees for my British Academy/Leverhulme application; to Jelena Dzankic for comments on the Montenegro section in Chapter 6; and to Martin Loughlin and Neil Walker who each read a complete draft of the manuscript, giving supportive and insightful advice. Neil also provided very helpful comments on my draft MLR article.

OUP has been extremely professional in delivering the project to completion. Alex Flach has supported my key idea from the beginning and I am delighted that the book will be part of the recently inaugurated constitutional theory series which is now flourishing. I have also received a great deal of practical help from Natasha Knight and Sally Pelling-Deeves who have been unfailingly encouraging and extremely efficient throughout. The copy-editing work done by Joy Ruskin-Tompkins was also first-rate and has helped move the manuscript from the draft stage to publication very quickly indeed.

Finally, my wife Ailsa has been a source of constant support in every way, intellectual and otherwise. In the course of writing this book we have been graced by the birth of not one, but two children. The arrival of Liam and Daniel inevitably slowed down progress on the book, but they have also brought a sense of fulfilment I could scarcely have thought possible. Despite the vast number of other commitments with which she has been faced during this period, Ailsa has read numerous drafts and offered searching insights on the structure and content of the manuscript without which the end result would be immeasurably weaker. I am deeply indebted for all of her love and support.

Contents

Chapter 1	The Referendum Revival and the Constitutional Moment	1
Chapter 2	Beyond Representation: Constitutional Referendums and Deliberative Democracy	19
Chapter 3	Framing 'the People': Constitutional Referendums and the Demos	58
Chapter 4	Elite Control and the Referendum Process	98
Chapter 5	The Referendum Challenge to Constitutional Sovereignty	129
Chapter 6	External Influences on Constitutional Referendums	153
Chapter 7	Participation in Constitutional Referendums	185
Chapter 8	Framing the Substantive Issue in Constitutional Referendums	226
Chapter 9	Referendums and Constitutional Decision-Making	260
Chapter 10	Constitutional Referendums: The Deliberative Challenge	285
Appendix: Referendums from 1898–2011 cited in the book		305
Bibliography		313
Index		339

1

The Referendum Revival and the Constitutional Moment

I. INTRODUCTION

The use of referendums around the world has proliferated remarkably in the past 30 years. It has been estimated that of the 58 functioning electoral democracies with a population of more than three million, 39 had conducted at least one national referendum between 1975 and 2000.[1] Although in some places, such as California and Switzerland, they act almost as adjuncts to the legislature, a particularly notable development is that referendums are being deployed increasingly in the settlement of fundamental constitutional questions, and often in countries with no tradition of direct democracy. Taking stock of this new wave of 'direct constitutional democracy' we can identify four types of constitutional process where the referendum is regularly used today: the founding of new states, most recently Montenegro in 2006 and South Sudan in 2011; the amendment of constitutions or the creation of new ones, for example in Iraq in 2005; the establishment of complex new models of sub-state autonomy, particularly in multinational states such as Spain and the UK; and the transfer of sovereign powers from the state to international institutions, with referendum use proliferating in the accession to and ratification of European Union treaties.

In this book I address the challenge which this important and under-theorized feature of contemporary politics poses for constitutionalism, many of the empirical and indeed normative precepts of which are built upon the implicit presupposition of an exclusively representative model of government and lawmaking. In this context, the central focus of the book will be the relationship between constitutional referendums and democracy. As direct democracy is used increasingly to supplement, and in some situations to supplant, representative democracy, it is important to revisit the age-old

---

[1] Lawrence LeDuc, *The Politics of Direct Democracy: Referendums in Global Perspective* (Broadview Press 2003) 29.

but now somewhat outdated debate over the respective merits and demerits of these two models. I will ask whether constitutional referendums can be truly democratic as an instrument of republican government. For defenders of referendum democracy the very question is oxymoronic—referendums encapsulate the democratic ideal of government by the people. For critics, however, it is the democratic failings of referendums that represent their principal weakness as a mode of constitutional decision-making, and it is in light of this critique that referendums bear an overwhelmingly negative association within political and constitutional theory today. My task then is in large part a normative undertaking. Adopting republican theory as a benchmark, and supplementing this analysis with the recent and related turn in constitutional theory towards deliberative democracy, I ask how well does, and how better could, the referendum fit within a democratic constitutional system.

II. TOWARDS CIVIC REPUBLICAN DELIBERATION

The framework theory which girds and contextualizes my normative approach is that of constitutional theory—a tradition which is itself enjoying something of a renaissance. Constitutional theory is both immanent and functionalist in its focus. Its methodology and content are therefore each distinguishable from the substantive normativity implied by both republicanism and deliberative democratic theory. As a way of thinking, constitutional theory differs from political philosophy in that it is not an exercise in ideal theorizing from first, abstract principles. Rather, it is an attempt both to understand constitutionalism as a form of political practice, and to frame evaluations of how this practice works against its own internal logic.[2] However, the fact that constitutional theory is not a Platonic quest from original normative principles does not imply that it operates in a normative vacuum, detached from morally informed political debate; quite the contrary. It is the very contingency of constitutional theory, and the centrality of political practice to its essence, that makes inoculation of constitutional analysis from value judgement impossible. In this sense, the approach adopted in this book might be characterized as 'functional normativity'. By this is meant a constitutionalist analysis which accepts that even in functional terms any account of constitutional law must recognize that normative presuppositions are inherent within any exercise of constitutional creation, reform, or practice. To take one example of how the empirical characteristics of contemporary constitutional practice are shaped by

---

[2] Martin Loughlin, 'Constitutional Theory: A 25th Anniversary Essay' (2005) 25 OJLS 183.

underpinning, if not always clearly articulated, normative principle, we need only reflect upon how in the practice of contemporary constitutionalism the terms 'constitution' and 'democracy' are invariably conceptually juxtaposed. Debates over constitutionalism within democracies are inevitably about the good and the bad (or more often, the better and the worse), set against a model of good democratic practice. Even positivist accounts that focus upon explicandum[3] as opposed to critique, recognize democracy as one of the very building blocks of present-day public law.[4] But given that arguably the most important function of constitutional practice is to create and secure a democratic system of government against some vision of the good, then an evaluation of how well that democratic system is working by the normative standards it sets itself is key to such a functional analysis. And it is by these lights that this book will assess the normative implications in the shift to direct democracy within the contemporary state.

It is in adopting at the methodological level such a functional normativity that we will address the rise of the referendum from the perspective of our two related—and as traditions of political theory, more avowedly normative—theoretical traditions, each of which, it will be argued, are central to justifying the place of the referendum within broader systems of representative government. Republicanism has itself been the focus of a considerable revival in the past three decades, particularly by those scholars and political practitioners who sense that modern representative democracy is losing much of its legitimacy as an effective vehicle for popular government. Republicanism is of course a very broad church, but if we are to encapsulate an encompassing goal, commonly shared by almost all who would describe themselves as 'republican', it is the commitment to 'government by the people'. For some, the primary focus is upon securing this goal by way of representative institutions, be they parliaments,[5] or even courts.[6] Another strain, what we might call 'popular republicanism', tends to accentuate the particular importance of politically engaged citizens. This emphasis can have either an instrumental purpose, namely that a politically active people is better able to call governmental institutions to account, or a more idealistic conviction that such engagement is central to the very idea of

---

[3] ibid 186.

[4] As seen, eg, in Loughlin's relational theory of sovereignty and in his focus upon constituent power and responsible government as foundational to the very idea of public law. Martin Loughlin, *Foundations of Public Law* (OUP 2010).

[5] Adam Tomkins, *Our Republican Constitution* (Hart Publishing 2005); Richard Bellamy, *Political Constitutionalism: A Republican Defence of the Constitutionality of Democracy* (CUP 2007).

[6] Philip Pettit, *Republicanism: A Theory of Freedom and Government* (OUP 1997); John Rawls, *Political Liberalism* (Columbia University Press 1993).

citizenship and the fuller realization of the individual as a political person.[7] It is this latter tradition of popular or civic republicanism—combining both its instrumental and inherent dimensions—which I will use to assess immanently the value of the referendum to contemporary democratic constitutionalism; and later in the chapter I argue further that a civic republican approach is particularly useful in assessing specifically *constitutional* referendums.

Deliberative democracy is an area of constitutional theory that has also been the focus of much recent attention. If we are to try to identify a principle that unites deliberative theorists across the spectrum it is that decision-making is best made in an open and reflective manner, where participants listen as well as speak, and in doing so are amenable to changing their positions. Deliberative democratic theory, like republicanism, encompasses many differing voices, from elite-focused accounts that tend to centre upon the decision-making of legislators, judges, and the like,[8] to those which are more concerned with the feasibility of 'popular deliberation' through which ordinary citizens can be directly engaged in the democratic process.[9] It is this latter approach, 'popular deliberative democracy', which, as a complement to civic republicanism, will be my focus as I ask whether constitutional referendums can meet the deliberative challenge. For Elkin, the principal weakness in deliberative theory is 'a lack of deep engagement by theorists with the question of how a political order that revolves around deliberation . . . will actually work'; or as he puts it: 'politics is precisely what ideal theory seeks to avoid'.[10] We are looking precisely at how deliberation might work within political practice; specifically in the engagement of citizens within constitutional decision-making.

In other words, as an exercise in constitutional theory, this book looks immanently at constitutional practice, assessing it by its own light. But since this by necessity implies some form of normativity I will thicken this analytical account by deploying recent turns in both republican and deliberative theory—both of which pose their own difficult challenges for referendum democracy. What I propose is a hybrid model of assessment

---

[7] Cass R Sunstein, 'Beyond the Republican Revival' (1988) 97 Yale LJ 1539; Sanford Levinson, *Our Undemocratic Constitution: Where the Constitution Goes Wrong (and How We the People Can Correct It)* (OUP 2006).

[8] John Rawls, 'The Idea of Public Reason Revisited' (1997) 64 U Chic L Rev 765; Amy Gutmann and Dennis Thompson, *Democracy and Disagreement* (Harvard University Press 1996).

[9] Benjamin R Barber, *Strong Democracy: Participatory Politics for a New Age* (University of California Press 1984); Bruce Ackerman, *We the People: Foundations* (Harvard University Press 1991); David Miller, *Citizenship and National Identity* (Polity Press 2000); John S Dryzek, *Deliberative Democracy and Beyond: Liberals, Critics and Contestations* (OUP 2000).

[10] Stephen L Elkin, 'Thinking Constitutionally: The Problem of Deliberative Democracy' (2004) 21 Social Philosophy and Policy 39, 40.

that adopts complementary elements of both. This allows me further to refine the key question this book will attempt to answer: can the referendum, from the perspective of civic republican deliberative democracy, be an appropriate mechanism with which to make democratic constitutional decisions, and if so when and how?

Although there is a considerable body of literature on the subject of referendums, theoretical assessments are fairly sparse, and in particular no systematic analysis from the perspective of constitutional theory has so far been undertaken.[11] Most of the existing work takes the form of empirical studies by political scientists and a number of these offer insightful accounts of the recent rise of referendums, how referendums are used, their impacts upon voters etc.[12] Mendelsohn and Parkin's collection of essays was one of the first to address referendums in thematic ways but, again, here the concerns of their book are mainly, and perfectly appropriately, those of the political scientist, focusing upon the important issues of electoral behaviour and the political motives and power of elite actors.[13] In the same field we also find useful case-by-case studies.[14] Many of these again are empirical contributions that address in detail the use of referendums in specific states or regions.[15]

---

[11] The most notable theoretical accounts in the tradition of political theory are: Markku Suski, *Bringing in the People: A Comparison of Constitutional Forms and Practices of the Referendum* (Martinus Nijhoff 1993) see esp 30–4; and Maija Setälä, *Referendums and Democratic Government. Normative Theory and the Analysis of Institutions* (Macmillan Press 1999).

[12] Francis Hamon, *Le Référendum: Étude Comparative* (LGDJ 1995); Ian Budge, *The New Challenge of Direct Democracy* (Polity Press 1996); LeDuc, *The Politics of Direct Democracy*; Matt Qvortrup, *A Comparative Study of Referendums: Government by the People* (2nd edn, Manchester University Press 2005); David Altman, *Direct Democracy Worldwide* (CUP 2011).

[13] Although the chapter by Brian Galligan in this collection does attempt to address the specificity of constitutional referendums. Brian Galligan, 'Amending Constitutions through the Referendum Device' in Matthew Mendelsohn and Andrew Parkin (eds), *Referendum Democracy: Citizens, Elites, and Deliberation in Referendum Campaigns* (Palgrave 2001) 109–24.

[14] David Butler and Austin Ranney (eds), *Referendums Around the World: The Growing Use of Direct Democracy* (Macmillan Press 1994); Michael Gallagher and Pier Vincenzo Uleri (eds), *The Referendum Experience in Europe* (Macmillan Press 1996).

[15] eg on Europe: Kris Kobach, *The Referendum: Direct Democracy in Switzerland* (Dartmouth Publishing 1993); Hanspeter Kriesi, *Citoyenneté et démocratie directe* (Seismo 1993); Anders Jenssen et al, *To Join or Not to Join: Three Nordic Referendums* (Scandinavian University Press 1998); Simon Hug, *Voices of Europe: Citizens, Referendums, and European Integration* (Rowman & Littlefield 2002). On New Zealand: Alan Simpson (ed), *Referendums: Constitutional and Political Perspectives* (Victoria University of Wellington 1992). In the US context, see: Thomas Cronin, *Direct Democracy: The Politics of Initiative, Referendum and Recall* (Harvard University Press 1989); Shaun Bowler, Todd Donovan, and Caroline J Tolbert (eds), *Citizens as Legislators: Direct Democracy in the United States* (Ohio State University Press 1998); John Haskell, *Direct Democracy or Representative Government?* (Westview Press 2001). On South America: Altman, *Direct Democracy Worldwide*. And on Canada: Patrick Boyer, *The People's Mandate: Referendums and a More Democratic Canada* (Dundurn Press 1991); Richard Johnston et al, *The Challenge of Direct Democracy: The 1992 Canadian Referendum* (McGill-Queen's University Press 1996). For references to other works written in German and

With the emergence of the referendum as such an important feature of the constitutional landscape across so many states, it is perhaps surprising therefore that the voices of constitutional theorists have largely been silent.[16] My quest in this book is to go beyond existing accounts of political practice, while drawing upon the helpful empirical and analytical findings that these works have produced. I do not propose to extract the referendum as an exotic constitutional device, detachable in some way from, or contrastable with, the broader system of representative constitutionalism operating within the state. Instead, the referendum is fully entwined with the changing dynamics of contemporary representative government as some of the established certainties both of constitutional supremacy and of citizen trust and efficacy erode in the face of normative, political, and economic pressures which today affect the established contours of statal constitutionalism. One key task then is to consider referendums in the context of the balance of power between legally codified constitutionalism on the one hand and active political capacity on the other, an issue which is itself of broader interest for theorists in an age of constitutional flux,[17] particularly as, both beyond and below the state, new constitutional actors enter the stage in processes of constitutional globalization.[18] The referendum in this sense becomes in fact a fascinating case study with which to address a changing normative architecture in which older territorial, institutional, and identificatory certainties which underpinned the unitary and hierarchical order of the constitutional state become ever more insecure and in which citizens increasingly look to new and often direct forms of political engagement to compensate for the perceived democratic failings of traditional constitutional models.

III. DIRECT DEMOCRACY IN AN AGE OF INSTABILITY

It is not a purpose of this book to explore in any depth *why* the referendum has emerged as such a key player in contemporary constitutional practice, but the reference to a changing normative order does lead us to think about

---

Italian see Simon Hug, 'Some Thoughts About Referendums, Representative Democracy, and Separation of Powers' (2009) 20 Constitutional Political Economy 251, 251–2.

[16] And it seems that this is a propitious time for a theoretical intervention. One scholar of referendums has recently concluded that much of the debate within political science as to the merits of referendums is in some respects at a 'dead end', having failed to ask the right questions. Simon Hug, 'Some Thoughts About Referendums, Representative Democracy, and Separation of Powers', 262.

[17] Martin Loughlin and Neil Walker (eds), *The Paradox of Constitutionalism* (OUP 2007).

[18] Neil Walker, Jo Shaw, and Stephen Tierney (eds), *Europe's Constitutional Mosaic* (Hart Publishing 2011); Colin Warbrick and Stephen Tierney (eds), *Towards an International Legal Community?: The Sovereignty of States and the Sovereignty of International Law* (BIICL 2006).

this question, even if only by way of speculation. In particular, it is notable that some of the trends that seem intuitively to have influenced this phenomenon also speak to the health or indeed infirmity of contemporary democracy.

First, we might note that there are three ways in which the proliferation of constitutional referendums (across the four constitutional processes outlined) is occurring. One is the increased application of ad hoc or discretionary referendums in states where the constitution does not require their use. An example is the UK, which hosted two referendums in 2011, one a statewide poll on the voting system and another in Wales on the devolution of further powers to the National Assembly. Another example is the Netherlands which, in 2005, conducted its first ever referendum, on the draft European Union Constitutional Treaty. Second is the growth in the number of constitutions that now mandate their use, a trend we find in the new orders emerging in Central and Eastern Europe after 1989. And third is the promotion of the referendum by international institutions as they intervene in post-conflict processes around the globe, for example in Bosnia-Herzegovina (1992), East Timor (1999), Montenegro (2006), and South Sudan (2011).

In some respects the rise of the referendum is clearly a product of circumstance. For example, one key driver was the break-up of multinational states which coincided with the collapse of communism in Europe. In this context the referendum offered dissenting political actors a vehicle for popular revolt, legitimizing and in due course foreclosing acts of constitutional rupture through direct popular intervention. A common usage for the referendum over the past quarter of a century, therefore, has been in the creation of new states and their subsequent constitutions, as well as the move to liberal democracy by many of the former USSR's satellite states. From 1989 to 1993 there were at least 16 referendums in Yugoslavia.[19] An additional 31 referendums were posed in Eastern Europe (six) and on the territory of the former Soviet Union (25). Of these 31, 12 were on sovereignty or independence, 7 on new constitutions or forms of government, and 12 dealt with policy matters.[20]

Another source for the spread of constitutional referendums has been European integration. The period since the early 1990s has also been one of fairly intense treaty-making within the EC/EU. Since the constitutions of some member states—most notably Denmark and Ireland—in effect

---

[19] It is difficult to be too precise; the referendum was used as a political tool by rival political actors at this time and the use of unofficial polls by small regions proliferated.

[20] Henry E Brady and Cynthia S Kaplan, 'Eastern Europe and the Former Soviet Union' in Butler and Ranney (eds), *Referendums Around the World: The Growing Use of Direct Democracy*, 180.

mandate referendums ahead of the ratification of such treaties, in this context again referendums emerge simply as the indirect result of other political processes.

But these three factors do not tell the whole story. As we have observed, an increasing number of states, including those emerging by way of referendum in Central and Eastern Europe, have seen fit to include the referendum in new constitutions as a key instrument of constitutional amendment. In other words, the referendum was not only instrumentally useful in the overthrow of communism or the securing of independent statehood, it retained sufficient salience to be included in the post-revolutionary constitution. There are, therefore, several features which suggest that the growth of the constitutional referendum is not simply a short-lived consequence of a particularly intense period of 'sovereignty politics'. One is the very fact that they came to be seen as an essential part in almost every move to new statehood by a sub-state people (one notable exception is the dissolution of Czechoslovakia, where the parties could not agree on a referendum question[21]). This can be contrasted with earlier periods of state-making in the twentieth century after both the First and Second World Wars, when the referendum was rarely used, even in the face of widespread empire collapse. This suggests that by the late twentieth century for the first time the referendum had become for many an automatic part of constituent constitutionalism and even of the constitutional amendment process. Second, another feature of the referendum revival is the influence of international actors in these processes. We see this in the international community's norm-creation processes, particularly in Europe, and in intervention in the cases mentioned earlier. Another element is the application of the referendum by countries with little or no constitutional tradition of using the referendum, but which now seem increasingly inclined to turn to the referendum at important constitutional moments. The political capital to be made from demanding a referendum and the danger in denying one suggests that this development is not only a consequence of political manoeuvring but of the changing expectations of citizens.

It seems, therefore, that while remaining mindful of the historical contingency of much recent referendum use, we also need to locate the rise of the referendum within broader changes in contemporary democratic practice and critique. One trend that has been identified is the increasing sophistication of contemporary electorates through better education and access to information. Dalton has called this development 'cognitive mobilisation'

---

[21] Stephen White and Ronald J Hill, 'Russia, the Former Soviet Union and Eastern Europe: The Referendum as a Flexible Political Instrument' in Gallagher and Uleri (eds), *The Referendum Experience in Europe*, 157–60.

and argues it is leading to stronger popular pressure for a greater say in governmental decision-making.[22]

If public demand is a factor, then another reason for referendum proliferation may be increasing disaffection among voters towards conventional representative politics. There is certainly evidence of a loss of public trust and efficacy within democracies, which has been well documented by political scientists.[23] Mendelsohn and Parkin identify both cognitive mobilization and heightened scepticism as important factors behind the rise of 'referendum democracy'. In their analysis: '[i]t is... likely... that a shift in political attitudes has taken place, the effect of which has been to make citizens either more confident in their ability to make key policy decisions or less confident in the ability of their elected representatives to do so'.[24] Various trends seem to have heightened citizen dissatisfaction with representative government: the elite monopolization of policy-making; the ever more efficient communications machinery of government that seems to be increasingly manipulative in 'spinning' stories; the expanding influence of big business in the political process; the hiving-off of government functions to technocratic and semi-private agencies, with concomitant breaks in the chain of accountability; the fall away in respect for the standards of behaviour of elected representatives; and the incongruous results within certain electoral systems which do not seem to reflect voter preferences. The parallel decline in levels of party membership and electoral turnout is therefore no coincidence.

Globalization has also nourished citizen disaffection with politics as people see power move away from the state not just to supranational 'constitutional' sites but also to private transnational corporations and structures. It seems, therefore, that the revitalization of direct democracy is in part a reaction not just to the declining standards of representative democracy but also to its emasculation in a world where its capacity for power is diminishing. It is interesting that the ad hoc referendum has emerged particularly as a feature of the recent EU constitution-making process, where France as well as the Netherlands turned to direct democracy for the draft EU Constitutional Treaty, even though the decision to hold a referendum was within the discretion of the French president and not

---

[22] Russell J Dalton, *Citizen Politics in Western Democracies: Public Opinion and Political Parties in the US, UK, Germany and France* (2nd edn, Chatham House 1996). See also Ronald Inglehart, *The Silent Revolution: Changing Values and Political Styles Among Western Publics* (Princeton University Press 1977).

[23] Neil Nevitte, *The Decline of Deference: Canadian Value Change in Cross-national Perspective* (University of Toronto Press 1996).

[24] Matthew Mendelsohn and Andrew Parkin, 'Introduction' in Mendelsohn and Parkin (eds), *Referendum Democracy* 1, 6.

mandated by the constitution. The acts of rebellion we saw in the Dutch and French processes and in Ireland over the subsequent Lisbon Treaty also hint at a growing popular disquiet with the trajectory, or at least the process, of integration.

The debacle of the draft Constitutional Treaty also reminds us that in recent times referendum use has begotten its own further proliferation. In the first place, precedents are being created.[25] We see this in the UK, for example, particularly in respect of devolution matters. Also, the use of referendums in Slovenia, Croatia, and Bosnia-Herzegovina, as well as in the former Soviet republics, in moves towards statehood seem to have made direct popular consultation an automatic assumption today for sub-state nationalist movements looking for statehood. There can also be a domino effect, where the proposal of a referendum in one state can pressurize others into holding one. President Chirac's decision to initiate a popular vote on the draft Constitutional Treaty can be explained in part by political pressure arising from the earlier commitment of the UK to hold a referendum. We see this also at the level of constitution-making. Surely one of the reasons why the referendum was introduced so systematically as a feature of constitutional amendment in the first constitutions to emerge in the new states of Central and Eastern Europe after 1989 was that it had been deployed to secure independence; once popular consultation had become part of state-framing processes it was easier to argue for, and harder to resist, its retention for constitution-framing exercises; and the people emerging from undemocratic models of government were in many cases reluctant to hand constitutional power back exclusively to elites. As other constitutions emerged, one example followed another, and the entrenchment of the referendum in the constitutional amendment process became again an almost universally adopted principle throughout the region, and one that has since been adopted more broadly, for example, in the new constitutions of Iraq and East Timor.

Finally, it seems that technology has been and is likely increasingly to be a factor in demands for more direct democracy. Anthony Giddens has observed that '[t]he downward pressure of globalization introduces not only the possibility but also the necessity of forms of democracy other than the orthodox voting process'. In his view referendums are one of the 'experiments with democracy' resulting from this by which government and citizens can 're-establish more direct contact' with one another.[26] Certainly,

---

[25] Morel talks of the 'politically obligatory' referendum: Laurence Morel, 'The Rise of Government-Initiated Referendums in Consolidated Democracies' in Mendelsohn and Parkin (eds), *Referendum Democracy*, 60–2.

[26] Anthony Giddens, *The Third Way: The Renewal of Social Democracy* (Polity Press 1998) 75.

with people taking part more and more in informal online polls, engaging more directly in politics through social networking, blogging, and micro-blogging etc,[27] the notion that their only engagement in constitutional politics should come indirectly through periodic representative elections is, for many, ever more incongruous.

IV. CONSTITUTIONAL REFERENDUMS

The category of 'constitutional' referendums is a broad one.[28] I take it to mean any direct citizen vote on the specific issue of constitutional change or constitutional creation.[29] In the context of the referendum–democracy nexus which I concentrate upon throughout the book, it is important to begin by distinguishing between two types of constitutional referendum which contain, respectively, very different implications for constitutional sovereignty. It is also in this context that what I have called a 'civic republican' approach to evaluating referendums will be further explained.

The referendum operating as an instrument of constitutional amendment either in place of, or alongside, parliamentary mechanisms (which may include, for example, a referendum used in the transfer of established constitutional powers to supra-state bodies), operates wholly within existing constitutional structures. As such, these are referendums internal to the constitution. By contrast, referendums deployed in the creation of new constitutions or new states are involved in processes which transcend the existing order, and can be said to supplant the constitution, becoming in some sense external to it. We might term these types of referendum 'constitution-changing' and 'constitution-framing', respectively.

The latter in particular causes us to reflect upon the concept of constitutional sovereignty. Kalyvas introduces a distinction between 'command sovereignty' and 'constituent sovereignty'.[30] The former is the classical model of the final word, central to modernist accounts of the legal system

---

[27] Robin Effing, Jos van Hillegersberg, and Theo Huibers, 'Social Media and Political Participation: Are Facebook, Twitter and YouTube Democratizing Our Political Systems?' (2011) 6847 Lecture Notes in Computer Science 25. See this volume more generally, which contains the proceedings of an International Conference in Delft on 'Electronic Participation'.

[28] As is that of 'referendum' more generally. By referendum I mean any poll where citizens vote on a specific issue rather than for a representative. The terms 'plebiscite' and 'direct democracy' will occasionally also be used largely synonymously in this general sense.

[29] In a similarly broad way the Venice Commission of the Council of Europe has defined constitutional referendums as: 'popular votes in which the question of partially or totally revising a State's Constitution... is asked'. European Commission for Democracy Through Law (Venice Commission), *Guidelines for Constitutional Referendums at National Level* (11 July 2001) COE Doc CDL-INF(2001) 10, I.

[30] Andreas Kalyvas, 'Popular Sovereignty, Democracy and Constituent Power' (2005) 12 Constellations 223, 224.

as *Rechtsstaat*. Within the Westphalian tradition of state-building, as conceptualized by Kelsen[31] and Hart,[32] it is considered that any legal order must have an absolute and final arbiter, and hence the sovereign is characterized, for example by de Spinoza, as he who 'has the sovereign right of imposing any commands he pleases'.[33] Constituent sovereignty, however, is for Kalyvas a neglected model which is concerned not with 'coercive power' but rather 'constituting power':

> Thus, contrary to the paradigm of the sovereign command that invites personification and can better be exercised by an individual who represents and embodies the unity of authority—from the ancient *imperatore* to the king to the modern executive—the constituent power points at the collective, intersubjective, and impersonal attributes of sovereignty, at its cooperative, public dimension.[34]

This involves seeing the sovereign as 'constituent subject', as the one who shapes not only the governmental structure of a community but also its juridical and political identity;[35] in other words, as the source of the constitution and of its authority.

It seems that different types of constitutional referendum are better conceptualized by either the 'command sovereignty' or 'constituent sovereignty' models, respectively. On the one hand internal, constitution-changing referendums, as part of a broader amendment process, are more accurately encapsulated by the command sovereignty model. The people are engaged directly in producing constitutional law, but it is highly debatable that they are engaged explicitly in '*constituting* power'. Rather, the use of the referendum is provided for by the constitution, its process is regulated by that constitution, and its result takes effect within the normative order of that constitution. As such, the command sovereignty of that constitution is not in any way overridden or replaced by the referendum. By contrast, the constitution-framing referendum, which intervenes in the making of a new constitution (Iraq 2005) or a new state (Eritrea 1993, East Timor, Montenegro, South Sudan) is categorically distinct as a popular constitutive act which brings about a new order.

The term 'popular sovereignty' is frequently used to describe 'referendum democracy'[36] in general. But such a generalization is, in light of this distinction, a category mistake, and one of some significance. There is

---

[31] Hans Kelsen, *The Pure Theory of Law* (2nd edn, M Knight tr, University of California Press 1967).

[32] HLA Hart, *The Concept of Law* (Clarendon Press 1961) 89–96.

[33] Benedict de Spinoza, *A Theologico-Political Treatise* (RHM Elwes tr, Dover 1951) 207, cited by Kalyvas, 'Popular Sovereignty, Democracy and Constituent Power'.

[34] ibid 235–6.   [35] ibid 226.

[36] Mendelsohn and Parkin (eds), *Referendum Democracy*.

certainly a sense in which, whenever the people are directly engaged in any lawmaking process, their exercise of collective will-formation and expression acts as a symbolic reminder that constitutional authority finds its democratic legitimacy in the consent of the people. But at the same time we must not lose sight of the fact that 'sovereignty' refers to the ultimate source of legal power within a legal system, identifying second-order competence to determine authoritatively the status of first-order rules; and, therefore, any reference to popular 'sovereignty', to remain a coherent concept for legal theory, particularly within the elaborate constitutional frameworks that exist today, must be concerned precisely with those situations where 'the people' can be shown to exercise direct control over second-order lawmaking—in other words, acting to 'produce' sovereignty in Kalyvas's sense. Just as we must not elide first- and second-order rules, nor should we confuse the modes of their respective creation, nor the role citizens play in these different lawmaking processes.[37]

I am concerned here with both types of referendum, since each is in its own way a vehicle for constitutional politics. However, at various points throughout the book we will return to this distinction. It is important first in relation to defining the relationship between direct and representative democracy. Since constitution-changing referendums are constrained to operate within mainstream *representative* democracy, subordinate to the second-order rules that provide them with their normative competence, even the categorization of these referendums as an instance of *direct* as opposed to *representative* democracy is perhaps something of an oversimplification. In playing a role within a broader representative system of government, where the legal effect of the referendums is dependent upon the overarching hierarchy of the existing constitution, they should perhaps more accurately be portrayed as part of that representative system, since the effect given to the outcomes they produce is ultimately subject to the representative competence of constitutional institutions; most obviously legislatures, but also courts. It will be important to bear in mind that constitutional referendums do not emerge, therefore, from a political vacuum, creating a hard-and-fast distinction between direct and representative democracy. Direct democracy is almost always a rarely activated constitutional device which is produced within a broader representative system. For example, a common model of constitutional amendment is a hybrid involving a role not only for a referendum but also requiring the complementary endorsement of representative institutions.[38] Whereas direct democracy is

---

[37] This argument is presented further in Stephen Tierney, 'Constitutional Referendums: A Theoretical Enquiry' (2009) 72 MLR 360.
[38] eg Australian Constitution, s 128.

often presented in contrast to representative democracy, constitutional practice shows this to be a caricature; in complex modern systems the two operate in parallel.

But we should also be alive to the fact that the second type, polity-framing/constitution-framing referendums—which I will generally term 'constitutive referendums'—can manifest a people's direct democratic capacity to act as the supreme source of constitutional law in foundational constitutional acts. In this latter type the people act as original constitutional authors, bringing about a clear break in the old order; and whether forming new states or new constitutions they imbue the new construct with a new popular source of legitimacy.

Civic republicanism is useful to address the specifically 'constitutional' aspect of these referendums, whether they be of a constitution-changing or constitution-framing character. Despite their differences, both types are deployed in higher order lawmaking, albeit the former in modifying rather than supplanting an existing system. There are two features specific to this broad role that, from the perspective of civic republicanism, seem to offer a strong prima facie defence of the deployment of direct democracy in both constitution-changing and constitution-framing acts. The first concerns the importance of the issues at stake. Civic republicans committed to the goal of an active citizenry may argue that when matters involving the very framing or reframing of a democratic system of government, whether in whole or in part, is at stake, the direct engagement of the people either supplementing, or indeed in place of, representative institutions is appropriate. This builds upon work within the republican revival that focuses upon constitutional politics as distinct from ordinary politics and in doing so stresses the desirability of engaging more overtly with ordinary citizens, particularly at the constitutional level per Ackerman's distinction between 'the will of We the People' and 'the acts of We the Politicians'.[39] The second argument is that in such decisions, particularly where they involve truly fundamental or constitutive constitutional issues such as the founding of a new state, the transformation of the constitution, or even the transfer of sovereign powers beyond the state, the very identity of the demos can be implicated. What is meant by this is that a constitution can come to embody the political selfhood of the people. In this sense, as well as serving the functional purpose of framing a system of government, by being 'popular' in orientation the constitution can also take on a symbolic representational role, encapsulating the very identity of the people, while also embodying emblematically

---

[39] See Ackerman, *We the People: Foundations*, 10.

its collective settled will.[40] In turn, individuals come reflexively to identify with one another through their shared commitment to this constitution. It is, therefore, also in this context of the polity-building or nation-building potential of constitutional lawmaking that we must address constitutional referendums. When referendums are used to make or recreate constitutions they can themselves take on a vital nation-building role. In light of these high stakes, from a civic republican perspective there again appears to be a strong prima facie case for direct popular engagement.

These two features—the importance of the issues at stake and the 'identity-forming' potential of certain constitutional processes—are more evidently present in constituent referendums. As such, throughout the book the specific potential of the constituent referendum and the particular issues it can raise for the operation of both representative government and constitutional supremacy will be an important point of distinction. That said, our overall focus is more broadly upon constitutional referendums in general, and in this light we should also note that there is not always a hard-and-fast line between constitutive and non-constitutive constitutional referendums, with the latter also capable of raising fundamental questions and issues which can also touch upon the identity of a constitutional people.

One final point about constitutional practice that brings home this point is that even constitutive referendums do not emerge in a political or legal vacuum. In many cases, the referendum comes at the end of a process that was not necessarily from the beginning a self-consciously constitutive one, or at least not one where the success of constitutive aspirations was certain. In a number of situations the referendum is in fact invoked within one constitutional order but in the course of the constitutional process of which it is the culmination the referendum comes to take on constitutive potential, rupturing and supplanting the existing system. The open-ended constitutive potential of the constitutional referendum will be returned to, particularly in the context of sub-state nationalism, in Chapter 5.

V. OUTLINE

In Chapter 2 we will begin the task of addressing whether, from the perspective of republican democratic theory, the referendum can be an appropriate mechanism for the direct engagement of the mass public in processes of constitution-framing or changing. I will scrutinize the main

---

[40] Rosenfeld discusses how modernist constitutionalism has played the role of constructing a form of collective self that builds upon but is, in its unitary and unifying functions, also different from diverse pre-constitutional cultural and ethnic attachments. Michel Rosenfeld, *The Identity of the Constitutional Subject: Selfhood, Citizenship, Culture and Community* (Routledge 2010).

criticisms aimed at referendums and will begin to assess the strength of these against the normative benchmark of civic republicanism. I will also turn to deliberative democracy, asking if this turn in democratic theory which focuses upon the procedural dimension of political decision-making offers a way in which republican theory might be deployed to construct referendum processes that go some way to answer the main charges of their critics.

The application of the arguments and principles outlined in Chapter 2 will be the main task of Chapters 4 to 9. But first, in Chapter 3, we will address how the constitutional referendum implicates the very idea of 'the people'. In the ordinary course of representative democracy this concept tends to lie dormant. However, the constitutional referendum by definition implicates an anterior act of demotic border-drawing—the framing of the collective self who will perform an act of constitutional self-determination and in doing so explicitly articulate itself as a constitutional people. This is often uncontroversial, but in some cases, particularly in the context of constitutive referendums, the referendum can expose tensions in the boundary question.

In Chapter 4 we will begin to assess in detail the main criticisms of the referendum set out in Chapter 2. The first issue is control. A common trope in contemporary democratic theory is that referendums are fundamentally undemocratic because they are controlled by and open to the manipulation of elites. In this chapter I will explore this question further, arguing that the issue of control must be broadened from the political context to examine the broader interplay of constitutional competence and political capacity throughout the referendum process, looking at the referendum as a series of stages, and addressing how the complicated motives of political actors all impact upon the control issue. Chapters 5 and 6 explore the control issue further, addressing situations where the constitutional referendum intervenes in some of the most contested debates today about the nature of sovereignty in both its internal (constitutional) and external (state-focused) dimensions.

In Chapter 7 we return in detail to the question of how it might be possible to facilitate deliberation in constitutional referendums by engaging direct citizen participation actively and meaningfully. The chapter asks whether it is feasible to introduce elements of deliberative participation into a referendum process which can overcome the allegation that referendums serve simply to aggregate pre-formed preferences and thereby fail to foster meaningful deliberation. One major conundrum for democratic theory is that deliberation is widely thought possible only within small groups.[41] As Fishkin puts it, 'we seem to face a forced choice between

---

[41] The paradox that efforts to extend participation and decision-making power to the mass public in a referendum must come at the expense of meaningful deliberation was an issue even at the

politically equal but relatively non-deliberative masses and politically unequal but relatively more deliberative elites.'[42] This is the key dilemma which the chapter confronts by addressing both the opportunity for participation and the quality of participation feasible within a referendum process. The focus is upon referendum practice, considering the prospects for deliberation within a referendum as they might arise in different ways over a range of stages, across various settings, and by means of a plurality of modes.

Referendums are criticized not just for obvious process defects but also on the basis that the subject matter is open to manipulation, which makes it difficult, if not impossible, to put a fair question to the people. In Chapter 8 we address this issue, asking what factors contribute to the fairness, and hence the legitimacy, of a referendum question. One issue is the clarity and intelligibility of the questions and the impediments to achieving a clear question. But another equally important concern is that the referendum represents a meaningful choice between options which a plurality of people consider important and worth both deliberating over and voting on. A particular concern is divided societies; I will ask whether a referendum is ever appropriate in such an environment and if so what issue-framing and other process factors would be needed for such an act to meet the demands of deliberative theory.

Finally, in Chapter 9 we will consider the issue of decision-making. The goal of constitutional politics is, in the end, political action. And it is by the benchmark of good or bad decision-making that constitutional referendums must in the end be assessed. The decision-making power of the referendum provides, for its supporters, much of its appeal and, for its detractors, much of its threat. In this chapter we address how deliberative theorists face up to the moment of decision, viewing it as an inevitable part of the imperfect and difficult business of democracy. But we will also see that it is in the moment of decision-making that the referendum faces some of its most compelling criticisms from deliberative theorists. One danger I will address is that the referendum can be used to foreclose a political conversation that should be kept open. In this context I will consider respectively how mechanisms can be built into the process to make the referendum so far as possible part of an ongoing constitutional process. Another issue is the danger to minorities posed by the decision-making potential of a referendum. Here we will address the use of threshold rules requiring some level of support beyond merely 50 per cent plus 1 of those who turn out to vote.

---

time of Rhode Island's referendum on the new American Constitution. James S Fishkin, 'Deliberative Democracy and Constitutions' (2011) 28 Social Philosophy and Policy 242, 243.

[42] ibid 243–4.

Throughout I will try to test theoretical claims in light of empirical evidence and against concrete examples. I will also use case studies to help illustrate some of the problems that referendums present for contemporary constitutional democracy and also to show how, by careful planning and the efforts of political actors and ordinary citizens, process design can be shaped which will help overcome the democratic problems that have at times beset the application of the referendum. This task is not one that can be avoided by the constitutional lawyer or theorist. The constitutional referendum, it seems, is here to stay, and the undertaking with which we are faced is how to make the best of that reality.

2

Beyond Representation: Constitutional Referendums and Deliberative Democracy

I. INTRODUCTION

For some it is an almost intuitive assumption that referendums represent an ideal model of democracy; they give a directly determining voice to the demos in a way that captures neatly both the people's collective, popular sovereignty, and the political equality of all citizens. As Bogdanor puts it: 'in the last resort, the arguments against the referendum are also arguments against democracy, while acceptance of the referendum is but a logical consequence of accepting a democratic form of government'.[1] But in contemporary democratic theory, where representative democracy has become a commonly accepted synonym for democracy itself, the counter-argument—that referendums are democratically problematic, and for some inherently anti-democratic—has tended to enjoy stronger support. My key enquiry in this book is whether, from the perspective of civic republican theory, the referendum can be an appropriate mechanism for the direct engagement of the mass public as constitutional authors in processes of constitution-changing or constitution-framing, the latter including also polity formation. There are a number of steps that can lead us to an answer to this question. The first of these, which I will address in this chapter, is to consider how the referendum has been appraised within contemporary theories of democracy, setting out the key debates, and establishing points of further enquiry that will enable a fuller answer to be offered in the latter chapters of the book.

In Section II of the chapter, I will address three main concerns raised by critics of referendums: how they are controlled; how popular participation is engaged within a referendum process; and the conditions under which decisions are reached by way of direct democracy. These issues also highlight how attitudes towards direct democracy can vary from one democratic

---

[1] Vernon Bogdanor, *The People and the Party System* (CUP 1981) 93. For a similar point see also Dennis C Mueller, *Constitutional Democracy* (OUP 1996) 189.

tradition to another. Behind these contrasting views of referendums are in fact alternative prioritizations of the multiple, and possibly conflicting, values that underpin democracy as a normative principle; as Bernard Crick once put it: 'Democracy is perhaps the most promiscuous word in the world of public affairs.'[2] For example, the key democratic goal for liberals is the guarantee of what they take to be fundamental rights based upon the overriding value of individual liberty. Liberals are often sceptical or indeed fearful of popular politics,[3] and consequently favour the legal entrenchment of substantive political values. Alternatively, civic republicans are apt to place greater emphasis upon the active participation of citizens in politics as an imperative democratic good, leaving open the political space to popular self-determination.

It is important that these differences in emphasis should not be framed in a Manichaean way; they can be more a matter of orientation than dichotomy, and indeed among democratic theorists and practitioners we often find a blend of both, despite a tendency among commentators towards pigeonholing people as either/or.[4] For example, it is not true that popular democratic participation is rejected by most liberals, nor that individual liberty is spurned by republicans—many of whom would also consider themselves to be liberals—but simply that the former tend to prioritize the *substance* of political decisions vis-à-vis their impact upon individual rights as they see them,[5] and the latter are apt to place greater stress on *process*, contending that a strong democratic procedure, wherein the people are engaged and well informed, is necessary both to ensure accountable government and to sustain popular commitment to that system, strengthening citizen loyalty to, and identification with, the polity.[6] The important

---

[2] Bernard Crick, *In Defence of Politics* (Pelican 1964) 56.

[3] A tradition that can be traced back to Madison: James Madison, 'No 10: The Union as a Safeguard against Domestic Faction and Insurrection (continued)', *The Federalist Papers* (New York, 18 January 1788) no 10.

[4] An unfortunate recent trend in constitutional theoretical debate has been the misplaced attempt to forge a clear ideological line between 'liberals' and 'republicans'. In fact, these two traditions (as seen eg in the work of Rawls and Bellamy) have far more in common than this bi-polar caricature would allow. In light of this, the model of republicanism adopted here is intended to help explicate the potential, and it is hoped better enhance the opportunities, for enhanced citizen participation within a liberal democracy.

[5] As Dworkin puts it: 'democracy is a substantive, not a merely procedural, ideal'. Ronald Dworkin, *Is Democracy Possible Here? Principles for a New Political Debate* (Princeton University Press 2008) 134. For the argument that substantive values are the principal concern in the democratic theories of both Hobbes and Locke see Martin Loughlin, 'Towards a Republican Revival?' (2006) 26 OJLS 425, 429. By this approach a thicker notion of justice is prioritized over democracy itself: 'democracy is not the main process by which political justice is constituted or achieved, but is merely instrumental to the preservation and expression of that goal'. Allan C Hutchinson and Joel Colon-Rios, 'What's Democracy Got To Do With It? A Critique of Liberal Constitutionalism' (2007) 3(5) CLPE Research Paper 29/2007, 5 <http://ssrn.com/abstractid=1017305> accessed 11 July 2011.

[6] Benjamin R Barber, *Strong Democracy: Participatory Politics for a New Age* (University of California Press 1984).

conclusion for our present purpose is that the different prioritizati
emphasized respectively by liberals, republicans, and other democr
mean that there is no one gold standard model of democracy again
which one can assess objectively and definitively the merits or demerits of
referendums. Bourke has recently observed: 'Democracy can... only be
understood as historical in all its dimensions, subject at once to institutional
change and to changes in ideological perspective.'[7] One's preferred model of
democracy will in many ways shape one's attitude to referendums.

Insofar as it does represent a discrete democratic strain, I will explore
further in Section III the tradition of 'civic republican democracy', setting
out its key aims and values. I will argue that this is a useful turn in
constitutional theory both for offering a powerful democratic critique of
how contemporary representative democracy has been overpowered by
hegemonic interests and in highlighting the importance of popular engagement
in processes of constitutional change as a partial remedy for this
malaise. However, in light of Section II there will remain serious questions
as to whether the referendum is an appropriate vehicle with which to
generate such engagement, and in particular whether it is an instrument
capable of fostering meaningful popular deliberation. In Section III, therefore,
I will turn also to deliberative democratic theory, asking if this
development in political philosophy and practice, which focuses upon the
procedural dimension of political decision-making, offers a way in which
civic republican theory can be deployed to construct referendum processes
that go some way to answer the three criticisms of referendums raised in
Section II. Here I will set out key principles of deliberative democracy
that are particularly relevant to constitutional decision-taking, and begin
to explore how these might help overcome the democratic deficiencies
that can afflict the referendum process. This will set the scene for the
remainder of the book, where these principles will be applied in analysing
the practice of constitutional referendums by the lights of 'functional
normative value' (per Chapter 1) as instruments of popular engagement
in processes of constitutional change. Not until the end of the book
will we have a comprehensive picture of the democratic challenges facing
constitutional referendums, but by the end of this chapter we will have set
out a template with which to approach this issue from the perspective
of republican democracy, identifying the problems that need to be
addressed and the principles of deliberative democracy theory that should
be applied in assessing and improving the different elements of the referendum
process.

---

[7] Richard Bourke, 'Enlightenment, Revolution and Democracy' (2008) 15 Constellations 10, 13. See also John Dunn, *Setting the People Free: The Story of Democracy* (Atlantic Books 2005).

II. REFERENDUMS AND DEMOCRACY: BACKGROUND AND CRITIQUE

In this section we will address several critiques of referendums. Since these debates are informed by the particular democratic principles or traditions which are most meaningful to the intervener, conclusions can be heavily influenced by ideological predisposition. Therefore, before turning to specific critiques and in order to provide these with some additional contextualization, we need also to be attentive to the following issues and questions:

- *Principle or practice?* In the contemporary literature we can distinguish between two main types of criticism. The first is that referendums are, as a matter of principle, an inherently undemocratic alternative to representative democracy—an argument that would exclude them entirely as an adequate tool of democratic decision-making. A less categorical critique might concede the intuitive attractiveness of referendums in principle but contend that there are problems—perhaps amounting to a pathology—in the practice of referendums, stemming from one or more of the three objections listed earlier. I will attempt to distinguish between these models of critique as we meet them. It is important to identify whether what seems to be a problem with referendums in principle is in fact concerned more with how they are conducted, and hence whether such criticisms of referendums might be remediable by good process design.
- *Elitism?* A second issue is concerned with the extent to which opposition to referendums is in fact a symptom of an elitist approach to politics and a concomitant distaste for popular democracy. Does a principled objection to referendums stem from a deeper distrust of the direct engagement of the people in political decision-making altogether? The elision that is sometimes to be found between legitimate criticisms of referendum practice and an elitist rejection of popular participatory politics is an unfortunate one which I will try to untie.
- *A wider problem for democracy?* A third issue is to what extent the problems identified with referendums are in fact broader issues for democracy as a whole, whether representative or direct. Referendums, after all, emerge from broader systems of representative government. Furthermore, decision-making in large, pluralistic, and often divided democracies is by definition an imperfect exercise, and we should be attentive to any instances where referendums are singled out for criticism that is of more general application to the messy business of contemporary democracy.
- *The specificity of constitutional referendums.* And finally, do the problems identified with referendums vary from constitutional referendums to

ordinary referendums? Is it the case that some of the democratic concerns which apply in respect of the widespread use of referendums as an alternative to representative lawmaking do not apply, at least to the same extent, to the occasional use of referendums for constitutional matters, and in particular for constitution-framing processes ('constituent referendums') as defined in Chapter 1?

The simplistic assumption that the referendum embodies an ideal model of democracy has been contested since the early nineteenth century, when the trend began of demagogues and empire builders exploiting plebiscitary mechanisms to pursue political goals, a process we will discuss in Chapter 4. Such abuses are self-evidently undemocratic, but the more interesting criticisms of referendums today are those aimed at their use within *democratic* systems, where direct democracy is playing an increasingly prominent role within otherwise healthy representative systems.[8] The three main criticisms of referendums we encounter in the literature are that in contradistinction to the institutional design of representative democracy: they lend themselves by definition to elite control and hence manipulation by the organizers of the referendum—*the elite control syndrome*; that there is an in-built tendency of the referendum process merely to aggregate pre-formed wills, rather than to foster meaningful deliberation—*the deliberation deficit*; and that referendums consolidate and even reify simple majoritarian decision-making at the expense of, and potentially imperilling, minority and individual interests—*the majoritarian danger*. I will address each in turn.

(i) The elite control syndrome

A recurring criticism is that referendums promise popular power, including control over elites, but are themselves so open to manipulation as to make a mockery of that promise. This critique is obviously valid when dictators use referendums to consolidate power, but it is also powerful in relation to seemingly more democratic processes. The charge is that elites can dominate the process of referendums in such a way as to procure a particular result. By Lijphart's famous formulation, 'most referendums are both controlled and pro-hegemonic'.[9]

---

[8] Mendelsohn and Parkin have used the term 'referendum democracy' to emphasize how embedded the referendum now is within representative systems. Matthew Mendelsohn and Andrew Parkin (eds), *Referendum Democracy: Citizens, Elites, and Deliberation in Referendum Campaigns* (Palgrave 2001). Critics of this development include: John Haskell, *Direct Democracy or Representative Government? Dispelling the Populist Myth* (Westview Press 2001) and David Broder, *Democracy Derailed: Initiative Campaigns and the Power of Money* (Harcourt 2000).

[9] Arend Lijphart, *Democracies: Patterns of Majoritarian and Consensus Government in Twenty-One Countries* (Yale University Press 1984) 203. Lijphart was adopting Smith's classification criteria that consider a

The essence of this criticism is that 'elites' (which, as we shall see, is itself an elusive term), have an array of exclusive powers at their disposal, such as deciding to initiate the referendum in the first place, setting the question, and determining the process rules by which the referendum will be conducted and the issue decided. This allows them to deploy the referendum only when they are certain of victory. Critics tend to contrast this position with the elite role in representative democracy. It is argued that representative democracy is less subject to manipulation by elites because of structured institutional mechanisms that allow, or if need be compel, representatives to act more cooperatively and/or deliberatively in making decisions in the broader public interest.

There are two issues at stake: the strength of representative democracy in diluting the power of particular elites, and the weakness of referendum democracy in failing to do so. First, it is often argued that the complex processes of decision-making by institutions within a representative system can be contrasted with the simplicity of the referendum. Decision-making within a representative system, unlike that in a referendum, begins rather than ends with an election. People take office and institutions are structured to produce good policy and good laws over time. A referendum, on the other hand, involves people directly making these important and difficult decisions in transient moments. Furthermore, according to this ideal model, the advantage of representative democracy lies in the opportunity for experts with time, ability, and public-spiritedness to exercise their informed judgement in the public interest. So when we address a critique of referendum democracy as elite-controlled, the point made by advocates of a representative alternative is not that elites are in fact involved in the process of referendum decision-making, but rather that these elites are able to exploit their role for narrow political advantage, undermining the public interest which they would be unable to do through the normal channels of representative government, where other elites as well as the electorate act as important checks on their behaviour and where representatives are inclined to operate in the public interest.

Since referendums are often criticized against the backdrop of this ideal image of representative democracy, much then hangs upon whether within the real, day-to-day operation of representative democracy these checks and balances do in fact operate effectively and this public-spiritedness is lived in a

---

referendum to be controlled if the government can decide to hold it and set the timing and the question, and pro-hegemonic if its results are 'supportive...to a regime': Gordon Smith, 'The Functional Properties of the Referendum' (1976) 4 European Journal of Political Research 1, 6. See also Matt Qvortrup, 'Are Referendums Controlled and Pro-hegemonic?' (2000) 48 Political Studies 821; and David Butler and Austin Ranney, 'Summing Up' in David Butler and Austin Ranney (eds), *Referendums: A Comparative Study of Practice and Theory* (American Enterprise 1978) 221.

meaningful way. But in recent times the ideal of representation embodied in free-thinking actors exercising independent judgement for the public good has increasingly fallen victim to internal and external manipulation of decision-making, resulting in a growing accountability gap between the making of decisions and processes of democratic control.[10] Political scientists and constitutional theorists alight upon several problems with modern representative democracy which we might summarize as: institutional imbalance; partisan control; and external influence. First, the principle of separation of powers that seeks to balance the influence of executive and legislature has become skewed in many cases, so the argument goes, in favour of the former, allowing executive government a virtual monopoly over the legislative agenda. Taking the UK as an example, the growth of government in the twentieth century brought with it particularly strong mechanisms of control over elected representatives.[11] These are largely incentive-based through the patronage of public office. The number of representatives holding ministerial office, from cabinet to junior ministerial positions, can be high; as at July 2010 there were 119 members of parliament across both houses in ministerial positions.[12] This guarantees a core of unconditional support for the government through the convention of collective responsibility. It has even been argued that one consequence of this unswerving loyalty to the government is a weakening of the doctrine of individual ministerial responsibility to Parliament, with ministers more and more protected by the government from parliamentary scrutiny.[13] Even in states with a formally entrenched constitutional separation of powers, the strength of the executive role has grown significantly.[14] Although of course this criticism varies depending upon shifts in power within the legislature and the personal strength of a particular executive head, the criticism of executive imbalance is now widespread across constitutional systems. Furthermore, this rise in executive government can bring with it a 'democratic deficit' as

---

[10] See eg John S Dryzek and Patrick Dunleavy, *Theories of the Democratic State* (Palgrave Macmillan 2009) 207–9.

[11] Lord Hewart, *The New Despotism* (Ernest Benn Ltd 1929); Hansard Society, *The Challenge for Parliament: Making Government Accountable* (Hansard Society 2001); Adam Tomkins, 'What is Parliament For?' in Nicholas Bamforth and Peter Leyland (eds), *Public Law in a Multi-Layered Constitution* (Hart Publishing 2003) 53–78.

[12] <http://www.cabinetoffice.gov.uk/sites/default/files/resources/lmr100701.pdf> accessed 12 July 2011.

[13] Diana Woodhouse, 'Individual Ministerial Responsibility and a "Dash of Principle"' in David Butler, Vernon Bogdanor, and Robert Simmons (eds), *The Law, Politics and the Constitution: Essays in Honour of Geoffrey Marshall* (OUP 1999).

[14] Andrew Rudalevige, *The New Imperial Presidency: Renewing Presidential Power after Watergate* (University of Michigan Press 2005).

power is outsourced more and more to officials,[15] who may not even be civil servants with their codes of impartiality and lines of democratic accountability.[16] This growth of 'technocratic' government at arm's length from scrutiny and regulation is another phenomenon of the accrescing functionalism of the state and the increasing complexity of government in a globalizing world.[17] All of this allows executives to consolidate power more and more by emasculating the power of backbench parliamentarians, co-opting administrators into the role of partisan advisers, and exploiting the growth—and growing complexity—of government to make decisions free from effective scrutiny.

A second and related critique focuses on the party system. Elites are able to use the heavily adversarial nature of modern politics to consolidate the partisan loyalty of elected representatives backed up by the whip system.[18] This in effect forces backbench MPs to vote with the government or risk losing party support or even face deselection in advance of the next election. Opposition parties can shadow this with the promise of future ministerial office for loyal MPs, by emphasizing (or exaggerating) the danger of electoral failure if the party appears disunited, and in a way similar to the government, by issuing the threat of deselection of disloyal MPs.[19] The heavily adversarial system extends into election campaigns, which are in the eyes of critics themselves a sham.[20]

A third factor is that elected legislators and governments also face an unprecedented level of scrutiny and pressure from the media,[21] lobbyists, and other interest groups (particularly representing business), all of which

---

[15] Adam Tomkins, *The Constitution After Scott: Government Unwrapped* (Clarendon Press 1998); Terence Daintith and Alan Page, *The Executive in the Constitution: Structure, Autonomy, and Internal Control* (OUP 1999).

[16] Matthew Flinders, *Delegated Governance and the British State: Walking without Order* (OUP 2008); Christopher Foster, *British Government in Crisis* (Hart Publishing 2005). Dryzek and Dunleavy call this 'low visibility networked governance'. See Dryzek and Dunleavy, *Theories of the Democratic State*, 208.

[17] Robert O Keohane, 'Global Governance and Democratic Accountability' in David Held and Mathias Koenig-Archibugi (eds), *Taming Globalization: Frontiers of Governance* (Polity Press/Blackwell 2003); Anne Marie Goetz and Rob Jenkins, *Reinventing Accountability: Making Democracy Work for Human Development* (Palgrave Macmillan 2005).

[18] Philip Cowley and Mark Stuart, 'Parliament' in Anthony Seldon and Dennis Kavanagh (eds), *The Blair Effect 2001–2005* (CUP 2005); Giacomo Benedetto and Simon Hix, 'The Rejected, the Ejected, and the Dejected: Explaining Government Rebels in the 2001–2005 British House of Commons' (2007) 40 Comparative Political Studies 755. See also Paul Craig, *Administrative Law* (5th edn, Sweet & Maxwell 2003) 76–87. It is, of course, the case that party discipline is particularly strong in the UK and much weaker, eg, in the US Congress, see Dryzek and Dunleavy, *Theories of the Democratic State*, 174.

[19] The whip system and role of mass parties is criticized by Adam Tomkins in *Our Republican Constitution* (Hart Publishing 2005) 136–9.

[20] One recent characterization of electoral campaigns is that they feature 'image-making, deception, the making of empty promises that cannot possibly be kept, [and] distortion of the record and positions of the other side'. Dryzek and Dunleavy, *Theories of the Democratic State*, 218.

[21] Lance Price, *Where Power Lies: Prime Ministers v The Media* (Simon & Schuster 2010).

diminish the scope for free deliberation.[22] In light of all these factors, the critique of elite control of referendum democracy should in large part be addressed in the context of a broader disaffection with how *representative* democracy operates.

What of the second issue raised by the 'elite control syndrome', namely that there are particular opportunities open to elites to exploit referendum democracy? We can now see that in addressing this we need to be wary not to reify the representative alternative. The failures of elected representatives to exercise independence and properly manage the power of executive elites is a broader issue for democracy in general. But turning to the referendum issue specifically, to some extent the notion of 'elite control' is itself vague and needs further elaboration. Which 'elites' are we talking about—executive or legislative, or the interplay between both? This is often not explained in the critical literature. Furthermore, it is a claim that is contested by advocates of the referendum who contend that in fact freedom from the elite control of representative democracy is one of the main benefits of direct democracy as an unmediated and hence 'pure' form of democracy; in other words, as one mechanism with which to overcome the malaise of elite domination of representative structures. These arguments will be tested in Chapter 4.

Given the opportunities to design checks and balances and its general success over the past century, the attractiveness and practical benefits of representative democracy as a general tool of government seem irrefutable, and it is certainly true that unscrupulous elites, in propitious constitutional circumstances, can exploit the use of referendums for political advantage. But just as we should avoid dichotomies that attempt to posit referendums as self-evidently democratic on the one hand or as inherently manipulable on the other, so too should we attend to the very real issues of hegemonic control within representative decision-making processes. We will return to these factors in our discussion of participation and inclusiveness in Section III.

(ii) The deliberation deficit

This criticism suggests that referendums by their nature facilitate or indeed encourage the mere aggregation of individual wills and in doing so fail to

---

[22] In the UK context see: Jacob Rowbottom, *Democracy Distorted: Wealth, Influence and Democratic Politics* (CUP 2010). And in relation to the US: Matthew A Crenson and Benjamin Ginsberg, *Downsizing Democracy: How America Sidelined Its Citizens and Privatized Its Public* (Johns Hopkins University Press 2002); and Theda Skocpol, *Diminished Democracy: From Membership to Management in American Civic Life* (University of Oklahoma Press 2003). In the context of globalization, see also Mathias Koenig-Archibugi, 'Transnational Corporations and Public Accountability' (2004) 39(2) Government and Opposition 1. Although for a more nuanced account of the varying roles of different interest groups, and the argument that some can be democracy-enhancing, see Grant Jordan and William A Maloney, *Democracy and Interest Groups: Enhancing Participation?* (Palgrave Macmillan 2007).

foster either the acquisition of information by, or the active deliberation of, citizens. By this argument people enter the referendum process with pre-formed views and the referendum, as a simple act of voting Yes or No, becomes a conduit through which these views can be expressed, often hastily, without discussion or reflection and, therefore, without any possibility that minds might be changed and preferences transformed. By contrast, representative institutions create the conditions for a more deliberative approach to decision-making and are therefore likely to result in objectively better decisions. As Haskell, a prominent critic of direct democracy, puts it: 'Only representative institutions can fill the need for informed deliberation, consensus, and compromise, all of which are necessary for good government in the public interest.'[23]

The debate concerning the respective merits and demerits of representative and direct democracy leads us to the recent turn in normative political theory towards deliberative democracy which will become our core benchmark as we assess the democratic credentials of referendums from a civic republican perspective. We will begin by addressing the contention that one advantage of representative government is in offering opportunities for meaningful deliberation. There are in fact three distinct arguments here. The first concerns a point touched upon in addressing the control syndrome, namely that representative institutions, by the way they are constituted and balanced one with another, create an environment conducive to fostering discussion towards policy which will involve the engagement of a broad cross-section of interests. The likely result is policy formed by a range of representatives with different attitudes, but all or mainly acting in the public interest. This can be contrasted with the quick, self-interested, and unreflective decision-making of the polling booth which we often find associated with direct democracy. The second is that elected politicians who compose these institutions have the competence and capacity to reach such informed judgements in a way that ordinary citizens acting together in direct democracy do not. A third is that one of the side effects of direct democracy is that it tends to oversimplify issues by artificially separating them into supposedly discrete questions. But any system of government should address policy in the full context of its myriad interconnections. To be effective, democratic government must attempt to arrive at agreement

---

[23] Haskell, *Direct Democracy or Representative Government*, 11. Mueller also expresses the view that a 'hands-off' version of democracy is preferable to the active participation of citizens. Democracy works because 'it does not require more from the human spirit than apathy, selfishness, common sense, and arithmetic'. In short, political apathy is the key to a healthy democracy. John Mueller, 'Democracy and Ralph's Pretty Good Grocery: Elections, Equality, and the Minimal Human Being' (1992) 36 Am J Political Science 983, 992. For another modern account of this 'Schumpeterian' view of democracy see Richard A Posner, *Law, Pragmatism, and Democracy* (Harvard University Press 2003).

on a range of issues, promoting compromise and give and take, and 'logrolling' a number of issues together in light of their financial and other points of interdependence. It should not attempt to separate them artificially one from another, overlooking the fact that a decision on one issue may have deleterious or restrictive implications for other decisions. Since our principal concern is with constitutional referendums, I will ask whether such a process of interconnection is equally important at the constitutional level as at the ordinary, legislative level.[24]

The first, institutional argument is in a number of ways compelling. Leaving aside for now whether referendums can ever foster deliberation in the public interest, representative democratic institutions, properly designed, do seem to offer this possibility. The partisan nature of modern politics can make the search for cross-party consensus more difficult, but the careful design of electoral systems can offer some way round this. Although a first-past-the-post system may be more likely to lead to single-party government and the likelihood of a winner-takes-all result, proportional representation often leads to no one party having a majority within legislatures, thus causing parties to negotiate outcomes with each other (although this can in turn lead to coalitions that act highly cohesively as majority governments). Other institutional mechanisms such as separation of powers, federalism etc can cause different institutions and branches of government to work together, or can at least moderate the opportunities open to elites to pursue narrow sectarian interests (always bearing in mind the criticisms we met earlier of how representative democracy operates in practice today). The notion that a referendum process is simply about the aggregation of individual wills is also one that carries considerable force. A referendum is a straight vote, with each individual having a formally equal say, the decision often being made by simple majority. This is certainly not a model that would seem to encourage consensus-building, particularly where a majority of citizens and their representatives framing the referendum process are aware that the referendum can be used to achieve key goals without the need for compromise.[25]

The second argument runs as follows: referendums give citizens responsibility for political decisions when in fact they lack the necessary capacity or the competence to make these.[26] Instead, politicians are better equipped on both grounds. In terms of capacity they have the time and energy to make

---

[24] Dominique Leydet, 'Compromise and Public Debate in Processes of Constitutional Reform: The Canadian Case' (2004) 43 Social Science Information 233, 235.

[25] For Hannah Arendt, it was the lack of deliberation in referendums that made them unacceptable to her as a vehicle of popular political participation. Hannah Arendt, *On Revolution* (Penguin 1977) 228.

[26] Giovanni Sartori, *The Theory of Democracy Revisited* (Chatham House 1987) 120.

decisions that ordinary citizens lack.[27] Competence refers to the superior ability of politicians: 'Representatives are expected to be more competent to make enlightened decisions because of their personal characteristics (e.g., their moral dignity or their intelligence).'[28] Competence is a difficult argument to evaluate conclusively since so much varies from system to system in terms of the political culture of the political class in question and the integrity or qualifications of individual politicians. We can say in support of the argument that many people enter politics with ideals, and it would be unduly cynical to assume that politicians do not retain integrity in public office. We can also note that governments in forming policy, and legislatures in passing law, are supported by expert civil servants who often adhere to a code of political neutrality. Their expertise is a vital component in the drafting of coherent law, supported by law commissions, external specialists who influence the design of particular policies and laws, expert draftsmen etc. But we should also be attentive to criticisms of the political class. In light of our earlier discussion, the influence of executive patronage, partisan loyalty, and the role of external lobbyists etc, the independence of representatives may not be as rarefied as a positive caricature of representative democracy might suggest. Professional politicians may have the time and resources to facilitate the enlightened and well-informed pursuit of the public interest, but that does not mean they will be motivated only or even mainly by this concern, nor does it mean they will necessarily be well educated on the issues before them.[29]

What we are left with then is a more nuanced conclusion, namely that representative models can offer the institutional framework for the kind of decision-making that involves discussion, agreement, and compromise, but that this can be undermined by other interests and influences which impact upon the independent application of whatever competence and capacity elected politicians might have. In other words, no matter the challenges faced in designing deliberative models of direct democracy, it should not be forgotten that representative democracy does not always arrive at the enlightened forms of decision-making to which its advocates aspire.

---

[27] Maija Setälä, 'On the Problems of Responsibility and Accountability in Referendums' (2006) 45 European J Political Research 699, 717. See also Anthony McGann, *The Logic of Democracy: Reconciling Equality, Deliberation, and Minority Protection* (University of Michigan Press 2006) 125.

[28] Setälä, 'On the Problems', 700.

[29] It is important that direct democracy is not evaluated by a different set of standards than representative democracy. Eg, the US Supreme Court has held that it could not invalidate legislation on the basis that Congress in passing it did not understand its implications. *US Railroad Retirement Board v Fritz*, 449 US 166 (1980): 'If this test were applied literally to every member of any legislature that ever voted on a law, there would be very few laws that would survive it.' 449 US 166 (1980), 179 (Chief Justice Rehnquist).

The argument that politicians have superior competence and capacity to conduct deliberative politics implies, of course, that ordinary citizens are comparatively lacking in these qualities and this is why the former should make decisions on the latter's behalf.[30] At least for some critics of direct democracy, most ordinary citizens have such a limited capacity for, and/or interest in, engaging in democratic politics that proper deliberation—although not perhaps perfect at the representative level—is really feasible only at that level.

Evidence that the citizen lacks the competence and the capacity to play an active role in politics is often deduced from the ignorance of and/or apathy for politics among the general public. Certainly there is empirical evidence that citizen engagement with traditional politics is diminishing. This is seen by markers such as party membership[31] and voter turnout.[32] But there are different ways to interpret this. Certainly one is that people do not have the inclination to engage, but this is only one. We should not discount the possibility that in some cases a lack of interest in politics may stem from high levels of citizen satisfaction rather than dissatisfaction. Furthermore, in Chapter 1 I suggested that in other cases high levels of political disaffection among citizens resulting in a backlash against the political class and a falling away of efficacy and trust might be one of the factors behind the recent proliferation of the referendum. LeDuc observes: 'Elected officials are often seen as unresponsive and out of touch... Ordinary citizens feel an

---

[30] Haskell discusses this debate and points to the level of disagreement among political scientists on the question of whether voters are informed enough for direct democracy. Haskell, *Direct Democracy or Representative Government*, 99–102. See also Donald Kinder and David O Sears, 'Public Opinion and Political Action' in Gardner Lindzey and Elliot Aronson (eds), *The Handbook of Social Psychology*, vol 2 (3rd edn, Random House 1985) 664–8; and Posner, *Law, Pragmatism, and Democracy*. In an assessment of voter competence in referendums Lupia and Johnson state:

> Voters are not well-informed as a rule, even about basic facts that seem relevant to connecting political means and ends. We take as fact the characterization of voters as commonly ignorant of political facts, for the burden of evidence is overwhelming.

Arthur Lupia and Richard Johnston, 'Are Voters to Blame? Voter Competence and Elite Manoeuvres in Referendums' in Mendelsohn and Parkin (eds), *Referendum Democracy*, 191–2. Their surprising conclusion, however, is that despite such ignorance 'referendum voters are not as incompetent as commonly portrayed' (191). And in fact the invariable two-option basis of the referendum means that 'the conditions for competent performance... are not as difficult to satisfy as much commentary suggests' (192). We return to this issue in Chapter 7.

[31] In the UK party membership numbered nearly 3,000,000 for the Conservatives and 876,000 for Labour in 1951 but only 250,000 and 166,000, respectively by 2005. John Marshall, 'Membership of UK Political Parties' (House of Commons Library paper, 17 August 2009) <http://www.parliament.uk/documents/commons/lib/research/briefings/snsg-05125.pdf> accessed 12 July 2011.

[32] Turnout is down in elections in a number of developed countries. Richard Flickinger and Donley Studlar, 'Exploring Declining Turnout in Western European Elections' (1992) 15 West European Politics 1; Richard Topf, 'Electoral Participation' in Hansdieter Klingemann and Dieter Fuchs (eds), *Citizens and the State* (OUP 1995); Mark Gray and Miki Caul, 'Declining Voter Turnout in Advanced Industrial Democracies' (2000) 33 Comparative Political Studies 1091.

increasing sense of political powerlessness and express little trust in the ability of existing political institutions to address their concerns.'[33] This might suggest that levels of disaffection are in fact to some extent a consequence of how contemporary representative democracy operates. The growth of government, the expansion in quangos etc, the growing influence of outside bodies, and the increasingly globalized nature of political decision-making can add to a sense that the citizen's role as periodic voter is increasingly symbolic, and that citizens are not being properly consulted or engaged by politicians in processes of policy-making.

These arguments seem to gain strength when we observe that many citizens who no longer join political parties or participate in more traditional forms of political activity remain engaged in protest politics and in other avenues of non-conventional politics, for example using the internet to communicate and mobilize. This suggests that the desire to participate, to be heard, and to influence remains strong but that citizens increasingly prefer new and direct networks of political mobilization.[34] A counter-argument to the 'competence and capacity deficit' line is that the ambition to take part deliberatively must be matched by opportunity; the ability and motivation of citizens to participate is difficult to evaluate when they are not actively engaged. It may be that what we are seeing in the rise of social movements is that the mobilization of political action in non-conventional fora is outstripping the supply of meaningful openings for political participation that can directly influence governmental institutions. Evidence for this is suggested by those who point to increased 'cognitive mobilization' of citizens as providing fertile ground for deeper popular engagement in politics.[35]

Civic republicans take citizen participation in politics as a good, even in a political system that well reflects popular opinion, arguing that such participation may be necessary to maintain a healthy political system by boosting accountability; elites will be more attentive to the views of an informed and

---

[33] Lawrence LeDuc, *The Politics of Direct Democracy: Referendums in Global Perspective* (Broadview Press 2003) 20. See also Russell J Dalton, *Citizen Politics: Public Opinion and Political Parties in Advanced Industrial Democracies* (3rd edn, Chatham House 2002); and Matthew Flinders, *Democratic Drift: Majoritarian Modification and Democratic Anomie in the United Kingdom* (OUP 2009).

[34] John A Guidry, Michael D Kennedy, and Mayer N Zald (eds), *Globalizations and Social Movements: Culture, Power and the Transnational Public Sphere* (University of Michigan Press 2000); James H Mittelman, *The Globalization Syndrome: Transformation and Resistance* (Princeton University Press 2000); Stephen Gill, *Power and Resistance in the New World Order* (Palgrave Macmillan 2003); Michael Hardt and Antonio Negri, *Multitude: War and Democracy in the Age of Empire* (Penguin Press 2004); John Holloway, *Change the World Without Taking Power* (Pluto Press 2005); David Featherstone, *Resistance, Space and Political Identities: The Making of Counter-Global Networks* (Wiley-Blackwell 2008).

[35] Stephen C Craig, Amie Kreppel, and James G Kane, 'Public Opinion and Support for Direct Democracy: A Grassroots Perspective' in Mendelsohn and Parkin (eds), *Referendum Democracy*, 25.

engaged public than an apathetic one. Furthermore, they tend to take a more positive view of the competence and capacity of citizens than the Haskell and Posner line of critics, who advocate an exclusively 'elitist' trustee approach to decision-making. One republican contention is that these qualities can only be enhanced by facilitating participation, with the felicitous consequence that the polity as a whole may well be strengthened by the fostering of bonds of social solidarity. This argument for both the inherent and instrumental goods of an active citizenry has, of course, classical provenance in the work of Aristotle,[36] but it is also a strong strain of the modern republican tradition.[37]

In this commitment to the good of citizen participation, popular republicanism links to a popular strain in the recent turn in democratic theory towards deliberative democratic theory. Sunstein highlights how deliberation is central to republican concerns: 'Republicans will attempt to design political constitutions that promote discussion and debate among the citizenry; they will be hostile to systems that promote lawmaking as deals or bargains among self-interested groups.'[38] It is through the linkages between these two traditions that we will in due course situate republican arguments that constitutional referendums can have functional normative value. Barber was one of the first thinkers to advance the modern popular republican position in his argument for 'strong democracy'.[39] He advances this as an alternative to a model of democracy within which citizens have little role in politics, and in doing so criticizes what he takes to be 'thin democracy' within which people vote for rulers, votes are counted, winners declared, and elites rule with little in the way of any ongoing engagement with citizens until the next set of elections.[40] Goodin also explains the republican critique of this model of inactive citizenry, which he characterizes as minimalist democracy:

> Minimalist democracy does not ask that citizens inform themselves before they vote. It does not ask them to pay attention to public debates on the

---

[36] Aristotle, *Politics* (Benjamin Jowett tr, Modern Library 1943). See also Pericles' Funeral Oration: Thucydides (*c* 460/455–*c* 399 BC), Peloponnesian War, Book 2.34–46.

[37] Ian O'Flynn, *Deliberative Democracy and Divided Societies* (Edinburgh University Press 2006) 66. See also JGA Pocock, *The Machiavellian Moment: Florentine Political Thought and the Atlantic Republican Tradition* (Princeton University Press 1975); Paul A Rahe, *Republics Ancient and Modern: Classical Republicanism and the American Revolution* (University of North Carolina Press 1992).

[38] Cass R Sunstein, 'Beyond the Republican Revival' (1988) 97 Yale LJ 1539, 1549.

[39] Barber, *Strong Democracy*, 145.

[40] As Rousseau famously expressed his criticism of British representative democracy: 'The people of England regards itself as free; but it is grossly mistaken; it is free only during the election of members of parliament.' Jean-Jacques Rousseau, *The Social Contract and Discourses*, Book III (GDH Cole tr, Everyman 1973) 266.

issues of the day. It does not ask them to get together with others to discuss the issues. It does not ask them to justify their voting decision to anyone else. Still less does it ask people to take a position publicly to get involved in campaigning to persuade others that they should vote the same way.[41]

Popular deliberative democrats therefore promote decision-making processes that involve ordinary citizens.[42] Dryzek neatly encapsulates the popular position: the 'essence of democratic legitimacy should be sought... in the ability of all individuals subject to a collective decision to engage in authentic deliberation about that decision'.[43] And in this advocacy of an active populace, pursuing direct engagement in matters important to their lives, again we see a strong link between the civic republican and populist deliberative democracy traditions, for example in the work of scholars such as Bruce Ackerman and James Fishkin.[44]

It has even been argued that an active citizenry is essential to develop an idea of 'the people' and that only this collective sense of peoplehood can properly foster deliberative interaction of citizens based upon a sense of mutual obligation.[45] The link between the civic republican commitment to citizen participation and deliberative democracy is also to be found in Iris Marion Young's work and in particular in her argument that the generation of more deliberative policies depends upon the fostering of an idea of 'a public' through a motivation of citizens to reach common decisions.[46] The contention that citizens lack the capacity and competence to participate deliberatively in politics is therefore challenged by this deliberative republican tradition as an elitist vision of democracy, and one that misses the communal ties that a society can build and to which citizens become committed to fostering. Hutchinson and Colon-Rios contend that if they are given

> extensive institutional opportunities to participate in their own governance, people will cultivate a greater appetite and aptitude for political engagement. If domination breeds largely subservients, then democracy will beget mainly democrats. In short, the best way to 'reinvigorate the argumentative dimension of our politics' is more democracy, not less.[47]

---

[41] Robert Goodin, *Innovating Democracy: Democratic Theory and Practice after the Deliberative Turn* (OUP 2008) 1.

[42] Ethan J Leib, *Deliberative Democracy in America: A Proposal for a Popular Branch of Government* (Penn State University Press 2004) 35–40.

[43] John S Dryzek, *Deliberative Democracy and Beyond: Liberals, Critics and Contestations* (OUP 2000) v.

[44] Bruce Ackerman and James S Fishkin, *Deliberation Day* (Yale University Press 2004).

[45] David Miller, *Citizenship and National Identity* (Polity Press 2000) 27.

[46] Iris Marion Young, *Inclusion and Democracy* (OUP 2002) 20.

[47] Hutchinson and Colon-Rios, 'What's Democracy Got To Do With It', 36. Another related strain in the modern republican tradition rejects market liberalism with its focus upon individual self-interest and the

It is clear that the referendum is likely to be looked upon negatively by those who are sceptical of the competence and capacity of ordinary citizens. But from the republican perspective it has been argued that the referendum might be one device with which to help re-engage people not just with democracy but with deliberation about the issues at stake. Setala takes the view that the 'argument that people lack the necessary competence to participate in politics can be used both for and against the use of referendums and popular initiatives'.[48] On the one hand the competence and capacity arguments might suggest people are ill-equipped to deliberate on these issues, but on the other:

> Supporters of deliberative and participatory democracy would point out the developmental potential of political participation, and argue that initiatives and referendums encourage public debate on political issues, which increases people's competence.[49]

We might expect that this would be the case especially with constitutional referendums which, by virtue of their exceptional nature and often acute importance, should be most likely to generate particular levels of popular engagement. As Arato argues: 'constitutional politics due to its extraordinary nature, has the potential to promote the public participation of individuals otherwise dedicated to private happiness, and whose political involvement is inevitably a shifting one'.[50] Frey also notes:

---

reduction of human relationships to the capitalist marketplace. Active political engagement offers a mode of resistance to the hegemony of dominant interests. James Tully, *Democracy and Civic Freedom, Volume I of Public Philosophy in a New Key* (CUP 2008); Hardt and Negri, *Multitude*.

[48] Setälä, 'On the Problems', 717.

[49] ibid 717. This does not, however, address the capacity issue:

> Unlike competence that may develop due to participation, there seems to be external constraints on people's capacities. People have limited resources to participate in politics in terms of how much time and energy they have to deliberate about political issues.

Setälä, 'On the Problems', 717. However, two commentators have argued that referendums can have an educative effect on citizens. Matthew Mendelsohn and Fred Cutler, 'The Effect of Referenda on Democratic Citizens: Information, Politicization, Efficacy and Tolerance' (2000) 30 British J Political Science 669–98. This is an issue we will return to particularly in Chapter 7, asking whether process design might help overcome this problem.

[50] Andrew Arato, 'Dilemmas Arising from the Power To Create Constitutions in Eastern Europe' (1993) 14 Cardozo L Rev 661, 669–70. Canovan observes that the idea of 'the people' intervening to rejuvenate politics is fed by myth. But that is not an invitation to cynicism:

> A less dismissive response might perhaps suggest that our familiar myths of the people as founder and redeemer of polities have rather more substance than that. If there is a kernel of truth hidden in the myths, it might be a truth about the basis of political power and political community. On that view, the hidden truth of the myth is that ordinary individual people do have the potential (however rarely exercised) to mobilise for common action. On occasion, such grass roots mobilisations generate formidable power, bringing down a regime; more rarely, they sometimes manage to make a fresh start and to lay the foundations of a lasting political community.

Margaret Canovan, 'Populism for Political Theorists?' (2004) 9 J Political Ideologies 241, 251.

As the voters are taken to be badly educated and ill informed, subject to manipulation and to emotional decisions it is often argued that referenda should be admitted for small and unimportant issues, only. In contrast, issues of great consequence—such as changes in the constitution—should be left to the professional politicians. The opposite position makes more sense.'[51]

There is good reason to believe that constitutional referendums in particular can lead to a heightened level of interest by citizens, as can be seen from the turnout figures set out in the Appendix, particularly in referendums on sovereignty and independent statehood.

Although it does seem that popular enthusiasm to engage in a constitutional referendum can be high, there is still the inveterate criticism that, methodologically, referendums are inherently antithetical to the institutionally path-dependent mode of compromise and consensus-building that characterizes properly designed representative democracy. In a referendum an issue is laid out as a take-it-or-leave-it Yes or No set of options, leaving no sound reason to deliberate with others, since this decision can be taken by simple majority. In other words, even if people are able and willing to engage deliberatively, the institutional structure of the referendum induces aggregative decision-making. As Chambers argues, the prospects of meaningful deliberation can be diminished when the referendum is introduced not because there is no debate but because sincere debate 'is often overshadowed by strategic campaign manoeuvring'.[52]

And so there are serious institutional problems with aspects of referendum design which do indeed seem to foster aggregative rather than deliberative decision-making. But we must ask whether this is an inherent

---

[51] Bruno S Frey, 'Direct Democracy for Transition Countries' (2004) University of Zurich, Institute for Empirical Research in Economics Working Paper Series No 165, 18 <http://www.iew.unizh.ch/wp/iewwp165.pdf> accessed 13 June 2011. Ackerman applies his notion of constitutional moments to argue that the referendum can intervene as a free-standing event thus helping to galvanize popular interest and participation at such a crucial time. He proposed a reform to the US Constitution Article V constitutional amendment process by adding a national referendum procedure in order to increase popular participation in constitutional decision-making. Bruce Ackerman, 'Transformative Appointments' (1988) 101 Harvard L Rev 1164, 1182; Ackerman, *We The People: Foundations*, 54–5. Giving people the opportunity to exercise direct popular sovereignty at constitutive moments suggests 'apathy will give way to concern, ignorance to information, selfishness to serious reflection on the country's future'. Ackerman, *We The People: Foundations*, 287. Specifically, the referendum 'can serve as a catalyst for the broad-ranging popular debate essential for the democratic legitimation of proposed constitutional initiatives' (54–5). For further consideration of whether referendums improve citizen participation in democracy etc see Matthew Mendelsohn and Andrew Parkin, 'Introduction: Referendum Democracy' in Mendelsohn and Parkin (eds), *Referendum Democracy*, 15. A perhaps surprising contributor to the debate was AV Dicey who took the view that civic education could be developed better in a referendum campaign than a general election campaign, in particular because there would be in the end a decisive outcome to the issue which would mobilize the interest of citizens. Qvortrup, *A Comparative Study of Referendums*, 62–3.

[52] Simone Chambers, 'Constitutional Referendums and Democratic Deliberation' in Mendelsohn and Parkin (eds), *Referendum Democracy*, 234.

pathology in the referendum itself or a specific defect of referendum design which might be overcome by innovative process methods, the introduction of the referendum into broader and ongoing processes of constitutional decision-making, and the building of deliberation into the process to help overcome the aggregative propensities in the referendum and ensure that citizens have a meaningful role in the framing of the issue and facilitating mass deliberation in the referendum campaign and process of decision-taking. We must also be attentive to how the tendency to dismiss the referendum as undemocratic on account of its aggregative propensities might stem from a broader argument that the capacity and competence to make informed and deliberative political decisions rests exclusively with professional politicians. Is the rejection of the referendum as an acceptable decision-making mechanism an instance of an elitist approach to politics, leaving us to conclude that what is problematic is not so much the citizen making decisions in a referendum but the citizen making decisions at all?[53] Given the danger that opposition to referendums as a matter of principle may itself stem from elitism, we need to be attentive again to the fact that many of the democratic debates surrounding referendum use are ideological in nature. The level of involvement one seeks for elected politicians and ordinary citizens respectively in making major constitutional decisions depends in large part on one's broader views of the aims of democracy.

There is, however, a third argument why representative government is preferable to direct democracy conducted through referendums, and it is highly compelling. It is the case that referendums by definition involve the siphoning-off of one particular issue to be put to the people. But government is a complex business that requires the weighing of a number of mutually dependent issues in making decisions. Again, Haskell highlights this advantage of representative democracy. Representative institutions are arranged to take account of 'the complexity and interrelatedness of controversial public policy questions'.[54] Referendums, however, are widely seen to fail this test:

> we might think that representative, deliberative institutions like parliaments are superior because they consider a large number of issues and thus build up more experience of how issues interlock and affect one another. Referendums, on the other hand, might encourage a kind of political myopia,

---

[53] There is something intuitively unappealing in such an approach. Young asks whether opposition to mass participation is in fact just snobbery and a mechanism for elite control of popular aspirations. Young, *Inclusion and Democracy*, 39. This distaste is a particular feature of contemporary liberal legal theorizing. As Unger puts it, 'discomfort with democracy' is among the 'dirty little secrets of contemporary jurisprudence'. Roberto Mangabeira Unger, *What Should Legal Analysis Become?* (Verso 1996) 72. And see Hutchinson and Colon-Rios, 'What's Democracy Got To Do With It', 6–7.

[54] Haskell, *Direct Democracy or Representative Government*, 16.

considering issues out of context and without weighing them against other, equally important considerations.[55]

For example, a referendum asking people if they want to keep a hospital open might well lead to a Yes vote, whereas a representative government would make this decision by weighing the financial implications against other commitments that need to be met.[56] Can the state afford to maintain the hospital? If it is to be built, what other priorities would need to be shelved? This amounts to a powerful argument to the effect that referendums are misconceived as a general tool of governmental or legislative decision-making. They can arguably also be dangerous if used by politicians to pass on decisions to the people which the political class is unwilling to confront.

Again, however, the fact that we are concerned specifically with *constitutional* referendums is relevant. It seems that the log-rolling issue raises one of the most significant distinctions between, on the one hand, the widespread use of referendums on individual matters of policy (eg in California) and the very occasional use of referendums for constitutional moments. It is arguable that processes of constitutional amendment or creation are as close as a society can come to free-standing political events. In this sense it might be argued that citizens can weigh up the individual merits or demerits of an issue such as a new electoral system, a new model of head of state, or even broader issues such as a new constitution or independent statehood, without having to connect these directly to a myriad of other policy considerations as they would in our hospital example.[57]

The challenges in attempting to achieve properly deliberative decision-making in either direct or representative processes are considerable. And simply to argue that citizens can be engaged in politics and encouraged to deliberate about issues does not tell us much about referendums specifically. Nor does it offer any conclusive rebuttal to the powerful argument that referendums can and do encourage aggregative and disconnected decision-making. But in due course we will investigate whether objections to the use of referendums are perhaps more practical than principled, in the sense that if it can be shown in practice that citizens can deliberate meaningfully and effectively in a referendum process, on a constitutional issue that is in large measure discrete and self-standing, then one of the powerful arguments that

---

[55] John Parkinson, 'Beyond "Technique": The Role of Referendums in the Deliberative System' (Referendums and Deliberative Democracy workshop, University of Edinburgh, 8 May 2009).

[56] On related problems which arise in those US states that use referendums frequently see LeDuc, *The Politics of Direct Democracy*, 43.

[57] Part of Ackerman's argument for a national referendum in the USA for constitutional moments is that, according to him, these can be abstracted from other elements of political discourse sufficiently to be free-standing constitutional moments. Ackerman, *We the People: Foundations*.

they should be excluded from the options available for democratic decision-making will be seriously undermined.

(iii) The majoritarian danger

Another criticism of referendums is that they represent a model of majoritarian decision-making that imperils the interests of dissenting individuals and minorities. For one political scientist who has written widely on referendums, the protection of minorities is 'the main objection against the referendum'.[58] Hence the opportunity for discussion and deliberation is not the only issue. Even if referendum processes are in theory venues where deliberation is possible, there is no guarantee it will take place or that it will result in a decision that seeks to accommodate the interests of all. Referendums do indeed often involve a simple 50 per cent plus 1 majoritarian model, which in turn can result in a winner-takes-all outcome; in other words, no matter what deliberative conditions are built into a referendum process, it is the mode of decision-making that is the danger; in the end, a majority may simply vote to harm a minority.[59]

This suggests that referendums may be particularly problematic in divided societies. By contrast, there are two advantages we have already identified in representative democracy which are often observed to be lacking in referendum democracy that can work to restrict the deleterious effects of crude majoritarianism. The distribution of powers among different institutions through separation of powers and checks and balances mechanisms is one, and proportional representation, one of the benefits of which in practice can be the forced cooperation of a plurality of political interests, is another. In principle both of these models of balance—institutional and electoral—offer safeguards against hegemony. The same institutional mechanisms that encourage consensus-building also, by definition, take stronger account of certain minority interests in a way that prima facie

---

[58] Matt Qvortrup, *A Comparative Study of Referendums: Government by the People* (Manchester University Press 2002) 158. The fear of majority tyranny is, more broadly, a strong trope in modern democratic thinking. Mill, eg, although committed to greater public participation in politics, was concerned by the accompanying danger of majoritarianism. John Stuart Mill, *Considerations on Representative Government* ([1862] Prometheus Books 1991) 116. We have noted Madison's fear of popular democracy; it is notable that he expressly rejected the use of direct democracy in the context of protecting minority interests. Madison, 'Federalist Paper No 10'. And see Haskell, *Direct Democracy or Representative Government?*, 11; Derrick A Bell, Jr, 'The Referendum: Democracy's Barrier to Racial Equality' (1978–79) 54 Washington L Rev 1; Priscilla F Gunn, 'Initiatives and Referendums: Direct Democracy and Minority Interests' (1981) 22 Urban Law Annual 135.

[59] However, we should also note the vigorous debate among scholars as to whether the empirical evidence from countries which have recourse to the referendum does in fact point to referendums harming minority interests, Avigail Eisenberg, 'The Medium is the Message: How Referenda Lead Us to Understand Equality for Minorities' in Mendelsohn and Parkin (eds), *Referendum Democracy*, esp 147–8.

referendums do not. Furthermore, within representative systems it is possible to model particular structures for divided societies, for example by way of consociationalism such as the power-sharing model used for Northern Ireland. In situations like this there is a particular danger that referendums will upset a carefully constructed applecart, further polarizing opinion and making problems worse.

But once again we need to nuance this account. We have identified flaws in the contemporary practice of representative democracy in terms of avenues for elite (particularly executive) control, external influences, and increasing distance between government and citizen. It is also important to note that representative democracy is not free from—nor is it intended to be free from—majoritarian decision-making. At the electoral level not all systems operate on a proportional representational system. First-past-the-post systems exist,[60] and even in proportional representational systems elections can be won by one party or a bloc of interests which is then able to control the policy agenda. There is a broader set of criticisms that asks whether voter intentions are ever accurately mirrored at the representative level even when institutions are shaped to encourage pluralism in decision-making. Indeed, no voting system is able to translate voting intention accurately; they each 'restructure opinion in all sorts of ways'.[61] There are also questions as to whether any 'representative' system can really lead to an accurate reflection of social differences given the myriad diversity of modern society and difficulties in securing, for example, accurate levels of representation of different groups etc.[62] It seems, therefore, that in any system the credibility of representative democracy comes down ultimately to faith in some form of Burkean trustee model.

Notwithstanding proportional representation and separation of powers, lawmaking within representative models tends to involve straight majority decisions. Certainly at the level of constitutional amendment many constitutions have provisions requiring super-majorities, but for ordinary laws a simple majority in parliament is usually sufficient. In a bicameral system this may need the endorsement of two houses, but legislation tends to be passed in either chamber on the basis of straight 50 per cent plus 1 majority decision-making. As much as direct democracy, representative democracy ends in decision-making that will always produce minority dissatisfaction. Nonetheless, the general point is a good one that the institutional and

---

[60] The UK model was recently strongly endorsed, ironically by way of a referendum.

[61] Chambers, 'Constitutional Referendums and Democratic Deliberation', 231 fn 3, points out that two identical deliberative processes which end in, respectively, a proportional representation and a first-past-the-post election, may well result in very different outcomes.

[62] Goodin, *Innovating Democracy*, 233–46.

electoral systems of representative democracy do work to constrain crude majoritarianism in a number of ways. While no system will be perfect by this criterion, a properly crafted representative system would seem better able to ensure some voice for minorities in decision-making than a referendum ending in a straight majority vote. Therefore, a challenge is set for those who advocate the use of referendums if they are to meet the charge of dangerous majoritarianism: can a mode of decision-making be built that respects rather than overrides minority interests, through a model of consensus-building?

One other point that does need to be made, however, is about the very merits and demerits of majoritarian decision-making itself. We have observed that liberals tend to be more sceptical of majoritarianism, one reason being that they tend to value the entrenched protection of what are taken to be fundamental individual interests over the value of free and unrestricted democratic political decision-making. Republicans, by contrast, are more concerned with the *process* of decision-making, hence their emphasis on the active participation of the people in decision-making as a political good. They contend that through participation and deliberation people will come together to find common cause before decisions are taken, and they will often conclude that majority decision-making, while not an inherent good, is the fairest way in which to make a decision in many circumstances. One argument for this is that it is difficult and often impossible to find a fairer alternative. While the danger to minorities in majority decision-making can be very real, we should also be alive to the opposite concern. To grant minority vetoes can be to replace the tyranny of the majority with the hegemony of the minority.[63] And so, although we should be attentive to the fact that representative democracy can build models that modify majoritarianism, or at least attempt to achieve broader and larger majorities in the making of decisions, this is not the same as accepting that majority decision-making has no place in a democracy, nor of accepting that minority constraints on majority will are necessarily democratically valid.

To sum up on the three main objections to referendum democracy, the following concerns have been identified: that referendums are susceptible to elite influence; that they can encourage aggregative rather than deliberative decision-making; and that they structurally favour majoritarianism with concomitant risks to individuals and minorities. These are significant dangers and they will require to be addressed fully. The control syndrome will cause us to consider the scope for legal and political regulation of referendums. The deliberation deficit has highlighted the general advantages of

---

[63] Hutchinson and Colon-Rios, 'What's Democracy Got To Do With It', 25.

representative democracy, even if this system does not itself work perfectly; but it has also left open the possibility that where referendums are to be used they may be better suited to constitutional situations than ordinary legislative decision-making. Finally the majoritarian danger alerts us to the pluralism of contemporary society and the dangers to minority interests posed by democracy, both representative and direct.

However, we have also seen that the force of existing critiques of referendums needs to be nuanced in various ways. To begin, these problems can also be a feature of representative models of democracy. Democracy in any form is never an ideal exercise and the perfect should not become the enemy of the good; therefore we should maintain a balanced approach to the possibilities and risks that attend representative democracy, just as we should in respect of those that attach to referendums. It is also important not to polarize the debate; as we have seen for example, a republican perspective may lead to a different response to the majoritarian danger than a liberal approach, but both traditions inevitably see a place for majoritarian decision-making, albeit with different caveats.

Therefore, our enquiry has narrowed as follows: given that neither direct nor representative democracy are free from criticism, are the legitimate criticisms of direct democracy, and referendums in particular, such principled objections that referendums are simply not suitable for the taking of constitutional decisions? It seems that an *ab initio* principled objection is more likely to stem from an ideological commitment on the part of the objector and an inherent preference for elite decision-making. Therefore, if one does not begin with such a predisposition it is possible that the criticisms we have encountered might be overcome by real-world models of direct democracy which can be shown, at least at the level of constitutional authorship, to facilitate proper deliberation. In the next section we will begin this task as we explore whether deliberative democratic theory offers us principles with which to design better referendum processes.

III. REPUBLICAN DEMOCRACY: THE LINK TO DELIBERATION

Republican calls for enhanced participation clearly relate to the turn in normative democratic theory in recent decades which has highlighted the potential advantages of deliberative democracy. The origins of this development are often ascribed to John Rawls's focus upon 'public reason'.[64] Since Rawls the field has broadened, with emphasis upon the deficiencies of

---

[64] John Rawls, *A Theory of Justice* (Harvard University Press 1971).

contemporary democracy,[65] the challenges of political and cultural pluralism,[66] and the divergence of deliberative theory along ideological lines.[67] This relatively new,[68] and still burgeoning, field engages scholars from widely different political traditions in assessing the prospects for an approach to the making of political and constitutional decisions that are more reflective and discursive than has traditionally been the case.[69]

A common commitment among deliberative democrats is that political decisions should be preceded by 'authentic deliberation'[70] if they are to be considered '*legitimate* expressions of the collective will of the people'.[71] But beyond this fairly open-ended commitment, the proliferation in deliberative democracy has been extensive and varied. Within such a broad church there are, inevitably, widely differing views among those who would describe themselves as deliberative democrats as to why a deliberative approach to politics is needed and what it should look like.[72] Two traditions divide, for example, on the question of who are the key actors in political deliberation. There are, on the one hand, those who concentrate upon deliberation

---

[65] Barber, *Strong Democracy*.

[66] Amy Gutmann and Dennis Thompson, *Democracy and Disagreement* (Harvard University Press 1996); James Bohman, *Public Deliberation: Pluralism, Complexity, and Democracy* (MIT Press 1996); Young, *Inclusion and Democracy*.

[67] Dryzek, *Deliberative Democracy and Beyond*. For references to other seminal accounts see Goodin, *Innovating Democracy*, 2 fns 1 and 2.

[68] Dryzek notes that 'prior to 1990 the term deliberative democracy was used but rarely'. Dryzek, *Deliberative Democracy and Beyond*, 2. See also James Bohman, 'The Coming of Age of Deliberative Democracy' (1998) 6 J Political Philosophy 400.

[69] For recent work see Goodin, *Innovating Democracy*; Simone Chambers, 'Rhetoric and the Public Sphere: Has Deliberative Democracy Abandoned Mass Democracy?' (2009) 37 Political Theory 323; John S Dryzek (with Simon Niemeyer), *Foundations and Frontiers of Deliberative Governance* (OUP 2010); and Karen Tracy, *Challenges of Ordinary Democracy: A Case Study in Deliberation and Dissent* (Penn State University Press 2010). According to Chambers, deliberative democratic theory has moved beyond the 'theoretical statement' stage and into the 'working theory' stage. Simone Chambers, 'Deliberative Democratic Theory' (2003) 6 Annual Rev of Political Science 307, 307. Other work that has passed beyond scene-setting to address its practical application includes: John Parkinson, *Deliberating in the Real World: Problems of Legitimacy in Deliberative Democracy* (OUP 2006); Robert Goodin and John S Dryzek, 'Making Use of Mini-publics' in Goodin, *Innovating Democracy*; Shawn Rosenberg (ed), *Deliberation, Participation and Democracy: Can the People Govern?* (Palgrave Macmillan 2007); and Janette Hartz-Karp and Michael K Briand, 'Institutionalizing Deliberative Democracy' (2009) 9 J Public Affairs 125. On the possibility of deliberation in institutions beyond the state see: James Bohman, 'International Regimes and Democratic Governance: Political Equality and Influence in Global Institutions' (1999) 75 International Affairs 499; and John S Dryzek, *Deliberative Global Politics: Discourse and Democracy in a Divided World* (Polity Press 2006).

[70] Joshua Cohen, 'Deliberation and Democratic Legitimacy' in James Bohman and William Rehg (eds), *Deliberative Democracy: Essays on Reason and Politics* (MIT Press 1997).

[71] Emily Hauptmann, 'Deliberation = Legitimacy = Democracy' (1999) 27 Political Theory 857, 858 (emphasis added); see also Seyla Benhabib, 'Toward a Deliberative Model of Democratic Legitimacy' in Seyla Benhabib (ed), *Democracy and Difference: Contesting the Boundaries of the Political* (Princeton University Press 1996) 67–94.

[72] For a discussion of divergent traditions see Gutmann and Thompson, *Democracy and Disagreement*, ch 1.

within elite constituencies, addressing how decisions are made at the level of representative politics either by politicians or judges,[73] and on the other are those who, in advocating a stronger popular role in decision-making, concentrate upon the possibility of enhanced political deliberation among ordinary citizens.[74] These traditions can be termed respectively, elite deliberative democracy and popular deliberative democracy. The latter does not exclude the importance of elite deliberation, but it is more inclined to stress an important role for, and believes in the possibility of, authentic deliberation by citizens as a good in itself and as an effective means of making representatives more accountable. In fact, much of the impetus for the recent turn in deliberative democracy theory stems from a reaction to the view that democracy had become too elite dominated and a sense that there is a need to re-engage the demos directly with democracy.[75]

In my account of referendums it is the latter, popular form of deliberation that is of primary, but importantly not exclusive, interest. In reflecting upon referendum democracy I am interested in the possibility of popular deliberation coexisting with elite deliberation, providing sites of interconnection and mutual reinforcement of deliberative decision-making, since referendums are always embedded within broader representative systems. For example, an elite role can be important in helping to foster and inform popular deliberation, just as debates within wider civil society seek to inform elite policy-making. In this sense we should not lose sight of the potential of deliberative democracy to act as a moderating influence between polarizing strains of republicanism and liberalism and of exclusivist approaches to either representative or direct democracy.[76]

---

[73] John Rawls famously focused upon elite avenues for reason, taking the US Supreme Court as 'the exemplar of public reason'. John Rawls, *Political Liberalism* (Columbia University Press 1993) 23. Gutmann and Thompson tend also to focus their work on public officials, eg Gutmann and Thompson, *Democracy and Disagreement*. This is criticized by Young, *Inclusion and Democracy*, 167. For a recent article focusing upon deliberation by judges see Eric Ghosh, 'Deliberative Democracy and the Countermajoritarian Difficulty: Considering Constitutional Juries' (2010) 30 OJLS 327, and for a ground-breaking exposition of the role of constitutional courts as deliberative fora see Conrado Hübner Mendes, 'Deliberative Performance of Constitutional Courts', PhD thesis (University of Edinburgh 2011).

[74] James Tully, *Strange Multiplicity: Constitutionalism in an Age of Diversity* (CUP 1995); Joshua Cohen and Charles Sabel, 'Directly-Deliberative Polyarchy' (2002) 3 European LJ 313; Iris Marion Young, 'Activist Challenges to Deliberative Democracy' in James S Fishkin and Peter Laslett (eds), *Debating Deliberative Democracy* (Blackwell 2003) 102–20; Dryzek, *Foundations and Frontiers*, 155–76.

[75] Dryzek and Dunleavy comment in relation to Rawls: 'The trouble with the Supreme Court is that it may be a deliberative institution, but it is not a democratic one.' Dryzek and Dunleavy, *Theories of the Democratic State*, 218. Dalton also argues: 'Unless citizens participate in the deliberation of public policy, and their choices structure government action, then democratic processes are meaningless.' Russell J Dalton, 'Citizenship Norms and the Expansion of Political Participation' (2006) 56 Political Studies 76, 78. See also James S Fishkin, *When the People Speak: Deliberative Democracy and Public Consultation* (OUP 2009).

[76] Chambers alights upon the moderating possibilities offered by deliberation at the constitutional level. Chambers, 'Deliberative Democratic Theory', 309–10.

(i) Principles of deliberative democracy and constitutional change: civic republicanism in action

Given that the recent turn in deliberative democracy theory has focused upon *constitutional* issues as an area of particular importance for those interested in enhancing deliberative engagement,[77] the constitutional referendum is a very useful case study with which to test this branch of democratic theory, and it is perhaps surprising that it has not hitherto received greater attention from deliberative democrats.

Our first task is to outline benchmark principles that should inform any exercise in the building of popular, constitutional decision-making mechanisms. I will identify principles of deliberation that are taken to be of generic importance when engaging the people directly in political or lawmaking processes, rather than those tailored specifically to referendums. These principles, whilst in no way exhaustive of the wide range of democratic principles considered important by deliberative democracy theorists working today, do seem to encapsulate the key concerns that are common to many accounts and in particular to those founded in a republican commitment to popular participation, especially at the constitutional level. I will identify four such broad principles which recur in a number of accounts, albeit in different combinations and with varying taxonomy, which are particularly appropriate in assessing referendum democracy. Notably these principles represent values which are often deemed to be missing from or impossible to achieve within a referendum process. Therefore, analysing them will allow us to consider further the critiques of direct democracy we met earlier. Finally, two other points might be made by way of introduction. First, the relevance of each of the four principles varies in different ways from small- to large-scale projects of citizen engagement, but all are to some extent relevant at both levels. Second, there are also situations where the challenges presented by these principles are greater than in others, deeply divided societies providing a stern test for any democratic process.

The principles I will address are: participation; public reasoning; equality as parity of esteem; and consent and collective decision-making. In the remainder of this chapter I will outline these principles and begin to explore what implications they might have for the use and design of constitutional referendums.

---

[77] James Tully, *Strange Multiplicity* (CUP 1995); Carlos Santiago Nino, *The Constitution of Deliberative Democracy* (Yale University Press 1996); Bohman, 'Public Deliberation'; Bruce Ackerman, *We the People: Transformations* (Harvard University Press 1998); Ackerman and Fishkin, *Deliberation Day*; Jürgen Habermas, *Between Facts and Norms: Contributions to a Discourse Theory of Law and Democracy* (MIT Press 1999); and James S Fishkin, 'Deliberative Democracy and Constitutions' (2011) 28 Social Philosophy and Policy 242.

(a) Participation

We have observed the criticism of elite control levelled at referendum decision-making and suggested that this should not be addressed as a problem exclusive to direct democracy. Nonetheless the role of elites and their capacity to manipulate electoral processes, marginalizing or excluding the meaningful involvement of citizens, is a genuine concern in any assessment of referendum democracy. In the chapters to follow I will ask whether a fully participatory process, inclusive of a wide range of citizens, is possible in a referendum, and in particular whether effective legal regulation can help facilitate it, hence limiting the scope open to a particular elite to manipulate a referendum result. For now, it is useful to develop further the deliberative value of participation, exploring why it is seen as a good by deliberative theorists.

I have already discussed how an active citizenry is seen by civic republicans to be of democratic value, touching on the reasons behind this. One reason mentioned in passing was that those affected by a decision should have the right to participate in the making of it. This is central to popular deliberative as well as republican thought.[78] For Young the important principle is that of inclusion: 'The normative legitimacy of a democracy decision depends on the degree to which those affected by it have been included in the decision-making processes and have had the opportunity to influence the outcomes.'[79] In a more targeted sense she argued for the inclusion of particularly marginalized people, but the more general point is that ordinary citizens who are otherwise excluded by the elite-driven processes of contemporary democracy should be able to play a fuller role.

In this we see how a popular approach to deliberative democracy links to a second and less instrumental argument for popular civic republicanism, namely the good that inheres in the politically active citizen. Although much contemporary deliberative democracy theory does focus upon elite deliberation,[80] this is perhaps unsurprising since the norm of political and legal decision-making is representative. But there is also a turn in deliberative democracy theory that focuses upon the importance of and the possibility for popular participation in decision-making; we saw this in the republican theory of Barber's strong democracy and Goodin's critique of minimalist democracy which each relate to popular deliberative theorists

---

[78] Dryzek, *Deliberative Democracy and Beyond*, v. Elsewhere he has stated: 'Deliberation only becomes deliberative democracy to the degree it provides opportunities for participation by all those affected by a decision.' Dryzek, *Deliberative Global Politics*, 27. See also Benhabib, 'Toward a Deliberative Model of Democratic Legitimacy', 68.

[79] Young, *Inclusion and Democracy*, 5–6.

[80] Chambers, 'Rhetoric and the Public Sphere'.

such as Dryzek who are committed to reviving deeper civic engagement. For example, Barber writes that 'in the end human freedom will be found not in the caverns of private solitude but in the noisy assemblies where women and men meet daily and discover in each other's talk the consolation of a common humanity'.[81] I have noted that prima facie referendums do offer the participation deliberative democracy theory seeks. Even Chambers, who has done much work on deliberative democracy theory and is a firm sceptic of referendums, has admitted that referendums are very attractive at first sight 'as mechanisms of constitutional renewal, ratification, and amendment. They can potentially serve as catalysts for a higher level of engagement and participation and this is a good thing.'[82] But even to admit this possibility, in light of the other criticisms we have seen of the referendum, merely moves us to the specifics of how participation is structured in a referendum process, how meaningful it is, and whether it has real influence in the framing of the referendum process and the issues to be put to the electorate.

In this context there are a number of issues to be addressed. How are referendums organized and structured? Are they controlled by particular elites, in particular the government, or is there in fact such competition among elites as to weaken the opportunity of any particular actor to manipulate referendum outcomes? What other factors can limit the role of elites, and in particular what role can legal regulation play in reining in elite domination? There is also, of course, the *content* issue. A commitment to popular participation is all very well but the focus for deliberative democracy must be upon *meaningful* participation. It is to this question that we now turn.

(b) Public reasoning: how deliberation takes place

A second principle common to deliberative democracy theory is public reasoning. This is variously described as publicity,[83] responsiveness,[84] accountability,[85] reciprocity,[86] or the exchange of reasons.[87] This is the core element of deliberative democracy since it provides it with its essential

---

[81] Barber, *Strong Democracy*, 311.   [82] Chambers, 'Constitutional Referendums', 240.

[83] The process should promote 'greater openness or transparency in political life'. O'Flynn, *Deliberative Democracy and Divided Societies*, 99.

[84] Amy Gutmann and Dennis Thompson, *Why Deliberative Democracy?* (Princeton University Press 2004) ch 1.

[85] A point that applies in particular to elites, requiring that they listen to and reason with the people they represent. For an interesting take on this see Dryzek, *Deliberative Democracy and Beyond*, 81–114.

[86] Gutmann and Thompson, *Democracy and Disagreement*, 53. This again involves taking the opinions of other people seriously and treating them with respect; in this way it links to the equality principle discussed later.

[87] John Rawls, *Political Liberalism* (expanded edn, Columbia University Press 2005) 446–7.

purpose—the public justification of ideas by participants, one to another. As we have observed, the last of these manifestations of the principle—exchange of reasons—is often taken to have provided the impetus for the modern revival of deliberative democracy in the influential work of John Rawls and the idea of public reason, which he took to be central to political legitimacy:

> our exercise of political power is proper only when we sincerely believe that the reasons we would offer for our political actions—were we to state them as government officials—are sufficient, and we also reasonably think that other citizens might also reasonably accept these reasons.[88]

This hints at Rawls's preoccupation mainly with elite deliberation. But he was alive too to the importance of popular participation. In this respect reasonable political engagement in turn depends upon reasonable citizens.

> Citizens are reasonable when... they are prepared to offer one another fair terms of cooperation according to what they consider the most reasonable conception of political justice... The criterion of reciprocity requires that when those terms are proposed as the most reasonable terms of fair cooperation, those proposing them also think it at least reasonable for others to accept them, as free and equal citizens.[89]

By the Rawlsian construction people will listen, consider other views (and where possible discuss their views with others); the implication being that this will be done in good faith, with participants open to changing their minds (transforming preferences)[90] and willing to compromise.[91] This

---

[88] ibid. [89] John Rawls, *The Law of Peoples* (Harvard University Press 1999) 137.

[90] Rawls wrote:

> The definitive idea for deliberative democracy is the idea of deliberation itself. When citizens deliberate, they exchange views and debate their supporting reasons concerning public political questions. They suppose that their political opinions may be revised by discussion with other citizens and therefore these opinions are not simply a fixed outcome of their existing private or nonpolitical interests.

Rawls, *The Law of Peoples*, 138–9. See also Benhabib, 'Toward a Deliberative Model of Democratic Legitimacy', 71. Again Dryzek observes: 'Deliberation occurs whenever the participants are amenable to changing their minds as a result of reflection induced by non-coercive communication.' Dryzek, *Deliberative Global Politics*, 27. So,

> deliberative democracy requires us to engage with one another in a highly open and reflective fashion—it requires us to advance reasons that we think others can accept, to recognise that our initial positions may be faulty or misguided and to be willing to alter those preferences should better arguments be forthcoming.

O'Flynn, *Deliberative Democracy and Divided Societies*, 89–90. Or as Miller felicitously explains, a deliberative forum is one where opinions and preferences are *formed*, not just *expressed*. David Miller, 'Deliberative Democracy and Social Choice' in David Held (ed), *Prospects for Democracy* (Stanford University Press 1993) 89.

[91] Barber, *Strong Democracy*, 151; Richard Bellamy, *Liberalism and Pluralism: Towards a Politics of Compromise* (Routledge 1999) 101; Dryzek, *Deliberative Democracy and Beyond*, 1; Young, *Inclusion and Democracy*, 26; Chambers, 'Deliberative Democratic Theory', 309. Chambers does find very mixed results

notion of compromise implies finally that the ultimate aim of deliberation is the search for consensus where that is feasible.[92] As such, this principle is directly opposed to the idea that democratic decision-making should simply involve the aggregation of pre-formed views.[93]

These dimensions also distinguish deliberation from mere strategy; a willingness to change one's mind, a preparedness to compromise, and a search for consensus are each underpinned by the actor's genuine commitment to a more objective public good (or at least to reaching a position that can be agreed to or acquiesced in by a plurality of actors) beyond the solipsism of narrow self-interest.[94] Strategic action involves individuals and other actors calculating what best serves their established goals.[95] By contrast, deliberation in this sense is captured in Habermas's idea of communicative action. Here human emancipation is embodied in deliberative discourses between citizens in which people in fact reflect upon their own interests and the ways these have been constructed by discourse; in a sense, to reason is, for Habermas, to communicate.[96] It is also possible to map the aggregative/deliberative distinction onto an ideological distinction between liberal and republican approaches to democracy. The latter, as we have seen, tends to argue against foreclosing political debate in the name of pre-entrenched, fixed preferences such as 'rights' and also sees democracy as being concerned with discursive participation rather than reducible to a competitive struggle to secure pre-determined interests. Chambers contends that the contemporary move by a number of theorists in the direction of deliberative democracy theory represents a 'turning away from liberal individualist or economic understandings of democracy and toward a view anchored in conceptions of accountability and discussion'.[97]

---

in the empirical literature (319) but for a very positive assessment of a recent exercise in popular deliberation in terms of preference formation see Andre Blais, R Kenneth Carty, and Patrick Fournier, 'Do Citizens Assemblies Make Reasoned Choices' in Mark E Warren and Hilary Pearse (eds), *Designing Deliberative Democracy: The British Columbia Citizens' Assembly* (CUP 2008) 127–44.

[92] Chambers, 'Deliberative Democratic Theory', 309.

[93] Although it is also the case that in many situations reaching consensus is impossible. Samantha Besson, *The Morality of Conflict: Reasonable Disagreement and the Law* (Hart Publishing 2005).

[94] Although a recent major article has argued that 'self-interest, suitably constrained, ought to be part of the deliberation that eventuates in a democratic decision'. Jane Mansbridge et al, 'The Place of Self-Interest and the Role of Power in Deliberative Democracy' (2010) 18 J Political Philosophy 64, 64.

[95] Note also Walzer's interesting distinction between debaters who only want to persuade others and deliberators who are open to changing their own minds. Michael Walzer, *Politics and Passion: Toward a More Egalitarian Liberalism* (Yale University Press 2004) 96.

[96] Jürgen Habermas, *Moral Consciousness and Communicative Action* (MIT Press 1990); Habermas, *Between Facts and Norms*. See also Erik O Erikson, *Understanding Habermas: Communicative Action and Deliberative Democracy* (Continuum 2003).

[97] Chambers, 'Deliberative Democratic Theory', 308. There is a strain of radical deliberative democracy theory which sees liberal constitutionalism as incompatible or at least as in some ways

At the epistemological level Rawls's idea of public reason and Habermas's discourse model each assume that political questions can be decided rationally—that there is such a thing as reason *shared* by all who participate.[98] For O'Flynn

> it is this basic idea that, above all others, has drawn deliberative democrats to his work—the idea that it is possible to identify shared standards of justification to which democratic citizens can appeal when debating matters of collective choice, but that cannot be reduced to any one comprehensive doctrine.[99]

This is a prerequisite to public reason and to 'communicative interaction' or what Dryzek calls 'recurrent communicative interaction';[100] we are dealing not only with internal reflection but public debate, where participants speak the same language with which they can persuade each other and form joint commitments, possibly even across otherwise deep differences and even divisions.

Another feature of public reason is that the importance of process is elevated as a crucial step *prior to* decision-making. Chambers suggests that deliberative models of decision-making are 'talk-centric' rather than 'vote-centric'.[101] Voting-focused approaches to democracy are essentially liberal approaches which consider people to have 'fixed preferences and interests' which compete; whereas talk-centric approaches focus on 'communicative processes of opinion and will-formation that precede voting'.[102] Similarly Goodin suggests: 'Democracy as deliberative democrats understand it centrally involves people in giving one another reasons, not simply in adding up people's votes. That is the central claim of deliberative democracy.'[103] In a sense deliberation is in the first place about energizing and improving democracy itself, the consequence of which it is hoped will be better decisions.

Therefore, such a principle which seeks to move decision-making away from a thin voting process which simply aggregates the pre-fixed preferences of voters is, of course, on a direct collision course with the caricature of referendums which we encountered in Section II. But can a referendum

---

inconsistent with deliberative democracy theory. By this understanding, the constitution acts to crystallize an 'aggregation of predetermined interests under the auspices of a neutral set of rules: that is, a constitution'. Dryzek, *Deliberative Democracy and Beyond*, 9.

[98] Rawls argues for 'a public basis of justification of questions of political justice given the fact of reasonable pluralism'. John Rawls, *Political Liberalism* (2nd edn, Columbia University Press 1996) 100.

[99] O'Flynn, *Deliberative Democracy and Divided Societies*, 27.

[100] John S Dryzek, *Discursive Democracy* (CUP 1990) 43.

[101] Chambers, 'Deliberative Democratic Theory', 308. See also Chambers, 'Constitutional Referendums', 231.

[102] Chambers, 'Constitutional Referendums', 231. See also Barber, *Strong Democracy*, 186–90.

[103] Goodin, *Innovating Democracy*, 93.

which is at least by one construction essentially a vote-centred decision-making mechanism, ever satisfy such a principle? According to the deliberative critique, a referendum cannot foster a meaningful deliberative process because it offers a winner-takes-all end point and so the faction able to secure a majority has no incentive to change minds or compromise and so need not deliberate in a genuine way with its opponents. Instead, people within a majority group can simply maximize the outcome they want. In other words, referendums offer citizens participation—hence the illusion of democracy—but by the standards we are addressing here, that participation will not be deliberative.

But decision-taking in the referendum vote is only one element of a referendum process, an element to which we will return in discussing the fourth principle (consent and collective decision-making) of deliberative democracy. There is also the pre-voting process, where the issue is itself framed. Thus we need to envisage the referendum process as a longer and more complex democratic engagement than it is often considered to be. It can in fact be seen as a series of stages. The first is the decision to initiate the referendum process; the second is the agenda-setting or issue-framing stage, where the matter to be put to the people is formulated; and the third is the campaign stage leading to the vote. We might ask, is it possible for deliberation to apply—perhaps in different ways—at each of these stages, and if so how?

We should not expect the same form of deliberation involving the same actors to be feasible at each stage of a referendum. The first stage is invariably an elite stage, where those with the constitutional power to initiate the referendum will decide whether or not to do so; and in a number of constitutions a referendum will in certain circumstances be triggered automatically. Deliberation at this point will depend upon the political culture of a particular society and also upon constitutional rules that might cause elites to try to find agreement with one another.

Our account in focusing upon the instantiation of *popular* deliberation is more concerned with the next two stages. Here we will distinguish between micro- and macro-level deliberation and consider how attempts to foster accountability can be built into both at different stages of the referendum—micro-level deliberation at the agenda-setting or issue-framing stage, and macro-level deliberation at the campaign stage. We will address this in Chapter 7, looking in particular at recent experiments in combining these two levels of deliberation within referendum processes; in other words, as a mixed model where small group exercises in public communication might be linked to processes of broader public engagement, including public education, at the macro-level prior to the referendum vote-taking. One case of particular interest in later chapters is the referendum on electoral reform held in British Columbia in 2003–04, which in novel ways did attempt to dovetail these two parts of the process.

But we are left with a question. Does such a campaign of public education necessarily make people more reflective and more open to changing their views? Campaigns are still run by elites who can give clear signals to voters and who can also attempt to entrench already fixed opinions. Furthermore, referendums do end in a vote and where polls show that a particular outcome has majority support, what incentive is there for people supporting that position to change their minds? In other words, can the decision-taking orientation of any referendum ultimately frustrate any attempt to craft deliberation into the process? These are considerations to which we now turn in addressing our remaining two principles.

(c) Equality as parity of esteem

Another objection levelled at the referendum process as a possible site for genuine deliberation is not simply that it involves voting but that when decisions can be made by a majority with no incentive to deliberate, this can inevitably endanger the interests of minorities. The principle of equality is central both to republican democracy and to accounts of deliberative decision-making, flowing from the notion of public reasoning: 'the requirement of providing acceptable reasons for the exercise of political power to those who are governed by it...expresses the equal membership of all in the sovereign body responsible for authorizing the exercise of that power'.[104]

We have addressed this concern as the majoritarian danger. I will now explore whether principles of deliberative democracy can help construct a referendum process that will adequately protect minority interests, respecting minorities but also properly including them as full co-authors in any process of popular constitutive decision-making. This is a profound issue, and potentially the greatest stumbling block for referendum democracy. We saw in Section II how representative democracy can build checks and balances both at the level of elections and in lawmaking processes and how some of the strongest arguments against referendums rest on the claim that this balancing of interests is not possible in a winner-takes-all process. And if this is a problem with referendums in general then it is arguably particularly problematic in referendums on major constitutional issues where great injustice can be done to voiceless minorities if a constitution and the constitutional identity of the polity can be shaped in the image of a dominant majority. Therefore, a key feature of participation is who has the opportunity to participate, how different voices are able to be heard, and, in particular, in increasingly pluralist societies where attention is often

---

[104] Cohen, 'Deliberation and Democratic Legitimacy', 416.

drawn to how minority voices have been marginalized, whether these different voices are able to engage meaningfully, their voices exerting genuine influence on proceedings.

We find the traditions of civic republicanism and deliberative democracy uniting around this principle. In the former tradition we observed earlier that Young emphasized the principle of inclusion. Exclusion can be 'from basic political rights, from opportunities to participate, from the hegemonic terms of the debate'.[105] The quest for inclusion of minority interests in democratic decision-making is part of her broader project of freedom as non-domination.[106] What is needed is real influence: 'Democratic inclusion means that all members of the given polity should have effectively equal influence over debate and decision-making within that polity.'[107] This is important not only in the context of divided societies but for any society, a commitment we also see in Rawls's notion of reasonable pluralism.[108] This means we need to think about the *quality* of deliberation in juxtaposition to the *equality* of deliberation—it must be inclusive not only of different people but of their different voices,[109] and of the pluralism that exists even within the context of a shared mode of communication.[110] Finally, and in a link back to the reasonableness principle, it is vital in this context that deliberative discussion is non-domineering and non-coercive.[111]

All of this presents another significant challenge for the referendum. In this context an issue that is particularly central to inclusiveness and respect for minorities is the substance of the issue. This is arguably even more vital than the referendum process itself, in order that the issue presented to the public in a referendum is one which a plurality of people in a territory consider it appropriate to determine in this way. This challenge becomes more difficult, and arguably impossible, in a divided society. In Chapter 8 we will address the framing of the question to be put to a people, and the danger that a referendum can be a zero-sum game in which a particular majority can claim constitutional legitimacy for its own dominant position. Here we will consider specific cases, and in particular that of Northern Ireland in 1998, leading up to the referendum on the Belfast Agreement,

---

[105] Young, *Inclusion and Democracy*, 6.

[106] ibid 258. In this she was influenced by Philip Pettit, who adopted this as the core principle in his account of republicanism. Philip Pettit, *Republicanism: A Theory of Freedom and Government* (OUP 1997).

[107] Young, *Inclusion and Democracy*, 7. See also Michael Walzer, 'Equality and Civil Society' in Will Kymlicka and Simone Chambers (eds), *Alternative Conceptions of Civil Society* (Princeton University Press 2002).

[108] Rawls, *Political Liberalism* (1993). And in Habermas: Jürgen Habermas, *Legitimation Crisis* (Thomas McCarthy tr, Beacon Press 1975) 108.

[109] William E Connolly, *Pluralism* (Duke University Press 2005).

[110] Young, *Inclusion and Democracy*, 52–80.   [111] Dryzek, *Deliberative Global Politics*, 27.

where a process was initiated that engaged people across a deeply divided community in a way that in the end won the trust even of the minority nationalist community. Here again we will see the idea of the referendum as a series of stages with scope for different elements of deliberation involving different actors to be built into each stage. There are a number of issues to which we will return, including the clarity of the question and the need before any referendum is held to build consensus that can transcend deep and often violent divisions within divided societies. An imperative aspiration of deliberative democracy is to maximize losers' consent and we will consider how this might be done in a constitutional referendum, particularly one held in such a volatile environment.

(d) Consent and collective decision-making
Another republican value is consent, which again echoes the point that those bound by a political decision or a law should have had the opportunity to agree or disagree with it. This moves us beyond participation and deliberation, from talking to voting, and hence to the most difficult but ultimately unavoidable function of the democratic polity—decision-making.

A number of aspects of consent have been addressed. First, there is the argument that consent is a chimera in referendums that are so controlled by elites. Second, we have addressed the argument that in direct democracy the electorate does not have the capacity in terms of knowledge of or interest in the issues to make complex decisions. And, third, we have considered *who* consents, contending that particularly in divided societies it is not enough to look for simple majority consent; it is also essential to address the complex plurality of the polity in question. However, we must also recognize that democracy is not just about talking but about reaching decisions. Although perhaps leading to a tension with the other ideals of deliberative theory, in the deliberative model the people of a polity can come to decide upon the mode of government for that polity. Deliberation is a good, but it is a good that ultimately serves the instrumental purpose of allowing a people to act. This is the commitment to demotic possibility; to the notion that the manifestation of a collective political self, the aspiration of the democratic state, is feasible, and that the people do develop a sufficient sense of collective membership to partake in legitimate collective decision-making.[112]

Of course, this raises another danger for minority or individual interests, but such a risk attends any exercise in democratic decision-making. At the extreme level, pluralist critiques in the 'agonistic' tradition challenge even the very idea that a political society can in any meaningful way unite around

---

[112] Michael Saward, 'Enacting Democracy' (2003) 51 Political Studies 161.

collective goals.[113] But for those democrats who see this as the essential project of a polity—that is, for those who accept the possibility of some form of shared reason and purpose operating in a democratic polity by way of 'recurrent communicative interaction'—the question rather is what decision-making processes best facilitate this. And our particular point of focus, of course, is whether in the formation of collective goals at the constitutional level, referendums might play a part.

This principle ultimately builds on the first three. It is a practical necessity that decisions, including foundational constitutional decisions, must be made in and for a democracy.[114] There is also a prima facie argument from a popular republican position that the people of the polity ought to be directly involved in constitutional decision-making, particularly at constitutive moments. But whether a referendum is an appropriate means of engaging the people is something that will largely hang on the final, decision-making stage and its democratic merits and demerits. For some the referendum is the ideal vehicle for consent: 'The one job that a referendum can do that no other device can is to provide the legitimacy that comes with a mass act of consent—by voting on the options that come out of the "debate" phase.'[115] But things are not so simple, as we have seen in identifying principles that offer safeguards against the three main dangers for which referendum democracy is criticized. It is, therefore, vital that these principles continue to inform the popular decision-making stage if the end result of the referendum is to be considered legitimate when set against the full set of demands set out within deliberative democracy theory. In Chapter 9 we will consider how deliberation might be facilitated and, where possible and appropriate, prolonged in the making of decisions. It is at this stage that the people as a whole are called upon most clearly to participate directly. This they do most obviously by voting, but importantly for the deliberative democrat, this stage should also be the product of reflection and communication. We will address various procedural models by which deliberation might be encouraged. For example, in respect of difficult and contested decisions which are the outcome of elite negotiations we will explore arguments for two referendums, one to empower the process of negotiation and another to decide upon its outcome. Another issue to be addressed is the use of thresholds to impose a super-majority requirement for the

---

[113] Chantal Mouffe, *The Democratic Paradox* (Verso 2000).

[114] Gutmann and Thompson point to the fact that deliberation has two functions. One is constructive in the sense of resolving moral disagreements; the other, however, is coercive in lending legitimacy to non-unanimous decisions about these moral disagreements. Gutmann and Thompson, *Democracy and Disagreement*.

[115] Parkinson, 'Beyond "Technique"', 16.

passage of a particular measure. This is a difficult issue in constitutional decision-making more broadly, but we will explore arguments for such thresholds particularly from the perspective of principles of deliberative democracy, addressing, for example, whether these might help offer minority protection, particularly within deeply divided societies and hence encourage a more inclusive model of deliberation, and resultingly, a more pluralistically legitimate model of constitutional decision-making.

IV. CONCLUSION

In this chapter we have encountered three standard democratic criticisms of referendums and have turned to deliberative democracy, asking if this model can help overcome these criticisms and make the constitutional referendum a democratically acceptable mechanism from the perspective of popular civic republicanism. We have identified four key principles of deliberative democracy theory. Whether these can meet the criticisms that referendum democracy faces will be our focus for the remainder of the book, as set out in Table 2.1.

Adopting the functional normativity of constitutional theory, this task will combine theory and practice. Examples from a number of relevant cases will be called upon, assessed against our normative principles; and recommendations for good practice will be offered based upon recent initiatives in deliberative theory and practical experiments in the implementation of deliberative principles.

Table 2.1 Key principles of deliberative democracy theory

The contribution of deliberation to the decision-making process	Principles of civic republican deliberation	Addressing the following criticisms of referendums	Elaborated upon in
Who deliberates?	Popular participation of the people within a broader system of representative government	Elite manipulation—'the elite control syndrome'	Chapters 4, 5, and 6 on control and Chapter 7 on participation
How should they deliberate?	Public reasoning: reflection and discussion	Aggregation—the 'deliberation deficit'	Chapter 7 on participation and Chapter 8 on the substantive issue
Under what conditions?	Equality and parity of esteem	Majoritarianism—the 'majoritarian danger'	Chapters 7 and 8
To what end?	Consent and collective decision-making	All of the above	Chapter 9 on decision-making

But before we turn to a detailed account of how law and constitutionalism are deployed to regulate referendum practice and the possibilities civic republicanism and deliberative democracy theory offer for the remedy of the democratic problems referendum practice raises, there is one other issue which, given its anterior importance to any account of constitutional democracy, must be addressed by way of context. This is the way in which the constitutional referendum can act to define the people itself. It is first necessary to consider how the demotic assumptions that underpin so much of this democratic theorizing can themselves be called into question by referendums, given the fact that constitutional referendums bring back the people directly in constitutional decision-making, supplanting not only the institutional monopoly over decision-making within a representative democracy, but also a number of presuppositions about the relational theory of sovereignty that accompanies the representation model. We will confront this issue in the next chapter.

3

Framing 'the People': Constitutional Referendums and the Demos

I. WHO ARE THE PARTICIPANTS? THE SELF-DETERMINATION QUESTION

The very existence of any democratic polity and any political act made in its name implies a manifestation of 'the people'. But this begs the question, how do we legitimately demarcate the political space within which a people can be said to exist and act politically? Political theorists call this the 'democratic boundary problem'. It is perhaps not surprising that this first question of democracy—who are the people?—invariably goes unarticulated in the day-to-day life of representative democracy. The most obvious, and indeed practical, reason is that there is no need to dwell on this: it is simply assumed that 'the people' is a synonym for the citizenry of the state.[1] The latter can be taken to encompass the former in most cases quite happily; and if the state works, leave it be. Another reason is that to explore this question too closely can in some cases be dangerous. In a number of polities the nature of the demos and even the territorial boundaries of the state are contested affairs. In such a situation, why not let sleeping dogs lie rather than invite a confrontation over inclusion and exclusion.

In referendums, however, and particularly constitutional referendums, a more explicit identification of the people cannot be avoided even, or indeed especially, in hard cases. In this chapter, we will explore the ways in which the constitutional referendum by definition implicates an anterior act of demotic border-drawing—the framing of the self who will perform an act of

---

[1] For Dahl, the great philosophers have ignored this question because 'they take for granted that a people has already constituted itself'. Robert A Dahl, *After the Revolution? Authority in a Good Society* (Yale University Press 1970) 60–1. Others consider its neglect to be more surprising. Canovan has observed: 'Unlike "freedom", "justice", or even "nation", "people" has attracted hardly any analysis, even by theorists of democracy', a fact she deems 'astonishing'. Margaret Canovan, 'Populism for Political Theorists?' (2004) 9 J Political Ideologies 241, 247. And Goodin comments: 'the first question for any democratic theory is who is included', but notes, '[t]his is a strangely under-explored issue within democratic theory'. Robert Goodin, *Innovating Democracy: Democratic Theory and Practice after the Deliberative Turn* (OUP 2008) 3.

constitutional self-determination and in doing so expressly articulate itself as a constitutional people. As we will see, this is most evident in those constitutional referendums we have called 'constitutive', but more broadly, any constitutional referendum as an act of popular self-determination requires a direct attribution of constitutional authorship.

Two interconnected definitional elements emerge in a constitutional referendum as act of self-determination: the first conceptualizes the polity as physical space; the second imagines it as a group of people. In this light the constitutional referendum sets the boundary of the people by way of both territorial demarcation and franchise rules. The former conceptualization envisages a discrete people in spatial terms, the participatory demos is composed of those eligible to vote within a particular geographical area. The territorial boundaries of the demos are often taken to be self-evident, as they are, of course, in the normal workings of representative democracy, particularly when the referendum is a state-wide affair. But this assumption can be contested and in this context the referendum can play an unsettling role either in merely highlighting or indeed by inflaming territorial disputes. My focal point here is sub-state nationalism. This phenomenon was given new life in the collapse of the USSR and the Socialist Federal Republic of Yugoslavia (SFRY). And in these dramatic struggles referendums were used both by the central state and by sub-state elites to define purportedly legitimate constituencies. What we see from these cases, and from more harmonious plurinational states such as Canada and the UK discussed in later chapters, is how the demos question lies unconfronted in a world dominated by a uni-national ideology that maps republican democracy and formal equality of citizens unreflectively onto each polity, assuming even in the face of sociological evidence and political strife that there is to one state always only one demos. In bucking this trend, the referendum has therefore become a key instrument in modern nationalism's challenge to the constitutional orthodoxies of state legal orders and implicitly to the theoretical orthodoxies underpinning the unitary conception of the demos.[2]

The second, franchise, issue can raise complex problems even when the territorial question is settled. There may be broad consensus that a referendum, if it is to be held, should take place within a particular territorial space, but the issue of who is entitled to vote can raise its own problems. Two questions surrounding the eligibility of voters have created controversy: are

---

[2] Normative challenges to the injustice of particular statal instantiations of the people have in recent times been offered by political theorists. Will Kymlicka, *Multicultural Citizenship* (OUP 1995); Margaret Moore, *Ethics of Nationalism* (OUP 2001); and Ferran Requejo, 'Liberal Democracy's Timber is Still Too Straight: The Case of Political Models for Coexistence in Composite States' in Neil Walker, Jo Shaw, and Stephen Tierney, *Europe's Constitutional Mosaic* (Hart Publishing 2011).

there or should there be people among those resident within the territory not entitled to vote? And, are there people resident beyond the territory to whom, nonetheless, the franchise is warranted? Hence, what seems intuitively to be a simple question—who can vote?—can be the site of intense dispute in constitutional referendums.

In these questions we see how ideology intervenes to define the demos not simply in spatial terms but by way of constructed identity markers such as legally defined residence, citizenship, nationality, and ethnicity.[3] Indeed, the way in which the franchise issue is dealt with in the design of a referendum can tell us much about the type of nationalist ideology dominant in a specific state or territory; for example, particular rules of inclusion or exclusion reveal whether the vision of the nation that prevails is more or less 'civic' or 'ethnic' in orientation. We will use as examples both referendums concerning independent statehood and those that involve the transfer of powers to supra-state organizations, concluding the chapter by taking the territory of New Caledonia as a case study of how these various issues of territory and franchise have played out in practice.

There is finally a broader issue at stake in the explicit confrontation of the demos issue in a constitutional referendum. The people, once defined, are then called upon to address together *as a people*, and on the basis of individual equality (invariably unmediated by issues of group membership and differentiation), an issue involving the shaping or re-shaping of the polity. In this sense, the referendum is significant not only in substantive terms as a mechanism of constitutional change, but also for its symbolic role in bringing together and hence declaring the voters to be—directly, equally, and communally—a determining 'self'. This is particularly apparent in the constitutive referendum, where we might even say that the referendum constitutes (or re-constitutes) not only the polity but possibly also the very people whose identity as citizens is reframed through their joint constitutive act; in other words, as a direct act of constitutional authorship the referendum explicitly confronts those authors with the relationship they now share in community with their co-authors. Another point therefore emerging here, and relevant to later chapters, is how the referendum can engage the self-awareness of citizens as a collective, constitutionally authoring people, a process of self-realization which might otherwise lie dormant in more detached processes of representative democracy.

---

[3] Which are complex for law to manage, since they are each in different ways and to different extents also sociological concepts. Rogers Brubaker, *Nationalism Reframed: Nationhood and the National Question in the New Europe* (CUP 1996) 10.

II. THE TERRITORIAL QUESTION IN CONSTITUTIONAL REFERENDUMS

After more than two centuries of constitutional practice the referendum is now a firm feature in the transition to independent statehood by colonized or sub-state peoples, as polls in Eritrea 1993, East Timor 1999, Montenegro 2006, and South Sudan 2011 exemplify. In this section we will trace the early emergence of the referendum in the nineteenth century and its more systematic application after the First World War; the limited use of referendums in post-Second World War decolonization processes; and its more recent reappearance in the deluge of sub-state referendums in Central and Eastern Europe after 1989, the effects of which are still reverberating in the aspirations of sub-state peoples across the globe who increasingly turn to the referendum to frame their purported international personality and their consequent political aspirations and constitutional claims. Finally, we will also observe how the referendum applied in a self-determination setting can, perhaps more than any other constitutional device, serve to explode the myth of national unity in plurinational states, and how its application to define the demotic question in a homogenizing way can in fact be highly dangerous in deeply fractured societies.

(i) Referendum as plebiscite: the early phase

Self-determination is not just a legal principle, it is a political claim of acute rhetorical power. And it is this intense political dimension that has served to make the legal norm of self-determination one of the most elusive, ambiguous, and hence unsatisfactory principles of international law. Its legal status is in many ways unimpeachable. Recognized as a founding purpose of the United Nations,[4] and declared to be a right of 'all peoples' in Article 1 of the two general UN human rights instruments,[5] it is often now said to enjoy the rarefied status of a norm that is both elevated as *jus cogens*[6] and applicable *erga omnes*.[7] But, as we will explore in this chapter, although international

---

[4] Charter of the United Nations (UN Charter) (San Francisco, 26 June 1945) Art 1(2). See James Crawford, *The Creation of States in International Law* (OUP 1979) 89.

[5] International Covenant on Civil and Political Rights (ICCPR) (New York, 16 December 1966, 999 UNTS 171) Art 1; International Covenant on Economic Social and Cultural Rights (ICESCR) (New York, 16 December 1966, 993 UNTS 3) Art 1. See also *Legal Consequences for States of the Continued Presence of South Africa in Namibia (South West Africa) notwithstanding Security Council Resolution 276 (1970) Advisory Opinion* [1971] ICJ Reports 16, paras 89–90.

[6] *Legal Consequences of the Construction of a Wall in the Occupied Palestine Territory Advisory Opinion* [2004] ICJ Reports 136, paras 155–6; John Dugard, *Recognition and the United Nations* (Grotius Publications 1987) 158–62.

[7] *Military and Paramilitary Activities In and Against Nicaragua (Nicaragua v United States) Merits* [1986] ICJ Reports 14.

law and its institutions have in spite (or because) of this status attempted to emasculate the application of the principle of self-determination in claims to independent statehood by nationalist movements, the referendum, infused as it is with the purported political legitimacy of a self-determining people, constantly re-emerges as political trump card to challenge the legal formalism of the settled order of states.

The intervention of the referendum as a source of tension between territorial sovereignty as the legal promise of statehood and the political ideal of self-determination of peoples can be traced back to the nineteenth century. Following the upheavals of 1848, as the demand for increased popular participation in politics grew, the plebiscite became a tool in the independence and reunification struggles of the latter part of the century.[8] Plebiscites had earlier been used to incorporate Avignon, Savoy, and Nice within France,[9] but by the 1860s they were to be deployed more systematically in several Italian provinces on the question of unification, culminating with a vote in Rome following the fall of the city to the army of unification in 1870.[10] Their use at this time was, however, sporadic and although Norway separated peacefully from Sweden in 1905 following near-unanimous support for independence in a referendum,[11] it was not until the end of the Great War that we see a turning point, with the plebiscite endorsed by the Paris peace settlements and League of Nations as a more structured, and internationally recognized, means of resolving territorial questions in Europe during the post-war period.

The principle of self-determination, formulated in the revolutionary ideology of the nineteenth century, was consolidated as a political commitment at this time, largely at the hands of US President Woodrow Wilson, who established the ideal of mapping territorial borders as closely as possible to the national boundaries of peoples.[12] It did not achieve the status of legal

---

[8] The term 'plebiscite' is used in this context to denote a referendum specifically on a territorial issue but, as I have noted, the terms 'plebiscite' and 'referendum' are generally used synonymously in this book.

[9] Jean A Laponce, 'National Self-Determination and Referendums: The Case for Territorial Revisionism' (2001) 7(2) Nationalism and Ethnic Politics 33, 38–9.

[10] Dennis Mack Smith, *Italy: A Modern History* (University of Michigan Press 1969) 66–7, 96.

[11] John T Rourke, Richard P Hiskes, and Cyrus Ernesto Zirakzadeh, *Direct Democracy and International Politics: Deciding International Issues Through Referendums* (Lynne Rienner Publishers 1992) 31–2.

[12] 'Peoples may now be dominated and governed only by their own consent. Self-determination is not a mere phrase.' Speech by Wilson, cited by Johannes Mattern, *The Employment of the Plebiscite in the Determination of Sovereignty* (Johns Hopkins University Press 1920) 76. See also Lloyd Ambrosius, 'Dilemmas of National Self-Determination: Woodrow Wilson's Legacy' in Christian Baecher and Carole Fink (eds), *The Establishment of European Frontiers after the Two World Wars* (Lang 1987). The influence of Lenin in linking the principle of democracy to resurgent nationalism is also an important backdrop to Wilson's intervention in Paris. Alfred Cobban, *The Nation State and National Self-Determination* (2nd edn, Collins 1969) 51.

principle, and accordingly, despite League of Nations endorsement and the early promise of widespread popular engagement, its application in the re-ordering of territory after the First World War was still heavily circumscribed. In fact, there were only seven territorial plebiscites in Central and Eastern Europe in 1920–21. The Schleswig process involved two plebiscites: on 10 February 1920 74.9 per cent in the northern territory voted to be part of Denmark and on 14 March 1920 80.2 per cent in the south voted for Germany—a process that informed the drawing of the new border. On 11 July 1920 Allenstein voted to be part of Germany, not Poland (98 per cent; 87 per cent turnout); on the same date Marienwerder did likewise (92 per cent; 87 per cent turnout); on 10 October 1920 Klagenfurt voted for Austria, not Yugoslavia (59 per cent; 96 per cent turnout); on 20 March 1921 Upper Silesia (60 per cent; 97.5 per cent turnout) voted to join Germany rather than Poland;[13] and on 17 December 1921 the people of Sopron voted for inclusion in Hungary, not Austria (65 per cent; 89.5 per cent turnout).[14] It is therefore notable how few rather than how many referendums were held in this period, given the scale of the territorial changes taking place. As Wambaugh commented: 'the Allies avoided a plebiscite in every region of first importance save that of Upper Silesia',[15] leading her to conclude: 'the principle of self-determination...was in the end honoured, save in the treaty with Germany, more in the breach than in the observance'.[16] Furthermore, the purpose for which they were used was also restricted. Notably in this period plebiscites involved decisions about whether particular territories should be part of one state or another, rather than offering discrete peoples a chance to vote on establishing a state of their own.[17] The most blatant restriction of the self-determination principle, of course, was in its availability only to Europeans. The overseas colonies of the defeated Germany were assigned as 'mandates' to the victorious powers under the thin veneer of League of

---

[13] Laponce, 'National Self-Determination and Referendums', 41–4.

[14] There was also one plebiscite held over from the early period, in which the people of the Saarland voted by 90.7 per cent (turnout 98 per cent) in 1935 to join Germany, not France. The classic account of the plebiscitary process is Sarah Wambaugh, *Plebiscites Since the World War* (Carnegie Endowment for International Peace 1933). Figures are also provided by Henry E Brady and Cynthia S Kaplan, 'Eastern Europe and the Former Soviet Union' in David Butler and Austin Ranney (eds), *Referendums Around the World: The Growing Use of Direct Democracy* (Macmillan Press 1994) 178. And see also Lawrence T Farley, *Plebiscites and Sovereignty: The Crisis of Political Illegitimacy* (Westview Press 1986) 33–6.

[15] Wambaugh, *Plebiscites Since the World War*, 42.

[16] ibid 41. See also Robert Lansing, *The Peace Negotiations. A Personal Narrative* (Constable and Company 1921) 88.

[17] As Laponce puts it: 'The question to be answered in a typical sovereignty-boundary referendum is not "Are you an X or an O?" but "Do you prefer to side with the Os or the Xs in matters of sovereignty?".' Jean A Laponce, 'Turning Votes into Territories: Boundary Referendums in Theory and Practice' (2004) 23 Political Geography 169, 171.

Nations oversight. Their independence, along with that of the other European colonies, would need the intervening event of yet another world conflagration.

Therefore, even in an age of collapsing empires no principle emerged in international law that considered a demonstration of popular support by a discrete sub-state national group to be, by itself, a legally consequential step towards independent statehood. New states were created by elites through political will or with international patronage through the peace settlements or other acts of external recognition, with the referendum playing only a marginal role to inform decisions on the limits of a few territorial boundaries. Of course, it was readily apparent that reconciling the national identities of the peoples of Central and Eastern Europe with territorial borders to their universal satisfaction was an impossible task, but the consequence of such a limited and highly selective application of the self-determination principle was that many disgruntled minorities found themselves unhappy with the outcome. In attempts to curtail this utopian dream it was no surprise that the plebiscite was rapidly seen as a dangerous tool and one whose use should be carefully and strictly truncated.

(ii) Decolonization: evading the boundary question

After the Second World War self-determination was consolidated as a norm in international law. The right to self-determination which would eventually be guaranteed by the International Covenant on Civil and Political Rights (ICCPR) as a right of all peoples became in reality the right of Europe's colonial possessions to free themselves.[18] But the tension between the promise of self-determination as a liberating tool for sub state peoples and its consolidation of state sovereignty emerged in the firm commitment to established state boundaries which marked the birth of the United Nations. By this principle the notion of the nation-state as depository of one national demos was crystallized in the law of the UN Charter through the recognition of the sovereign equality[19] and territorial integrity[20] of states. This reflected an ideological norm of 'one state, one people', accepted across the globe;

---

[18] UNGA Res 1514 (XV) (14 December 1960). On the self-determination entitlement of Mandate and Trust territories, see *Legal Consequences for States of the Continued Presence of South Africa*, para 52. See also Antonio Cassese, *Self-Determination of Peoples: A Legal Reappraisal* (Hersch Lauterpacht Memorial Lectures, CUP 1999); James Mayall, *Nationalism and International Society* (CUP 1990) 50 and 55–7 (on the 'domestication' of the principle); Karen Knop, *Diversity and Self-Determination in International Law* (CUP 2002) 277–326; and Gerry Simpson, *Great Powers and Outlaw States: Unequal Sovereigns in the International Legal Order* (Cambridge Studies in International and Comparative Law, CUP 2004) 275.

[19] UN Charter Art 2.1.

[20] UN Charter Art 2.4.

indeed, this was one of the few generalizable principles agreed to by both sides in the Cold War.[21] In line with the principle of territorial integrity of states, the borders of colonies were not open to change in the vast majority of cases; instead, through the principle of *uti possidetis juris* the colonial regime would simply be replaced by an indigenous system of government within the same borders fixed by the colonial powers.[22]

Given that decolonization in general brought only a change of government rather than of borders, the means by which territories legitimized claims to independence were invariably regular representative party elections.[23] The use of referendums in the decolonization era was again rare. There was a limited number held on the issue of independent statehood (eg Cambodia 1945, Algeria 1961, Western Samoa 1961, Anguilla 1967, the Comoras 1974), but otherwise, like the post-First World War period, the few that did take place centred upon the re-drawing of boundaries between existing entities. One area where a number of these border polls took place was the British possessions in West Africa. For example, the UN Trusteeship Council recommended the staging of plebiscites in the UN Trust Territory of British Cameroons. This was endorsed by the General Assembly,[24] and in the end four were conducted between 1959 and 1961, asking the people of different parts of the territory if they wanted to join with Nigeria or the independent republic of 'Camerun', both of which were moving towards statehood.[25] Another case is that of Togoland and its relationship to the Gold Coast, which was also approaching independence at this time. The General Assembly requested the Trusteeship Council to send a special mission to the Trust Territories of Togoland and again this recommended that 'a formal consultation with the people will be necessary to decide' the question of its political future; all of the leading political parties in the territory agreed that there should be a plebiscite.[26]

One notorious case where the internationally endorsed plebiscite remains unfinished business is the territory of Western Sahara, where the United

---

[21] This has been called the 'territorial covenant'. Robert H Jackson and Mark W Zacher, 'The Territorial Covenant: International Society and the Stabilisation of Boundaries' (1997) University of British Columbia Institute of Internal Relations Working Paper No 15 <http://www.ligi.ubc.ca/sites/liu/files/Publications/webwp15.pdf> accessed 13 July 2011.

[22] Antonello Tancredi, 'A Normative "Due Process" in the Creation of States through Secession' in Marcelo G Kohen (ed), *Secession: International Law Perspectives* (CUP 2006) 191.

[23] A Rigo Suredi, *The Evolution of the Right of Self-Determination: A Study of United Nations Practice* (AW Sijthoff 1973) 303.

[24] UNGA Res 1350 (XIII) (13 March 1959).

[25] Farley, *Plebiscites and Sovereignty*, 40–1. Antonio Cassese, *Self-Determination of Peoples*, 78.

[26] Rigo Suredi, *The Evolution of the Right of Self-Determination*, 295. In the end, a majority (56 per cent) of people of British Togoland voted in 1956 to merge with the Gold Coast to form Ghana.

Nations peacekeeping mission (MINURSO) was established in 1991.[27] MINURSO's task was both to monitor the ceasefire between Morocco and the Polisario Front (the Sahrawi national liberation movement which pressed for independence) and to organize a referendum which would enable the Sahrawis of Western Sahara to exercise self-determination by choosing between integration with Morocco and statehood. The referendum was originally scheduled for 1992 but has never taken place, largely due to the influence of Morocco in frustrating the process.[28]

The rarity with which the UN encouraged or endorsed the use of the referendum in the post-war era is probably due to the fear that it would serve to mobilize separatism within emerging states in the developing world, and indeed beyond. While international law applied the principle of self-determination to colonized people, international institutions and states moved quickly to ensure that the right did not extend beyond the decolonization process to offer sub-state nationalists elsewhere a green light for secession.[29] In light of this, a distinction emerged between the 'external' and 'internal' dimensions of the right to self-determination. Colonies were entitled to the former manifestation of the right resulting in independent statehood. Elsewhere those claiming to be sub-state peoples, insofar as international law did extend the principle to them, were entitled only to an internal manifestation of self-determination, an inchoate concept that is generally taken to mean some form of representative government.[30] There was certainly no right to statehood, whether sub-state peoples could mobilize massive support for such a claim by way of a referendum or not.

Turning to the third stage of the self-determination story, however, by the early 1990s the Pandora's box of self-determination seemed to have been opened. Although international law and practice had attempted to delimit carefully which peoples were entitled to external self-determination in the form of independent statehood, the symbolic political potential of the plebiscite as a road to national independence made it impossible to constrain. Therefore, the referendum was set to re-emerge as the vehicle of choice for sub-state nationalists, ironically in Eastern Europe and the Balkans, over 70 years after the Paris peace process had so strictly circumscribed its use in this region.

---

[27] UNSC Res 690 (29 April 1991), UN Doc S/RES/690.

[28] East Timor was another case where decolonization was delayed. Eventually, after years of brutal oppression by Indonesia, on 30 August 1999 78.5 per cent of the people of this former Portuguese colony voted for independence in a UN-sponsored referendum.

[29] Martti Koskenniemi, 'National Self-Determination Today: Problems of Legal Theory and Practice' (1994) 43 ICLQ 241.

[30] Anne Bayefsky (ed), *Self-Determination in International Law: Quebec and Lessons Learned* (Kluwer Law International 2000) 323–5.

(iii) State collapse after 1989: sub-state nationalism unleashes the referendum

Referendums deployed by both the central government and the republics played a key role in the constitutional struggle for power in, and ultimately in the collapse of, the USSR in the early 1990s. The referendum gatekeeper power that lay in the hands of individual republics enabled them to transform what was initially one state-wide plebiscite aimed at consolidating the federation into a series of separate nation-building referendums, allowing republics to position themselves symbolically as discrete peoples, asserting their own sovereignty, in some cases notionally alongside that of the state, but in reality in direct challenge to it. The referendum process therefore facilitated the expression of sub-state nationalism which, once mobilized, proved to be impossible for central political actors to control. Here we see a strong practical example of how the constitutional referendum is not only a vehicle for nationalism but potentially an important framing device in the reconstruction of the political identity of the people.

With the first stirrings of secessionism, particularly in the Baltic republics, and the indication that referendums would be used to legitimize nationalist aspirations, the Soviet government responded in 1991 with its own national referendum, which in hindsight can now be seen as a last, desperate attempt by Secretary General Gorbachev to hold the state together.[31] The death throes of the USSR offer an interesting study in how the referendum can expose and perhaps even accentuate the demotic fractures that exist within a multinational state.

Gorbachev's political reforms in 1989 and 1990 came at a time of rising nationalism throughout the Union. Although he enjoyed relative success in parliamentary elections in each of these years, so did the nationalist opposition, both in the Baltic states and also in the important republic of Ukraine.[32] Gorbachev decided to go directly to the people with a plan for a reconstituted USSR in the face of opposition not only from sub-state nationalists but also from reformists on the one hand who felt his liberalization was not going far enough and the conservative Communist Party on the other.

The pan-USSR referendum on a new Union Treaty, held on 17 March 1991 ('the Gorbachev referendum'), asked the question: 'Do you consider it necessary to preserve the USSR as a renewed federation of equal sovereign republics in which human rights and freedoms of all nationalities be fully

---

[31] Stephen White and Ronald J Hill, 'Russia, the Former Soviet Union and Eastern Europe: The Referendum as a Flexible Political Instrument' in Michael Gallagher and Pier Vincenzo Uleri (eds), *The Referendum Experience in Europe* (Macmillan Press 1996) 157–60.

[32] Roman Szporluk, *Russia, Ukraine, and the Breakup of the Soviet Union* (Hoover Institution Press 2000) 299–300; Stephen White, *Communism and its Collapse* (Routledge 2001).

guaranteed?'[33] This poll was in part an attempt to see off referendums threatened by 9 of the 15 republics: Estonia, Latvia, Lithuania, Armenia, Georgia, Ukraine, Russia, Kirghizia, and Uzbekistan. But the strategy backfired. Indeed, by the time the Gorbachev referendum was announced, Estonia, Latvia, and Lithuania had already made moves towards independence. Here the issue was complicated by the number of Russians living in these republics, a fact which presented nationalists with a dilemma. To go ahead and hold the Gorbachev referendum would give the Russian populations in the three Baltic republics the chance to articulate their support for continued union with the USSR. On the other hand, to boycott could lead to military intervention from Moscow.[34] The republics got round this problem by replacing the Gorbachev referendum with their own on independence: Lithuania on 8 February and Estonia and Latvia on 3 March.[35] The votes for independence were high.[36] As Brady and Kaplan report, even in heavily Russian areas 50 per cent or more of the population voted for independence.[37] The move towards independence for the Baltic republics was now unstoppable.

But the Gorbachev referendum was also adapted by other dissenting republics keen to avoid such a blatant choice: immediate independence versus the Central Committee's constitutional plan to consolidate the Union. A number of the other 12 republics either changed the question or added additional questions. One example is Kazakhstan, which amended the question to stress the sovereignty of the republics. 'Do you think it necessary to maintain the USSR as a Union of equal *sovereign states*?'[38] Kirghizia, Uzbekistan, and Ukraine meanwhile added questions on their own specific 'sovereignty' within the new Union. Ukraine was a crucial case on account of its strategic importance to the USSR and also given that its 'two-question' approach was such a direct challenge to the USSR's sovereignty. The first question was that set by Gorbachev and resulted in a vote of 71.5 per cent for

---

[33] Cited by Gregory Gleason, 'The Federal Formula and the Collapse of the USSR' (1992) 22(3) Publius 141. For a slightly different linguistic translation see White and Hill, 'Russia, the Former Soviet Union and Eastern Europe', 157–60.

[34] Brady and Kaplan, 'Eastern Europe and the Former Soviet Union', 192.

[35] Juris Dreifelds, *Latvia in Transition* (CUP 1997) 78. Following this, Georgia also decided to boycott and hold its own referendum on independence.

[36] Lithuania: 93 per cent on 85 per cent turnout; Estonia: 78 per cent on 83 per cent turnout; Latvia: 75 per cent on 88 per cent turnout.

[37] Brady and Kaplan, 'Eastern Europe and the Former Soviet Union', 193–4. They provide a breakdown of the voting figures by republic: 190–1.

[38] Emphasis added. See Nikolai Troitsky, '20 Years Without the Soviet Union', *Baltic Review* (Vilnius, 27 March 2011) <http://baltic-review.com/2011/03/20-years-without-the-soviet-union/> accessed 21 October 2011.

a renewed federation and 28.5 per cent against. The second was: 'Do you agree that Ukraine should be part of a Union of Soviet Sovereign States on the basis of the declaration of sovereignty of Ukraine?' (that declaration adopted on 16 July 1990).[39] The Yes vote was an even more decisive 80 per cent with a turnout of 83.5 per cent.

These seemingly contradictory results served to intensify both Ukrainian nationalist aspirations and unionist retrenchment. As LeDuc puts it: 'Strong nationalists were inclined to vote NO on the union question and YES on sovereignty, while hard-line communists favoured the opposite combination.'[40] Ukraine was another multinational republic with a Russian population of over 20 per cent, concentrated in the Crimea and the eastern provinces. Not surprisingly the Gorbachev question enjoyed stronger support in the east. But it is notable that, as in the Baltic states, ethnic Russians were divided on the issues.[41]

The result across the Union was, therefore, at best a pyrrhic victory for Gorbachev. He won a majority of votes on his question in every republic that took part, but only four republics offered the question to the voters as he had intended. And when we take into account the strong Yes vote on Ukraine's second question, a result mirrored elsewhere, and consider the uncertainty implied by Yes votes on amended questions in other republics, it becomes very difficult to reconcile these results with a clear endorsement for a reformed USSR.

Events moved quickly as Gorbachev put forward a new draft Union Treaty. Ukraine and a number of other republics held back from considering it and in the meantime the attempted coup d'état against Gorbachev by hard-line communists in the government in August 1991 destroyed any vestige of authority the Secretary General could claim. This in turn led the republics to stage further referendums, which were now unequivocally on the issue of independence. On 21 September Armenia voted for statehood and soon Turkmenistan (October), Azerbaijan, and Uzbekistan (both December) followed suit. In Ukraine also a referendum was held on 1 December 1991 with overwhelming support for independence.[42] As LeDuc

---

[39] Szporluk, *Russia, Ukraine, and the Breakup of the Soviet Union*, 300.

[40] Lawrence LeDuc, *The Politics of Direct Democracy: Referendums in Global Perspective* (Broadview Press 2003) 109. For details on the geographical breakdown of the vote see Szporluk, *Russia, Ukraine, and the Breakup of the Soviet Union*, 300–7.

[41] As Brady and Kaplan conclude, the sovereignty question was 'fairly successful in gaining support from Ukrainians and Russian alike'. Brady and Kaplan, 'Eastern Europe and the Former Soviet Union', 201.

[42] The vote for separation was Yes 90.3 per cent; No 9.7 per cent; turnout 84 per cent. And in due course the referendum was set to be used throughout the Union to secure independence, with only four republics—Russia, Kazakhstan, Tajikistan, and Belarus—not using this device on their eventual roads to statehood.

observes: 'More than any other single event, the Ukrainian referendum signalled the end of the Soviet Union.'[43]

The dissolution of the Soviet Union demonstrates the potent mix of sub-state nationalism and referendum democracy. At an institutional level we see some of the assumptions within political science about elite control in referendum processes being called into question (an issue we return to in Chapter 4). Although Gorbachev had strong institutional authority with which to initiate a referendum, carefully choosing a question in the hope of contriving a positive result, the autonomy already enjoyed by republics within the federal state brought with it the institutional infrastructure through which local elites could also use the referendum as a mechanism to mobilize sub-state constituent power. The referendum which Gorbachev had intended to be a constitution-building exercise, allowing one Soviet people to speak both together and directly, over the heads of the republics' elites, thereby consolidating the unity of the state, in fact served only to expose that the Soviet Union was fracturing along national lines.

The constitutional referendum opened up the possibility for the peoples of the republics to articulate their discrete territorial identities *constitutionally* rather than merely *politically* in a way that was impossible in any other forum. The referendum process both allowed and caused them to reflect upon their own identities and to mobilize their emerging sense of national selves in nascent acts of constitutional authorship. And crucially these processes took on lives of their own, changing as they did from being acts inside the existing constitution to constitutive acts for new polities emerging beyond that constitution. And in this we see how the trajectory of the referendum can result in outcomes that surprise elite actors. Since the very staging of a constituent referendum begs the demotic question—which people are you?—it can lead to the answer: we are Ukrainian, we are Estonian, we are Georgian etc, rather than we are Soviet citizens, as centrists had anticipated. Gorbachev believed he was engaging with one Soviet people, but he underestimated the extent to which the peoples of the Union felt primary national affinity with their own republics either alongside or in direct contradiction to this sense of Soviet citizenship. In the end, the former identities won over; the peoples of the USSR became authors of their own destinies and the device which both facilitated and legitimized their constitutional aspirations was the referendum.

(iv) Referendums and the implosion of divided societies

The application of referendums in the dissolution of the USSR was not untroubled by political violence. The central state made some early

---

[43] LeDuc, *The Politics of Direct Democracy*, 110. See also White, *Communism and its Collapse*, 78.

attempts to resist secession by force,[44] and minorities within republics rebelled against the process, often seeking the same right of self-determination as the republics, resulting in the carnage of Chechnya, civil war within Azerbaijan over Nagorno-Karabakh,[45] and the attempted secession of Abkhazia and South Ossetia from Georgia. But in general the use of referendums by the republics of the USSR did not pour oil on the flames of widespread civil war as it was to do in the collapse of the SFRY.

From 1990 onwards, moves towards independence by Slovenia, Croatia, and Bosnia-Herzegovina (Bosnia) caught the central Yugoslav state unawares and led to a violent backlash by both Belgrade and minority groups in Croatia and Bosnia. A vital step in the break-up of the state was the staging of referendums on independence by Slovenia and Croatia on 23 December 1990 and 19 May 1991 respectively, with overwhelming votes in favour.[46] The Croatian case in particular serves as another reminder that the process of breaking-up a state is not always one in which one ethnically homogeneous people, contained within an agreed territorial boundary, decides almost unanimously to press for statehood. The SFRY was characterized by the presence of minorities of different nationalities across the republics, and into such a complex environment the crude application of the referendum to settle territorial claims was incendiary.

The use of a referendum in this type of situation is particularly dangerous not only because with an in-built majority there can only be one outcome, which can further entrench the power of the majority. It is also problematic because this clear act of hegemony is presented as being democratic, offering a spurious constitutional legitimacy for political power play. The referendum is paraded as a self-evidently democratic device. It asks 'the people' to speak, and each person can do so with an equal say. But this simplistic notion of fairness is based upon what Avigail Eisenberg calls 'undifferentiated equality'.[47] Voters as individuals are decontextualized from their discrete communal settings. Their votes are then aggregated across communities and the total is taken to be the voice of one demos.

---

[44] Dreifelds, *Latvia in Transition* 78; Juri Ruus, 'Estonia' in A Auer and M Bützer (eds), *Direct Democracy: The Eastern and Central European Experience* (Ashgate 2001), 47, 51; Szporluk, *Russia, Ukraine, and the Breakup of the Soviet Union*.

[45] On 10 December 1991 the dominant Armenian population in Nagorno-Karabakh voted for independent statehood in a referendum that was boycotted by Azerbaijanis and led to an armed conflict.

[46] In Slovenia turnout was 93.2 per cent, with 95.7 per cent voting for independence. Despite a Serb boycott, with a turnout of nearly 80 per cent, 93.2 per cent in Croatia voted for independence and on 25 June 1991 both republics declared their independence.

[47] Avigail Eisenberg, 'The Medium is the Message: How Referenda Lead Us to Understand Equality for Minorities' in Matthew Mendelsohn and Andrew Parkin (eds), *Referendum Democracy: Citizens, Elites, and Deliberation in Referendum Campaigns* (Palgrave 2001) 149.

A referendum in this scenario takes no notice of multinational realities, of the existence of discrete constituencies, or of the relative patterns of power that define the relations between these groups; in fact it traduces these in the interests of the majority, creating resentment among minorities not only because their interests have been defeated by political power but because democratic legitimacy is prayed in aid to justify that defeat. As the events we will now discuss have shown, such a scenario can serve to escalate inter-communal conflict.

The most difficult case as the SFRY dissolved was, of course, Bosnia-Herzegovina. Bosnia sought the recognition of European states and, as a republic of the collapsing SFRY, was encouraged by the western powers to hold a referendum in order to indicate a democratic mandate for independence (see Chapter 6). Given the ethnic mix of the territory and prevailing tensions, the referendum had a disastrous impact on inter-ethnic relations. The ethnic composition in Bosnia in 1992 was approximately 43 per cent Muslims (later known as Bosniaks), 31 per cent Serbs, and 17 per cent Croats. Despite this complex demotic composition and the levels of animosity across communities, a referendum was duly organized by the Assembly of Bosnia-Herzegovina. This took place between 29 March and 1 April 1992. On a turnout of 63.4 per cent there was overwhelming support (99 per cent) for independence.[48] But participation was very uneven, and ominously the Serbian population boycotted the vote and rejected the result. There remained in Bosnia sizeable numbers of troops of the pro-Serbian Yugoslav National Army, and it became clear well before the referendum that a smouldering civil war in the territory would only be inflamed by such a vote and a subsequent process of state recognition. This is indeed what happened, with catastrophic results, particularly for the Muslim people. The Demographic Unit of the Office of the Prosecutor of the International Criminal Tribunal for the Former Yugoslavia (ICTY) estimates that some 104,000 people were killed between 1992 and 1995.[49] Added to this, of course, must be those wounded, tortured, raped, and the hundreds of thousands displaced from their homes.

Although the international community attempted to constrain how both the USSR and the SFRY collapsed, by offering the prospect of state recognition only to republics within both states, the referendum became a mode of resistance to such a seemingly arbitrary demarcation; other territories which had some degree of ethnic cohesion and institutional autonomy also used local plebiscites to assert the legitimacy of their own discrete constituent

---

[48] Daniel Bethlehem and Marc Weller, *The Yugoslav Crisis in International Law* (CUP 1997) xxxiv.

[49] <http://www.icty.org/sid/10591> accessed 12 July 2011.

power. Referendums started to proliferate among these self-proclaimed 'peoples' from the moment Croatia made its move towards statehood. For example, in August 1990 a referendum was held among the Serbs of the Krajina region of Croatia. In this unofficial poll there was almost unanimity for union of this territory and the Serbian region of Bosnia.[50] Similarly, on 9–10 November 1991, the Serbs in Bosnia-Herzegovina held a referendum with an overwhelming majority voting to remain in Yugoslavia,[51] while between 26 and 30 September 1991 Kosovar nationalists held an unofficial referendum to validate an earlier declaration of independence.

The Bosnian experience echoed an earlier referendum held in Northern Ireland in 1973, which also served to expose rather than settle the demotic question, with similarly troubled consequences. This sovereignty referendum which became known as the Border Poll, was held on the question of whether Northern Ireland should remain part of the UK or join with the Republic of Ireland to form a United Ireland.[52] The outcome was never in doubt: 99 per cent voted for the 'remain in UK' option on a 58 per cent turnout. Irish nationalist parties, including the moderate Social Democratic and Labour Party (SDLP), called upon voters to boycott the referendum as a democratic farce, with the Yes vote secured by the unionist majority in Northern Ireland. It is perhaps no coincidence that 1973 was Northern Ireland's bloodiest year. Bogdanor, who is highly critical of this referendum, has argued that in such a situation of polarized conflict, 'the referendum has little to offer'.[53]

In Chapter 8 we will discuss how the referendum in 1998 in Northern Ireland on the Belfast Agreement was, by contrast, a genuine and in the end largely successful attempt to understand and accommodate a situation where two groups within one territory, each having primary affinity to different kin states, can come together to agree upon a way of governing the disputed territory together, at least for the time being. There are a number of reasons for the success of the Belfast Agreement and the parallel

---

[50] See Laura Silber and Allan Little, *The Death of Yugoslavia* (BBC 1996) 92–104.

[51] The referendum would remain a key device, with another one held on 15–16 May 1993 by Serbs in Bosnia, which led to the rejection of the Vance-Owen peace plan.

[52] The referendum was held on 8 March 1973 and asked: 'Do you want Northern Ireland to remain part of the United Kingdom?' or 'Do you want Northern Ireland to be joined with the Republic of Ireland outside the United Kingdom?'

[53] Vernon Bogdanor, 'Western Europe' in David Butler and Austin Ranney (eds), *Referendums Around the World: The Growing Use of Direct Democracy* (Macmillan Press 1994) 38. Another example of the referendum intensifying national divisions is Canada, where in 1942 a referendum held on the subject of conscription resulted in different outcomes in Quebec and the other provinces. According to Marquis this 'exacerbated the division' between the two parts of the country on the issue. Pierre Marquis, 'Referendums in Canada: The Effect of Populist Decision-Making on Representative Democracy' (Government of Canada, Political and Social Affairs Division 1993).

referendum process by which it was endorsed,[54] but there is no doubt that the first and most fundamental reason, which was missing in 1973 just as it was in Bosnia in 1992, was a full accommodation of the territory's demotic complexity and full engagement and inclusion of both national communities in the decision-making process *prior to* the referendum.

Finally, the 1999 referendum in East Timor is different in that it cannot be said to have disadvantaged a particular minority, but it has parallels to Bosnia in demonstrating how a referendum, introduced into a volatile situation, can be the spark for a powerful group or state to react violently. After the UN-sponsored referendum on 30 August 1999, militias opposed to independence and acting on behalf of the Indonesian government spent several weeks destroying much of East Timor's infrastructure, making hundreds of thousands of refugees and killing between 1,000 and 2,000 people. The brutality was finally stopped by the belated deployment of the International Force for East Timor (INTERFET) on 20 September 1999. The lesson here seems to be one for international intervention. When the international community sponsors a referendum the result of which is likely to be deeply unpopular with an aggressive state, it must provide protection for the people concerned before and during such a poll.

Struggles for independent statehood by sub-state peoples offer radical challenges to assumptions present in international law, state practice, and in settled republican theory about the nature of a self-determining people. In particular, they call into question the notion that the ideal of a unitary republican demos maps perfectly onto the state as a juridical person. The constitutive referendum has continued to manifest itself in recent decades as an act of subversion through which sub-state elites—for example, in Quebec and the Basque Country[55]—have sought to bypass (or at least augment) established constitutional law and process in calls, inter alia, to have their discrete personality as peoples recognized on the international plane. These referendums, which are seen by central state actors to be unconstitutional in terms of the dominant constitutional norms of the state, serve to question a number of preconceptions that attend standard statist constitutionalism: first, the state's perception of itself as a unitary demotic space; second, an

---

[54] Kieran McEvoy and John Morison, 'Beyond the "Constitutional Moment": Law, Transition and Peacemaking in Northern Ireland' (2003) 26 Fordham Int'l LJ 960.

[55] Where a two-question, non-binding referendum was proposed in 2008 but in the end not held following a decision of the Constitutional Court of Spain on 11 September 2008. The referendum proposed an open-ended process of constitutional negotiations among the Basque parties 'to reach a democratic agreement about the right to decide of the Basque People'. See Ferran Requejo and Marc Sanjaume Calvet, 'Secession and Liberal Democracy: The Case of the Basque Country' (2009) Universitat Pompeu Fabra Political Theory Working Paper No 7 <http://www.recercat.net/bitstream/2072/43036/1/GRTPwp7.pdf> accessed 21 October 2011.

assumption that the constitution permits of but one unitary understanding of the locus of sovereignty; and, third, the notion that the paradoxical relationship between constituent power and constitutional form can be resolved by asserting positively entrenched legal sovereignty to be an inherently superior norm to any claim of discrete constitutive power by a sub-state people. We will return to the latter two issues in particular in Chapter 6.

The Bosnian referendum of 1992 and its boycott by Bosnian Serbs remains the classic example of how a referendum can serve merely to raise the demotic question, rather than answer it. In all of this we see the danger of using referendums in deeply divided societies where they can serve to expose and indeed inflame what is often a dormant disjuncture between the boundaries of territorial government and the nature of the demos/demoi within that territory.[56] Inter-communal relations in many parts of the world have survived uneasily through often unarticulated modes of understanding which have ensured the demotic issue is not openly confronted by way of self-conscious constitutional declarations, allowing each side to hold to different understandings of the nature of the state and even of the constitution. But the referendum, by attempting to create the conditions for collective constitutional authorship, can expose the fact that there is no consensus on the existence of one demotic author within the polity. The international recommendation of a referendum in Bosnia was fatally misguided. The people were being asked to decide, but optimistic assumptions about the cohesion of 'the people' were merely exposed in consequence. In Ivor Jennings's well-worn aphorism, 'the people cannot decide until someone decides who are the people',[57] this is the central challenge which the referendum has posed for almost a century in multinational states.

III. WHO ARE THE PEOPLE? WHO ARE THE VOTERS?

The issue of who within the agreed territorial space is warranted to vote is generally non-controversial. This entitlement will usually mirror the franchise rules for other elections, which tend to follow standard principles based upon some relationship between citizenship and residency. For example, in UK referendums the electorate has been modelled upon either existing local government or parliamentary electoral franchises. The former includes other EU nationals and peers, but not British citizens who have

---

[56] For a critique of the failure to implement boundary-type referendums in the former Yugoslavia, like those used after the First World War, realigning borders to fit better the ethnic composition of the territory, see Laponce, 'National Self-Determination and Referendums'.

[57] Ivor Jennings, *The Approach to Self-Government* (CUP 1956).

registered as overseas voters. The latter does include overseas voters, but not EU citizens or peers. For example, in the devolution referendums in the late 1990s, the local electorate was used for referendums in Scotland, Wales, and London,[58] and the parliamentary electorate for the Northern Ireland referendum.[59] But despite these straightforward cases history has shown that it is not uncommon in constitutional referendums, particularly those staged on territorial autonomy or independence in substate territories, for the franchise question to be deeply contested. In such cases there are two types of claim that deviate from a typical residence- or citizen-based approach to voting, each of which have proven to be controversial. The first is in respect of categories of people not resident in the territory whom it is asserted should be entitled to vote, and the second is that the franchise should be restricted to exclude some who are resident.

On the first point, an obvious argument is that all citizens of the existing state should be entitled to take part in a referendum involving the constitutional future of part of that state; after all, the whole state will be affected by any such decision. For example, we might ask why, when referendums were held in Scotland and Wales in 1997 and Northern Ireland in 1998 on devolution, the whole of the UK was not able to vote in a referendum on such dramatic constitutional change.[60] Such arguments are likely to arise again, and more forcefully, in the event of referendums on Scottish independence (discussed in Chapter 5) or Irish reunification.[61]

There are two possible arguments for this 'expanded franchise' position, which we might call 'the nested identity argument' and 'the affected interests argument'. The first contends that the sub-state territory belongs to a larger demos. This may deny that the sub-state group is credibly a free-standing 'demos', arguing that the state is comprised of but one national people; that is, the relevant nation is the UK and all UK citizens should have a say. Or it may accept the notion of a discrete demos at sub-state level—that there is such a thing as the Scottish or Welsh nation—but still contend that the Scots and the Welsh are also nested within a broader UK demos at

---

[58] Referendums (Scotland and Wales) Act 1997, ss 1(3) and 2(3); Greater London Authority (Referendum) Act 1998, s 1.

[59] This followed earlier practice in the 1973 Northern Ireland border poll, Northern Ireland (Border Poll) Act 1972, s 1(a). European Guidelines have recommended that where a residence requirement is imposed it should not 'as a rule' exceed six months. European Commission for Democracy Through Law (Venice Commission), 'Code of Good Practice on Referendums' Study No 371/2006 (20 January 2009), COE Doc CDL-AD(2007)008rev, para I.1.1.c.

[60] Oonagh Gay, 'Referendums: Recent Developments' (1999) House of Commons Library Research Paper 99/30, 26–7 <http://www.parliament.uk/briefing-papers/RP99-30.pdf> accessed 25 January 2012.

[61] Northern Ireland Act 1998, s 1.

the state-wide level. In either case it is wrong to consult only part of the people of the state on such a major issue. The second argument can leave aside questions of national identity altogether and contend that a state-wide referendum should be held on the basis that the issue of secession involves the vital interests of all the peoples of the state, on the basis of which they each have a right to a say.[62] A response to this is that the entire UK did have a say through representative voices expressed in Parliament which passed the devolution legislation and whose consent would be needed for any future constitutional separation of the country that might result in an independent Scotland. In other words, the affected interests argument can still be satisfied, even where the referendum is held exclusively in a sub-state territory, provided the other peoples of the state have a say, and in 1998 in the UK Parliament the rest of the UK did indeed have the final say, through their representatives in the legislature who came together to pass the required legislation or constitutional amendment.

Different arguments are presented for the inclusion of more limited categories of people, all with a purported tie in some way to the sub-state demos itself. It is sometimes argued that there are categories of people not resident in the territory who should nonetheless be entitled to vote on the basis that they are 'co-nationals' of the sub-state people, and hence part of the territorial demos. Therefore, the argument goes, they should have the franchise extended to them even though they live elsewhere. There can be two groups on whose behalf such claims to inclusion are made. The first are those who live in other parts of the state but who are perceived either by themselves or by those organizing the referendum to be co-nationals of the people of the territory voting for secession or autonomy. This is a more selective argument than that which says everyone living elsewhere in the state should be entitled to vote. It requires that these others, to be entitled to vote, be possessed of some attribute (such as place of birth) that specifically ties them to the territory in question. So, for example, at the time of the referendum on Scottish devolution in 1997 it was asked whether people born in Scotland but living elsewhere in the UK should be permitted to vote. The overwhelming counter-argument, however, accepted by all of the political parties, was that only those resident in Scotland should be entitled to participate in the referendum. This argument was based upon an interest test. Those resident in Scotland would be bound by the laws of a devolved administration and would contribute financially to the tax base of the country. Accordingly, only they should have a say in whether government should be devolved. This argument that voting rights should be tied to

---

[62] In the last chapter we discussed how the 'affected interests' argument is a key principle of deliberative democracy.

residence was accepted and the franchise was not extended beyond those already eligible to vote in local government elections in Scotland.

Second are those perceived to be co-nationals of the people of the territory who live in another state. These may be people who voluntarily emigrated or are descendants of such people—sometimes called 'out-voters'.[63] In the period leading up to the Montenegro referendum in 2006, Montenegrin law provided that only those citizens of Montenegro who had been permanent residents of Montenegro for at least 24 months prior to the referendum were entitled to vote.[64] Some objections were raised to this, since it made ineligible not only people in other states with some sense of belonging to Montenegro, but also those citizens of the FRY born in Montenegro but now living in Serbia. But in the end it met with international approval. In a 2001 report the Organization for Security and Co-operation in Europe/Office for Democratic Institutions and Human Rights (OSCE/ODIHR) supported this position, noting that as such citizens were in any case entitled to vote in Serbian elections they should not be entitled to a 'double franchise'.[65]

Alternatively, an argument may be made for those who through no choice of their own, for example due to forcible population transfer, ethnic cleansing, or displacement, moved to another state, or who are the descendants of such people—in other words, a refugee exception permitting out-of-country voting.[66] The argument runs that in such a situation tying the franchise rigidly either to citizenship or residence would be unfair when some element of coercion or necessity forced the expatriation. Examples of states that have in recent times allowed citizens living abroad to participate in elections or referendums include East Timor, Eritrea, and Iraq.[67]

During the League of Nations plebiscites, this issue arose. One difficult case was the plebiscite in North Schleswig, where the Danes were insistent that the franchise be extended to those who had lost their domicile through expulsion. The ejection of Danes from the territory had occurred in a campaign of Germanization conducted by Prussia from 1886 onwards,[68]

---

[63] Farley, *Plebiscites and Sovereignty*, 97.

[64] Law on the Election of Municipal Councillors and Representatives (Parliament of the Republic of Montenegro) (1998, 2000, 2001, and including amendments of 20 July and 11 September 2002), Art 11.

[65] OSCE/ODIHR, 'Assessment of the Referendum Law, Republic of Montenegro, Federal Republic of Yugoslavia' (Warsaw, 6 July 2001) 8.

[66] Patrik Johansson, 'Putting Peace to the Vote: Displaced Persons and a Future Referendum on Nagorno-Karabakh' (2009) 28 Refugee Survey Quarterly 122.

[67] Notably, the Venice Commission has recently taken the view that as a general principle 'it is desirable that the right to vote be accorded to citizens residing abroad'. Venice Commission, 'Code of Good Practice on Referendums', para I.1.1.c.

[68] Sarah Wambaugh, *A Monograph on Plebiscites: With a Collection of Official Documents* (OUP 1920) 51–2.

made more intense by German excesses in the First World War.[69] The Commission of Belgian and Danish Affairs agreed that all persons male and female aged 20 should be able to vote who 'were born in the zone in which the plebiscite is to be taken, even if they have lost their domicile there, in consequence of their expulsion by the German authorities—or have been domiciled there since a date before 1 January 1900'.[70] Turning to other cases, the degree of population transfer in Alsace-Lorraine after 1871 was one reason cited by France against a plebiscite there in 1919. Patterns of expulsion of Palestinian communities by Israel in 1948 and the strategic planting of Jewish settlements in the West Bank since 1967 would similarly cast a shadow on any attempt to use plebiscites as part of a future state-building process for Palestine.[71]

As well as arguments for the inclusion of voters resident elsewhere, in certain situations it has also been argued that the franchise should be restricted to *exclude* some who are living in the territory in question. This is prima facie a highly contentious proposition which would in effect deny membership of the demos to residents. Many states have legally defined residence criteria which require a certain period of residence for non-citizens before voting rights are acquired. But it becomes more controversial when the residence period is a particularly long one, or where this is applied on a discriminatory basis, and especially should ethnicity be used as a basis for inclusion or exclusion.

This area of demarcation can again highlight how different models of nationalism are at work in informing alternative approaches to the franchise. One of the tropes in nationalism theory is that there is a binary distinction between ethnic nationalism and civic nationalism. The former is characterized as stressing the common ethnicity of a particular group. This is widely criticized as exclusivist, atavistic, and reactionary. The latter identifies national belonging along largely civic and even residential lines. All citizens (and/or residents) are deemed to belong to the demos regardless of ethnic or racial markers. It is this model of nationalism that is commonly held by liberals and republicans alike to be the only acceptable code of citizenship—and franchise allocation—of any progressive, democratic society based upon the equality and freedom of all individuals.

Although this binary relationship is in many ways idealized,[72] when we reflect on the franchise issues that arise in referendums, the normative

---

[69] ibid 53.   [70] ibid 61. See also Laponce, 'National Self-Determination and Referendums', 51.

[71] Farley, *Plebiscites and Sovereignty*, 54.

[72] For arguments that nationalism in practice rarely appears in such pure formulations, and that much of the analysis of these principles is philosophically suspect, see Stephen Tierney, *Constitutional Law and National Pluralism* (OUP 2005) 23, esp fn 9.

principles of civic nationalism offer fairly clear guidance. As we saw in the UK referendums on devolution, residence rules were applied in line with civic conceptions of belonging and eschewing essentialist marks of distinction such as ethnicity. The argument for exclusion of non-resident, so-called co-nationals is similarly easily dismissed by those who argue that if you are not resident in the territory, not affected by laws subsequently passed within or for it, and not eligible to contribute to the tax base, then you have no claim to the franchise.

The issue of exclusion of residents is therefore highly charged. From the perspective of civic nationalism it is immediately repugnant, particularly when ethnic criteria are applied in demarcating the boundaries of the franchise. But as with the argument for inclusion of 'co-nationals' who were forced to flee from a territory (refugee outvoters), particular circumstances can argue against an absolutist approach. One complicating factor can arise in certain colonized or formerly colonized states where it is argued that an undifferentiated approach to the franchise in a particular referendum, especially one on independence, which does not take account of historical circumstances, is itself unjust to an oppressed native population. For example, it might be argued that an incoming group of residents from a colonial power is so great as to overwhelm the numbers belonging to a vulnerable and possibly small indigenous group. To take proper account of the ramifications of historical injustice, it is argued, it may be necessary to qualify a simplistic approach to demotic inclusion based upon the standard application of civic criteria alone.

Let us take several examples of situations where residents have been denied equal franchise rights. The first is the approach taken by Estonia and Latvia following their transition to independence from the Soviet Union.[73] A complication here was the large Russian-speaking communities settled in the Baltic states under the Soviet era. By 1989 ethnic Russians comprised less than one-tenth of Lithuania's population but about one-third of Estonia's and one-half of Latvia's.[74] This made the franchise issue particularly volatile in the latter two countries.[75]

As we have seen, Estonia held a referendum in March 1991 on independence, with an overwhelming vote in favour.[76] Notably all residents, citizens, and non-citizens were eligible to vote. In the next referendum on the draft constitution held in 1992 (in which ethnic Russians, most of whom

---

[73] Nils R Muiznieks, 'The Influence of the Baltic Popular Movements on the Process of Soviet Disintegration' (1995) 47 Europe–Asia Studies 3.

[74] Szporluk, *Russia, Ukraine, and the Breakup of the Soviet Union*, 44–7 and 269–71.

[75] Ole Nørgaard et al, *The Baltic States after Independence* (Edward Elgar 1996).

[76] See also White and Hill, 'Russia, the Former Soviet Union and Eastern Europe', 164–5.

were non-citizens, could not vote) 91.3 per cent voted in favour. A subquestion in this referendum was whether Russian-speakers who had applied for Estonian citizenship by 5 June 1992 should be allowed to participate in the upcoming presidential and parliamentary elections: 53—47 per cent—voted against allowing them the franchise. As Auers et al explain: 'The prevailing viewpoint was that only Estonian citizens should have the right to make decisions concerning the Estonian state. Moreover the majority of non-citizens had voted against independence in the referendum on independence.'[77] Under Estonian law the right to vote in elections to the national parliament or European Parliament is still restricted to citizens. From 1992 the opportunity to apply for citizenship was opened up, but with naturalization dependent to some extent upon knowledge of Estonian language and history the process was very slow[78] and by 2007, 8 per cent of Estonians were still stateless.[79]

In Latvia the 1991 referendum on independence asked: 'Are you in favour of a democratic and independent Latvia?' This was open to all permanent inhabitants in Latvia aged over 18, including ethnic Russians. All residents had also been able to participate in the first multi-party elections to the Supreme Council in March/April 1990.[80] But, as in Estonia, later referendums were limited to citizenship holders, in this way excluding one-third of the Latvian population, which was still denied automatic citizenship following reforms in 1994.[81]

The Latvian government came under pressure from the OSCE, NATO, and the EU, and in consequence the parliament changed the citizenship law on 22 June 1998 making naturalization easier, with liberal campaigners citing this as key to Latvia joining these bodies. The law removed the 'windows' system which gave people according to age a particular time limit within which to apply for citizenship.[82] It also proposed granting automatic

---

[77] Daniel Auers, Jüri Ruus, and Algis Krupavicius, 'Financing Referendums and Initiatives in the Baltic States' in Karin Gilland Lutz and Simon Hug (eds), *Financing Referendum Campaigns* (Palgrave Macmillan 2009) 83. Pettai also discusses how this referendum proposal split Estonia along ideological lines: 'Right-wing parties and members of the Congress of Estonia campaigned against it, while many moderate Estonian politicians simply avoided taking a public stand.' Vello Pettai, 'Estonia: Positive and Negative Institutional Engineering' in Jan Zielonka (ed), *Democratic Consolidation in Eastern Europe* (OUP 2001) vol I, 128.

[78] Pettai, 'Estonia: Positive and Negative Institutional Engineering', 134–6.

[79] Arch Puddington et al, 'Estonia' in Freedom House, *Freedom in the World: The Annual Survey of Political Rights and Civil Liberties* (Rowman & Littlefield 2007) 248.

[80] Adolf Sprudzs, 'Rebuilding Democracy in Latvia: Overcoming a Dual Legacy' in Zielonka (ed), *Democratic Consolidation in Eastern Europe*, 146.

[81] Auers, Ruus, and Krupavicius, 'Financing Referendums and Initiatives in the Baltic States', 87. See Dreifelds, *Latvia in Transition*, 97–8; Dzintra Bungs, 'Latvia' (1992) 1(27) Radio Free Europe/Radio Liberty Research Report, 62–6.

[82] Sprudzs, 'Rebuilding Democracy in Latvia', 151.

citizenship to children born in Latvia after 1991. However, in order to challenge this, the nationalist movement managed to force an initiative by gaining over 10 per cent of the citizens' signatures. And so a further referendum was held in Latvia in which voters were offered the chance to repeal the law. The referendum was held on 3 October 1998: 73 per cent of eligible voters took part and 53 per cent voted against repeal of the new liberalizing law against 45 per cent for its repeal. Thus the citizenship law was approved, making access easier for ethnic Russians. However, as in Estonia, disenfranchisement remains a major issue. By 2010 there were still 343,279 non-citizens in Latvia,[83] the majority members of the Russian minority and most of the others minorities from other former Soviet republics. A report by the European Commissioner for Human Rights in 2007 was deeply critical, stressing that the continued existence of the status of non-citizen is 'deeply problematic in terms of real or perceived equality and social cohesion'.[84]

Another example of the way in which the referendum exposes sharply how the demos is conceived is the whites-only referendum in 1992 in apartheid South Africa asking voters if they supported the negotiated reforms orchestrated by President FW de Klerk to end the apartheid system, in place since 1948.[85] This referendum, like the apartheid system itself, belied the most basic principle of republican democracy. All that can be said for it is that in political terms it allowed de Klerk to move ahead towards transition and on this basis the ANC, while condemning the principle of a racist referendum, advocated a Yes vote as strategically important in moves to end apartheid.

Another extremely troubled case which we mentioned in the decolonization context is Western Sahara. MINURSO was commissioned to conduct a referendum to enable the Sahrawis of Western Sahara to complete their exercise of the right to self-determination.[86] The referendum has not taken place over disagreement as to who constitutes a Sahrawi. Polisario seeks to rely on a Spanish census taken before the Moroccan occupation in 1975, as the basis of voter registration. Morocco, on the other hand, seeks to include people who have since moved into the territory, including many people who are widely considered by the Sahrawis to be illegal settlers, relocated

---

[83] Central Statistical Bureau of Latvia, IS09 Resident Population of Latvia by Citizenship <http://www.csb.gov.lv/en> accessed 14 October 2011.

[84] Commissioner for Human Rights of the Council of Europe, 'Memorandum to the Latvian Government' (16 May 2007), CommDH(2007)9, s 30.

[85] On 17 March 1992, 68.7–31.3 per cent voted Yes on an 85 per cent turnout. Other racially exclusivist referendums were held in 1960 among white South Africans on the issue of a republic and in 1969 by white Rhodesians on the declaration of unilateral independence.

[86] UNSC Res 690 (29 April 1991), UN Doc S/RES/690.

there specifically to water down the indigenous vote. The latest round of negotiations in 2007–08[87] at Manhasset, New York ended in deadlock.

The Nisga'a Final Agreement (Nisga'a Treaty) was concluded between the Nisga'a people and the governments of British Columbia and Canada on 27 May 1999 and again highlights the difficulty of the referendum for small indigenous peoples. It is a limited autonomy agreement, through which the Nisga'a government can run its own affairs in certain areas, but subordinate to provincial and federal law. It also recognizes a large area of land as belonging to the Nisga'a, creates a large water reservation for their use in the north west of British Columbia, and includes fishing rights. Political opponents in British Columbia argued for a provincial referendum on this.[88] But such a suggestion was rejected, partly in the context of the small Nisga'a population of 5,500. The treaty was the end of a century-long campaign for land by the Nisga'a, whose claim was largely based upon original entitlement and historical injustice.[89] Therefore the proposed referendum, premised upon a unitary conception of the demos, would in this situation overlook the fact that one demos, the settlers of British Columbia, would massively overwhelm the small Nisga'a people.[90] As a postscript, in 2002 British Columbia held a province-wide referendum on First Nations treaty negotiations. This was conducted by post and asked voters their views on eight principles, each of which was potentially restrictive of aboriginal rights and prerogatives, with Yes votes compelling the provincial government to adopt that principle in treaty negotiation. There was a widespread boycott and only approximately one-third of the ballots were returned. Of these, more than 80 per cent said Yes to all eight principles. Again, this is clearly the use of a referendum by an overwhelmingly dominant population purportedly to legitimize a particular agenda in relation to small minorities. It was also in many ways a political exercise since it was unclear how, if at all, the principles could be implemented.

These cases highlight how the franchise issue is, in a constitutional referendum, in fact about the very framing of the demos. In general the principles of liberal nationalism which are also, on this issue, largely

---

[87] Flowing from UNSC Res 1754 (30 April 2007), UN Doc S/RES/1754.

[88] Refe Mair, 'Nisga'a Treaty Must Go to Referendum', *Vancouver Courier* (Vancouver, 26 August 1998) 9. See also John Borrows, 'Tracking Trajectories: Aboriginal Governance as an Aboriginal Right' (2005) 38 UBC L Rev 285; Joseph Quesnel and Conrad Winn, 'The Nisga'a Treaty. Self Government and Good Governance: The Jury Is Still Out' (2011) Frontier Centre for Public Policy Series No 108.

[89] In a case itself emerging from British Columbia, the Supreme Court of Canada recognized such claims as a basis for aboriginal title to land and the right to use this land for traditional purposes. *Delgamuukw v British Columbia* [1997] 3 SCR 1010.

[90] Avigail Eisenberg, 'When (if ever) Are Referendums on Minority Rights Fair?' in David Laycock (ed), *Representation and Democratic Theory* (University of British Columbia Press 2004); Avigail Eisenberg, 'Presentation to the Select Standing Committee on Aboriginal Affairs for the BCCLA' in *Proceedings of the Select Standing Committee on Aboriginal Affairs Victoria, BC* (2 November 2001).

consonant with modern democratic republicanism, would set a default rule based upon citizenship, which would also open the franchise to permanent or long-term residents. But where a society is multinational and where the territory has suffered from patterns of historical injustice in consequence of colonialism in its various manifestations, these social realities can be brought to the surface in contentious disputes about inclusion and exclusion of voters, particularly since the constitutional reforms at stake may involve either the alleviation or the consolidation of relative patterns of hegemony. And it is in this context that historical injustice and societal pluralism can complicate simplistic approaches to equality and fairness. We will now turn to the case of New Caledonia, where again members of small and vulnerable indigenous groups find their interests undermined as a result of colonialism. Here an innovative approach to the franchise has been taken in preparation for a new referendum scheduled to take place by 2019.

IV. NEW CALEDONIA: A CASE STUDY IN DEMOTIC BOUNDARY-DRAWING

In the gradual decolonization of New Caledonia the application of the referendum has raised complex issues of territory and franchise. In time this very process has instigated a revision of civic republican orthodoxy in the French constitution which had long pre-supposed the existence of one undifferentiated national identity across France and its colonies. Furthermore, in determining voting entitlement in light of this new-found recognition of pluralism, the French state has begun to accept that the consequences of historical injustice and the subordination of the indigenous community should permit franchise rules that discriminate in favour of a marginalized indigenous people—principally for the purpose of a self-determination referendum—in an attempt to account for this legacy. In this way the evolution of referendum practice in New Caledonia is also the story of a growing international recognition that the exercise of self-determination must take account of historical injustice, which in turn has implications for democratic practice, particularly at popular constitutive moments.

New Caledonia has been a colony of France since 1853 and as a matter of international law the territorial issue is straightforward. In 1986 the UN General Assembly took the opportunity to affirm 'the inalienable right of the people of New Caledonia to self-determination and independence in accordance with resolution 1514 (XV)'.[91] At present it is a non-self-governing

---

[91] UNGA Res 41/41 (2 December 1986), UN Doc A/RES/41/41. Reference to UNGA Res 1514 is to the landmark Declaration on the Granting of Independence to Colonial Countries and Peoples, UNGA Res 1514 (XV) (14 December 1960).

territory (one of the largest remaining) under the supervision of the UN Special Committee on Decolonisation, and as such its final international status remains to be determined in an ongoing process of self-determination. This status is contested by France. It declared New Caledonia a French 'overseas territory' along with many such colonies in 1946 but one year later it withdrew New Caledonia from the UN list of non-self-governing territories. Nonetheless, international momentum has in time pushed France towards constitutional reforms[92] and in the constitutional changes of 2003 a new *sui generis* constitutional status of New Caledonia—secured after a series of constitutional agreements—was encapsulated in Title XIII of the constitution.[93]

Referendums have hitherto been used on three occasions in New Caledonia. The first took place in 1958 but did not bring about any change to direct rule from France. This poll was part of an empire-wide process in which President de Gaulle offered the new French constitution to many of France's colonies. Another was held in 1987 on what would become a new constitutional settlement for the territory—the Matignon–Oudinot Accords of 1988. Again, a majority voted for the status quo but by now, with an increasingly assertive nationalist movement in the territory, this was heavily contested against a backdrop of violence involving disaffected indigenous people (the Kanaks). The third referendum took place on the Noumea Accord—the most elaborate and, from the perspective of New Caledonian nationalism, progressive, move towards independence—on 8 November 1998, with 72 per cent voting Yes to the pre-negotiated constitutional agreement.[94] Another referendum is anticipated by 2019, which may or may not settle the final status of the territory. This story of gradual decolonization through a succession of very different referendums all set against the very uneasy relationship between New Caledonia and France, makes this territory a fascinating case study in how the act of constituting 'the people' is a fundamental move anterior to the constitution of the polity, and how the sovereignty referendum can become such a demos-constituting act.

The ethnic mix of New Caledonia is highly complex and this is one factor that has served to complicate the use of the referendum as a device with which to settle the territory's future on the basis of consent. The population

---

[92] This momentum was reinforced by the General Assembly declaring the 1990s to be the International Decade for the Eradication of Colonialism. UNGA Res 43/47 (22 November 1988), UN Doc A/RES/43/47.

[93] *Titre XIII Dispositions transitoires relatives a la Nouvelle-Calédonie* (Constitution of France, Titre XIII 'Transitional provisions relating to New-Caledonia') gives constitutional effect to the Nouméa Accord 1998.

[94] Nic Maclellan, 'Voters Say Yes to Noumea Accords', *Islands Business* (Suva, December 1998) 30–2; Nic Maclellan, 'From Eloi to Europe: Interactions with the Ballot Box in New Caledonia' (2005) 43 Commonwealth & Comparative Politics 394, 401.

of New Caledonia—itself very small[95]—is divided into four main ethnic groups. The indigenous Kanak language groups were found to amount to 45 per cent of the population when studied in a census of 1996.[96] These Melanesian groups have been marginalized in economic and political terms as a consequence of French colonialism; they are also geographically concentrated, forming a large majority of the population of the Loyalty Islands and Northern Province (New Caledonia is made up of a number of island groups, the largest of which is the main island or Grand Terre).[97] A second group known as Caldoches or Calédoniens descend from white French settlers, many of whom were convicts who arrived in the territory in the latter half of the nineteenth century. They have accumulated the bulk of the wealth of New Caledonia through farming and mining in a territory that is particularly rich in nickel;[98] they are often compared to Afrikaners. There are also more recent—and generally temporary—residents from France, known as *métropolitains*, who typically work in civil administration.[99] Finally, there are also Asian and Polynesian immigrants who have typically arrived fairly recently from other French territories such as Wallis and Futuna and the New Hebrides as well as from Indonesia, Vietnam, and other Asian states.[100] These three non-Kanak groups form a significant majority of the population of the Southern Province.[101]

---

[95] Calculated to be 231,000 by a census carried out in 2004. Cited by Jacques Ziller, 'French Overseas: New Caledonia and French Polynesia in the Framework of Asymmetrical Federalism and Shared Sovereignty' in Jorge Oliveira and Paulo Cardinal (eds), *One Country, Two Systems, Three Legal Orders—Perspectives of Evolution* (Springer 2009) 445.

[96] David A Chappell, 'The Noumea Accord: Decolonization without Independence in New Caledonia?' (1999) 72 Pacific Affairs 373, 373; Maclellan, 'From Eloi to Europe', 403. It is also a proportion of the population that has declined in the long term—down from 60 per cent in 1891. Rumley ascribes this to a French immigration policy: Dennis Rumley, 'The French Geopolitical Project in New Caledonia' in Dennis Rumley, Vivian Louis Forbes, and Christopher Griffin (eds), *Australia's Arc of Instability: The Political and Cultural Dynamics of Regional Security* (Springer 2006) 236. Notably, the data here are quite old, since questions based on ethnicity were not asked in the 2004 census: Ziller, 'French Overseas', 449. On a visit to New Caledonia in 2003 President Chirac stated that France did not recognize ethnic origin. People 'are all French and there are French people of all ethnic origins'. Therefore, questions on ethnicity were 'irresponsible and illegal'. Quoted by Rumley, 'The French Geopolitical Project in New Caledonia', 243. In the end, and after an 18-month delay, the census finally proceeded in late 2004 without the ethnicity questions which led to a 'significant boycott': Maclellan, 'From Eloi to Europe', 404–5.

[97] For these groups the territory is often referred to as Kanaky rather than New Caledonia.

[98] Chappell, 'The Noumea Accord', 375.

[99] Europeans and their descendants (including Caldoches) constituted 34 per cent of the population in the census of 1996.

[100] Chappell, 'The Noumea Accord', 376 and 381.

[101] Maclellan, 'From Eloi to Europe', 398. This includes the capital Noumea, which is also largely controlled by non-Kanaks.

(i) French republicanism and moves towards independence

Although New Caledonia has a clear international legal right to self-determination, the 2004 census example exposes how this right collides with the embeddedness of French classical republican ideology, which has envisaged France and its overseas territories as one, indivisible territory containing one, indivisible demos; a self-perception which has only begun to change in recent years through gradual constitutional processes that now offer some recognition of the national pluralism of French territories.

The French republican *idée fixe* is summed up in Article 1 of the Constitution of the Fifth Republic of 4 October 1958, which provides that 'France is an indivisible, secular, democratic and social Republic. It ensures the equality of all citizens before the law, without distinction of origin, race or religion. It respects all beliefs.' In consequence, the French constitution has long embodied a mono-cultural and mono-national vision of the French state which brings with it a centralized governmental system; both this national vision and this governmental centralization were extended to the governance of its empire.[102] This vision has only fairly recently been modified in constitutional amendments made on 8 March 2003, which added a sentence to Article 1: 'It is organised on a decentralised basis.' Title XII of the Constitution on Territorial Units was also rewritten in these amendments. This contains provisions on all of France's overseas territories, with Article 74-1 in Title XIII covering New Caledonia.[103] And, therefore, in large part the story of French engagement in New Caledonia over the past half-century is one of tension between a dogmatic civic nationalism, a heritage of colonial chauvinism, and the newly emerging recognition of national difference that is central to the concept of self-determination.[104]

The referendum in 1958 explicitly exposed the traditional nationalist mentality. As noted, New Caledonia voted to remain in France but with the indigenous people so marginalized the fairness of such a vote is seriously questioned. As Marrani observes, this outcome:

> was perhaps under the pressure of the French settlers present on the territory and not by the will of all the different populations within the territory. The right of cohesive national groups applied to New Caledonia in 1958 seems to

---

[102] David Marrani, 'Principle of Indivisibility of the French Republic and the People's Right to Self-Determination: The "New Caledonia Test"' (2006) 2 J Academic Legal Studies 16.

[103] Constitution of France, Titre XIII. See also Alan Berman, 'The Noumea Accords: Emancipation or Colonial Harness?' (2001) 36 Texas Int'l LJ 277.

[104] For more on the history of French policy in the South Pacific see Robert Aldrich and John Connell (eds), *France's Overseas Frontier* (CUP 1982).

have only considered the inhabitants of French origin and not the other 'peoples' like the Kanak, for example.[105]

The referendum of 13 September 1987 still bore the hallmarks of colonialism and French dominance. Although again the vote was in favour of remaining in France, it led to stronger autonomy. These changes, taking effect through the Matignon–Oudinot Accords, divided New Caledonia into three provinces (Northern Province, Southern Province, and the Province of Loyalty Islands), each with its own system of government. This was designed to provide autonomy for the Kanaks since, although the Southern Province is composed mainly of European settlers and other more recent immigrants, the Northern Province has a majority of Melanesians, and the Loyalty Islands is overwhelmingly Melanesian. The three provincial assemblies came together to constitute the Congress of New Caledonia which was given legislative powers, while a consociational arrangement was put in place for the appointment of the government.[106] Despite these changes, there was also resentment within the indigenous population that, as far as many nationalists were concerned, a model of autonomy was being imposed upon the territory and that the territory seemed no closer to independence.[107]

Although many Kanaks remained deeply unhappy, the 1988 Accords did mark the point at which France started to acknowledge New Caledonia as a discrete demos with a right to determine its own future. The French state recognized that New Caledonia was a self-determining entity and from this time any decision on its future would be for the people of the territory to make. The 1988 Accords not only created a new system of autonomy, they also set out a ten-year period in which the territory would prepare for a referendum on sovereignty. As Marrani comments: 'This was a definite move departing from the idea of indivisibility of the French Republic.'[108]

However, France as a whole remained part of the self-determining process with, as was noted earlier, a referendum also in France on 6 November 1988 to approve the constitutional provisions that would give effect to the new statute for New Caledonia. This suggests that the relevant self-determining demos was not only the people of New Caledonia but also the people of France. And indeed the following period was not an easy one, as a backlash occurred within the French political class itself. As late as 1996 Gaullist Premier Juppe said that France would not consider independence or

---

[105] Marrani, 'Principle of Indivisibility of the French Republic', 18. See also Chappell, 'The Noumea Accord', 376–7.

[106] Ziller, 'French Overseas', 450–1.

[107] Indeed, Kanaks rioted in protest at the Matignon–Oudinot Accords.

[108] Marrani, 'Principle of Indivisibility of the French Republic', 20.

Framing 'the People': Constitutional Referendums and the Demos 89

independence-association as possible options.[109] The socialists, when in power in 1997, took a less chauvinistic line but it was in this tense environment that the Noumea Agreement was struck on 5 May 1998 and approved by a referendum on 8 November of that year.

Although this was the first to recognize the discrete territorial integrity of New Caledonia, another issue continued to linger, and that was whether account would be taken of the specific ethnic composition of New Caledonia, and in particular of the historical injustice suffered by the indigenous Kanaks. To some extent the Noumea Agreement recognizes the pluri-ethnic reality of the territory. Importantly, it concedes that the annexation by France in 1853 was not a legal agreement with the indigenous people;[110] takes account of the distinctiveness of Kanak civilization; creates a strong and indeed unique autonomy structure for New Caledonia in a complex document of some 261 articles; considers that a New Caledonian citizenship should be created;[111] and establishes voting rules (discussed later) for a future referendum. This system of autonomy is specific to New Caledonia[112] and asymmetrical,[113] creating a formulation of shared sovereignty;[114] which at least on its face is a radical innovation for a state such as France.[115] But still, this was not the referendum on independence that many Kanaks had envisaged in 1988.[116]

Since the Noumea referendum ended in a 72 per cent vote in favour on a 74 per cent turnout[117] it is also notable for its popularity across New Caledonia's ethnic divisions.[118] In particular, within the big Yes vote for

---

[109] Chappell, 'The Noumea Accord', 382.

[110] eg the Preamble acknowledges the fact of colonization and European domination of the rest of the world. But this is also coupled with a claim that the 1853 occupation was 'in accordance with the conditions of international law' at the time; an assertion described as a 'fallacy' by Berman, 'The Noumea Accords', 283.

[111] Ziller, 'French Overseas', 451.

[112] See Constitution of France, Titre XIII.

[113] New Caledonia's legislative powers are unique among French overseas territories, as is the fixed timetable for a self-determination referendum. Maclellan, 'From Eloi to Europe', 397.

[114] The Noumea Accord comes with the commitment that power transferred cannot be taken back. This has been called 'irreversible transfer'. Maclellan, 'From Eloi to Europe', 400. See also Chappell, 'The Noumea Accord', 385.

[115] 'On this basis, New Caledonia is a separate country (*Pays*) which shares sovereignty with the French Republic, with the perspective of "full sovereignty", i.e. independence, if the majority of the population so wishes in the future.' Ziller, 'French Overseas', 450. The reference to a move from shared sovereignty with France to 'full sovereignty' also appears in the preamble to Noumea.

[116] Chappell, 'The Noumea Accord', 373.

[117] The Accords were then approved by the French National Parliament with a vote of 827 to 31 to change the French constitution to include the provisions of the Accord. The Agreement was adopted in France by *Loi organique*, giving it constitutional status.

[118] Chappell, 'The Noumea Accord', 386.

Noumea there was massive indigenous Kanak support estimated at 87 per cent in the Islands and 95 per cent in the north of the territory.[119] The support among Kanaks may be attributed to the fact that Noumea is itself a half-way house agreement, which gives constitutional autonomy with a fixed timetable towards a future referendum on sovereignty,[120] and provides for the next referendum to take place between 2013 and 2019.[121] By Article 217, if the outcome is positive, the territory will be 'sovereign'. But if not, that will not be the end of the matter and a new period of consultation will be initiated.

It seems that these Accords did mark a definite change not just in the constitutional status of New Caledonia but in the mentality of French republicanism. A disaggregated concept of the demos was now entrenched, the discrete identity of New Caledonia accepted, and the stain of colonialism admitted. However, we still wait to see what role France might play in a future referendum and what it might do in the event of a vote for independence.

In short, the independence of New Caledonia is still far from a foregone conclusion. The different sides see the implications of Noumea very differently. For the Kanaks it is a clear road to independence, while the opposition see it as an opportunity to forestall further status change.[122] There is also considerable scepticism. Berman describes the Noumea Accord as 'a convenient guise for maintaining more than a century-old colonial harness'.[123] Although the preamble envisages the prospect of 'full sovereignty for New Caledonia', the document never mentions independence. Rumley sees it as a compromise by the French government, buying it time 'to manipulate local public opinion in its favour'[124] and by the Kanak people, who as a minority would probably have lost any independence vote at that time.[125] If immigration could be halted, 'sooner or later, it was felt, the Kanak population would be in the majority'.[126] But this tense situation has meant that the

---

[119] ibid 387.

[120] Organic Law No 99-209 of 19 March 1999 on New Caledonia, Title XI: 'la consultation sur l'accession á la pleine souveraineté'.

[121] Organic Law No 99-209 of 19 March 1999 on New Caledonia, Art 217; Marrani, 'Principle of Indivisibility of the French Republic', 24; Maclellan, 'From Eloi to Europe', 400; Chappell, 'The Noumea Accord', 386.

[122] Maclellan, 'From Eloi to Europe', 401–2.   [123] Berman, 'The Noumea Accords'.

[124] Rumley exemplifies the ongoing suspicion, shared by many, that France is at all willing to end its control over New Caledonia and other mineral-rich territories in the South Pacific. Rumley, 'The French Geopolitical Project in New Caledonia'.

[125] See also Berman, 'The Noumea Accords', 281.

[126] Rumley, 'The French Geopolitical Project in New Caledonia', 239.

future battleground seems set to centre on the issue of franchise in the next referendum.

(ii) A franchise fit for self-determination?

The complex ethnic mix within the territory of New Caledonia itself and the situation of deep power imbalance among communities has made the referendum franchise issue incendiary, particularly in light of a French republican ideology centred upon an undifferentiated concept of equality. However, the French state's gradual move towards recognizing for limited purposes the ethnic pluralism of New Caledonia, and the acceptance that this should lead to a differentiated conception of citizenship, carry concomitant implications for the franchise in the anticipated self-determination referendum. As a point of principle the French constitution still does not recognize the existence of a New Caledonia 'nation', but it does accept in practice ethnic specificity for the purposes of electoral law. A temporary model of citizenship—'New Caledonia citizenship-French nationality'—accepts that only citizens of the territory should be able to participate in elections to its institutions and to the final consultation for self-determination.[127]

With a small population in which the indigenous people are a minority, and indeed a shrinking minority in the context of inward migration,[128] it was recognized by France in 1998 that a referendum on independence would probably have failed. The electoral question is historically controversial, with Kanaks excluded from voting altogether until 1946.[129] Although this was corrected by the time of the 1958 referendum, Kanaks were still not encouraged to vote. The demographic reality by the 1990s meant that by normal franchise rules based simply on residence, Kanak aspirations for self-determination would be undermined by the likely outcome of a referendum. In this context the Noumea Accord contains franchise provisions that serve to privilege the indigenous peoples as a corrective for a post-colonial situation where settlers have become such a powerful force.

The new rules for a future referendum contained in the Noumea Accord restrict voting rights to long-term residents.[130] The category of New Caledonian 'citizenship' is distinguished from French 'nationality'. Only those

---

[127] Although France was willing to amend normal franchise rules based on residency, it still does not recognize ethnicity, as we saw in the controversy surrounding the 2004 census.

[128] One Kanak political party estimated that by the late 1990s 20,000 people had migrated to New Caledonia since 1988—out of a population of approx 230,000. Chappell, 'The Noumea Accord', 385 cites this figure. Maclellan, 'From Eloi to Europe', 403 offers a more modest assessment that immigrants in this period numbered over 10,000.

[129] Maclellan, 'From Eloi to Europe', 399.

[130] Chappell, 'The Noumea Accord', 386. Noumea Accord, Art 2.2.

possessing the former are entitled to vote.[131] According to the new regime, the potential franchise for the proposed referendum between 2013 and 2019 is restricted mainly to those born in New Caledonia with some exceptions including for those born before 1988 who have reached the age of majority and resided in New Caledonia from 1988 to 1998; those born after 1998 having one parent who met or could have met the requirements for participating in the 1998 referendum, and those who in 2013 can prove 20 years of unbroken residence.[132] Maclennan describes the purpose of the law as 'to effectively freeze the electoral body in 1998' as only those people resident for ten years after 1988, and their descendants of voting age, can take part in future referendums.[133]

Inevitably these franchise rules have provoked controversy. However, they have been found not to violate the ICCPR by the UN Human Rights Committee. In a complaint brought before the Human Rights Committee (HRC)[134] 21 French nationals, resident in New Caledonia but excluded from the 1998 referendum and potentially excluded from future referendums from 2014 onwards, challenged this law, claiming it violated their rights under Articles 2 (right to an effective remedy), 12 (right to freedom of movement), 25 (right to participation in public life), and 26 (right to be free from discrimination).

There were two central questions for the Committee to address: were the voting rules discriminatory? And, were the residence rules for each election proportionate? On the first issue the Committee found no unlawful discrimination. It accepted the French government's argument that difference of treatment for different people is not discriminatory if it is objectively justifiable. By this measure the residence requirements for both the 1998 referendum and future plebiscites were permissible. It is notable that the Committee also accepted the French argument that it was valid to restrict participation in the referendums to persons 'concerned' by the future of New Caledonia.[135] A central reason why a move from simple residence was deemed permissible was that the issue involved self-determination under Article 1 of the Covenant, and because the ongoing effect of the restricted

---

[131] Maclellan, 'From Eloi to Europe', 404. [132] Noumea Accord, Art 2.2.1.

[133] Maclellan, 'From Eloi to Europe', 404. See Organic Law No 99-209 of 19 March 1999 on New Caledonia, Art 218 for further detail on who can be registered as a potential voter for the future referendum. The hope of independence leaders is that the limits on immigration and restrictions on the franchise will create the winning conditions for an independence vote in the next referendum. Maclellan, 'From Eloi to Europe', 404. It should also be noted that any French citizen residing in New Caledonia may still vote for municipal elections and the election of the representatives of New Caledonia in the French parliament whether or not they are New Caledonian citizens. Ziller, 'French Overseas', 452.

[134] *Gillot v France*, HRC, Comm No 932/2000, UN Doc CCPR/C/75/D/932/2000 (2002).

[135] ibid para 13.16.

franchise would only apply to future referendums in the framework of a self-determination process, and not general elections.[136]

Neither did the Committee find the length of residence requirements to be disproportionate. Again, these were considered justified because they limited participation to persons 'concerned' by the future of New Caledonia. The Committee accepted that this was justified 'in order that those residents able to prove a sufficiently strong tie are able to participate in each referendum'.[137] This does raise the question, what is meant by a strong tie? And why is it justified to demand this for a referendum but not for general elections?

There was a subsequent case taken to the European Court of Human Rights by a temporary resident of New Caledonia who had since returned to metropolitan France and was unable to vote in the elections to the Congress and provincial assemblies of New Caledonia due to the ten-year residence rule, a more limited franchise restriction than that imposed for a future referendum, but still a residence rule of considerable length. Once more, a similar finding was made. The applicant alleged that the restrictions imposed on his right to vote had violated the right to free elections guaranteed by Article 3 of Protocol No 1 and constituted discrimination on grounds of national origin, in breach of Article 14. Although this exclusion was not directly related to a future self-determination referendum, again the French government justified the residence condition on the basis that self-determination was indirectly relevant. The representative bodies in the territory were engaged in preparing for a self-determination referendum. These consultations should reflect the will of 'interested' persons and the result should not be altered by a huge vote cast by recent arrivals on the territory who lacked solid links with it. Furthermore, the restriction on the right to vote was a direct and necessary consequence of establishing Caledonian citizenship.

The European Court, as had the HRC re the ICCPR, found no violation of the European Convention. New Caledonia's current status amounted to a

---

[136] ibid paras 13.17, 14.7.

[137] ibid para 14.6. The Committee concluded that

> the cut-off points set for the referendum of 1998 and referenda from 2014 onwards are not excessive inasmuch as they are in keeping with the nature and purpose of these ballots, namely a self-determination process involving the participation of persons able to prove sufficiently strong ties to the territory whose future is being decided. This being the case, these cut-off points do not appear to be disproportionate with respect to a decolonization process involving the participation of residents who, over and above their ethnic origin or political affiliation, have helped, and continue to help, build New Caledonia through their sufficiently strong ties to the territory.

Gillot v France, para 14.7. <http://www.unhcr.ch/huricane/huricane.nsf/0/E87101B9D41869DEC1256C40005417C6?opendocument> accessed 13 July 2011.

transitional phase prior to the acquisition of full sovereignty and was therefore part of a process of self-determination. The Court also took account of the territory's troubled history and viewed the ten-year residence condition in the context of resolving the long conflict in New Caledonia. Therefore, in light of the history and status of New Caledonia such 'local requirements' warranted the restrictions imposed on the applicant's right to vote. The Court found unanimously that there had not been a violation of Article 3 of Protocol No 1 and that in consequence it was unnecessary to examine the complaint based on Article 14.[138] This endorses the right of France to set restrictive electoral laws in these circumstances.

It is interesting that proportionality was linked to the self-determination issue by both tribunals, and particularly by the HRC. The provisions were found to be proportionate, but the key to justifying such discrimination as there was, was the importance attached to self-determination as a legitimate value. What we see is in effect the justification of differentiated equality for the purposes of the franchise, but crucially this applies with particular weight to self-determination referendums.[139] The HRC's finding that the restriction of the franchise to those with 'strong ties' seems to validate indirectly a privileging of the indigenous population. In this sense the referendum is being singled out for special treatment, justifying a restriction of who constitutes the demos. For other elections different rules of residency and citizenship should apply. This is recognition that the constitution of the demos logically predates that of the polity, and that the polity's constitutional order derives its legitimacy from that demos, properly constituted. It is this recognition of the referendum as playing such a dual role—that is, not only of creating the constitution but in a sense also creating the constitutional people—that the referendum franchise rules in this case were found not to be illegitimately discriminatory or disproportionate.

And this is consistent with the broader UN position, in particular a statement made by the UN Secretary-General calling upon the administering powers of non-self-governing territories to 'ensure that any exercises of the right of self-determination are not affected by changes in the demographic composition of the Territories under their administration as a result of immigration'.[140] And in many ways the New Caledonia franchise rules are a compromise position. Kanak leaders have argued that only Kanaks as

---

[138] *Py v France* App no 66289/01 (ECtHR, 11 January 2005); see also Maclellan, 'From Eloi to Europe', 402–3.

[139] Although the European Court focuses upon restrictions of the franchise more broadly, it does appear to endorse the HRC's finding in para 14.7—*Py v France*, para 63—and in doing so seems to accept the indirect connection to the self-determination issue alluded to by France.

[140] Report of the Secretary-General, 'International Decade for the Eradication of Colonialism' (2001), UN Doc A/56/61. See also UNGA Res 43/47.

the original inhabitants should be entitled to vote. France on the other hand rejected this, citing the guarantee of equality in the French constitution, and also Article 1 of the UN Charter which, while citing 'the principle of equal rights and self-determination of peoples' as a purpose of the UN, also sets out 'promoting and encouraging respect for human rights and for fundamental freedoms for all without distinction as to race, sex, language, or religion' as another purpose. France also made reference to General Assembly Resolution 1514, which demands that:

> Immediate steps shall be taken, in Trust and Non-Self-Governing Territories or all other territories which have not yet attained independence, to transfer all powers to the peoples of those territories, without any conditions or reservations, in accordance with their freely expressed will and desire, *without any distinction as to race, creed or colour*, in order to enable them to enjoy complete independence and freedom.[141]

On the other hand, Berman argues: 'It is highly arguable that Kanaks are the only peoples entitled to vote on self-determination because they are the original inhabitants who have been subjected to "alien subjugation, domination and exploitation" in violation of the Charter of the United Nations.'[142] Furthermore: 'Allowing other groups to vote on self-determination is farcical because France pursued a calculated policy of encouraging new migrants to the territory to squelch Kanak moves for independence.'[143]

The findings of the HRC and the European Court of Human Rights endorse the more moderate franchise restrictions introduced in New Caledonia. In many ways they leave the Kanak nationalists dissatisfied, and it is not clear whether these provisions will suffice to secure a Yes vote for independence in the coming years. However, they do demonstrate just how the constitutional referendum puts the anterior demotic issue, which generally lies dormant in constitutional politics, at the front and centre of processes of polity formation and change.

V. CONCLUSION

The demos issue in New Caledonia exposes two problems in the use of the referendum in an ethnically divided society which we encountered earlier in

---

[141] Declaration on the Granting of Independence to Colonial Countries and Peoples, adopted by the UNGA Res 1514 (XV) (emphasis added).

[142] Berman, 'The Noumea Accords', 282 fn 125. For another endorsement of such restrictions see Harry Beran, 'Who Should be Entitled to Vote in Self-Determination Referenda?' in Martin Warner and Roger Crisp (eds), *Terrorism, Protest and Power* (Edward Elgar 1990) 156–63.

[143] ibid 282 fn 125. This is contrary to Art 8 of the Plan of Action for the Full Implementation of the Declaration on the Granting of Independence to Colonial Countries and Peoples, UNGA Res 35/118 (11 December 1980), UN Doc A/RES/35/118.

the chapter. The first is that a constitutive referendum implies the pre-existence of a relatively unified demos. But when this is lacking, the referendum threatens simply to expose the fault-lines between groups as it was to in Northern Ireland in 1973 and Bosnia in 1992. The referendum, by instantiating a territorially bounded act of collective constitutional authorship, can cause people to reflect upon their own sense of territorial belonging. More instrumentally it can allow elites, particularly sub-state territorial elites, to turn a claim to demotic distinctiveness into reality by institutionalizing it; that is, by mobilizing the people of the territory in a discrete act of self-determination. The referendum, of course, is not the only way in which sub-state nationalism can be mustered, and the break-up of the former USSR and SFRY would probably have happened even without the use of plebiscites. But at the same time, they were a highly useful resource for sub-state nationalists, presenting the modernist democratic promise in full.

New Caledonia is enlightening secondly because it offers a detailed illustration of how France, with a deep ideological commitment to undifferentiated equality, has had to come to terms with the fact that when a referendum is in effect a polity-constituting act, franchise rules for such a constitutive referendum, to be relevant to the justice issues involved, must also take account of demotic difference and historical injustice if self-determination is to be meaningful. A distinction has been drawn here between the polity-constituting demos and what we might call the demos *toujours*. The republican instantiation of the referendum in the former sense as in some cases different due to the fundamental nature of the issue at stake, and the implications it has for the identity of a constitutional people, have each in some measure been accepted by France and by international tribunals, even if neither justification has been fully articulated or explained.

As we saw with the Baltic states, many modern democracies as a consequence of history are faced with difficult issues concerning inclusion and exclusion. It has not been the task of this chapter to illustrate all of these or to solve these problems, but rather to show how they are more fully exposed by referendum processes which call to the fore 'the people' who in a republican sense claim the right of self-government over a particular territory. In the remainder of the book we return to the key question of whether, when set against principles of deliberative democracy, a constitutional referendum can be considered a legitimate act of democratic republican authorship. In seeking to address the normative implications of the constitutional referendum, we cannot leave undisturbed the question 'Who are these authors?', not only because this is presupposed by the referendum process itself, but primarily because this first question for constitutional referendums can be, as we have seen, a deeply troubled one. In territorial terms the referendum can only function successfully if the people or peoples have some sense of collective attachment, no matter how pluralistically that attachment manifests itself, to the territory as locus for a discrete political enterprise. And in franchise terms, the principle of inclusion is central to the inherent fairness of the referendum from a republican perspective. These are issues which will continue to speak to the very suitability of the referendum at all, particularly for divided societies.

4

Elite Control and the Referendum Process

I. INTRODUCTION

Many observers are deeply sceptical that referendums are, or are even capable of being, a genuine manifestation of direct, popular democracy. This is a long-standing criticism. Underlying the issue of control is the persistent doubt as to whether in a referendum there is really an opportunity for ordinary citizens to play a meaningful part in constitutional decision-making or whether referendums, including constitutional referendums, are merely a democratic chimera, symbolizing popular power when in reality direct democracy acts as a cover for elite manipulation.

Addressing the issue historically, it is in part their somewhat ignoble origins that have given referendums a bad name. In Section II we will trace the overtly exploitative application of referendums which came to characterize this early period. Elite manipulation of constitutional referendums—and of elections in general—remains a feature of undemocratic states to the present day. However, since our interest in this book is in the relationship between referendums and democracy, those referendums that are manifestly undemocratic will not be a major point of focus. A more important objection to referendum use is the charge that manipulation is also an inherent pathology even in otherwise relatively healthy democracies. We will begin this section by revisiting the charge that referendums are, almost by definition, 'elite driven and pro-hegemonic'.[1] A referendum, like any electoral process, is of course organized by political elites. The elite-driven objection then is not that elites are involved in framing referendums (indeed, this criticism tends to be levelled by those who defend elite-led representative democracy as universally preferable to direct democracy), but rather that within the broad category of electoral processes, referendums are particularly prone to exploitation by elites.

---

[1] Arend Lijphart, *Democracies. Patterns of Majoritarian and Consensus Government in Twenty-One Countries* (Yale University Press 1984) 203.

As demonstrated earlier, attitudes towards referendums hinge to a large extent upon the particular aims and values that one considers to underpin democracy. The normative benchmark I have adopted in this book is 'civic republican democracy'. From this tradition, I concluded Chapter 2 with a prima facie defence of the limited use of referendums in the constitutional context, provided these can be shown to foster—at least to the same extent as representative democracy—a deliberative approach to democracy among ordinary citizens. In this context the first principle I identified as central to a deliberative referendum process was 'participation'. The problem we confront in this chapter is therefore stark, preceding as it does even the deliberation question. If a referendum is inherently prey to the control and manipulation of elites, then participation, no matter how deliberative the process is, will be pointless. In other words, recalling the central question we have posed—can the referendum play a democratically defensible role in an exercise of constitutional authorship by a people?—if constitutional referendums are shown to be pathologically prone to elite abuse to a significantly greater extent than representative models of constitutional decision-making, then clearly the answer will be no.

The initial point to be made is that the issue of control has perhaps been oversimplified in much of the literature, which tends to focus upon the initiation of the referendum process in fairly narrow terms, seeking to identify a key actor who organizes the referendum. Certainly this gate-keeper power can be crucial, but my contention is that the control issue is both wider and more complex than this, requiring analysis of the broader interplay of constitutional competence and political capacity throughout the referendum process. Initially this task requires that the referendum be broken down into a number of process components: the initiation stage begins the process, but we must also consider a second agenda-setting stage, which encompasses question-formation and process planning including timing issues; and, third, the campaign process itself, embracing the campaign rules, provision of information to voters, funding and expenditure rules etc. We will address these at the beginning of Section III before turning also to consider how constitutional rules interact with political factors to disperse power among political actors and how the complex motives of political actors also affect, in some ways counterintuitively, standard accounts of control. Finally, the research on control tends not to disaggregate legislative from constitutional referendums in a categorical way. We will address the question of control generically insofar as it raises common issues. However, as we will see, there are some aspects of control that are specific to constitutional referendums and these will be addressed in the following two chapters.

II. BONAPARTISM: OLD AND NEW

The presentation of the referendum as a seemingly democratic act, when the reality of its use is in fact to subvert democratic ideals, is as old as modern republican self-government itself. France was the first modern state to hold a national referendum on the draft of a new constitution in 1793 in a process that was heavily manipulated by the French revolutionaries to validate with popular endorsement their insurrection of 1789; and the Jacobins were to continue to deploy the plebiscite to add a democratic veneer to what was de facto dictatorial authority until the turn of the nineteenth century.[2] The plebiscite also proved useful to Napoleon Bonaparte, who held three separate polls between 1799 and 1815 to secure his control over the French state.[3] In doing so, the term 'bonapartism'—more typically associated with strong executive government—is also used to describe the way in which referendums have been applied to offer some form of purported legitimacy either for the internal constitutional and political manoeuvrings of autocratic regimes, or for the acquisition of territory by imperial powers.[4] Indeed, Napoleon used 'musket democracy' in the republican aftershock of the French Revolution not only to consolidate power at home but also to build his empire abroad, with plebiscites held within subjugated territories to validate conquest.[5]

---

[2] Referendums were also held in 1795 and 1799 to approve subsequent iterations of the constitution.

[3] In 1800, 1802, and 1804 to approve him respectively as consul, consul for life, and Emperor. See Frédéric Bluche, *Le Bonapartisme. Aux origines de la droite autoritaire (1800–1850)* (NEL 1980) 26–33; Stephen Holmes, 'Two Concepts of Legitimacy: France after the Revolution' (1982) 10 Political Theory 165; Martyn Lyons, *Napoleon Bonaparte and the Legacy of the French Revolution* (Macmillan Press 1994) ch 9; Laurence Morel, 'France: Towards a Less Controversial Use of the Referendum' in Michael Gallagher and Pier Vincenzo Uleri (eds), *The Referendum Experience in Europe* (Macmillan Press 1996) 67–8; Arthur Lupia and Richard Johnston, 'Are Voters to Blame? Voter Competence and Elite Manoeuvres in Referendums' in Matthew Mendelsohn and Andrew Parkin (eds), *Referendum Democracy: Citizens, Elites, and Deliberation in Referendum Campaigns* (Palgrave 2001) 204–7 on the falsification of votes and turnout.

[4] Melvin Richter, 'Toward a Concept of Political Illegitimacy: Bonapartist Dictatorship and Democratic Legitimacy' (1982) 10 Political Theory 185; Henry E Brady and Cynthia S Kaplan, 'Eastern Europe and the Former Soviet Union' in David Butler and Austin Ranney (eds), *Referendums Around the World: The Growing Use of Direct Democracy* (Macmillan Press 1994) 175.

[5] Notably plebiscites were held to legitimize the annexation of territory but never to permit secession from 'greater France'. Johannes Mattern, *The Employment of the Plebiscite in the Determination of Sovereignty* (Johns Hopkins University Press 1920) 79. See also Lawrence T Farley, *Plebiscites and Sovereignty: The Crisis of Political Illegitimacy* (Westview Press 1986) 31. The referendum remained a favoured constitutional instrument into the middle of the nineteenth century in France for both executive consolidation and empire-building. Louis Napoleon held one in 1848 electing him President of the French Republic; one in 1851 to approve a new constitution and reinforce his personal authority, making him president for ten years; and another in 1852 conferring upon him the hereditary title of emperor: Mattern, *The Employment of the Plebiscite* 27. The trend for plebiscites extended to Italy, where several were held during the unification of the republic. Mack Smith comments on how a number of these votes were 'rigged'. Dennis Mack Smith, *Italy: A Modern History* (University of Michigan Press 1969) 66–7.

The twentieth century was also to witness the distortion of the referendum to provide faux legitimacy for the acquisition of territory, most egregiously in Hitler's plebiscite held in Austria in 1938 after the *Anschluss* in mockery of the emerging international principle of national self-determination.[6] Overwhelming victories are another feature of the bonapartist referendum.[7] Further examples can be found from Nazi Germany[8] and Fascist Italy,[9] and after the war the few referendums that were used in Eastern Europe were the subject of abuse. This can be seen, for example, in the blatant rigging of the constitutional referendum in Poland in 1946 through the intimidation of voters and the falsification of ballot papers.[10] From 1947 to 1987 three further referendums were held in Eastern Europe and the USSR, each of which had an official turnout of nearly 100 per cent and approval ratings little below this. The grand farce culminated in a referendum in Romania in 1986 with signed ballots, no negative votes, and only 228 abstentions from an electorate of 17 million.[11] And we continue to see further examples of abuse. In 1996 a referendum in Belarus served to strongly consolidate the powers of the president in a process that effectively usurped the existing constitution of 1994 and in the face of opposition from both the parliament and the Constitutional Court. As Elgie and Zielonka comment: 'The procedures, form and substance of the referendum were imposed by the president, who also enjoyed a total monopoly over the mass media.'[12] Other constitutional referendums where high degrees of abuse

---

[6] In fact, prior to German annexation there had been a plan by Austria's Chancellor Kurt Schuschnigg to hold a referendum asking the Austrian people whether they wished to remain independent or merge into Germany, but this was cancelled following a coup by the Austrian Nazi Party on 11 March 1938.

[7] In light of the officially calculated 99.7 per cent vote in Austria in favour of the *Anschluss*, inevitably there were allegations of vote rigging: Evan Burr Bukey, *Hitler's Austria: Popular Sentiment in the Nazi Era, 1938–1945* (University of North Carolina Press 2000) 25–42. Although an uncomfortable truth is that the takeover was nonetheless tremendously popular: Rolf Steininger, *Austria, Germany, and the Cold War: From the Anschluss to the State Treaty* (Bergahn Books 2008) 10. Overwhelming victories also marked Bonaparte's use of referendums, which each resulted officially in over 99 per cent support on between 43 and 51 per cent turnouts. Peter J Emerson, *Defining Democracy: Decisions, Elections and Good Governance* (The De Borda Institute 2002) 105. This was also a feature of Italian reunification: Mack Smith, *Italy: A Modern History*, 66–7.

[8] Hitler used a series of four referendums between 1933 and 1938 to consolidate his rule. Arnold J Zurcher, 'The Hitler Referenda' (1935) 29 Am Political Science Rev 91.

[9] Mussolini held two: one in 1929 on the issue of recognizing Vatican sovereignty and another authorizing Fascist rule in 1934.

[10] Richard F Staar, 'Elections in Communist Poland' (1958) 2 Midwest J Political Science 200, 201–3; Neal Ascherson, *The Struggle for Poland* (Michael Joseph 1987) 144; Brady and Kaplan, 'Eastern Europe and the Former Soviet Union', 182.

[11] Brady and Kaplan, 'Eastern Europe and the Former Soviet Union', 183.

[12] Robert Elgie and Jan Zielonka, 'Constitutions and Constitution-Building: A Comparative Perspective' in Jan Zielonka (ed), *Democratic Consolidation in Eastern Europe* (OUP 2001) vol I, 41. See also 'Constitutional Watch' (1996) 4 East European Constitutional Rev 5. Notably, international organizations

were reported include those held by Francois Duvalier to strengthen his grip on Haiti. The first in 1961 saw no negative votes recorded and in a second in 1964 only 0.1 per cent of the population voted against a new constitution according to official figures. Other notorious examples include the constitutional referendums in Chile in 1980, Egypt, 2007, and Burma, 2008.[13]

It is no surprise therefore that the brazen use of the referendum by Napoleon in land-grabbing exercises and the association of the referendum with revanchist nationalism, bureaucratic socialism, and autocracy in the twentieth century has led to a general aversion among constitutional theorists. Plebiscitary democracy was criticized by de Tocqueville in the Bonapartist context[14] and by Arendt, who despite her commitment to popular political participation, with the shadow of Hitler's abuses in the background, described the plebiscite as 'the unbridled rule of public opinion'.[15] And so even today the association of the plebiscite with these abuses inevitably shapes the deep scepticism we see of the very idea that the referendum might be a meaningful vehicle for democratic self-determination.

As we turn to address control in more democratic environments we must pay full heed to the reasons for this scepticism but in recognition of its contextual provenance we should also be ready to temper the critique it offers. We should especially be wary if this aversion to referendums has become a contemporary generalism stemming from jaundice induced by a very particular historical experience. The egregious manipulation of referendums tends to occur in countries where broad patterns of illegitimate electoral practices prevail. As such this does not necessarily point to a pathology particular to referendums, but to the way in which democracy in general can be undermined by powerful and self-serving elites. We also need to observe that attempts to use the referendum in an exploitative way can backfire. General Pinochet of Chile relinquished office in 1989 after his plans to extend his presidency were resoundingly defeated in a referendum

---

refused to send monitors since the referendum was considered to be so blatantly unconstitutional. For other abuses surrounding the use of the referendum in Belarus as well as democratic problems with referendum use in Romania, Estonia, Lithuania, and Poland see Alexander Lukashuk, 'Constitutionalism in Belarus: A False Start' in Zielonka (ed), *Democratic Consolidation*, 297–8, 309, and 313–17.

[13] For a review of referendums within non-democratic systems see David Altman, *Direct Democracy Worldwide* (CUP 2011), 88–109.

[14] His preference for limited government on the US model in preference to Bonapartist plebiscitary democracy is a theme of Democracy in America—Alexis de Tocqueville, *Democracy in America* (Harvey Mansfield and Delba Winthrop eds and trs, University of Chicago Press 2000). See also Richter, 'Toward a Concept of Political Illegitimacy', 202, 210–11.

[15] Hannah Arendt, *On Revolution* (Faber and Faber 1963) 231. See also Margaret Canovan, 'The People, the Masses, and the Mobilization of Power: The Paradox of Hannah Arendt's "Populism"' (2002) 69 Social Research 403, who discusses (417) the 'conundrum' of how 'Arendt could be a "populist" while deploring most cases of what others might classify as popular mobilization'.

on sweeping constitutional reform.[16] And in 1987 a referendum in Poland which sought to validate top-down economic and political reforms, with questions that were designed to enhance support, resulted in failure for the government and in doing so seemed to hasten the collapse of the regime two years later.[17] These examples hint at the fact that as we turn to democratic systems, controlling the result of a referendum is not as easy as the stereotyped image may suggest.

III. REFERENDUM CONTROL IN DEMOCRATIC SYSTEMS

By the charge that referendums are 'controlled and pro-hegemonic' Lijphart meant: 'when governments control the referendum, they will tend to use it only when they expect to win'.[18] This begs a question about the nature and detail of control, however. The degree to which a controlling elite within an otherwise properly functioning democracy can influence the result of a referendum has been the focus of recent empirical work by political scientists. But in some respects we still lack research that presents this issue in the fullness of its complexity. Existing political science focuses principally, and not surprisingly, upon the *political* power of actors in staging a referendum. But this work, while valuable, can perhaps underestimate the importance of the detailed *legal* rules that condition the boundaries within which this political power can be exercised. The existing literature on control also tends to concentrate upon the power to initiate a referendum, whereas it is important to address the opportunities for, and challenges to, elite influence throughout the referendum process as a whole.[19] To seek a more complete

---

[16] 91 per cent voted Yes on reforms to the constitution in the referendum on 30 July 1989. In a more democratic context President de Gaulle, who used referendums extensively to consolidate his executive power (discussed in Chapter 5), resigned office in 1969 after defeat in a referendum on Senate and local government reform.

[17] In light of a widespread boycott, the Yes vote on each of two questions on reform did not achieve the threshold of 50 per cent of eligible voters. Stephen White and Ronald J Hill, 'Russia, the Former Soviet Union and Eastern Europe: The Referendum as a Flexible Political Instrument' in Gallagher and Uleri (eds), *The Referendum Experience in Europe*, 156. A referendum in Hungary in 1989 had a similar effect in stimulating political transition: Alan Renwick, 'The Role of Non-Elite Forces in Hungary's Negotiated Revolution' in Andras Bozoki (ed), *The Roundtable Talks of 1989: The Genesis of Hungarian Democracy* (Central European University Press 2002) 204–8.

[18] Lijphart, *Democracies*, 204.

[19] For work that does address the referendum campaign more broadly see Mendelsohn and Parkin (eds), *Referendum Democracy*; David M Farrell and Rüdiger Schmitt-Beck (eds), *Do Political Campaigns Matter? Campaign Effects in Elections and Referendums* (Routledge 2002). For other attempts to categorize referendums in the context of process control see Markku Suksi, *Bringing in the People: A Comparison of Constitutional Forms and Practices of the Referendum* (Kluwer 1993) 30–4; Gallagher and Uleri (eds), *The Referendum Experience in Europe*; Simon Hug and George Tsebelis, 'Veto Players and Referendums Around the World' (2002) 14 J Theoretical Politics October 465; Maija Setälä, 'On the Problems of Responsibility and Accountability in Referendums' (2006) 45 European J Political Research 699, 705–7;

story of how referendums are controlled and regulated, therefore, we will distinguish three distinct environmental factors that can condition and make more complex the exercise of political control over time: (i) the constitutional framework under the authority of which referendums are organized; (ii) the way in which constitutional rules interact with political factors to disperse power among a number of actors at different stages of the referendum process, and not only at the moment of initiation; and (iii) the motives of political actors who seek to control referendums. These motives can vary from strong support for a measure being proposed, relative indifference to the measure, and even a desire for the measure to fail, whether that aspiration is publicly articulated or not. In other words, the motives of elites may be multiple, complex (even seemingly self-contradictory), and can face frustration at the hands of other elites and the voting public. This broader picture also suggests that the scope for control will vary greatly from one constitutional order to another and even from one referendum to another.

(i) Constitutional framework of referendums

Since the constitutional framework and legal context within which they emerge and by which they are regulated is often left underexplored in accounts of control over referendum processes, we will address control with greater emphasis on constitutional factors (mindful of the interaction of constitutional and political factors), and in linear terms from start to finish: initiation; referendum process; effect of the referendum result. Some of these matters will be dealt with in outline only since we will return to them in greater detail in later chapters.

(a) Initiation

A constitution can regulate referendums in one of three ways: making explicit provision for referendums and requiring their use in certain situations (mandatory referendums); permitting a referendum either by express provision, or by silence in the constitutional text which is taken to be permissive (discretionary referendums);[20] or forbidding the use of referendums, either entirely or by restricting them to certain issues. In this third scenario constitutional silence on referendum use might be read as prohibitory rather than permissive.

Claes H de Vreese, 'Context, Elites, Media and Public Opinion in Referendums: When Campaigns Really Matter' in Claes H de Vreese (ed), *The Dynamics of Referendum Campaigns: An International Perspective* (Palgrave Macmillan 2007) 2–3.

[20] Setälä calls these 'facultative referendums'. Setälä, 'On the Problems of Responsibility', 705. Eg the unwritten nature of the UK constitution means that every British referendum is in this sense discretionary and ad hoc.

The respective levels of legal regulation and political discretion therefore vary from constitution to constitution. The power to initiate any particular referendum can be situated on a scale with maximal legal regulation at one end and maximal political discretion at the other. Mandatory referendums are the most closely controlled by law and hence most clearly limit the scope for discretion of political actors.[21] Some constitutions require referendums as part of the constitutional amendment process in general,[22] while others only require them for exceptional constitutional matters: for example, Austria[23] and Spain[24] reserve mandatory referendums for fundamental constitutional revisions and Iceland for an amendment to the status of the established Evangelical Lutheran Church.[25]

One reason why elite control amounting to manipulation is criticized by democratic theorists is, of course, that it can distort the true intentions of voters. Voters are lured into voting for something which in fact does not reflect their preferences or at least their interests. It is notable therefore that we find evidence of a direct correlation between constitutional regulation and citizen choice. Hug and Tsebelis in an extensive study, and one of the few to take significant account of the role of constitutions in the issue of referendum control, argue that when referendums are regulated by constitutions the results of these polls are more likely to align with the preferences of voters.[26]

Let us turn to discretionary referendums where the constitutional regime is taken to permit referendums but is either silent on them or offers few if any guidelines or regulations as to their use. In such a situation we might assume that the scope for political discretion—and hence control—will be greater than in those which are closely regulated by the constitution. The very power of political actors to decide whether to hold a referendum or not is a significant discretion. The contrast between the leeway open to UK governments on how to ratify recent draft EU treaties compared to the mandatory referendums in Ireland is illustrative. In the former case, referendums that may well have led to a popular rejection of both the draft Constitutional Treaty and the draft Reform Treaty were avoided, whereas the Irish government had no option but to hold referendums and confront the political difficulties that resulted (see Chapter 6).

---

[21] De Vreese, 'Context, Elites, Media and Public Opinion in Referendums', 2–3.

[22] We find these across the globe, eg Australian Constitution, s 128; Constitution of Denmark, s 88; Constitution of Ireland, Art 46; Constitution of Japan, Art 96; Constitution of the Republic of Mauritius, Art 47; Federal Constitution of the Swiss Confederation, Title 4, ch 2.

[23] Federal Constitution of Austria, Art 44.   [24] Constitution of Spain, Art 168.

[25] Constitution of the Republic of Iceland, Art 79.

[26] In reaching this conclusion they assessed 52 constitutions containing provisions for required referendums. Hug and Tsebelis, 'Veto Players and Referendums Around the World', 491.

Typically, this type of permissive constitutional regime leaves discretion in the hands of the executive. In states with mandatory referendums such discretion is usually reserved for non-constitutional matters,[27] or requires the support of the legislature.[28] But in practice those where the constitution is silent also require the support of the legislature by way of an enabling Act. And the discretionary power can also be dispersed, and may in fact work against the authority of the executive. Some constitutions permit referendums at the behest of oppositional voices, allowing political representatives to press for a referendum, often as a form of recall or veto power.[29] One avenue to activate this is through a minority in the legislature; for example, the constitutions of Denmark[30] and Ireland[31] offer this possibility. Although the constitutional referendum can be a powerful veto in this context, it is not a mechanism by which the people can set their own agenda.

Another variation on this permits referendums to be instigated by citizens. These are often termed 'initiatives' and they offer the opportunity for popular movements to force a popular vote. Most Swiss referendums commence as initiatives[32] and notably the results are legally binding. We also see this process in New Zealand,[33] Italy,[34] and widely at the sub-national level in the USA.[35] Only the Swiss among the citizens of Europe can initiate a legislative measure by way of referendum. In Italy the initiative power also exists in respect of ordinary laws, but here it only has a veto function, with the power to abrogate but not initiate legislation.[36] Therefore these initiative referendums—like oppositional referendums—most commonly take the form of a veto power.

There has been empirical work—similar to that by Hug and Tsebelis cited earlier—looking at US states which use the initiative. Again, this suggests

---

[27] eg in Ireland in the case of non-constitutional Bills the President can decide not to submit a measure to referendum if 'the subject of a petition...does not contain a proposal of such national importance that the will of the people thereon ought to be ascertained'. Constitution of Ireland, Art 27(6). For a similar provision see Constitution of the Portuguese Republic, Art 118.

[28] eg Constitution of Greece, Art 44.

[29] These have been called abrogative or rejective referendums, the former addressing a law that is already enacted and the latter a law not yet in force. Setälä, 'On the Problems of Responsibility', 706.

[30] Constitution of Denmark, s 42.   [31] Constitution of Ireland, Art 27.

[32] Federal Constitution of the Swiss Confederation, Arts 138, 139, and 141.

[33] The Citizens Initiated Referenda Act 1993.

[34] Constitution of the Italian Republic, Art 138(2)—constitutional amendments, following approval by both chambers of parliament must be submitted to a referendum 'when, within three months of their publication, a request is made by one fifth of the members of either chamber, by 500,000 electors, or by five regional councils'.

[35] Thomas E Cronin, *Direct Democracy: The Politics of Initiative, Referendum and Recall* (Harvard University Press 1989).

[36] Constitution of the Italian Republic, Art 75.

that policies tend to correspond more closely to the voters' preferences than in states without the initiative.[37] Gerber's findings also seem to suggest that initiatives are less easily controlled by elites than referendums held at the discretion of elites or even than mandatory referendums initiated by government. This initiative power tends to apply in respect of the recall of ordinary laws rather than on matters of constitutional amendment, and hence they are of less interest to this study. But in some cases a constitutional power to force a referendum can impact on the constitutional arena, as we will see in Chapter 6 in light of Denmark's referendums on the European Union.

Constitutional silence can create its own controversies, in some cases leaving a legal black hole. The question begged, of course, is whether silence in a constitution should be taken to permit or forbid referendums.[38] And if it permits referendums, how is the discretion to hold a referendum distributed? This can result in a dispute between the executive and the legislature. Is the executive empowered to hold a referendum without the need for legislative authority, or is the passage of an enabling act needed which will set out the process rules etc?[39] A second type of dispute can arise within a multi-level state over whether the different levels of territorial authority are each empowered to hold referendums and on which issues. There has been little coverage of this issue in the literature on control, but from a legal perspective it is hugely controversial and one of the most significant challenges in the use of constitutional referendums today. Again, in Chapter 5 we will return to the particular issues that have arisen in multinational states, discussing Quebec, where dispute over the 1995 referendum on sovereignty led to an important reference to the Supreme Court of Canada, and the potential for similar territorial disputes in other states such as Spain and the UK.

Another important issue that must be taken into account where a constitution is otherwise silent on referendums is constitutional conventions. Over time conventions as to when and how referendums should be

---

[37] Elisabeth R Gerber, *The Populist Paradox: Interest Group Influence and the Promise of Direct Legislation* (Princeton University Press 1999); Elisabeth R Gerber, 'Legislative Response to the Threat of Popular Initiatives' (1996) 40 Am J Political Science 99. See also John G Matsusaka and Nolan M McCarty, 'Political Resource Allocation: Benefits and Costs of Voter Initiatives' (2001) 17 J Law, Economics and Organization 413.

[38] In Germany the constitution is taken only to permit referendums at the local level. Article 146 of the Basic Law provided that it 'shall cease to apply on the day on which a constitution freely adopted by the German people takes effect'. However, despite the suggestion that this envisaged a direct say for citizens on reunification of the country, no referendum was ever held to validate this process in 1990. For a criticism of the lack of direct popular engagement on this issue see Simone Chambers, 'Democracy, Popular Sovereignty, and Constitutional Legitimacy' (2004) 11 Constellations 153, 164–8.

[39] In Chapter 5 we will see how this became a controversial issue in France in the 1950s and 1960s.

held can emerge. To take the UK, for example, it has been suggested that there is now a constitutional convention that the devolution of legislative powers or any major legislative changes to devolution would require a referendum.[40] This seems to limit the opportunity for either the executive or Parliament to proceed with constitutional change in certain areas without consulting the people. For example, it now seems unthinkable that any government would try to take the UK into Economic and Monetary Union (EMU) within the EU without a referendum.[41]

In addition to constitutional rules, we should also observe that ordinary legislative regulation is very common both in states where there is no constitutional provision for referendums (eg Political Parties, Elections and Referendums Act 2000 in the UK[42]) and also in states with mandatory constitutional regimes (eg Australia[43] and Ireland[44]). This can be highly significant since, even when an elite has some degree of discretion under the constitution, perhaps through a lack of detail in the relevant constitutional provisions, on the decision to trigger a referendum, a detailed referendum law can tightly circumscribe how this process can be conducted. Thus the backdrop to referendum initiation can be a complex legal picture of higher order constitutional norms, including conventions, interacting with detailed lower order legislative rules, often supplemented further by secondary legislation.[45]

We might end this section on the trigger power with a small case study. Of the three countries acceding to the EC in 1973, two held referendums. Ireland was required to by its constitution. In effect, so too was Denmark

---

[40] Interestingly, calls for a referendum in this context can be traced back to AV Dicey and his unsuccessful intervention on the issue of Irish Home Rule. Rivka Weill, 'Dicey was not Diceyan' (2003) 62 CLJ 474. See also AV Dicey, 'Ought the Referendum to be Introduced into England?' (1890) 57 Contemporary Rev 489. Bogdanor has argued that by convention a referendum is required prior to 'any significant devolution of powers away from Westminster' or 'when a wholly novel constitutional arrangement is proposed'. See HL Select Committee on the Constitution, *Referendums in the United Kingdom* (HL 2009–10, 99) evidence by Vernon Bogdanor, 45–6. Certainly, it has been the practice to hold a referendum for significant devolution processes. Most recently a referendum was held on 3 March 2011 to extend the powers of the Welsh Assembly under the Government of Wales Act 2006, s 103. The Northern Ireland Act 1998, s 1, provides for a referendum prior to any moves to reunify Ireland. However, one qualification to the notion of a new convention at least in the devolution of powers from Westminster to the sub-state legislatures must be entered in light of the Scotland Bill 2010–2011 (HC Bill 164), which was laid before the UK Parliament proposing the extension of significant powers to the Scottish Parliament, including fiscal powers, without a referendum.

[41] European Union Act 2011, s 2.

[42] This sets out detailed rules on campaign organization, funding, and expenditure, which we will discuss later in this chapter and in Chapter 8.

[43] Referendum (Machinery Provisions) Act 1984.

[44] A number of laws have been passed in Ireland, eg the Referendum Act 1994; the Electoral (Amendment) Act 1996; the Referendum Act 1998; the Referendum Act 2001.

[45] eg the Regional Assembly and Local Government Referendums Order 2004 (UK).

since the consent of a majority of five-sixths in the *Folketing* (Danish Parliament) was required to avoid one.[46] Britain, with no constitutional requirement either as a matter of law or convention, was not so required; but it is notable that one was held on continued membership in 1975, which was the result of political rather than constitutional factors. The initiation/trigger power is first of all an issue of law, and therefore one that must be set in the constitutional context. The more directive and detailed a constitution, the less room for manoeuvre exists for political elites. But the British experience in 1975 also reminds us that control of the initiation process often involves a delicate interplay between constitutional and political concerns.[47]

When Qvortrup analysed 128 referendums around the world between 1945 and 1997 he found that 'pro-hegemonic' referendums which could be said to be controlled by particular elites only accounted for 15.6 per cent of the referendums studied. Instead, 103 of the 128 were either the product of a constitutional requirement or were instigated by citizen initiative or by the opposition. These results he argues 'clearly falsify Lijphart's assertion'.[48] In this light it seems that the simplistic notion of referendums as elite-controlled and manipulated needs considerable qualification, demanding an account of the actual level of constitutional and legal regulation of each referendum, from case to case.

(b) Agenda-setting

Law also acts to condition political discretion at the second stage of the referendum—agenda-setting—, where matters such as the framing of the question and the timing of the referendum are settled (this can also embrace preparations for the third, campaign stage in setting rules on funding and expenditure, ballot, and counting processes etc). In much of the existing literature the issue of control is often taken to be synonymous with who sets the question. This is an oversimplification, since drafting the question is but part of the broader agenda-setting stage, albeit a crucial one. An elite actor might be bounced into holding a referendum, or see a referendum as a last resort. This actor may have some discretion in defining the question, but

---

[46] Constitution of Denmark, s 20. See Palle Svensson, 'Five Danish Referendums on the European Community and European Union: A Critical Assessment of the Franklin Thesis' (2002) 41 European J Political Research 733.

[47] Political pressure rather than constitutional obligation also led to President Chirac proposing a referendum in France on the draft Constitutional Treaty—'Chirac Bows to Pressure for a French Vote on EU Constitution', *Irish Independent* (Dublin, 25 January 2011) <http://www.independent.ie/world-news/europe/chirac-bows-to-pressure-for-a-french-vote-on-eu-constitution-163228.html> accessed 14 October 2011.

[48] Matt Qvortrup, 'Are Referendums Controlled and Pro-hegemonic?' (2000) 48 Political Studies 821, 823.

this is not synonymous with setting the issue.[49] It seems, therefore, that we need to address this stage of the referendum in broader context.

I will return to political difficulties that face would-be agenda-setters later but for now it is useful to develop further the legal constraints that act at the various stages of the referendum process. Let us outline three main areas where legal regulation can play a significant role: first, the framing of the question which should be seen as part of the broader task of defining the issue to which the question relates; second, setting the timetable for the referendum; and, third, campaign funding. Here I set out issues which I will return to in later chapters when I consider how a referendum process that fosters deliberation at each stage might be constructed. By treating these as discrete components of the agenda-setting stage of the referendum we will see that there are a number of challenges and opportunities for political actors in seeking to coordinate control of the referendum agenda. Each of these different components also raise normative issues from the perspective of deliberative civic republicanism. In later chapters specific recommendations will flow as to how the process might be made more open, inclusive, and participatory, and ultimately less subject to narrow elite control, in reference back to the *control objection* identified in Chapter 2.

CONTROL OF THE QUESTION

Since question-setting is too narrow a focus with which to address control in the round, the first step in any constitutional referendum is, more broadly, to conceptualize the constitutional issue at stake before it is turned into a question.[50] This enables a number of matters to be separated out, such as: is the issue one that gives rise to a mandatory referendum? In discretionary constitutional regimes, is it a suitable issue to be put to a referendum, or one in respect of which constitutional convention or previous practice suggests that a referendum would be appropriate or required? And, can the issue be made into an intelligible question?

In this chapter our interest is in how the framing of the question is open to manipulation. There are, of course, many ways in which this can be done, for example by wording the question to maximize support or the running together of different issues in one question (see Chapter 8). There are two ways in which law can intervene to regulate this. The first is by limiting elite control of the agenda-setting and question-setting processes. This might be

---

[49] Uleri drew the distinction between the agenda-setter and the initiator of the referendum. Pier Vincenzo Uleri, 'Introduction' in Gallagher and Uleri (eds), *The Referendum Experience in Europe*; Hug and Tsebelis, 'Veto Players and Referendums Around the World', 466.

[50] Hamon discusses how various actors can be involved at this stage. Francis Hamon, *Le Référendum: Étude Comparative* (Librairie générale de droit et de jurisprudence 1995) 24.

done by introducing a deliberative process involving a number of actors, thus diluting the power of each. Traditionally the articulation of the issue and the subsequent setting of the question has been left to elites. But in recent times there have been experiments in popularizing this process, where a meaningful role for citizens has started to emerge in influencing the agenda. In Chapter 7 we will address both the Constitutional Convention in Australia which preceded the setting of the referendum question in the 1999 referendum on the head of state, and the British Columbia Citizens' Assembly, which had the power to set the referendum question on electoral reform in 2004. Second, the regulatory function of law can be important, for example to ensure that the question be approved by an independent body for issues such as intelligibility, and to offer scope for legal challenges on issues of clarity etc.[51]

TIMING

There are a number of ways in which timing can be used by an elite to attempt to influence the outcome of a referendum.[52] One is to keep the referendum process short. In general a hastier process would seem to increase the risk of manipulation by restricting the opportunities of oppositional voices to mobilize and influence voters.[53] Another opportunity open to organizers is to track polls or in general gauge the most propitious moment for the referendum; creating the 'winning conditions'. This is most incongruous in a system that otherwise has fixed, periodic election dates provided for in the constitution. Indeed, most polities do so and one of the major arguments for fixed election dates is precisely to reduce the opportunity for such exploitation.[54] But with discretionary referendums, which by definition are more ad hoc, responding to events as they arise, then the timing of the referendum is also a question of circumstances.

If the decision to hold a referendum is entirely at the discretion of government, then it is likely that the government can also timetable the referendum as it wishes, but this privilege can also arise with mandatory

---

[51] Controversy arose over the question initially proposed by the UK coalition government for the referendum on electoral reform held on 5 May 2011. The Electoral Commission investigated the question and took the view that it was too difficult to understand. The question was subsequently changed. Electoral Commission, 'Referendum on the UK Parliamentary Voting System: Report of views of the Electoral Commission on the proposed referendum question' (Electoral Commission 2010).

[52] Matthias K Polborn and Gerald Willmann, 'Referendum Timing' (2004) SSRN Working Paper No 527548 <http://ssrn.com/abstract=527548> accessed 14 July 2011.

[53] eg the Egyptian government was accused by critics of bringing forward the referendum planned for 4 April 2007 to 26 March 2007 in order to frustrate the effective mobilization of an opposition campaign.

[54] Jon Elster, 'Introduction' in Jon Elster and Rune Slagstad (eds), *Constitutionalism and Democracy* (CUP 1988) 3.

referendums since constitutions that provide for referendums often do not set out precise timing rules.[55] This issue is perhaps less noticeable in the UK, where the calling of elections is in large part a political decision of the Prime Minister.[56] Although the timing of referendums is also to some extent in the hands of the government, in practice each referendum needs a specific Act of Parliament to set out the process rules etc and this can also fix the date of the referendum.[57] This does not preclude manipulation of timing, but it does to some extent disperse control.

The importance of such 'timing discretion' can be seen from the Quebec referendum in 1995, where the date was changed in the course of the campaign from June to October as opinion polls in the spring showed that the measure would probably fail.[58] In fact the date of 30 October was not fixed until 7 September, and not formally adopted by the National Assembly until 20 September. Similarly, the French referendum on the EU Constitutional Treaty was brought forward as the government sensed support for the No side was growing.[59] Originally planned for the second half of 2005, on 4 March it was announced that the French referendum would be brought forward to 29 May.

Another tactic is to hold a referendum along with another election, as in Russia in December 1993, where the referendum—asking four questions concerning confidence in the president, the government's economic and social policy, and the calling of early elections—took place alongside parliamentary elections.[60] This can be an attempt to associate the referendum with a particular party or presidential candidate or to improve—or suppress—turnout.[61] Alternatively, a referendum can be situated far enough away from an election so that it is not an issue at the election. It has been

---

[55] One exception is Australia, which does regulate this in the Referendum (Machinery Provisions) Act 1984, ss 9–10.

[56] Although this is likely to change. The Fixed Term Parliaments Act 2011 will introduce fixed-term elections from 2015. Fixed dates already exist for elections to the devolved legislatures of Scotland, Wales, and Northern Ireland.

[57] Political Parties, Elections and Referendums Act 2000, s 103.

[58] Robert A Young, *The Struggle for Quebec: From Referendum to Referendum?* (McGill-Queen's University Press 1999) 13, 18, and 27.

[59] 'Chirac accelerates EU referendum after gains for no camp', *EU Business.com* (18 February 2005) <http://www.eubusiness.com/europe/france/050218132610.w1ahja9o/> accessed 14 July 2011. See also Sally Marthaler, 'The French Referendum on Ratification of the Constitutional Treaty', Referendum Briefing Paper No 12, European Parties Elections and Referendums Network, 29 May 2005.

[60] LeDuc argues that this 'made it more likely that the winners of the constitutional battle would be able to prevail within the new political structures that were being established'. Lawrence LeDuc, *The Politics of Direct Democracy: Referendums in Global Perspective* (Broadview Press 2003) 61–2.

[61] Bolstering turnout seemed to be one aim behind the decision of the UK government to hold a referendum on the UK voting system on 5 May 2011, the same date as devolved and local government elections.

argued that this was a factor in the timing of the Swedish referendum in 1994.[62] Or two referendums can be run together in the hope that people will see the two as a combined issue.[63]

Another issue can be sequencing. When there is to be more than one referendum on a particular issue, either within different territories in a state or across a number of states, referendums can be sequenced so that the referendum most likely to produce a favourable result is held first, in the hope that this will help build momentum, encouraging sceptical voters in other territories to vote this way when their turn comes. This has been called 'the domino strategy' and seemed to occur for the referendums on EU membership for Austria, Finland, Norway, and Sweden with those most likely to vote in favour going first: Austria June, Finland October, Sweden and then Norway two weeks apart in November.[64] The latter were most reluctant. Although there was not recognition of this as EU policy, 'it nonetheless clearly served the agenda of officials in Brussels'[65] as well as their supporters in these countries. It is also notable that of the nine referendums that eventually led to another process of accession in May 2004, the last three were held in the Czech Republic, Estonia, and Latvia, the states 'whose populations were perceived as the most Eurosceptic'.[66] According to Szczerbiak and Taggart it was hoped for a 'cascade effect', where earlier Yes votes would encourage support in these states 'for fear of exclusion'.[67] Another example is the decision to hold the referendum on devolution for Wales in 1997 one week after that held in Scotland. For a long time polls had shown Scots to be much more enthusiastic for devolution, and so it proved with a high Yes vote. The Welsh who in polls were far less keen on devolution in the end voted Yes by the narrowest of margins (50.3 per cent to 49.7 per cent), perhaps suggesting that the momentum of the Scottish result influenced swing voters in Wales.

But aspects of timing can, of course, be regulated. For example, referendum law can set out the permissible length of a referendum campaign; it can provide that the referendum must be held within a fixed period after the enabling legislation is passed; or it can even fix the date of the referendum in this legislation. Each of these to different extents limits the power of elites to

---

[62] Olof Ruin, 'Sweden: The Referendum as an Instrument for Defusing Political Issues' in Gallagher and Uleri (eds), *The Referendum Experience in Europe*, 177–8.

[63] The Slovenia referendum on accession to the EU in 2003 was held simultaneously with one on joining NATO.

[64] Detlef Jahn and Ann-Sofie Storsved, 'Legitimacy through Referendum? The Nearly Successful Domino-Strategy of the EU-Referendums in Austria, Finland, Sweden and Norway' (1995) 18 West European Politics 18.

[65] LeDuc, *Politics of Direct Democracy*, 89.

[66] Aleks Szczerbiak and Paul A Taggart (eds), *EU Enlargement and Referendums* (Routledge 2005) 6.

[67] ibid.

wait for the most propitious moment to call a vote. Another issue with timing is whether a referendum is a once-only event or whether it can be restaged where a particular elite is dissatisfied with an earlier result. In some cases, as a matter of constitutional law, referendums can be repeated time and again. Montenegro's Law of the Referendum 2001 ahead of the 2006 referendum on independence provided for only a 12-month delay between referendums: Article 12. This was potentially unsettling since it offered the prospect of an early second referendum had the threshold for the Yes vote not been secured. But again legal rules can reduce the scope for the 'neverendum'. For example, the Northern Ireland Act 1998 contains a rule that the Secretary of State shall not make an order for a referendum on the unification of Ireland earlier than seven years after the holding of a previous poll.[68]

A second issue, besides date-fixing, is the length of a campaign once a process begins. Here legal regulation is certainly feasible, and fixed rules on campaign length can also have an indirect impact on the discretion of elites to set a date.[69] In trying to construct a deliberative referendum it is important that the process is long enough for meaningful participation of interested parties. If a campaign is of sufficient duration to foster, and actively encourage, a deliberative process, then the power to set the actual date of the referendum as well as being more closely controlled will arguably be less important. Law can play a role in ensuring that such time is available. This does not guarantee that meaningful deliberation will take place, but it gives space for alternative views to be expressed, opposition campaigns to be mobilized, and voters to become better informed.

FUNDING AND EXPENDITURE

Campaign funding and expenditure are among the most contested issues in referendum design, so central are they to the respective levels of control open to interested parties.[70] However, there is disagreement as to the influence a campaign can in fact have over voters. Some argue it is effectively determinative.[71] It does seem that the USA is a particular case, with

---

[68] Northern Ireland Act 1998, s 1 and Sch 1(3).

[69] Of course, it may not always be possible to leave a long period between the decision to hold a referendum and the vote itself, particularly if the issue is an emergency.

[70] The de Gaulle government in France was accused of manipulating successive referendum campaigns in 1958, 1961, and 1962 'as much as it decently could in a democratic system'. This included the official position dominating broadcasts, official envelopes with ballot papers containing 'sheets giving de Gaulle's reasons for a "yes" vote', and strong personal appeals by de Gaulle for a Yes vote. Andrew Shennan, *De Gaulle* (Longman 1993) 112–13.

[71] Broder argues that, in the context of the USA, with sufficient spending in a referendum campaign one side could virtually ensure victory. David Broder, *Democracy Derailed: Initiative Campaigns and the Power of Money* (Harcourt 2000). See also Daniel A Smith, *Tax Crusaders and the Politics of Direct Democracy* (Routledge 1998).

the widespread use of the initiative in certain states and campaign spending taking place in a largely deregulated environment.[72] Even so, others are less categorical, listing it as only one of a number of important factors.[73] Some contend that in states where the referendum is used at the national level, and where other more orthodox levels of legal regulation apply, the influence of campaign expenditure may not be highly significant.[74] We can certainly identify cases where one side was unable to sway a result even by heavily outspending the other campaign. In Canada in 1992 the side backing the draft Charlottetown Accord spent $11.25 million as against $883,000 by the No side, but the Accord was still rejected by voters.[75] In these situations, of course, we need to nuance these findings against the possibility that strong voices in the media were also opposed to, or at least sceptical of, a particular proposal. It seems safer to conclude that the effects of spending, which can be significant, might well be mitigated by other factors, including the entrenched attitudes of voters,[76] but that even here they can be significant in tight races.[77] Such an effect may have been felt in the Wales devolution referendum in 1997, where the Yes side heavily outspent the No side and won by such a narrow margin.[78] It is also the case that much more was spent on the Yes campaign in the referendum on EC membership in the

---

[72] Thomas Stratmann, 'The Role of Money in Ballot Initiatives' in Karin Gilland Lutz and Simon Hug (eds), *Financing Referendum Campaigns* (Palgrave Macmillan 2009).

[73] Elizabeth R Gerber, 'Does the Popular Vote Destroy Civil Rights?' (1996) 42 Am J Political Science 1342; Thomas Stratmann, 'Campaign Spending and Ballot Measures' in Gilland Lutz and Hug (eds), *Financing Referendum Campaigns*. However, there is evidence that campaigns in referendums can be particularly important compared to other elections: 'since voters are asked to decide on often relatively unfamiliar topics with no partisan labels of candidate names on the ballot to guide them'. Sara Binzer Hobolt, 'Campaign Financing in Danish Referendums' in Gilland Lutz and Hug (eds), *Financing Referendum Campaigns*, 64. Butler and Ranney also argue that campaigns make a difference. David Butler and Austin Ranney, 'Conclusion' in Butler and Ranney (eds), *Referendums Around the World*, 262.

[74] De Vreese makes a more general point about the specificity of referendum campaigns: 'Most campaign effects are conditional. We should not expect to find large across-the-board effects.' De Vreese, 'Context, Elites, Media and Public Opinion in Referendums', 15–16. See also Thomas Stratmann, 'Is Spending More Potent For or Against a Proposition? Evidence From Ballot Measures' (2006) 50 Am J Political Science 788.

[75] Richard Johnston, 'Regulating Campaign Finance in Canadian Referendums and Initiatives' in Gilland Lutz and Hug (eds), *Financing Referendum Campaigns*, 27. The referendum in the North East of England in 2004 on a regional assembly resulted in a No vote of 78 per cent despite the Yes side spending considerably more than their opponents. Navraj Singh Ghaleigh, 'Sledgehammers and Nuts?: Regulating Referendums in the UK' in Gilland Lutz and Hug (eds), *Financing Referendum Campaigns*, 191–5.

[76] Attitudes can be particularly entrenched in constitutional referendums when matters of identity are at stake.

[77] Zaller points to the specific nature of these campaigns and of media influence in such contests. John Zaller, 'The Statistical Power of Election Studies to Detect Media Exposure Effects in Political Campaigns' (2002) 21 Electoral Studies 297.

[78] Ghaleigh, 'Sledgehammers and Nuts', 185.

UK in 1975[79] and here polls that suggested a tight race were proved wrong in the victory of the 'remain in Europe' side by 67.2 per cent to 32.8 per cent.[80]

The picture is therefore highly mixed and de Vreese seems correct that the impact of expenditure will vary from campaign to campaign, combining with so many additional factors such as elite cues, party loyalty, the strength of voter attitudes, the influence of the media etc, meaning that there is no definitive test applicable from one referendum to another on the influence of expenditure.[81] But it does seem that in the ordinary course of events legal controls on expenditure will moderate the scope open to powerful actors to influence the outcome of a referendum. The UK's Political Parties, Elections and Referendums Act contains detailed provisions on funding and expenditure and information dissemination,[82] but even here funding controls on the ground can be hard to manage.[83] The courts can also play an important role; for example, the Irish courts have intervened to control public expenditure in referendum campaigns[84] and the use of the state television network.[85]

(ii) Political power and referendums: a complex mosaic

Legal regulation is an important factor in conditioning political discretion but we need also to turn to the political constraints and the complex—even ambiguous—political motives that can combine with law in these situations to create the complex environment within which referendums are organized and controlled. Just as what might seem at first glance like wide-ranging political discretion can be subject to subtle but still important legal and constitutional strictures, similarly, what might seem to be a liberal licence offered by a lack of legal restraints might be heavily conditioned by political considerations.

In addressing political discretion we are drawn back to Lijphart's claim that governments tend only to use the referendum when they expect to win.

---

[79] David Butler and Uwe Kitzinger, *The 1975 Referendum* (Macmillan Press 1976) 284–5. See also *Referendums in the United Kingdom*, evidence presented by Professor David Butler, 6.

[80] Butler and Kitzinger, ibid 263–4.

[81] Johnston, 'Regulating Campaign Finance in Canadian Referendums and Initiatives', 30.

[82] Political Parties, Elections and Referendums Act 2000, ss 111–27.

[83] See *Referendums in the United Kingdom*, evidence presented by Robert Hazell, 3–4 and 7.

[84] *McKenna v An Taoiseach (No 2)* [1995] IESC 11, [1995] 2 IR 10.

[85] *Coughlan v Broadcasting Complaints Commission* [2000] IESC 44, [2000] 3 IR 1. On the other hand, courts can restrict efforts by political actors to moderate spending. One option is to create two campaign umbrella organizations. But attempts by Quebec to force campaign groups into such umbrella committees to the exclusion of all third-party spending was found to be too restrictive of freedom of expression and hence a violation of the Canadian Charter of Rights and Freedoms, see *Libman v Quebec (Attorney General)* [1997] 3 SCR 569. More broadly, in the USA the Supreme Court has recently struck down attempts to limit electoral campaign spending: *Citizens United v Federal Election Commission*, 558 US 08-205 (2010).

We have noted that control of initiation is not the same thing as controlling the entire process of the referendum. And even if we take the issue of initiation on its own, this is a more complex story than it often appears to be, involving the intermingling of constitutional issues with political factors. This also reminds us that a thorough assessment of the constitutional apparatus of each state is needed rather than theories of control which are presented as universally generalizable.

There are at least five political factors that can each combine with the overall constitutional context in any one referendum to make the issue of control through the whole referendum process both complex and particular: separation/sharing of powers;[86] the role of the opposition; the party system; electoral unpredictability; and the intervention of the media. This is doubtlessly not an exhaustive list but it will at least serve to offer a sense of the complexity involved.

First, in many instances the initiating power should not be viewed merely as the power of one elite actor but the interplay of numerous, and often dissonant, political voices. Therefore, we need to break down the notion of 'elites'. Are we talking about executives or legislatures or both? (And in the background we might expand the notion of elite influence to include also the courts, the media, and other interest groups.) In some situations the way the constitutional rules are framed can cause different branches to cooperate—or compete—in the staging and running of a referendum, with the potential to make this a site of dispute. In constitutional regimes that offer an executive figure some discretion to hold a referendum, this role can invariably be exercised only with the approval of the legislature. Under the Australian constitution, which requires a referendum for any constitutional amendment, a referendum is initiated by the government, but this proposal must first be approved by an absolute majority of each house of parliament.[87] And in constitutions which are silent on the use of referendums, again although the executive may have discretion, such a power will in practice require enabling legislation to be passed, and in this situation the legislature may curtail the executive's ambitions.[88] This notion of elites

---

[86] Neustadt famously talked of a separation of institutions but a sharing of powers within the US constitutional system. Richard E Neustadt, *Presidential Power and the Modern President: The Politics of Leadership* (Macmillan Press 1960).

[87] Australian Constitution, s 128. Often referendums are only constitutionally triggered after approval of a measure by the legislature, in some cases requiring a high threshold of support at this stage. Eg the Constitution of Gambia, Art 226, indicates that constitutional amendments are to be put to referendums only after passage by three-quarters of the legislature.

[88] One recent example is the SNP minority government in Scotland, which published a draft referendum Bill in 2010 but did not proceed with this during the 2010–11 session of Parliament. It is likely the Bill would have faced strong opposition from the majority unionist parties.

118   Constitutional Referendums

competing for political power, and drawing upon purported constitutional legitimacy in doing so, is brought out in a detailed study of referendum strategy by Walker. He focuses upon how referendums have been the focus of intense rivalries between competing elites in post-Soviet Russia; in this case between president and parliament, and between state and sub-state level in the context of a multinational federal state.[89]

A second environmental issue that complicates the notion of elite control and shows it to be a contested area is the power of oppositional forces, in particular oppositional political parties. We have addressed how the constitution can provide opportunities both for oppositional voices and the direct initiative of citizens (which are usually mobilized in practice by oppositional political actors) to initiate a referendum. This leads to Hamon's classification of referendums as being either 'the recourse of the prince', 'the recourse of the citizens', or 'the recourse of the parties'.[90] We have also observed that this power is usually a reactive one, permitting a referendum to be instigated in relation to an act or proposed piece of legislation by the government, forming in effect a veto power. Hug and Tsebelis, whose empirical work on the 'veto player' concentrates on the power of oppositional voices, argue that there is 'considerable leeway to the veto player who may trigger a referendum, and even more so if this veto player may also formulate the referendum question'.[91] They go so far as to argue that in certain situations: 'If an actor prefers the status quo to the proposed policy and has the capacity to trigger a referendum, it can assure that the outcome will remain the status quo.'[92] One example cited by Hug and Tsebelis is the first Danish Maastricht referendum. Here the overwhelming majority within the Danish political class was in favour of ratification. But a minority in the Parliament, invoking the constitutional provision that allows one-sixth of the members of parliament to force a referendum on such an issue, did so. This led to a referendum in which the voters also rejected the Maastricht Treaty.

In this case, certainly, the constitutional provision was crucial; the particularity of the Danish constitution allowed the people directly to emerge as a veto power through the mobilization of elite political opposition.[93] It is also often the case that in other situations the people are most often not consulted on constitutional change where the constitution does not require it and where there is broad cross-party consensus on the issue. But this is not the whole story. There can be cases, even when such a constitutional trigger

---

[89] Mark Clarence Walker, *The Strategic Use of Referendums: Power, Legitimacy, and Democracy* (Palgrave Macmillan 2003). We will return to some of these cases in the next chapter.

[90] Hamon, *Le Référendum: Étude Comparative*.

[91] Hug and Tsebelis, 'Veto Players and Referendums Around the World', 480.

[92] ibid 485.   [93] How this was reversed in the second referendum will be discussed in Chapter 6.

is lacking, where political power may enable the opposition to mobilize popular support and perhaps also the media to put pressure on the governing party to concede a referendum. Morel talks about 'politically compulsory referendums', by which he means situations where 'all relevant political actors unanimously demand a referendum on a particular issue, and a legitimate decision cannot be made without a referendum'.[94] We see here again the interplay of constitutional law and convention on the one hand and politics on the other. The political power of the opposition in pressing for a referendum is heavily contingent on the constitution. Where a constitution is silent on referendums, much will depend upon whether they are seen to be acceptable, whether there is precedent for them, and whether a reasonable claim might be made that constitutional convention requires one. In other words, the power of the political opposition, if it can point plausibly to existing referendum practice, and argue for its extension, can help create a new constitutional convention, as we discussed earlier in the UK context.[95]

A third, and related, political factor, again structural in nature, is, therefore, the party system in the state. This enters the mix, shaping further the relationship between political discretion and legal regulation. In a two-party system the level of political discretion which already exists with discretionary as opposed to mandatory referendums can be significantly strengthened. This has been shown to be the case in the Swiss context but it is an interesting finding that may have more general application. As Mueller puts it:

> Given that the party in control of the parliament could pass any proposal it puts up to a referendum, and tends to put up only proposals it expects to win, it is not clear that giving parliament the right to call referenda serves any desirable purpose in a two-party system.[96]

---

[94] He cites the Norwegian referendum on EU membership in 1994 as an example. Laurence Morel, 'The Rise of Government-Initiated Referendums in Consolidated Democracies' in Mendelsohn and Parkin (eds), *Referendum Democracy*, 61.

[95] A factor here is that pressure for a referendum as a device used in opposition can force the hand of that party if it comes into government. Eg the Labour Party in opposition in 1970 accepted the principle of a referendum but it was unable to force the Conservative government to hold one on entry in 1972–73. But Labour re-negotiated the terms of British membership of the EEC when re-elected in February 1974 and was then politically bound to hold a referendum in 1975. Vernon Bogdanor, 'Western Europe' in Butler and Ranney (eds), *Referendums Around the World*, 39. Labour, in opposition in the 1980s and 1990s, also pushed for constitutional change through such mechanisms as the Scottish Constitutional Convention, which stressed the popular sovereignty of the Scottish people. This meant that the use of a referendum for its proposals for Scottish devolution when returned to office in 1997 was a political inevitability. A third example is the pressure applied by the Conservative Party since 1997 for referendums on further treaty-based integration within the EU. This seems to bind the Conservatives politically to hold a referendum in respect of any further significant treaty changes emanating from Brussels during their tenure in office, leading to the European Union Act 2011.

[96] Dennis C Mueller, *Constitutional Democracy* (OUP 1996) 183.

The scope of available discretion seems likely to be weaker in a multi-party system due to the need for coalitions.[97] But matters are not always as straightforward as this. First, as we saw in the context of veto power, a party even with a majority and unwilling to hold a referendum, may come under considerable pressure to do so. In other words, a popular front can unite either for or against a referendum on a certain matter. Second, in a two-party system the governing party may have a small majority and so even a small rebellion can be decisive. Rourke et al offer the assessment that in general governments 'lose referendums unless they first build a broad coalition among major parties and interest groups'.[98] In the next section we will return to UK referendums in the 1970s in this context. Again constitutional structure remains an important conditioning factor, with evidence to suggest that political parties can influence mandatory referendums and initiatives more readily than discretionary votes.[99] In other words, with relatively low levels of discretion open to the governing party in mandatory referendums, and relatively high levels of discretion open to opposition parties in constitutions that permit initiatives, the political power of parties can vary widely from constitution to constitution.

This leads to a fourth political issue which must be factored into the idea of control—the unpredictability or even volatility of the electorate, which can be considerably greater in referendums than in parliamentary elections. There seems to be a number of reasons for this. Much will depend upon the degree of party or ideological familiarity attached to the issue and also how familiar it is to the electorate to begin with; the more novel the issue, the higher the likelihood of volatility.[100] And while elite cues can certainly be important for many voters,[101] the lack of clear party identification on a particular issue may make these harder to pick up.[102] In any case, in many

---

[97] ibid 185. However, a referendum on an issue may be a bargaining chip that one party offers to another as an enticement to form a coalition, as we saw in the UK in 2010 with the promise by the Conservatives to the Liberal Democrats of a referendum on electoral reform.

[98] John T Rourke, Richard P Hiskes, and Cyrus E Zirakzadeh, *Direct Democracy and International Politics: Deciding International Issues Through Referendums* (Lynne Rienner Publishers 1992) 175.

[99] Alexander H Trechsel and Pascal Sciarini, 'Direct Democracy in Switzerland: Do Elites Matter?' (1998) 33 European J Political Research 99, 119–20.

[100] Lawrence LeDuc, 'Opinion Change and Voting Behaviour in Referendums' (2002) European J Political Research 711, 727–8. In a related way, the frequency of referendums can be a factor. Where the referendum is a rarely used mechanism or where the issue is put before voters for the first time, then the lack of familiarity with the issue (compared to a situation where voters vote for parties with which they are very familiar) may lessen the degree of pre-disposition in the voting intentions of the electorate.

[101] Ian Budge, 'Political Parties in Direct Democracy' in Mendelsohn and Parkin (eds), *Referendum Democracy*, 86.

[102] Claes H de Vreese and Holli A Semetko, 'News Matters: Influences on the Vote in the Danish 2000 Euro Referendum Campaign' (2004) 43 European J Political Research 699, 701. See also Richard Sinnott, 'Cleavages, Parties and Referendums: Relationships between Representative and Direct Democracy in

referendums party loyalty will not be triggered as obviously as in other elections where one is choosing among parties or party candidates. People might sense that they can vote as they wish in a referendum without directly damaging the party they support, a phenomenon that has been called 'the punishment trap'.[103]

Conversely, in situations where parties seek to distance an issue from the popularity of a particular party (often the party of government), such a strategy can backfire. Referendums do not take place in a vacuum. LeDuc observes that referendum voters are not simply 'issue voters' and that 'attitudes towards issues are only one of the variables affecting voting choice'.[104] Voters may look beyond the referendum issue and use it as a 'second-order election'.[105] In other words, the popularity of political actors or the government can be a vital issue, as can leadership.[106] There are arguments that domestic political factors were influential in the EU referendums in Ireland, France, and the Netherlands, although in Chapter 6 we will address findings that question how far this was the case. In addition, we can point to other cases where ancillary issues were influential in the referendum process. For example, the French government used a referendum on the Maastricht Treaty in 1992 as, in effect, a confidence vote.[107] The

---

the Republic of Ireland' (2002) 41 European J Political Research 811. However, others do stress that partisan cues remain important: Sara Binzer Hobolt, 'How Parties Affect Vote Choice in European Integration Referendums' (2006) 12 Party Politics 623; Sara Binzer Hobolt, *Europe in Question: Referendums on European Integration* (OUP 2009).

[103] Gerald Schneider and Patricia A Weitsman, 'The Punishment Trap: Integration Referendums as Popularity Contests' (1996) 28 Comparative Political Studies 582. And even when the party may suffer, voters in referendums will not always display loyalty. With only a narrow majority vote for devolution in Wales in 1997 large numbers of Labour and Liberal Democrat supporters clearly voted against the position taken by their favoured parties. David Denver, 'Voting in the 1997 Scottish and Welsh Devolution Referendums: Information, Interests and Opinions' (2002) 41 European J Political Research 827, 841. This reminds us that we need also to consider the political factors in Section IV to get the full picture of the control issue. But again it is important not to overstate the degree of volatility. One study argues that supporters of government parties in Ireland, France, and Denmark in 1992 voted much more strongly in favour of the Maastricht Treaty than supporters of opposition parties did. Mark Franklin, Michael Marsh, and Lauren McLaren, 'Uncorking the Bottle: Popular Opposition to European Unification in the Wake of Maastricht' (1994) 32 J Common Market Studies 455. See also Simon Hug and Pascal Sciarini, 'Referendums on European Integration' (2000) 33 Comparative Political Studies 3. But it does seem that, overall, partisan loyalty cannot perform a predictive function to the same extent in referendums as in general elections.

[104] LeDuc, 'Opinion Change', 729.

[105] Karlheinz Reif and Hermann Schmitt, 'Nine Second-Order National Elections: A Conceptual Framework for the Analysis of European Election Results' (1980) 8 European J Political Research 3.

[106] This image of different political leaders has been identified as a factor in the Australian referendum on the head of state of 1999. Clive Bean, 'Political Personalities and Voting in the 1999 Australian Constitutional Referendum' (2002) 14 Int'l J Public Opinion Research 459. See also de Vreese, 'Context, Elites, Media and Public Opinion in Referendums', 1.

[107] For work on whether government signals to party supporters can be significant when the issue is flagged as a 'confidence' measure see Hug and Sciarini, 'Referendums on European Integration', 32.

government was very confident of the outcome but in fact this strategy by President Mitterrand almost backfired. Only a narrow Yes vote was secured despite government expectations of an easy victory. On the other hand, oppositions who provoke a referendum on a particular issue can suffer either from voters who may agree with the opposition on the referendum issue but who do not want to undermine the government, or from those citizens who see the whole referendum as a transparent case of attempted manipulation, or a waste of time and money, and therefore rebel against the organizers on this basis.[108]

The people might also use the referendum to rebel against the political class as a whole. I have mentioned the first Danish referendum on the Treaty of Maastricht as a dramatic example of the people doing just this. Again, in Denmark in 2000 on EMU the Prime Minister and government threw support and resources behind the Yes campaign, backed by all of the main political parties, unions, business leaders, and media outlets.[109] But the people said No. There are a number of possible reasons for this rejection. The opposition was able to raise doubts about the issue, and the euro itself was falling in value. But popular rebellion was also a factor. As LeDuc puts it: 'In the end... one of the strongest weapons that the No side possessed was the psychology of the underdog. For many, left or right, the campaign was an epic battle of the Danish people against the political elites—or little Denmark against the European superstate.'[110] Another example is Italy in 1991 on preference voting, where the people supported abrogation by 95.6 per cent to 4.4 per cent on a 62.5 per cent turnout, even though neither the Christian Democrats nor the Socialists were in favour of changing the electoral system.[111] Finally, voter rebellion against the political class is often cited for the rejection of the draft Charlottetown Accord in Canada in 1992 (see Chapter 9).

Within such complex political environments the scope for political discretion can manifest itself in different ways at different points in the referendum process, with influence being lost or gained unpredictably, and not only at the time when the process starts. In an intense political environment a referendum campaign can be affected by new and surprising dynamics. As LeDuc puts it: 'the uncertainties of a campaign can place at risk even the most carefully structured referendum proposal'.[112] He discusses how the focus of the Australian referendum in 1999 moved from the simple binary of whether Australia should be a republic rather than a constitutional monarchy, and

---

[108] The referendum in the North East of England on a regional assembly is an example.
[109] LeDuc, *Politics of Direct Democracy*, 95–6.   [110] ibid 97.
[111] Bogdanor, 'Western Europe', 68.   [112] LeDuc, 'Opinion Change', 727.

centred instead on what kind of republican head of state was envisaged by the Yes campaign: the divisive split between those who favoured an elected and an appointed president respectively led many in the former camp who might have voted Yes to vote No.[113] The kind of unpredictable results that we have seen lead to considerable uncertainty among political scientists as to the predictability of referendums. De Vreese points out that traditional theories of voting behaviour based upon party support or attachment, economic perceptions, understandings of issues, and evaluations of leaders or candidates do not offer the same guidelines in referendums: 'despite the apparent simplistic nature of the referendum vote (Yes/in favour or No/against), the referendum issue is often multifaceted and different aspects may trigger diverse perceptions of the issue among voters'.[114]

A fifth political factor is the role of the media which can, of course, influence the electorate and compound unpredictability.[115] A governmental elite may have formal control over initiation and even question-setting but in the face of a hostile media and a strong opposition not only through political parties but also through interest groups, it can face a stern challenge. As we have seen, governments and parliaments can be harried into holding referendums by the opposition and the media even when they would prefer not to. Tony Blair, under an intense media spotlight, in April 2004 eventually announced to Parliament his intention to hold a referendum on the draft Constitutional Treaty, a promise repeated in the Labour manifesto for the 2005 election. He was saved from this by the defeat of the Treaty elsewhere. Although notably no such promise was made by Labour on the Lisbon Treaty, as media pressure was faced down, and a legal challenge to this change of position was unsuccessful.[116]

Jenkins and Mendelsohn, focusing on the 1995 Quebec referendum, found that news coverage in this referendum was similar to that in elections in that it looked to political elites for 'the provision of information and interpretation of the issue'. Their conclusions were that this type of coverage 'almost inevitably frustrate[s] voters who may already feel they have no control over the process'.[117] Furthermore, it did not help facilitate meaningful deliberation since there was 'little opportunity for deliberation to emerge

---

[113] See also John Higley and Ian McAllister, 'Elite Division and Voter Confusion: Australia's Republic Referendum in 1991' (2002) 41 European J Political Research 845.

[114] De Vreese, 'Context, Elites, Media and Public Opinion in Referendums', 1, 14.

[115] De Vreese and Semetko, 'News Matters: Influences on the Vote in the Danish 2000 Euro Referendum Campaign'.

[116] 'Stuart Wheeler Loses High Court Challenge to the EU Lisbon Treaty', *The Times* (London, 26 June 2008) <http://www.timesonline.co.uk/tol/news/uk/article4214748.ece> accessed 14 July 2011.

[117] Roy Jenkins and Matthew Mendelsohn, 'The News Media and Referendums' in Mendelsohn and Parkin (eds), *Referendum Democracy*, 229.

from or be stimulated by the news coverage'.[118] Citizens were being treated more as spectators than participants. The conclusion of these authors is clear: 'In order for referendums to function as devices of popular sovereignty, the public must be active participants in the discourse.'[119] To help facilitate meaningful deliberation the media has a role to give voice to a wider range of actors and perspectives of voters. Since this is, of course, only one study of one referendum there is much work to be done on how media coverage shapes political discourse during referendum processes more broadly, but the role of private actors in either frustrating or helping to facilitate deliberation is potentially great.

And so we are left with a very complex picture of multiple actors interacting in different ways in each process by which a referendum is staged. As de Vreese puts it, we need a holistic picture of the categories of actors involved in a referendum campaign:

> (i) the political elites (including parties and candidates); (ii) civil society, interest organizations and lobbyists; (iii) the media and public opinion, and (iv) the electorate. These actors (understood in the broadest sense of the word) interact differently in a referendum campaign than, for example, in a general election campaign and the parameters of this interaction are contingent upon the specific context of the referendum.[120]

Political scientists are themselves increasingly aware of the unpredictability of referendums in light of these complexities,[121] to which we might add the country's constitutional tradition, the role of finance, the erratic application of political triggers, the volatility of the electorate etc. What this suggests is that each referendum has to be assessed in forensic detail, since attempts to establish broadly applicable comparative models can easily miss the complex particularities of each case.

It is surprising that this complex matrix has not hitherto been a standard backdrop for any assessment of elite control in referendum processes. The evidence from this account of political discretion in referendum processes makes clear that the notion of elite control of referendums must be approached very cautiously. What we see is a complex and highly variable political environment where different political actors can have significant and competing roles to play and where the electoral behaviour of citizens can be volatile and unpredictable. Into this mix we must also add a focus upon the constitutional system itself, whereby political discretion must

---

[118] ibid.   [119] ibid.

[120] De Vreese, 'Context, Elites, Media and Public Opinion in Referendums', 7.

[121] Michael Gallagher, 'Conclusion' in Gallagher and Uleri (eds), *The Referendum Experience in Europe*, 237.

be assessed in light of legal regulation. All of these variables, which are by no means a conclusive catalogue of the complex relationship between political discretion and legal regulation, at least heavily qualify the thesis that referendums are 'controlled and pro-hegemonic'. I will now address further complicating factors as I turn to political motives.

(iii) The complex motives of political actors

Much of the literature on elite control assumes that elites seek a Yes result when they initiate a referendum. But in fact a referendum might be held with more complex motivations than this. I will consider how a referendum might be held either in order to save a group from taking a controversial decision, in which case its views on the preferred outcome might be mixed or ambiguous, or in order to surmount an impasse in the political or lawmaking process. I will also address how unconventional alliances might form on the issue, a fact which again complicates the notion of governmental or oppositional control; and, finally, I will note the impact of these ambiguities and mixed motives on the voting public, which returns us to the issue of electoral volatility or unpredictability. The lack of clear political signals to voters, including those with strong partisan loyalty, a factor already alluded to, can be made more acute in these scenarios.

One feature of referendums that has been observed by commentators is that they can be used by elites to evade responsibility, something they cannot do so easily in representative models of decision-making. There are a number of instances of governments using referendums, not necessarily to increase the prospects of winning on a particular issue, but in order to avoid a controversial decision. A government might see no other way to move a matter forward. It may not want a referendum and may not even have a clear view on what outcome it would like, but in political terms it may feel backed into a corner. The referendum may not produce a victory for the proposition but it will provide a government with an excuse for failure. This can occur, for example, in the context of EU treaty-making. If a treaty is rejected by the people the government can wash its hands of the decision, while at the same time the government cannot be blamed by the electorate at the next election for a decision the electorate itself has taken.

Another situation where we find allegations of abdication of responsibility is where not only the government but the political classes in general cannot agree on a way forward and so there is no majority able, or willing, to take a position.[122] The referendum can be used to surmount such

---

[122] Referendums have frequently been used in Lithuania to solve political deadlock. Daniel Auers, Jüri Ruus, and Algis Krupavicius, 'Financing Referendums and Initiatives in the Baltic States' in Gilland Lutz and Hug (eds), *Financing Referendum Campaigns*, 92–4.

an impasse. Morel labels one category of referendums 'legislative referendums', which are held when there is an impediment to securing the measure through parliament such as the government's minority status, a threshold requirement, or a division between or within the houses of parliament which prevent its passage by normal parliamentary procedures.[123] Again, we need to factor into the equation the constitutional framework within which these difficulties emerge. When the constitution allows oppositional groups or citizens to initiate referendums, another avenue is open to push for such an impasse-resolving referendum; the Danish referendum on the Single European Act in 1986 is an example.[124]

A third issue can be alliances that cut across the usual adversarial lines of a particular party system, both in initiating a referendum and consequently on the conduct of it. The governing party may be so divided by the issue that it cannot form a united front. In fact, we have seen situations where rather than a referendum being used by a government to advance a party interest, it is instead used as an attempt to get round a divisive split in the party. These have been called 'division-resolving' referendums, which are 'motivated by internal divisions within the governmental party or coalition'.[125]

The UK in the 1970s provides a useful case study first on the EEC and then on devolution. In the early 1970s the Labour Party feared that a damaging split could emerge over membership of the EEC and so, in deciding to hold a referendum in 1975 on continued membership, it allowed a free vote for MPs, including ministers.[126] James Callaghan described the referendum as a 'lifeboat' into which the party was climbing in order to see off the danger of fission.[127]

Labour turned to the referendum on devolution in similar circumstances. Proposals were put forward for devolution for Scotland and Wales in 1976 and these were widely opposed within the party. Bogdanor comments that the promise of a referendum which accompanied these proposals 'was a device that would enable Labour backbenchers opposed to devolution nevertheless to vote for it in the House of Commons while campaigning against it in the referendum'.[128] The legislation was in the end withdrawn in March 1977. But when it was revived in 1977–78 referendums were again

---

[123] Morel, 'The Rise of Government-Initiated Referendums', 57.

[124] Palle Svensson, 'Denmark, The Referendum as Minority Protection' in Gallagher and Uleri (eds), *The Referendum Experience in Europe*.

[125] Setälä, 'On the Problems of Responsibility', 712.

[126] Although seven cabinet ministers argued for withdrawal, as we have seen the referendum approved continued membership. See also LeDuc, 'Opinion Change', 711–12.

[127] David Butler and Uwe Kitzinger, *The 1975 Referendum* (Macmillan Press 1976) 282.

[128] ibid 42.

proposed and these were held in 1979. Again, Bogdanor points to how the 1979 referendums were used 'to defuse an issue'.[129]

A further subset of the 'responsibility avoiding' or 'division-resolving' referendums is where one is held on an issue that is seen as a potential election loser. A government may decide to stage a referendum on a particularly controversial issue, perhaps one that might not only split the party, but whichever way it is decided might lead to popular dissent, in order to get it out of the way and at the same time dissociate the government from any decision the public reach in the referendum. The government may have a particular view on the issue and may not wish to concede this position. But if the option is to lose a general election on account of this position it may well prefer to put the matter to a referendum, even if it means losing it. In a related way we have noted earlier that the government's decision on timing may be determined in order to bury the matter as an election issue, as far as possible.[130]

Such a complex range of possible motives behind referendums inevitably has knock-on consequences for electoral behaviour, at least insofar as the kinds of elite cues that voters might expect to see in an election will be absent or confused through mixed messages from parties. In light of these complex and often heavily ambivalent motives, it is no surprise that volatile and unpredictable behaviour can be the result, as we have discussed. Finally, in addressing the complex motives of elites in staging referendums we must again note that this power can be heavily conditioned by the constitutional framework. In a system of strictly regulated, mandatory referendums many of the political calculations open in discretionary regimes simply cannot be made.

IV. CONCLUSION

In this chapter I have argued for an expanded notion of 'control', setting out three distinct but related factors: legal regulation of referendums, political power, and political behaviour. In light of this broader picture of control and influence it seems we need a much more nuanced account than the simple 'controlled and pro-hegemonic' claim we encountered in Chapter 2, and that what is needed is a more thorough account of the details of each referendum process, taking account in full of the legal and political environment in which it operates. In the same way, such recourse to the details of the referendum process are needed to inform us of the scope for deliberation in a referendum process.[131]

---

[129] ibid 45. [130] Setälä, 'On the Problems of Responsibility', 712, 713.

[131] Mendelsohn and Parkin are surely correct that direct democracy is part of representative democracy and the actions of voters are 'significantly mediated by elites, institutions and electoral law'. Mendelsohn and Parkin (eds), *Referendum Democracy*, 4. But we need to expand how we address this

The first question that was set in Chapter 2 was whether referendums are inherently too controlled and pro-hegemonic to facilitate the very possibility of meaningful popular participation and inclusiveness. In this chapter we have seen that this is something of a caricature; that there is no compelling evidence to show that a referendum, by definition, is more open to easy elite manipulation than elections; that legal regulation backed up by judicial review can intervene to circumscribe carefully the scope for political discretion;[132] that political power in a referendum is often more a story of competition than control; and that voting behaviour can be unpredictable and hence not necessarily easy to control even when a strong elite-led campaign clearly favours a particular outcome.

Finally, we have seen enough to suggest that there are issues of control which apply particularly in the constitutional context. For example, it has been in respect of referendums on matters of the highest constitutional consequence that we have seen some of the most stringent levels of constitutional regulation (eg the mandatory use of referendum in Australia etc); that some of the most important cases have been decided by higher courts; situations where the motivations of political actors have been most complex and even ambiguous (for example, the intentions of successive UK governments on EC treaty processes); and where voting behaviour has been particularly volatile and unpredictable, and attempts to assert political control most obviously frustrated (Denmark on Maastricht; Italy on electoral reform). In the next two chapters our focus narrows to some particularly challenging issues of control that emerge in the specific context of constitutional sovereignty.

---

complex environment, looking at the range of this influence in full context and how it operates to control elites as well as voters.

[132] One international recommendation to protect the law itself from manipulation is that fundamental aspects of referendum law should not be open to amendment less than one year before a referendum and a recommendation that this law should have constitutional status superior to ordinary law. European Commission for Democracy Through Law (Venice Commission), 'Code of Good Practice on Referendums' Study No 371/2006 (20 January 2009), COE Doc CDL-AD(2007)008rev, para II, 2. It will be argued in later chapters that various aspects of process design, reinforced by legal regulation, can be used to make a referendum less inherently pro-hegemonic than it might otherwise be.

5

The Referendum Challenge to Constitutional Sovereignty

I. INTRODUCTION

In this chapter and the next I will turn to two situations where the constitutional referendum intervenes in some of the most contested debates today about the nature of sovereignty in both its internal constitutional and external state-focused dimensions. The first, addressed here, is where the very constitutionality of holding a referendum is itself in question. This may not at first glance appear to raise specifically problematic issues about the nature of constitutional authority—legal and political acts are frequently questionable for their constitutionality, and the constitutional state is designed to handle such disputes. But as we will see, the constitutional referendum can become the focus for a deeper struggle over the very *ascription* of constitutional sovereignty, bringing into question generally accepted understandings both concerning the locus of sovereignty within a polity and the authority of constitutional institutions—in particular courts—to resolve disagreements concerning this locus in ways that are seen to be legitimate by all sides. In many referendums, particularly those engaged in ordinary, legislative decision-making, the issue of the constitutionality of the referendum rarely arises, or if it does the authority of national courts to adjudicate upon the legality of a particular measure is invariably accepted as the final word. Things are not always so simple with constitutional referendums. In a trite sense any referendum is controlled in that it is organized under a legal framework of some kind. But as will be discussed, it is in disputes concerning the competence to stage a referendum that the constitutional legitimacy of this framework can come into question, bringing normative argumentation into the interstices between formal positivist legality and political constitutionality, at times unsettling traditional understandings of the site, and even the nature, of constitutional supremacy.

The intervening factor that can complicate otherwise accepted understandings of constitutional legality is the reappearance of the people directly as claimants—or at least as a simulacrum—of *pouvoir constituant*. I will explore how at the heart of a number of disputes has been the claim that a particular referendum is in fact a constitutive act of popular sovereignty, which even if structured outside the normal pathways of constitutional process that otherwise might proscribe or at least closely circumscribe such an act, offers its own and, so the argument goes, higher source of constitutional legitimacy. I will address two examples of this situation in Sections II and III, respectively. One is a separation of powers struggle, where one branch of government initiates a referendum in a way that threatens to supplant the existing balance of powers among institutions established by the constitution. In doing so, it invokes the purported legitimacy of the popular sovereignty of the whole people of the state to counter arguments that this stretches, or even violates, constitutional legality. The other is territorial disputes, which can arise in federal or even unitary states between the central organs of the state and sub-state actors. In this situation actors within a sub-state territory aspire to use the referendum to effect greater autonomy or independence, in this case calling upon the discrete identity of the sub-state people as justification for such a unilateral act, even where this initiative runs up against constitutional constraints. This latter example in particular also recalls our account in Chapter 3 of how the constitutional referendum can raise important questions about the nature of the demos.

II. REFERENDUMS: CONSTITUTIONAL OR EXTRA-CONSTITUTIONAL?

I begin by addressing the situation where an actor—usually a powerful executive figure—attempts to initiate a referendum which will test the limits of constitutional legality, but in doing so mobilizes popular democracy in purported legitimization of any constitutional corner-cutting. In such a scenario, legal and political claims may run together. Such actors defend the constitutionality of their actions but at the same time invoke *pouvoir constituant* as a higher source of authority in the event of any dispute over the referendum's legality. In other words, if required, *pouvoir constituant*—instantiated as popular sovereignty—is called upon, in response to charges that the referendum is unlawful, as authority to trump such positivist legal concerns.

This type of dispute is, of course, much more likely to arise in situations where the constitution is silent on the use of referendums. Invoking *pouvoir constituant* in something of a constitutional vacuum allows the initiator to argue that constitutional silence offers a licence to hold a referendum—if the people were to be denied the right to decide directly, the constitution should have made this explicit; it is considerably more difficult to do so in a constitutional system that mandates referendums and which also makes clear how and by whom a referendum can be triggered. To deploy the referendum in an apparently extra-constitutional way in this latter scenario can be a far more brazen contestation of the normative supremacy of the written constitution. But such deployments are to be found. This use of what we might call 'executive-led, extra-constitutional referendums' can arise in a situation of crisis or of impasse, where constitutional change is difficult to achieve, where the temptation to surmount constitutional impediments can be great, and crucially where the constitutional culture pays homage—at least symbolically—to the resilience of a popular *pouvoir constituant* even within a formally entrenched constitutional structure. This latter component offers an avenue to the elite actor to invoke the referendum in the name of latent popular sovereignty, perhaps also claiming it necessary to do so in order to circumvent political and constitutional stasis.

This is precisely the scenario we see in the constitutionally troubled postwar period in France under President de Gaulle, who invoked the referendum several times during his presidency (1959–69). Here constitutional referendums were deployed by the President unilaterally, despite provisions within the constitution that seemed to preclude this. The referendum in France—a legacy of the post-revolutionary period, as we have seen—had already been revived immediately after the Second World War in constitution-transforming processes.[1] But de Gaulle was set to invoke this device for a series of controversial measures that tested the Fifth Republic's (1958–) constitution to the limit. These measures involved two referendums on self-determination for Algeria (January 1961 and April 1962); one on the direct election of the president (October 1962) and another on the powers of the Senate and regional devolution (April 1969). French constitutional culture was is some ways conducive to this process. In the French constitutional tradition, informed by the radical republicanism of Rousseau, *pouvoir constituant* has always lurked as an unsettling political trump card in relation to the entrenched republican constitution, the volatility of which is evident in the five iterations of the republican constitution over one-and-a-half centuries. And as we saw in Chapter 4, the referendum has been an important tool in the hands of executive elites from the beginning of modern French constitutionalism. But although a number of referendums

---

[1] Referendums were held on 21 October 1945 on the drafting of a constitution and on interim power for the new Assembly and on 5 May 1946 and 13 October 1946, both to approve the constitution of the Fourth Republic (1946–58).

were held between 1793 and 1815,[2] the referendum was not used at all in the Third Republic (1870–1946) and was only deployed at the end of the Fourth Republic (1946–58) to ratify the new constitution in 1958; the period has indeed been characterized by the term 'le peuple absent'.[3]

President de Gaulle, in reaction to the perceived weaknesses of the Third and Fourth Republics, considered that his role as head of state was in effect to act as the political representative of the nation, entitling him to engage directly with the people at important constitutional moments.[4] The defining characteristic of the Fifth Republic was a move away from the strong, and in de Gaulle's view stultifying, parliamentary system, to one where a strong president would become a more assertive political actor, crucially in direct dialogue with French citizens (as legitimized by his direct election—the subject matter of the particularly controversial 1962 referendum).[5] And in de Gaulle's resort to the referendum we again see the link between France's history of intermittently strong executive leadership and its radical approach to popular sovereignty, which has kept alive the emblem, and at times the reality, of *pouvoir constituant* as ultimate constitutional resource; it was in this context that a more executive-led 'directorial' form of government in the constitution of the Fifth Republic brought with it a revival of the bonapartist referendum.[6]

The constitution of the Fifth Republic provided for the use of referendums in two provisions: Articles 89 and 11. Before addressing these, it is important to note by way of context Article 3, which encapsulates a key

---

[2] The Jacobin constitution of 1793 allowed for popular referendums, as did the constitutions of 1800 and 1851. We have also discussed those referendums held by Louis Napoleon in the middle of the century.

[3] Vernon Bogdanor, 'Western Europe' in David Butler and Austin Ranney (eds), *Referendums Around the World: The Growing Use of Direct Democracy* (Macmillan Press 1994) 47.

[4] Guy Carcassonne, 'France (1958): The Fifth Republic after Thirty Years' in Vernon Bogdanor (ed), *Constitutions in Democratic Politics* (Gower 1988) 241–56; Lucien Jaume, 'Constituent Power in France: The Revolution and Its Consequences' in Martin Loughlin and Neil Walker (eds), *The Paradox of Constitutionalism* (OUP 2007) 82.

[5] Anthony Hartley, *Gaullism: The Rise and Fall of a Political Movement* (Routledge & Kegan Paul 1972); Serge Berstein, *The Republic of de Gaulle, 1958–1969* (Peter Morris tr, CUP 1993) 8–11.

[6] This model of referendum democracy is indeed characterized by de Gaulle's France, where the referendum was used to consolidate the direct relationship between a strong president and the people. In constitutional terms the doctrine of 'reserved domain' was deployed to suggest a strong reserve power vested by the constitution in the office of the president. Berstein, *The Republic of de Gaulle, 1958–1969*, 59. See also Rene Redmond, *The Right Wing of France: From 1815 to de Gaulle* (James M Laux tr, University of Philadelphia Press 1968); Berstein, *The Republic of de Gaulle 1958–1969*, 11–18. As Hamon puts it: 'each [of de Gaulle's referendums] was planned by the executive, triggered by the executive, and their purpose was at least as much to confirm or strengthen the legitimacy of this power as to adopt a new statute or a new constitution'. Francis Hamon, 'The Financing of Referendum Campaigns in France' in Karin Gilland Lutz and Simon Hug (eds), *Financing Referendum Campaigns* (Palgrave Macmillan 2009) 107. Indeed, in reference to the 1958 referendum, Carcassone describes the Fifth Republic as being born 'through a legal *coup d'etat*'. Carcassone, 'France (1958)', 241.

totem of French republicanism: 'National sovereignty belongs to the people who shall exercise it through their representatives and by means of referendum.' This seems by one reading at least to embody a restatement of the radical *pouvoir constituant* of the French body politic, returning us to the age-old paradox[7]—does the constitution become the only source for any legitimate exercise of popular constitutional power or does popular sovereignty in France contain its own source of legitimacy? In other words, does Article 3 constitute mere recognition of popular sovereignty rather than legitimacy for it, acknowledging that a higher power vested in the people resides outside and above that of the constitution itself? But there is another element to the equation: the specific reference to the referendum in Article 3. Since the constitution explicitly invokes the referendum as the mode of expression of this power, a further question is begged: even if this higher power of the people above and beyond the constitution does indeed survive constitutional instantiation of lawful authority, are *expressions* of this power only legitimate when exercised through a referendum? In other words, it may be that the constitution cannot contain (as in circumscribe) the sovereignty of the people, but can it contain (as in facilitate) the vehicle for the exercise of this sovereignty. And if so, how and by whom may such referendums be triggered?

Turning to the detailed provisions, Article 89 provides that the President of the Republic has the right to initiate amendments to the constitution to be put to a referendum, but only with the approval of both Houses of Parliament.[8] Article 11 provides another power for the President to submit to a referendum any government Bill on a range of matters detailed in the article, and importantly allows him to do so 'on a recommendation from the Government', which in effect could be virtually a unilateral power.[9] It was around the respective scope of these two articles that the use of referendums by de Gaulle provoked such controversy.[10] It seems clear that Article 89 was

---

[7] Loughlin and Walker (eds), *The Paradox of Constitutionalism* (OUP 2007).

[8] Constitution of Fifth Republic of France, Art 89: 'The President of the Republic, on the recommendation of the Prime Minister, and Members of Parliament alike shall have the right to initiate amendments to the Constitution...'

[9] 'The President of the Republic may, on a recommendation from the Government when Parliament is in session, or on a joint motion of the two Houses...submit to a referendum any Government Bill which deals with the organization of the public authorities, or with reforms relating to the economic or social policy of the Nation, and to the public services contributing thereto, or which provides for authorization to ratify a treaty which, although not contrary to the Constitution, would affect the functioning of the institutions...'

Constitution of Fifth Republic of France, Art 11.

[10] Laurence Morel, 'France: Towards a Less Controversial Use of the Referendum' in Michael Gallagher and Pier Vincenzo Uleri (eds), *The Referendum Experience in Europe* (Macmillan Press 1996) 71–2.

intended to be the exclusive mechanism by which constitutional amendments would be proposed to the people. But crucially a referendum could only be held under this provision on a measure already agreed to by the legislature. Article 11, on the other hand, although intended for other matters (and seemingly not framed as an alternative way to effect constitutional amendments), did not expressly offer a veto to the legislature. In his efforts to initiate constitutional change in a unilateral way, it was Article 11 which de Gaulle invoked.[11]

By generally accepted principles of constitutional interpretation this invocation of Article 11 relied upon a dubious argument. One of the bases on which Article 11 allows the President to hold a referendum is 'the organization of the public authorities'. It was by way of this clause—effectively deployed as a catch-all provision—that de Gaulle attempted to justify his use of referendums for high constitutional issues. This was at the very least a strained interpretation of the clause when one considers the subject matter for each of the referendums he initiated. How, for example, could the referendums held in 1961 and 1962 on the status of Algeria be interpreted as concerning 'the organization of the public authorities'? An argument can perhaps be made that it was not so obviously clear in this context that *constitutional amendments* as such were being proposed which should definitively require the use of Article 89. However, constitutional change was clearly at issue in the third referendum held in October 1962 on the issue of direct election of the President (to be done by electoral college as provided for within the constitution[12]). This led to vociferous claims that the President was acting unconstitutionally in subverting the purpose of Article 11.[13] De Gaulle's unconvincing argument was that while Article 89 provided for referendums on issues of constitutional change, it should not be taken as exclusive authority for these. Article 11 did not exclude such

---

[11] Notably since this time and despite the widely held assumption that the main way of invoking referendums in the constitutional amendment process would be Art 89, Art 11 was in fact used for each of the referendums staged during de Gaulle's presidency, and indeed has been applied for those held since: enlargement of the EEC in 1972; approval of constitutional amendments in respect of the Matignon Accords for New Caledonia in 1988; ratification of the Maastricht Treaty in 1992; reduction of the President's term of office to five years in 2000; and ratification of the Treaty establishing a European Constitution on 29 May 2005.

[12] Per the original Art 6 of the Constitution of the Fifth Republic, amended following the 1962 referendum.

[13] Alec Stone, *The Birth of Judicial Politics in France: The Constitutional Council in Comparative Perspective* (OUP 1992) 65. It has been observed that non-Gaullist politicians, and most leading jurists, viewed the adoption of the Art 11 in place of the Art 89 process in this context to be unconstitutional: Vincent Wright, 'France' in David Butler and Austin Ranney (eds), *Referendums: A Comparative Study of Practice and Theory* (American Institute for Public Policy Research 1978) 152–4; Morel, 'France: Towards a Less Controversial use of the Referendum?', 73; Shennan, *De Gaulle*, 111.

matters from its ambit, and so could be used as an alternative source of authority.[14]

If indeed de Gaulle's claim goes beyond a reasonable positivist interpretation of the two articles, we must look elsewhere for any possible constitutional legitimation of his actions. One argument is that an overriding goal of the constitution was to consolidate executive power. A purposive approach to Article 11 would therefore allow the President to read the term 'the organization of the public authorities' very widely, even in the face of the seeming exclusivity of Article 89. Bogdanor is sympathetic to this argument:

> Whether de Gaulle was or was not justified on juridical grounds in using Article 11 to amend the Constitution, he was certainly acting in the spirit of the Constitution he had promulgated. For the essence of de Gaulle's interpretation of the Fifth Republic Constitution lay in the proposition that, in the last resort, the government should be insulated from, so as not to be dependent on, the legislature.[15]

Others took a different view. The legacy of Napoleonic abuses had led to a deep suspicion of the referendum in France, with former President Vincent Auriol arguing: 'the referendum is an act of absolute power... While ostensibly making obeisance to the sovereignty of the people, it is, in fact, an attempt to deprive the people of its sovereignty, for the benefit of one man.'[16] Bogdanor in turn questions these claims of dictatorship. In fact de Gaulle situated the referendum within representative government: 'Not least among de Gaulle's achievements is his showing that these fears were groundless. He domesticated the referendum, so that it was no longer associated with dictatorship.'[17] But this is, of course, a defence from a primarily political rather than legal perspective. It does not answer the legal objection that the meaning of Article 11 was being stretched beyond breaking point.[18]

A second argument is that popular sovereignty survived the creation of the constitution not just as symbol but as normative force, and in light of this the President was entitled to trigger that power regardless of the niceties of proper constitutional procedure. De Gaulle certainly used the rhetoric of this radical tradition—seemingly embodied in Article 3—to suggest that the legal power of the French people had been left unaffected, or at least

---

[14] Bogdanor, 'Western Europe', 52. See also Stone, *The Birth of Judicial Politics in France*, ch III.

[15] Bogdanor, 'Western Europe', 52–3.

[16] ibid 48. See also Hartley, *Gaullism*, 190–1.

[17] Bogdanor, 'Western Europe', 48. Shennan puts this somewhat differently. For him the 'legalism' of de Gaulle's opponents 'ran into a kind of collective common sense, which told voters that it was, after all *his* constitution and that so soon after the war France still needed de Gaulle'. Shennan, *De Gaulle*, 111–12.

[18] Stone, *The Birth of Judicial Politics in France*, 65–6.

unsettled, by the positivist constitutional frame. As Hartley puts it: 'The plebiscitary procedure of the referendum, which on so many occasions sealed the "compact" between de Gaulle and the French people, circumvented the "intermediary" powers of party and parliament and assured the triumph of the general will.'[19] But does Article 3 validate de Gaulle's application of Article 11 and effective suspension of Article 89? Such an argument seems to confuse the symbolic power of popular sovereignty with the very real power of a particular constitutional actor to mobilize it as he sees fit. Article 3 states that national sovereignty belongs to the people, who shall exercise it *through their representatives and by means of referendum*. Article 89 provides an avenue for referendums on constitutive questions but in doing so it ties this to a constitutional procedure that disperses the trigger power among the people's representatives. The danger in one particular elite upsetting this balance and appealing directly to the people is not the subordination of law to the people—arguably the subjection of legal sovereignty to the will of the people is the perhaps unsettling (although for republicans, in many ways invigorating) implication of Article 3 itself and of the enduring paradox of popular sovereignty—but that he moves *himself* beyond legal control, at which point the president could exploit this power to manipulate the referendum process, for example setting a question in a biased way, introducing (or overriding constitutionally provided) threshold rules etc.[20] Article 3 recognizes popular sovereignty, but it also constitutionalizes this by attempting to condition the procedure for its exercise. Article 89 therefore acts inter alia to complement and at the same time consolidate the delimitations contained in Article 3, restraining any potential it might have to act as an unrestricted pathway to de facto presidential sovereignty. And in this we glimpse a broader point about the complex interplay between constitutionalism and democracy in a developed polity—that popular sovereignty and representation can never be separated one from the other. 'The people' is too large and diverse a body to manifest itself without the intervention of representational forces; popular sovereignty insofar as it survives constitutional instantiation, must live with this practical reality and hence with the constraints that constitutionalism imposes upon

---

[19] Hartley, *Gaullism*, 302; Carcassone, 'France (1958)', 241–56. And notably the constitutionality of the referendum was effectively upheld by the Constitutional Council, which concluded that it was not within the jurisdiction of the court to rule unconstitutional a matter already approved by the people in a referendum: Décision no 62-20 DC of 6 November 1962 <http://www.conseil-constitutionnel.fr/conseil-constitutionnel/francais/leself-determinationecisions/depuis-1958/decisions-par-date/1962/62-20-dc/decision-n-62-20-dc-du-06-novembre-1962.6398.html> accessed 15 July 2011. Stone describes the reasoning of the court 'an absurdity'. Stone, *The Birth of Judicial Politics in France*, 66.

[20] As we will discuss in Chapter 8, de Gaulle also used his power to set favourable questions in a number of referendums.

how popular sovereignty might be exercised; this is the very promise of popular republicanism's own democratic manifestation, if it is not to fall prey to manipulation.

The final argument that Article 89 sets out the exclusive conduit for the exercise of popular sovereignty, as with constitutional entrenchment as a whole, is that it was itself ratified by the people through the referendum that endorsed the constitution of the Fifth Republic as a package. The people agreed that their sovereignty would be exercised henceforth through a referendum, and agreed to a mechanism by which this would take place. However, again, although this might seem at one level conclusive, it also reminds us that the authority of the constitutional text depends upon its own bootstrapping[21]—the paradox of constituent power and constitutional form remains unresolved, as indeed, as a paradox, it must.[22] What we can say, however, is that it is in the constitutional referendum that we see many of the dormant complexities of this paradox emerge, with the potential to force their way to the surface in a number of constitutional polities, and unsettling more generally so many of the positivist assumptions we might hold about constitutionality, as they did in de Gaulle's France.

III. SUB-STATE NATIONALISM AND THE REFERENDUM CHALLENGE TO CONSTITUTIONAL POSITIVISM

A second setting for intense disputes as to whether constitutive referendums can be held and if so by whom has arisen in recent times over questions of sovereignty for sub-state territories. Sub-state elites in a number of states have claimed the right to stage 'sovereignty referendums' within their territory. In some sense these claims can be compared to those made by de Gaulle in France in that they either combine standard positivist justifications that constitutional authority exists for such a referendum with a political appeal to popular sovereignty, or at other times subordinate the former to the latter, asserting that the discrete identity of the people of the territory can entitle such a unilateral act even if it is unconstitutional by standard positive constitutional interpretation. But these claims take on another dimension that stretches traditional conceptions of statal constitutionalism even further. Whereas de Gaulle and his opponents would be agreed upon the existence of one sovereign and indivisible French people as

---

[21] Elster describes 'constitutional bootstrapping' as 'the process by which a constituent assembly severs its ties with the authorities that have called it into being and arrogates some or all of their powers to itself'. Jon Elster, 'Constitutional Bootstrapping in Paris and Philadelphia' (1992–93) 14 Cardozo LJ 549, 549.

[22] Hans Lindahl, 'Constituent Power and Reflexive Identity: Towards an Ontology of Collective Selfhood' in Loughlin and Walker (eds), *The Paradox of Constitutionalism*.

the underpinning principle of the French state—the argument turning upon which central institution or institutions were empowered, and how, to activate the articulation of that sovereignty through one, state-wide referendum—the claims of sub-state nationalists can call into question this very principle of demotic unity that underpins and indeed characterizes the Westphalian *Rechtsstaat*.

This difficult issue brings us back to the demotic question encountered in Chapter 3 and the implications it holds for constitutional control. By the received understanding of western democratic constitutionalism, the legitimacy of any constitution, resting upon the consent whether expressed or tacit, of *one* constitutional people, is a given. And as we have discussed, normative principles surrounding deliberative democracy have been built upon this presumption by political theorists. This is implicit in the work of Rawls[23] and Habermas.[24] Therefore, the sub-state challenge, particularly when it tries to mobilize the referendum as a vehicle of legitimacy, tests not only the limits of authority of a given constitution, but the almost universally accepted understandings of the monistic demotic environment within which traditional liberal constitutionalism plays out. Constitutionalism in the traditional statist mode also conditions actors to formulate their claims internally within the constitution, framing them by its syntax. Sub-state sovereignists in their assertions of demotic plurality and corresponding claims to 'sovereignty' in relation to a particular sub-state territory, bring to the constitutional table a radical challenge to these assumptions, a challenge with empirical and normative dimensions. On the former level, they present claims to the existence of a discrete national society (or a plurality of societies) below the level of the state. At the normative level they argue that the constitution, as instrument of a dominant demotic unit,[25] fails to recognize the depth of plurality within the state. This in turn calls the very legitimacy of that constitution into question. It may seem by a certain type of positivist constructionism to be internally valid and coherent, but the a priori popular legitimacy which must underpin any democratic constitution[26] is by this measure deficient.

This scenario reopens the constitutional form/constituent power paradox in a new setting. The problem of constitutional legitimacy is, of course, an

---

[23] For a discussion see Ferran Requejo, 'Democratic Legitimacy and National Pluralism' in Ferran Requejo (ed), *Democracy and National Pluralism* (Routledge 2001) 167–9.

[24] Jürgen Habermas, 'Struggles for Recognition in the Democratic Constitutional State' in Amy Gutmann (ed), *Multiculturalism: Examining the Politics of Recognition* (Princeton University Press 1994) 107.

[25] Stephen Tierney, 'Crystallising Dominance: Majority Nationalism, Constitutionalism and the Courts' in Alain Gagnon, André Lecours, and Geneviève Nootens (eds), *Dominant Nationalisms* (University of Montreal Press 2008).

[26] Martin Loughlin, *The Idea of Public Law* (OUP 2003) 95.

old one, given that by logic a sovereign founder must precede a sovereign constitution.[27] How then does or indeed can that founder really relinquish that sovereign power? It is this tension that Article 3 of the French constitution tries to embody and contain, but the de Gaulle referendums show how this tension can irrupt in certain conditions. Habermas attempts to circumvent this paradox with a theory of the 'equiprimordiality' of democracy and the rule of law.[28] But Lindahl explains how Habermas's account is ultimately unsatisfactory in the context of sub-state nationalism. Although Habermas acknowledges the gravity of the problem by referring to the foundation of a constitutional democracy as a 'groundless discursive self-constitution', he argues that it is possible to escape endless circularity through recognizing the 'future-oriented character, or openness, of the democratic constitution'.[29] But in the context specifically of sub-state nationalism Lindahl suggests that this kind of elaborate bootstrapping 'surely begs the question'.[30] The issue cannot just be about future orientation when the very legitimacy of the constitution—and by implication, its historical origins—is in question. As Lindahl puts it, some feel they were included against their will and now no longer wish to be included or at least seek to renegotiate the terms of union with others on an equal basis. Such an understanding, although barely articulated, seems to underpin the French recognition in the Noumea Accord of franchise restrictions in favour of the indigenous New Caledonians for any future act of self-determination, and of the acceptance of these rules, even in the face of liberal non-discrimination criteria, by two international tribunals (Chapter 3).

But as we have observed, assertions of national pluralism cannot be reduced simply to assertions of political sovereignty thrown against the positivist authority of the constitution. Sub-state nationalist positions often assert constitutionally grounded claims (by one argument the true meaning of the constitution as a pluralistic enterprise has been distorted by a unitary interpretation adopted by the state[31]), although they are then, at moments of crisis or impasse, ready to assert claims to discrete demotic sovereignty founded in residual pre-constitutional or contemporary supra-constitutional

---

[27] 'The constitutional assembly cannot itself vouch for the legitimacy of the rules according to which it was constituted. The chain never terminates, and the democratic process is caught in a circular self-constitution that leads to an infinite regress.' Jürgen Habermas, 'Constitutional Democracy: A Paradoxical Union of Contradictory Principles?' (2001) 29 Political Theory 766, 774.

[28] Habermas, 'Constitutional Democracy', 774.

[29] ibid. See also Hans Lindahl, 'Recognition as Domination: Constitutionalism, Reciprocity and the Problem of Singularity' in Neil Walker, Jo Shaw, and Stephen Tierney (eds), *Europe's Constitutional Mosaic* (Hart Publishing 2011) 205, 210.

[30] Lindahl, ibid.

[31] Stephen Tierney, *Constitutional Law and National Pluralism* (OUP 2004) 15–17.

legitimacy. These deep-seated, indeed ontological, disputes tend to lie dormant within the ordinary workings of contemporary constitutionalism in the multinational state. It is significant, therefore, that it has been the deployment of the referendum by sub-state elites that has caused these latent constitutional/political arguments for segmented or pluralized demotic supremacy to break through the wall of positivist legitimacy that has hitherto supported the 'imposed' constitution.

But in the sub-state context we should also nuance this conclusion by recognizing that the extent to which the referendum does in fact challenge existing constitutional authority is a matter of degree. It is important to distinguish referendums that seek to consult the people on their views and perhaps seek authority to negotiate sovereignty within the generally accepted rules of the existing constitution, and those more radical initiatives that assert an authority rivalling that of the constitution as expressions of self-determining sovereignty. What we will see as we address Quebec and Scotland as case studies is that the arguments deployed by nationalists tend to shift between an 'inside' and 'outside' approach to the constitution in ways that are both strategic and, at the same time, intended to be mutually reinforcing. Where a strong body of opinion exists within the sub-state territory that the constitution is legitimate, there is a concomitant politically (as well as legally) motivated inclination on the part of sub-state nationalists to 'play by the rules', with a referendum fitting within existing constitutional structures. Where relations between centre and periphery are more fraught, there is a greater risk that the referendum will be called upon to instantiate the purportedly higher level of constitutional legitimacy—that of the sovereignty of one of its founding peoples—rather than a positivist interpretation from 'inside' the existing constitution.

Any model of constitution—whether federal (Canada), decentralized (Spain), or unitary but devolved (UK)—can be vulnerable to the sophisticated constitutional claims of sub-state nationalism, but there are institutional features that can make them especially so. As we have observed, the ground for dispute over both the power to initiate a referendum and what its effect can be, is more fertile in situations of constitutional silence. The Canadian constitution makes no reference to referendums. It has, however, been accepted that federal authorities are entitled to stage referendums, as they have done on three occasions: on prohibition (29 September 1898); on conscription (27 April 1942); and on the draft Charlottetown Accord (26 October 1992).

It has also long been accepted that provinces can hold referendums. Quebec held its own referendum on prohibition as long ago as 1919 and today provincial referendums are commonplace; for example, British Columbia and Ontario staged referendums on electoral reform in 2005 and 2007, respectively.[32] Indeed, the Charlottetown experience is interesting for the way in which provinces initially brought the referendum onto the constitutional change agenda. With negotiations coming to a close, there had been no plan on the part of the federal government to stage a referendum. But as several provinces intimated their intention to hold one, the federal government decided to stage a national poll as a way of keeping control of events.[33] The Canadian Referendum Act 1992, passed to facilitate the process, was permissive, allowing provinces to conduct parallel referendums,[34] but seeming to require that the referendums be held on the same day and with the same question.[35]

These examples provoked no significant arguments concerning the constitutional authority of the provinces. But the issue of control did become heavily disputed when the National Assembly of Quebec organized two referendums on the issue of 'sovereignty association' in 1980 and 'sovereignty and partnership' in 1995. The Quebec case remains the paradigm example of how sub-state elites, when their demands for constitutional change are not met by the central state through constitutionally recognized channels of deliberation and amendment, feel entitled to appeal directly to the people. The Quebec case has, therefore, inspired sub-state nationalists in other states in recent years to view the referendum as a device with which to stake claims to independent statehood or enhanced autonomy. We will address Quebec before turning to the UK, another multi-level polity where the referendum is also firmly on the sub-state nationalist agenda.

In both the 1980 and 1995 referendums a majority voted No to the proposals for change. The latter process in particular resulted in a deluge of academic and other commentary,[36] legislative interventions,[37] a pronouncement by the Supreme Court of Canada,[38] and a parliamentary

---

[32] Indeed, British Columbia held a second referendum on this issue in 2009, as well as a referendum on First Nations treaty rights in 2002; and in 2001 New Brunswick held a referendum on lottery gaming.

[33] Richard Simeon, 'The Referendum Experience in Canada' (Referendums and Deliberative Democracy workshop, University of Edinburgh, 8 May 2009).

[34] Referendum Act 1992, s 3(1).

[35] Quebec held a referendum on Charlottetown on the same day but followed its own referendum law. See Richard Johnston, 'Regulating Campaign Finance in Canadian Referendums and Initiatives' in Gilland, Lutz and Hug (eds), *Financing Referendum Campaigns*, 26.

[36] eg Robert A Young, *The Struggle for Quebec: From Referendum to Referendum?* (McGill-Queen's University Press 1999). See also Sujit Choudhry and Robert Howse, 'Constitutional Theory and the Quebec Secession Reference' (2000) 13 Canadian J Law and Jurisprudence 143.

[37] The federal Clarity Act (Bill C-20, 2nd sess, 36th Parliament, 48 Elizabeth II, 1999 (as passed by the House of Commons 15 March 2000) (Clarity Act 2000)) and Quebec Bill 99 (An Act respecting the exercise of the fundamental rights and prerogatives of the Québec people and the Québec State, Quebec National Assembly, 1st sess, 36th leg Bill 99 (assented to 13 December 2000)).

[38] *Reference re Secession of Quebec* [1998] 2 SCR 217.

motion signalling some attempt at constitutional renewal.[39] The questions these processes raise for constitutional theory are largely counterfactual. What legal weight would a Yes vote have had? Would it have automatically changed the constitutional relationship between Quebec and the rest of Canada? How would it have related to the detailed provisions for constitutional amendment set out in Article V of the Constitution Act 1982? Would Quebec's secession have been permissible only after negotiations between the two sides? Would the rest of Canada have been constitutionally obliged to negotiate? At the time and in light of the narrow No vote in 1995 these seemed to demand urgent attention. As a matter of Canadian constitutional practice they are far less pressing today,[40] but given that the Quebec referendum experience is now a precedent for sub-state nationalists elsewhere,[41] these theoretical issues remain important.

The situations in 1980 and 1995 were constitutionally similar. In 1980 the Quebec legislature sought in effect to bypass the constitution, going directly to the people and seeking a mandate to negotiate sovereignty and 'an economic association' with Canada.[42] The referendum failed but constitutional relations did not improve, with Quebec refusing to sign the latest iteration of the federal constitution, 'patriated' from the UK in 1982. Matters came to a head when in 1995 the National Assembly once again sought to circumvent the generally accepted constitutional amendment process and engage directly with the people on the question of the province's constitutional status, claiming the sovereign constituent power of the people of Quebec as the legitimacy for doing so.[43] Although an at times uneasy constitutional coexistence had prevailed since 1982, the 1995 referendum was nonetheless held against an ongoing backdrop of deep constitutional dissensus, with the unresolved dispute centred upon the most fundamental issue of all, the very legitimacy of the constitution itself. Quebec's constitutional status, was (and indeed remains) in the eyes of many nationalists, conceived as being partially inside the Canadian constitutional order,

---

[39] 'That this House recognize that the Québécois form a nation within a united Canada.' Hansard, 39th Parliament, 1st sess; No 087, 27 November 2006.

[40] There has been no serious legislative proposal for a referendum since 1995 and in December 2008 the people of Quebec returned the sitting (federalist) Liberal Party to office in provincial elections while the sovereignist Bloc Quebecois representation in the House of Commons fell from 47 to 4 seats in the federal election of 2 May 2011.

[41] Zoran Oklopcic, 'The Migrating Spirit of the Secession Reference in Southeastern Europe' (2011) 24 Canadian J Law and Jurisprudence 347.

[42] Peter W Hogg, *Constitutional Law of Canada* (2nd edn, Carswell 1997) 132–3.

[43] In response to a legal challenge to this move, Quebec Premier Jacques Parizeau announced: 'We can't subjugate Quebecers' right to vote to a decision of the courts. That would be contrary to our democratic system. Quebecers want to vote. They have the right to vote. And they will vote.' Cited by Young, *The Struggle for Quebec*, 106.

through formal positivist control as well as levels of lingering political attachment to Canada as a union state, and partially outside, in the realm of vernacular normative legitimacy, stemming from the popular sovereignty of the people of Quebec. To some extent, acting within the constitution was an article of faith: Quebec nationalists have long claimed that the moral authority of the Canadian constitution rests upon the ideal of a real binational vision which has been belied by constitutional practice, most egregiously through the patriation process.[44] This internal cooperation also has pragmatic reasons—the authority of the Canadian state is a political fact. Furthermore, to refuse to behave as constitutional actors can lead to the accusation of being undeliberative, since as we have seen in the constitutional theory of Rawls and Habermas, deliberation is contextualized within and conditioned by the contours of existing constitutional authority.[45] The consequence of overt extra-constitutional action would be to disenchant moderate nationalists. On the other hand, patriation had driven Quebec to a crossroads. To act within the constitution and submit entirely to its authority was arguably to legitimize the 1982 constitution. The way of remaining partly outside was to refuse to accept patriation and, should the occasion arise, call upon the higher order authority of the people of Quebec to initiate a new constitutional relationship with Canada.

The referendum was certainly a challenge to the authority of the Canadian constitution. While the question put to the voters in 1995 sought authority to negotiate sovereignty on the basis of an 'offer to Canada for a new economic and political partnership',[46] the referendum would also have authorized the unilateral assumption of sovereign status in the event of failure of these negotiations to conclude within one year. A referendum which in effect purported to authorize secession was, understandably in light of constitutional precedent, assumed by the federal government to be illegal under the Canadian constitution. Intervening in an ongoing legal challenge brought by a Quebec resident the federal government sought an Advisory Opinion from the Supreme Court of Canada (SCC). Interestingly, the SCC, when addressing the hypothetical point of the legality of any future attempt by Quebec to secede, offered a complex opinion that was far from the unequivocal statement sought by the federal government. The SCC declared that although there was not a unilateral right to secede within

---

[44] Paul Romney, *Getting it Wrong: How Canadians Forgot Their Past and Imperilled Confederation* (Toronto University Press 1999).

[45] Lindahl, 'Recognition as Domination', 210.

[46] 'Do you agree that Québec should become sovereign after having made a formal offer to Canada for a new economic and political partnership within the scope of the bill respecting the future of Québec and of the agreement signed on 12 June 1995?'

the Canadian constitution, should the people of Quebec vote Yes in a future referendum on this issue, the rest of Canada 'would have no basis to deny the right of the government of Quebec to pursue secession', and would be constitutionally required to enter into negotiations over the terms of Quebec's secession.[47]

What is remarkable about the Opinion is that an issue upon which the text of the constitution is silent was deemed by the court to be filled by unwritten but 'fundamental and organizing principles of the Constitution': federalism; democracy; constitutionalism and the rule of law; and respect for minorities. It was by reflecting upon these principles and their implications that the Court concluded that a positive referendum result could constitute a prima facie right to secede[48] for Quebec, provided the province met important process requirements with a 'clear majority of Quebecers' voting 'on a clear question' in favour of secession,[49] and provided Quebec's side of the negotiations was conducted in good faith, respecting the interests of the other provinces, the federal government, and the rights of others, including minorities.[50]

It seems that the Court, applying the unwritten constitutional principles of federalism and democracy in conjunction with the other unwritten principles and the written text of the constitution, was giving weight to the idea that Quebec did indeed have discrete constituent power separate from that national constituent power of the Canadian people as a whole, which if expressed clearly in a referendum in favour of secession, created a constitutional obligation on the part of the rest of the country to facilitate that secession.[51] The power of the people of Quebec to exercise self-determination was being taken seriously, even to the point of trumping the will of the rest of Canada to retain the federal union, and the use of a referendum, as the manifestation of political sovereignty, was deemed to be

---

[47] *Reference re Secession of Quebec* [1998] 2 SCR 217.

[48] Stephen Tierney, 'The Constitutional Accommodation of National Minorities in the UK and Canada: Judicial Approaches to Diversity' in Alain-G Gagnon, Montserrat Guibernau, and François Rocher (eds), *Conditions of Diversity in Multinational Democracies* (Institute for Research on Public Policy 2004) 169–206.

[49] Which, according to the court, 'would confer democratic legitimacy on the secession initiative which all of the other participants in Confederation would have to recognize'. *Secession Reference* preamble. See also paras 93, 150.

[50] *Secession Reference*, paras 95 and 151.

[51] 'The continued existence and operation of the Canadian constitutional order cannot remain indifferent to the clear expression of a clear majority of Quebecers that they no longer wish to remain in Canada.' *Secession Reference*, para 92. Such indifference: 'would amount to the assertion that other constitutionally recognized principles necessarily trump the clearly expressed democratic will of the people of Quebec'. *Secession Reference*, para 92. In short, it seems clear that Quebec has a right to secede, albeit following negotiations (which the other provinces and the federal government have a duty to enter into) if a clear answer to a clear question is achieved in the preceding referendum.

of the highest constitutional relevance.[52] Although the Court did not expressly say so, it seems almost certain that a mere piece of legislation passed by the National Assembly of Quebec claiming sovereignty would not have been treated in this way by the Court. It is inconceivable that the SCC would have decided that such a resolution could force the hand of Quebec's 'partners in confederation'. Instead, it is a 'clear expression of self-determination by the people of Quebec'[53] that carries this weight. Certainly the Court was careful to say that it was not recognizing a *unilateral* power of Quebec to secede following a referendum. This would require negotiation in good faith with Quebec's partners in confederation. But the very fact that these partners would be compelled to negotiate in good faith, and that these negotiations should not hold up secession unreasonably,[54] is a remarkable conclusion for the Court to read into the constitution, and a remarkable level of weight to give to a sub-state referendum. This seems to be clear recognition that there is a particular normative significance attaching to a constituent referendum, even when the written constitution does not ascribe such significance to it.

The Quebec situation is not unique, as elites among other sub-state peoples seek to use the referendum as a pathway to independence. In Scotland the prospect of a referendum on Scottish independence is very real, particularly following the achievement of an overall majority by the Scottish National Party (SNP) in the Scottish Parliament elections of May 2011. The UK, of course, has a wholly unwritten constitution and therefore has no constitutional provision permitting or proscribing referendum use. Referendums have been used in the UK both at state and sub-state levels. The first state-wide referendum was held on continued membership of the EC in 1975 and the second on 5 May 2011, which proposed changing from a 'first-past-the-post' to an 'alternative vote' model of electoral system for elections to the House of Commons.[55] Sub-state referendums (Northern Ireland 1973; Scotland 1979; Wales 1979; Scotland 1997; Wales 1997; Northern Ireland 1998; London 1998; North East of England 2004; Wales 2011) have all been organized by the central government with enabling legislation passed by Parliament.

But with devolution has come the opportunity for sub-state administrations to hold their own referendums. The long-held Scottish National Party

---

[52] 'The clear repudiation by the people of Quebec of the existing constitutional order would confer legitimacy on demands for secession.' *Secession Reference*, para 88.

[53] ibid para 88.   [54] ibid para 103.

[55] Parliamentary Voting Systems and Constituencies Act 2011. The proposal was defeated by 67.9 per cent to 32.1 per cent on a 42.2 per cent turnout.

commitment to Scottish independence was restated in its manifesto for the 2007 elections to the Scottish Parliament, in which it proposed a referendum on the issue and after which it constituted a minority government within the Scottish Parliament from May 2007 to May 2011. The Scottish Government during the term of that parliament slowly built on its plans to hold a referendum. First in August 2007 a 'National Conversation' consultation exercise was launched. On 30 November 2009 the Scottish Executive published the White Paper, *Your Scotland, Your Voice: A National Conversation*, which set out an examination of various constitutional options for Scotland's future—the status quo, further devolution, and independence—the Government, of course, declaring its support for the third of these options. And in 2010 it published a Bill and a paper seeking consultation on the Bill.[56] The draft Bill provided the framework for the conduct of the referendum. The Government intended to introduce the Bill to the Scottish Parliament in 2010 but its plan for a referendum was in the end, and in the face of opposition from the other parties, shelved until after the 2011 Scottish Parliament elections. In this Bill nonetheless we see an example of a proposal that, in contrast with the Quebec initiatives, fits within—rather than directly challenges—generally agreed constitutional contours.

What is interesting from the Consultation Paper is that the declaration of the Scottish people as sovereign is modestly and briefly stated: 'This Government believes in the sovereignty of the people of Scotland. We are committed to giving the people the opportunity to express their views in a referendum.'[57] However, it is also clear that the referendum was intended to be advisory only, and the proposal did not claim the kind of constitutional authority to effect secession, as did that in Quebec in 1995. Instead the approach taken by the SNP was framed to be much more 'inside' than 'outside' the constitution. The Union is explicitly reserved by the Scotland Act 1998 which created devolved government for Scotland.[58] This constitutional orthodoxy is respected by the Consultation Paper:

> Scottish Parliament legislation must conform to the provisions of the Scotland Act 1998.... It is...legitimate for a referendum held under an Act of the Scottish Parliament to ask the people questions related to an extension of its powers insofar as this is within the framework of the Scotland Act.[59]

---

[56] The Draft Referendum (Scotland) Bill was an annex to the Consultation Paper: *Scotland's Future: Draft Referendum (Scotland) Bill Consultation Paper* (The Scottish Government 2010).

[57] *Scotland's Future*, 3, foreword by the First Minister.

[58] Scotland Act 1998, s 30, Sch 5, para 1(1)(b). [59] *Scotland's Future*, 16.

This constitutional conservatism should, of course, be set against the conditioning backdrop of the Scotland Act, which contains a sophisticated set of gatekeeper controls that in practice prevent the passage of potentially *ultra vires* legislation. A Bill proposing a referendum that would authorize unlawful action would arguably be itself unlawful. There are also strong political reasons for this attention to existing law. Since the Scottish Government ruled as a minority administration until 2011, unlike Quebec where nationalists had a majority in the National Assembly in 1994–95, the SNP was dependent upon the support of some of its unionist political opponents if any referendum Bill was to pass. It is also the case that the Scottish nationalist attempt to secure independence is staged against the backdrop of a much more consensual recent constitutional history. The legitimacy of the Canadian Constitution Act 1982 was called into question as neither the people of Quebec nor the National Assembly had ever directly endorsed it. The Scotland Act, by contrast, resulted from a referendum held in Scotland which overwhelmingly approved its proposal for devolution. The SNP was clearly aware that it would be democratically perverse, as well as politically and legally impossible, to try to override the legal legitimacy of the Act by way of an extra-constitutional referendum.

The intention to remain within *vires* is reflected in the draft questions. Two questions were proposed—termed Proposal 1 and Proposal 2. It was made clear that both were consultative only.[60] The former proposed to ask the people to choose between the status quo and some form of enhanced devolution. Two versions of this first question were published in the Bill, each set against the status quo, one offering a very strong version of extended devolution, the other a more modest version based upon the Commission on Scottish Devolution (the 'Calman Commission') report of 15 June 2009. Taking the former as our example, the draft question read: 'Increased powers and responsibilities for Scotland: The Scottish Parliament should have its powers and responsibilities extended as described earlier. Do you agree with this proposal?' The second draft question, on the subject of independence, was also framed as a consultation only: 'The Scottish Government proposes that, in addition to the extension of the powers and responsibilities of the Scottish Parliament set out in Proposal 1, the Parliament's powers should also be extended to enable independence to be achieved. Do you agree with this proposal?'

The Consultation Paper goes on to explain what would have happened in the event of a Yes/Yes vote: 'Following the necessary negotiations between the Scottish and UK Governments, it would then be for the Scottish and UK

---

[60] The preamble to each read: 'The Scottish Parliament has decided to consult people in Scotland on proposals to seek the transfer of more powers to the Parliament.'

Parliaments to act on the expressed will of the Scottish people... in line with the position set out in paragraph 1.32.'[61] The reference to paragraph 1.32 made clear that the Scottish Government accepted that the devolved institutions have no authority to effect unilateral secession.[62] It seems to have fully accepted that, according to the doctrine of parliamentary sovereignty, secession would be illegal until negotiated with the UK government and, presumably, endorsed by Act of the UK Parliament.

Nonetheless, the Quebec process is an example of how a referendum on self-determination can take on a life of its own and how the courts can intervene unexpectedly, for example by declaring a duty on the rest of the state to negotiate independence in good faith. In other words, once sub-state constituent power is mobilized through a referendum, traditional understandings of the limits of constitutional control can be challenged. We are a long way from any such scenario in the UK, but it is interesting how within UK law the referendum has in at least one context seemingly assumed a particular constitutional status. In *Robinson v Secretary of State* the Northern Ireland Act 1998 was described as 'a constitution for Northern Ireland' by Lord Hoffmann, whereby the Belfast Agreement upon which the Act was based should be used as an aid to interpretation of the statute.[63] The role of the referendum in endorsing this Agreement (or 'constitution for Northern Ireland') was taken to be a significant factor by the High Court in Northern Ireland[64] in validating a new policy on police recruitment. This has led McEvoy and Morison to argue that the 1998 Act has such a constitutional status in part because 'it is a manifestation of the wishes of the Northern Ireland people'.[65] McEvoy and Morison go further in arguing:

> The judiciary has begun to address, however tentatively, the idea that the Northern Ireland Act represents something more than simply one more Act of Parliament... It represents, in our view, a fundamental 'constitutional moment' wherein the Agreement and the Act that implemented it, are *constituent* acts in the establishment of a new polity.[66]

---

[61] *Scotland's Future*, 18–19.

[62] '1.32. While the referendum will have no legal effect on the Union, the Scottish Government would expect the UK and Scottish Parliaments and the respective Governments to listen to the views of the Scottish people and act on them.' *Scotland's Future*, 17.

[63] 'The 1998 Act is a *constitution for Northern Ireland*, framed to create a continuing form of government against the background of the history of the territory and the principles agreed in Belfast.' *Robinson v Secretary of State for Northern Ireland and Others* [2002] UKHL 32, per Lord Hoffmann, para 25 (emphasis added); see also Lord Bingham, para 11.

[64] *In the Matter of an Application by Mark Parson for Judicial Review* [2002] NIQB 46, para 34.

[65] Kieran McEvoy and John Morison, 'Beyond the "Constitutional Moment": Law, Transition, and Peacemaking in Northern Ireland' (2003) 26 Fordham Int'l LJ 961, 968.

[66] ibid 969. Notably the constituency is itself a wide one, embracing multiple constituents: unionists and nationalists within Northern Ireland but also the two kin states of the UK and Republic of Ireland.

We do not as yet find a similar explicit connection between the popular endorsement of devolution in Scotland and the constitutional status of the Scotland Act. The courts have generally been very cautious in defining the constitutional status of the Scottish Parliament.[67] But implicit recognition of this can be found. In *Jackson*, Lord Steyn argued, albeit obiter, that the nature of the Act might even call into question the supremacy of Westminster: 'The settlement contained in the Scotland Act 1998...point to a divided sovereignty.'[68] In the recent *AXA* case the Inner House of the Court of Session tightly circumscribed the extent to which Acts of the Scottish Parliament might be susceptible to common law grounds of judicial review. The court did not refer to the Scotland Act as a new constitution for Scotland, or make reference to its provenance in a popular referendum, but we may be seeing tentative and indirect acknowledgement of an enhanced status of the Scotland Act in the court's ascription to Acts of the Scottish Parliament of '*sui generis*' constitutional status, in light of the fact that the Scotland Act is of 'real constitutional importance'.[69] The Supreme Court in the same case appears to go further in drawing a link between popular endorsement and the constitutional status of the Scottish Parliament. In a leading judgment Lord Hope states: 'The Scottish Parliament takes its place under our constitutional arrangements as a self-standing democratically elected legislature. Its democratic mandate to make laws for the people of Scotland is beyond question.'[70] Lord Hope goes on to draw an analogy between the Scottish Parliament and Westminster. While the former does not enjoy sovereignty: 'The dominant characteristic of the Scottish Parliament is its firm rooting in the traditions of a universal democracy. It draws its strength from the electorate.'[71] This evolving juridical backdrop might yet be significant. The SNP Government returned to office in May 2011 with an overall majority intends to revive its plans for independence and seems likely to pass enabling legislation to hold a referendum within the life of the current Parliament. In this environment a number of legal issues remain to be confronted, in particular what if any constitutional duty would fall upon the UK government to negotiate independence in the event of a Yes vote. In such a situation, the courts of Scotland and the UK Supreme Court might well have to venture into the murky territory of constituent power and constitutional principle, finding, as did the Supreme Court of Canada, that the popular political momentum carried by a referendum can bring with it

---

[67] *Whaley v Lord Watson* 2000 SC 340 (IH), 348 (the Lord President (Rodger)) and 357–8 (Lord Prosser).

[68] *Jackson and others v Her Majesty's Attorney General* [2005] UKHL 56, para 102.

[69] *Axa General Insurance Ltd v The Lord Advocate* 2011 SC 31 (IH), para 87.

[70] *AXA General Insurance Limited v The Lord Advocate* [2011] UKSC 46, para 46.

[71] ibid para 49.

vital constitutional imperatives which a supreme court, to remain relevant, can neither ignore nor approach through the mode of a narrow traditional positivism that does not speak to political reality.

IV. CONCLUSION

In these situations we see how the referendum can expose the unsettled foundations of a constitutional order, the authority of which is based upon a form of real or imagined popular endorsement at some time in the past. The fact that the referendum is an instantiation of 'today's people' speaking in a self-conscious way as constitutional author allows it to be presented as a new constitutional moment that legitimizes the supercession of earlier self-conscious—or imagined—expressions of the popular will.[72] The popular democratic promise is at once repressed and latent in representative constitutionalism. And so, when the people emerge directly in constitutional voice, in ways that are inconsistent with the mechanics of change embedded in the constitution, the question is raised: can this purported act of authorship be declared illegitimate simply because its mode of expression is somehow procedurally defective in light of an entrenched constitutional authority which derives its own legitimacy from an earlier manifestation of popular authorship?

We have seen in two contexts how popular constituent power, which its proponents claim underpins the legitimacy of constitutionalism, can be mobilized in direct challenge to the positivist authority claims of a particular constitution. In the first, the executive actor overrode the constitutional procedure which required some measure of consensus across the representative institutions before the door was opened to the voice of the national people. In the second, sub-state actors made possible the direct constitutional manifestation of what they claimed to be a distinct people within the state—one of the *pouvoirs constituant*—which as co-sovereign had discrete legitimacy to trump, or at least to challenge, that of any positivist impediment entrenched in the constitution, particularly when such an impediment is—as was claimed—simply a mask for domination by another co-sovereign.

In these referendums the claim is that, in the end, every democratic constitution falls back for its political legitimacy, and ultimately its lawful authority, upon the people it claims to represent. Although overly simplistic in light of the complex reality of modernist constitutionalism, this claim posits that the constitution does not create the people; rather, the people

---

[72] Akhil R Amar, 'Popular Sovereignty and Constitutional Amendment' in Sanford Levinson (ed), *Responding to Imperfection: The Theory and Practice of Constitutional Amendment* (Princeton University Press 1995) 89–115.

created, and continue to recreate, the constitution. As Lindahl puts it: 'the procedural rules of liberal democracies, as articulated and justified by Habermas, presuppose prior acts of inclusion and exclusion that resist legitimation within the constitutional order these acts contribute to creating'.[73] The Supreme Court of Canada's conclusion that the established positivist understanding of supremacy within the constitution could not frustrate the directly expressed will of the people of Quebec is implicit recognition of this hierarchical assertion. But just as the legal authority of the constitution cannot be separated from, and held in supremacy over, its political legitimacy, the reverse also applies. We saw in the cases of de Gaulle's France, Quebec, and Scotland how the legitimizing claims of popular sovereignty are presented alongside positivist constitutional claims in different ways. The mobilization of popular sovereignty claims by way of referendum is not necessarily a revolutionary act. It can take place fully within the constitution (Scotland 2010), with a partial bending of constitutional procedure (France), or as a claim to be a true reading of the constitution that has been belied by dominant actors (Quebec). The people exist as final legitimizer in the face of rival authority claims, but those authority claims can also be accommodated internally as well as contested externally.

This partly inside and partly outside mobilization of the people (or *a* people) as constitutional subject leads us to a further conclusion which we touched upon re France: that direct democracy even at the constitutional level is not separable from, but relates symbiotically with, representative democracy. In the first place, the institutional triggers that initiate the referendum invariably come from within the constitution, and this sets the stage for a power struggle which is conditioned to be *constitutional* rather than crudely *political*. In France we saw a classic separation of powers contest between executive and legislature; the illegitimate use of referendums by de Gaulle was not in reality about constituent power vs constitution, but about the executive attempting to hijack the popular will in order to pursue its own agenda. In Quebec and Scotland, claims to territorial sovereignty are also constitutional claims. In each case, the referendum emerges within and *from* the constitution, and its use is partially—albeit to differing extents—justified in this context.[74] It is also part of a process rather than an event final in itself. In Canada the Supreme Court became involved, and tellingly it set out constitutional hurdles for both sides to meet in the

---

[73] Lindahl, 'Recognition as Domination', 5.

[74] And not surprisingly, international standards set by states are keen to contain the authority of the referendum outcome within existing legal frameworks. European Commission for Democracy Through Law (Venice Commission), 'Code of Good Practice on Referendums' Study No 371/2006 (20 January 2009), COE Doc CDL-AD(2007)008rev: 'referendums within federated or regional entities must comply with the law of the central State', para 32, and see Explanatory Memorandum, para 26.

construction of a future referendum process and in subsequent negotiations over secession, thereby reinforcing the sense that any future process towards Quebec sovereignty would be constitutional rather than extra-constitutional in nature. The referendum, therefore, can certainly expose the limits of a traditional constitutionalism that does not fully account for the power of the latent constituent power or multiple constituent powers which it contains, but it also exposes the limits of democracy conceived as popular political power to itself entire. In the end, the constitutional referendum may unsettle established patterns of constitutional authority in modern democracies, but it does not overthrow these; it is itself, like the popular power it seeks to facilitate, also relational to them.

6

External Influences on Constitutional Referendums

I. INTRODUCTION

It is clear from Chapter 5 that the referendum can play a key role in contemporary struggles over constitutional sovereignty. But sovereignty itself is a highly contested term today as observers identify changes in the nature of the authority of the state. As Keating puts it, 'the old constitutional categories are losing their meaning'.[1] Therefore, we must address the specificity of constitutional referendums in a context of flux where the traditional coordinates of constitutional authority no longer accurately map emerging layers of normative authority.[2] Today a number of alternative constitutional sites at both supra-[3] and sub-state[4] levels challenge the state's claims both to retain exclusive territorial sovereignty and to offer a unitary resource for the identity and loyalty of citizens. The constitutional referendum is a useful case study in addressing these changing patterns since it serves to expose how, in a number of situations, constitutional control is slipping from the hands of national governments.

Having looked at how referendums can raise complex problems concerning how sovereignty is allocated *within* the polity, here I address the broader issue of how they can also manifest the present destabilization in the concept and practice of state sovereignty itself, a situation which stems from the ever more complex and involved sets of relations between the state and external actors and institutions. In other words, we are moving from how disputes over *internal* constitutional sovereignty can play out in the context of the referendum to examine how in a globalizing normative environment referendums can pose troubling questions for the *external* sovereignty of the state. We will

---

[1] Michael Keating, *Nations Against the State—The New Politics of Nationalism in Quebec, Catalonia and Scotland* (2nd edn, Palgrave 2001) 275.

[2] Neil Walker, 'Out of Place and Out of Time: Law's Fading Co-ordinates' (2010) 14 Edinburgh L Rev 13.

[3] Jurgen Habermas and Max Pensky, *The Postnational Constellation: Political Essays* (Polity Press 2001).

[4] Stephen Tierney, 'Reframing Sovereignty: Sub-State National Societies and Contemporary Challenges to the Nation-State' (2005) 54 ICLQ 161.

consider two types of referendum where international law, international institutions, and powerful states can play a part in a referendum process. The first concerns the transfer of power to supranational institutions. Taking further integration in the European Union as our case study we will see how referendums have taken place in an environment where considerable external pressure is brought to bear, even to the point of encouraging a particular result. The second is referendums concerning new statehood, where again in recent years external actors, both other states and international organizations, have exerted an influence on referendum processes.[5] A prominent example is the referendums that played a part in the emergence of new states from the collapse of the USSR and SFRY. In particular we will consider: the criteria of recognition for new states adopted by the EU and applied by the Badinter Commission as Yugoslavia dissolved in the early 1990s; the way the referendum acted as a spectre lurking in the background during international intervention in Kosovo from 1998–99; and then in more detail the Montenegrin referendum of 2006, which is a particularly useful case study in illustrating just how broadly and deeply external engagement can influence the referendum process within a nascent polity.

In both types of situation we see how the simplistic vision of the referendum as an expression of popular sovereignty can be little more than chimerical. 'The people' as ultimate sovereign *within* the state is being invoked, but the reality is that the state's *external* sovereignty is diminishing, and international involvement in the referendum symbolizes this latter reality. And this raises deeper questions: can we really address referendum democracy in such situations as a sovereign act, self-contained within the state? Indeed, since the capacity of internal popular sovereignty is increasingly conditioned by changes in the external dimension of state sovereignty, can we still envisage the constitutional referendum in such a situation as in any meaningful sense an exercise in popular 'self-determination?'[6]

II. INTERNATIONAL INSTITUTIONS AND SUPRANATIONAL INTEGRATION

Whereas the cases we looked at in the last chapter call into question the resilience of constitutional form in the face of incipient constituent power,

---

[5] It has even been suggested that the use of referendums in the settlement of certain territorial issues is now a requirement of international customary law. See Visuvanathan Rudrakumaran, 'The "Requirement" of Plebiscite in Territorial Rapprochement' (1989) 12 Houston J Int'l L 23.

[6] For the paradoxes and contradictions inherent in the very notion of self-determination as a right of 'peoples' see Martti Koskenniemi, 'National Self-Determination Today: Problems of Legal Theory and Practice' (1994) 43 ICLQ 241, 249; Zoran Oklopcic, 'Populus Interruptus: Self-Determination, Independence of Kosovo and the Vocabulary of Peoplehood' (2009) 22 Leiden J Int'l L 677.

the situations we now address question the health or even the viability of exclusively territorially situated constructions of both concepts, and in particular whether we should still envisage them playing out within the state through the traditional and absolutist paradigm of coherent and exclusive constitutional authority—'sovereignty'. Referendums in the context of EU integration—where we see the 'transformation of the Community from an international to a constitutional legal order'[7]—stand out against this type of conceptualization. The referendum, rather than settling the sovereignty question by pre-defining a sovereign demos, here seems to exacerbate a contest between an internal conceptualization of sovereignty—the ultimate and discrete constitutional power of a particular people making decisions about how much power to relinquish—and an external conceptualization within which nation-states, as traditional masters of international law, and the EU, increasingly asserting itself as would-be incipient sovereign, compete over the normative significance of this new legal order.[8]

The referendum has become an important actor at different stages of the EU's treaty development and its usage has grown as an instrument of accession[9] and treaty ratification.[10] Interestingly, the increased use of referendums has, through several instances of rejectionism, brought with it a threat to the integrationist strategy of the EU and as such this has prompted the intervention of the EU in these constitutional processes in a number of ways. In this section I will highlight two issues. The first is how referendums can become vehicles for the expression of popular resistance to certain levels

---

[7] Paul Craig, 'Constitutions, Constitutionalism, and the European Union' (2001) 7(2) European LJ 125, 128.

[8] Certainly the 'integrationist referendum' is not entirely new. It was used in French (late eighteenth century) and Italian (mid-nineteenth century) unification processes and was part of the process bringing the Australian colonies into federation in 1898. The plebiscites after the First World War also served the purpose of integrating territory into newly emerging or already established states. But in these cases the issues were more obviously in line with the traditional prerogatives of the Westphalian model. Territories were clearly surrendering whatever legal autonomy they had in the goal of establishing a new and again clearly sovereign state. With EU integration the issue is far more elongated and inchoate. The EU has a *sui generis* form, but whatever that is it is not (yet) a state. At the same time member states, whatever powers they have transferred to Brussels, remain states. It is in the slow and somewhat open-ended transfer of state functions that the referendum has emerged as such a strange device. It is the tool of a self-determining people settling sovereignty questions, but here the sovereignty question is so complex and unclear in its trajectory that several matters: the self, what it is determining, and which other actors are also central to this determination, remain uncertain.

[9] eg nine of the ten states acceding to the EU in 2004 sought popular assent through referendums held between March and September 2003 (only Cyprus did not).

[10] The referendum was not used by any of the original six signatories to the Treaty of Rome. Since the 1970s Denmark and Ireland have used them frequently, and at the time of the draft Constitutional Treaty we also saw referendums in Spain, Luxembourg, France, and the Netherlands. Notably, however, we saw a rolling back of the referendum in respect of the Lisbon Treaty, with only Ireland going directly to the people for its ratification.

of integration, a rejectionism that is in part facilitated by the fact that referendums are, paradoxically, mobilizations of *national* constituent power even though the issue being determined aims to transcend this supposedly modernist relic in favour of a new supranational constituent framework; and the second is the way in which the institutions of the EU and pro-integrationist national governments have seen fit to involve themselves in attempts to influence referendum outcomes in other states.

(i) National identity: frustrating integration

The referendum has served to frustrate the trajectory of EU integration mainly at the hands of states whose constitutions mandate their use in this context: Denmark and Ireland in particular. As we saw in Chapter 4, under the Danish constitution a referendum is required to be held for transfers of powers to international bodies unless the very high threshold of a five-sixths majority in the Folketing votes in favour of the transfer without a referendum. Therefore, even a small minority in parliament has been able in a number of situations to force a referendum, making direct democracy a fixed feature of Denmark's relations with the EC/EU since the poll held in 1972 on Denmark's accession. Since then there have been referendums in 1986 on the Single European Act;[11] in 1992 on the Treaty of European Union (Treaty of Maastricht) and subsequently in 1993 on the Edinburgh Agreement,[12] which modified Maastricht; in 1998 on the Treaty of Amsterdam; and in 2000 on Economic and Monetary Union.[13]

A number of referendums in Denmark have proven to be a thorn in the side of European integration, but in the end they have not impeded the drive of this movement in a significant way. Although the Danish people said No to the Maastricht Treaty,[14] a compromise was agreed by the EC with Denmark by way of the Edinburgh Agreement and this was approved in the 1993 referendum. Again, although the Danes rejected EMU in 2000, by then the Eurozone had been created for participating states and so Denmark merely opted out of this initiative. Therefore, Danish referendums have

---

[11] Note the 1986 referendum on the Single European Act was not held under Section 20 but was only a consultative referendum which the executive had the general authority to stage without express constitutional authorization.

[12] Although the former was conducted under Section 20, the latter referendum was in fact held under Section 42, which is the general referendum provision typically for non-constitutional matters.

[13] No referendum was held on the draft Treaty establishing a Constitution for Europe after this was rejected in both the French and Dutch referendums before the Danish vote could take place. The Treaty of Lisbon was ratified by the Folketing on 24 April 2008, again without a referendum.

[14] Maastricht was supported by 80 per cent in the Folketing but was rejected by the voters in the referendum by 52–48 per cent.

been more an irritant than a serious obstacle to integration. However, the preparedness of Danish voters to say No in 1992, the only country to do so, was a shock to the relentless centralization of the system. For some this has been seen as the beginning of a new strain of political contestation[15] which has had lasting effects across a number of states, articulating 'the reservations that many observers outside the political elites felt about the speed and direction of European integration'.[16]

In Ireland too the constitutional requirement of a constitution has resulted in two famous cases of rejection. Although the Irish constitution provides for the use of a referendum for constitutional amendments,[17] it was not altogether clear that the ratification of every new EC treaty constituted a constitutional amendment until an important case in 1986 when the Supreme Court ruled that further transfers of constitutional powers to the EC amounting to changes to the 'essential scope or objectives' of the EC would require constitutional amendment and a consequent referendum.[18]

Referendums have since been used for all of the significant treaty processes. And it has been a bumpy ride, with evidence that over time Euroscepticism has steadily been growing. This can be seen in the rise of the No vote: 17 per cent on accession in 1972; 30 per cent in 1987 (on the Single European Act); 31 per cent in 1992 on the Treaty of European Union; 38 per cent in 1998 on the Amsterdam Treaty. This process culminated in rejection of the Treaty of Nice in 2001. Following a minor concession by way of the Seville Declaration recognizing Ireland's policy of military neutrality, a second referendum was held and the Nice Treaty was eventually accepted by Irish voters in 2002. But the more dramatic rejection was that of the Treaty of Lisbon in 2008, intensifying as it did the shockwaves still reverberating from the failure of the draft Constitutional Treaty.[19] Once again, the Irish government negotiated minor compromises and Lisbon was eventually accepted by the Irish people in 2009.

---

[15] Mark Franklin, Michael Marsh, and Lauren McLaren, 'Uncorking the Bottle: Popular Opposition to European Unification in the Wake of Maastricht' (1994) 32 J Common Market Studies 455.

[16] Lawrence LeDuc, *The Politics of Direct Democracy: Referendums in Global Perspective* (Broadview Press 2003) 95. See also Cees van der Eijk and Mark Franklin, 'Potential for Contestation on European Matters at National Elections in Europe' in Gary Marks and Marco Steenbergen (eds), *European Integration and Political Conflict* (CUP 2004).

[17] Constitution of Ireland, Art 46.

[18] *Raymond Crotty v An Taoiseach and Others* [1987] IESC 4. See also Gavin Barrett, 'Building a Swiss Chalet in an Irish Legal Landscape? Referendums on European Union Treaties in Ireland and the Impact of Supreme Court Jurisprudence' (2009) 5 European Constitutional L Rev 32.

[19] John O' Brennan, 'Ireland says No (Again): The 12 June 2008 Referendum on the Lisbon Treaty' (2009) 62 Parliamentary Affairs 258, 274.

158   Constitutional Referendums

While Ireland's occasional rejectionist stance has, like Denmark's, been viewed as something of a minor inconvenience in the treaty-making process, a broader and more significant popular challenge to integrationist momentum came in response to the draft Constitutional Treaty, which was put to a referendum in four states. To the surprise of many, the draft Treaty was rejected by voters in France and the Netherlands.[20] These results, together with the rejection of the Lisbon Treaty in the first Irish referendum, have led to extensive commentary on the reasons behind the No votes. Although it is impossible to offer a definitive account of these reasons since they are many and complex, varying from one referendum to another, there is evidence that national identity has played a significant role in each of these cases.

It has become commonplace to dismiss these No votes as the outcome of popular ignorance about the EU, but it seems that this simplistic conclusion is misplaced. Qvortrup, commenting on the first referendum in Ireland on the Treaty of Lisbon, argues:

> Voters, as has been pointed out in several empirical studies, are not ill-informed, but tend to have a good basic understanding of the issues put before them. It is perfectly conceivable that the voters simply did not like what was on offer, and that they, consequently, made a decision consistent with their preferences.[21]

Instead, he points to the high levels of Euroscepticism which marry up with indicators of a strong Irish national identity. Eurobarometer readings show that in 2007 Irish citizens had the second lowest European identity in the EU, and nearly 60 per cent identified themselves as exclusively Irish rather that wholly or partly European.[22] His conclusion is that 'the voters, while not opposed to the EU as such, were unhappy with further integration or transfer of sovereignty'.[23]

Another possibility which we encountered in Chapter 5 is that voters are using the referendum as a 'second-order' election to vote on domestic issues and in particular on the record in office of the incumbent government. But this effect, although often claimed to explain a high No vote in EU referendums, is deeply contested, with the political science literature 'sharply

---

[20] Meaning that the planned referendum in Ireland, like that in Denmark, was postponed indefinitely. It was approved in referendums in Spain and Luxembourg.

[21] Matt Qvortrup, 'Rebels without a Cause? The Irish Referendum on the Lisbon Treaty' (2009) 80 Political Quarterly 59, 65.

[22] Cited by Qvortrup, 'Rebels without a Cause', 65. See also Richard Sinnott, 'Attitudes and Behaviour of the Irish Electorate in the Referendum on the Treaty of Nice' (2003) University of College Dublin Working Papers <http://www.ucd.ie/dempart/workingpapers/nice2.pdf> accessed 10 October 2011; 'Deeper Look at Poll Illuminates Complex Reasons for Result', Irish Times (Dublin, 14 June 2008).

[23] Qvortrup, 'Rebels without a Cause', 65.

divided on the matter'.[24] Again, commentators who have carried out detailed studies question the extent to which people really are voting on the performance of domestic elites. Garry, March, and Sinnott, in their study of voting in the Irish Nice referendums, conclude that both 'were closer to being processes of deliberation on EU issues than to being plebiscites on the incumbent government'.[25]

Turning to the French and Dutch referendums on the draft Constitutional Treaty, the outcome was a particular surprise as each of these countries had hitherto played vanguardist roles in the integrationist drive. And in France opinion polls predicted a Yes vote until shortly before the referendum. By September 2004 the Yes side had a 64–36 per cent lead[26] but lost on 29 May 2005 with a 54.8 per cent No vote. More emphatically, on 1 June 2005 61.5 per cent of Dutch voters voted No. The reasons for these results seem multiple and complex, particularly in light of the ad hoc nature of the referendums.[27] For example, according to the Eurobarometer (a survey body itself working for the European Commission) the No vote in the Netherlands was due to a range of factors, the most common being: a lack of information (32 per cent); loss of national sovereignty (19 per cent); opposition to the national government/certain political parties (14 per cent); and Europe being too 'expensive' (13 per cent).[28] Since these findings suggest

---

[24] John Garry, Michael Marsh, and Richard Sinnott, ' "Second-order" versus "Issue-Voting" Effects in EU Referendums: Evidence from the Irish Nice Treaty Referendums' (2005) 6 European Union Politics 201, 202.

[25] Garry, Marsh, and Sinnott, ' "Second-order" versus "Issue-Voting" ', 215. Binzer Hobolt also argues that preferences on EU issues can override partisan loyalties and triggers. Sara Binzer Hobolt, 'How Parties Affect Vote Choice in European Integration Referendums' (2006) 12 Party Politics 623. For Binzer Hobolt the role of parties is certainly not irrelevant, but nonetheless she concludes (641): 'people's EU preferences are a stronger predictor of vote behaviour and... many voters "defect" from the party line. In other words, partisan loyalties may not be sufficient to persuade voters to vote in a certain way.' Petithomme finds that EU referendums upset normal party system dynamics and one effect is to reinforce the role played by protest parties. Also, for parties of government 'it is more difficult to predict the ability of incumbent parties to attract their voters and campaign effectively'. Mathieu Petithomme, 'Awakening the Sleeping Giant? The Displacement of the Partisan Cleavage and Change in Government-Opposition Dynamics in EU Referendums' (2011) 12 Perspectives on European Politics and Society 89, 108.

[26] Matt Qvortrup, 'The Three Referendums on the European Constitution Treaty 2005' (2006) 77 Political Quarterly 89, 91.

[27] As we have seen, France has a tradition of direct democracy, but referendums have rarely been used in the ratification of EU treaties (one was held in 1972 concerning the proposed accession of the UK, Denmark, Ireland, and Norway and one in 1992 on the Treaty of Maastricht). The 2005 referendum in the Netherlands was the first, and so far only, referendum in Dutch history, and it came in the wake of evidence that Dutch voters were increasingly supportive of the use of referendums. Eg a Dutch Parliamentary Election Study found that 76 per cent 'fully agreed' with the statement 'On some of the important issues in our country voters should be able to vote by means of a so-called referendum'. Qvortrup, 'The Three Referendums', 90.

[28] European Commission, 'The European Constitution: Post-Referendum Survey in the Netherlands' Flash Eurobarometer No 172 (March 2005). See also Paul Taggart, 'Questions of Europe—The Domestic

that only 14 per cent explicitly treated the referendum as a second-order election, while the loss of national sovereignty and the expense of Europe together represent a strong focus by voters on European issues, this would seem to refute the idea that this referendum was fought principally upon domestic political issues.[29] Analyses of the French vote display similar patterns.[30]

In highlighting the role of European issues in motivating No votes, the point is not to suggest a trend of growing Euroscepticism across Europe. Certainly some do read such a development into these results. Schuck and de Vreese, for example, consider that fear of globalization is likely to grow and this process could have serious repercussions for the EU in future referendums.[31] But we should also temper such a conclusion first with the more modest conclusion that these referendums simply suggest that first levels of Euroscepticism were significant in the Netherlands and France at the time of these referendums and cannot be assumed to lead to broader trends from that fact alone and, second, with the fact that a large majority in Ireland voted Yes in the second Lisbon referendum,[32] a result which is widely attributed to the global economic downturn and the security many Irish people seemed to see in the EU as a bulwark against its worst consequences.[33] In other words, globalization can be a double-edged sword when it comes to attitudes to European integration. What can be said, however, quite clearly is that when the issue of sovereignty arises in a way that also implicates national identity, voting behaviour can become

Politics of the 2005 French and Dutch Referendums and their Challenge for the Study of European Integration' (2006) 44 J Common Market Studies 7, 19.

[29] Schuck and de Vreese are among those who consider Euroscepticism among the Dutch electorate to be a more significant factor behind the No vote than domestic, second-order issues: Andreas RT Schuck and Claes H de Vreese, 'The Dutch No to the EU Constitution: Assessing the Role of EU Skepticism and the Campaign' (2008) 18 J Elections, Public Opinion & Parties 101, 120.

[30] In fact, commentators have argued that the level of contestation on display provoked a moment of crisis for the entire French political class:

> the outcome of the referendum shows the emergence of a split between politicians and the entire electorate. Euroskepticism not only impeded the construction of a more federal European Union but also undermined the credibility of mainstream French politicians.

Bruno Jerome and Nicolas G Vaillant, 'The French Rejection of the European Constitution: An Empirical Analysis' (2005) 21 European J Political Economy 1085, 1091. See also Andrew Glencross and Alexander Trechsel, 'First or Second Order Referendums? Understanding the Votes on the EU Constitutional Treaty in Four EU Member States' (2011) 34(4) West European Politics 755.

[31] Schuck and de Vreese, 'The Dutch No to the EU Constitution', 120. And others argue this can be attributed to a failure of the EU to engage citizens. Imogen Sudbery, 'Bridging the Legitimacy Gap in the EU: Can Civil Society Help to Bring the Union Closer to Its Citizens?' (2003) 26 Collegium 75.

[32] 67.1 per cent voted Yes—a swing of 20.5 per cent from the result of the first referendum in 2008.

[33] We should also note the Yes vote in other referendums held in Spain (February 2008) and Luxembourg (July 2008) on the draft Constitutional Treaty. See Taggart, 'Questions of Europe', 14.

volatile and hence unpredictable, and in light of this, elite control is harder to effect, as highly mobilized cross-party Yes campaigns across Europe have begun to realize to their cost. We must also factor in the likelihood that the use of the referendum in the ratification process is here to stay and may well proliferate. One trend is a domino impact or 'multiplier effect' in those countries where the referendum is discretionary. We are seeing evidence that once one state commits to holding a referendum, pressure can grow on others to do so.[34] Also the requirement to hold referendums which we find in so many of the constitutions of recently acceding states may again have long-term implications.[35] Most of the new member states have been very enthusiastic about the EU, no doubt anticipating the economic benefits of membership, but these attitudes can change, as we have seen, for example, with the Netherlands and Ireland.

(ii) EU influence on national referendums

Perhaps as a result of their volatility the EU has itself become involved in referendum processes, in effect forming part of the campaign for pro-treaty votes. As Min Shu observes, 'the more significant a particular referendum is in the integration process, the more enthusiastic the involvement of EU institutions becomes'.[36] The influence from the EU has come in several forms. The first is financial. There is significant evidence, for example, that the Commission helped fund the pro-euro campaign in the 2000 Danish referendum on EMU.[37]

The second is in the provision of information, or as some argue, propaganda during referendum campaigns. For example, during the 1998 Irish referendum campaign on the Amsterdam Treaty there were complaints that the European Commission was violating Irish law by distributing 'The Citizens' Guide to the Amsterdam Treaty'. This document was described by Patricia McKenna, a Green MEP, member of the Irish Parliament, and prominent No campaigner, as a 'tendentious and one-sided document'.[38]

---

[34] We noted in Chapter 5 that in France President Chirac committed to a referendum on the draft Constitutional Treaty under political pressure, mainly due to an earlier commitment by the UK government to hold one. The irony is that the French No vote, which in effect killed the draft Treaty, saved the UK government from having to stage a referendum.

[35] Patricia Roberts-Thomson, 'EU Treaty Referendums and the European Union' (2001) 23 J European Integration 105, 131.

[36] Min Shu, 'Referendums and the Political Constitutionalisation of the EU' (2008) 14 European LJ 423, 439.

[37] William M Downs, 'Election Report—Denmark's Referendum on the Euro: The Mouse that Roared...Again' (2001) 24 West European Politics 222.

[38] Ms McKenna wrote to the Commission questioning its legality under Irish and European Community law. Shu, 'Referendums and the Political Constitutionalisation of the EU', 438.

There have been various strategic attempts by the EU in recent years to boost its profile and ostensibly to help build a sense of European citizenship, but it seems these efforts are linked to the achievement of successful referendum outcomes. The European Commission published its own 'Action Plan for Communicating Europe' in July 2005. This document set out 50 internal practical measures to improve communication. In 2007 the Commission also issued 'Communicating Europe in Partnership', a strategy document 'to give to European citizens well organised information about the EU'.[39] This coincided with the Lisbon Treaty and set as one of its goals 'a new set of... civil society projects... with the overall objective of supporting the ratification process for the Reform Treaty'.[40] A considerable sum of money, estimated by some at €88 million, was allocated for this information campaign.[41] Although not tied directly to this, a lot of energy was expended, for example in Ireland, particularly during the second referendum on the Lisbon Treaty, where the EU spent heavily on information and also on an advertising campaign.[42]

A third is the direct involvement of either EU actors or prominent pro-integrationist figures from other member states in the referendum campaign. A study of the level of foreign involvement in France's referendum on the draft Constitutional Treaty shows some remarkable results. This found that every foreign intervention was in favour of a Yes vote.[43] Several representatives of the EU institutions appeared in public debate during this campaign, including President of the European Commission José Manuel Barroso, his predecessor Romano Prodi, German Chancellor Schröder, and Spanish Prime Minister Zapatero who, with President Chirac, launched

---

[39] European Commission, 'Communicating Europe in Partnership', COM(2007) 568 final.

[40] ibid 16.

[41] '88 Million Euros to help EU sell Lisbon Treaty' (*Democracy International European Referendum Campaign*, 24 November 2008) <http://www.erc2.org/> accessed 10 October 2011.

[42] Again, there were allegations that the Commission was interfering illegitimately in the referendum. One controversy involved the insertion of 1.1 million copies of a 16-page EU booklet on the Lisbon Treaty into Irish newspapers on 27 September 2009. This claimed inter alia:

> Today, members of the EU enjoy a wealth of benefits: a free market with a currency that makes trade easier and more efficient, the creation of millions of jobs, improved workers' rights, free movement of people and a cleaner environment... These are major goals. The Lisbon Treaty is designed to give the EU the tools to achieve them.

See Bruno Waterfield, 'EU Intervention in Irish Referendum "Unlawful"', *The Telegraph* (London, 29 September 2009) <http://www.telegraph.co.uk/news/worldnews/europe/eu/6239933/EU-intervention-in-Irish-referendum-unlawful.html> accessed 10 October 2011.

[43] Arsène Richard and Ronald Pabst, 'Evaluation of the French Referendum on the EU Constitution' (*Democracy International*, May 2005) <http://www.democracy-international.org/fileadmin/di/pdf/monitoring/di-france.pdf> accessed 10 October 2011, para 4.2 citing the television programme *Arrêt sur images* of 8 and 15 May entitled 'Référendum: les médias sont-ils neutres?'

a joint Yes campaign on 11 February. Schröder and Zapatero even spoke twice in front of the National Assembly.[44]

External actors can also put pressure on states after a negative vote, suggesting that this should not be treated as final. After the first Lisbon Treaty referendum in Ireland for example, French Foreign Minister Bernard Kouchner notoriously described the Irish as 'ungrateful'.[45] Similarly, shortly after the French and Dutch votes against the Constitutional Treaty, French President Chirac declared that 'the process of ratification had to proceed forthwith'.[46] And of course we saw how the Danes were led towards the Amsterdam Treaty and a Yes vote after Maastricht in processes that would be mirrored in Ireland re the Lisbon Treaty. Indeed, during the campaign on the second Lisbon Treaty referendum, the Italian commission vice-president and transport commissioner Antonio Tajani was flown across Ireland by the supportive Ryanair, to promote a Yes vote, in a campaign plane displaying 'Vote Yes for Europe' logos.[47]

(iii) Referendums and European integration: exposing dual constitutionalization

On one level these referendums seem to reflect the same impulse as the sub-state referendums we looked at in the last chapter. They become vehicles to articulate and empower resilient national identities and national aspirations

---

[44] ibid para 4.2.

[45] Honor Mahony, 'France Warns Ireland on EU Treaty 'No' Vote', *EUObserver.com* (10 June 2008) <http://euobserver.com/9/26299/?rk=1> accessed 10 October 2011; Ian Traynor and Nicholas Watt, 'Lisbon Treaty: Pressure on Ireland for Second Vote', *The Guardian* (London, 19 June 2008) <http://www.guardian.co.uk/world/2008/jun/19/lisbon.ireland> accessed 21 October 2011. In an internal memorandum Margot Wallstrom, European Commission Vice-President responsible for 'communicating' the EU wrote: 'We cannot treat the Irish "no" as merely a national issue or only a Treaty ratification problem.' Bruno Waterfield, 'EU Steps Up Pressure on Ireland to Hold Second Lisbon Treaty Referendum', *The Telegraph* (London, 10 October 2008) <http://www.telegraph.co.uk/news/newstopics/eureferendum/3173967/EU-steps-up-pressure-on-Ireland-to-hold-second-Lisbon-Treaty-referendum.html> accessed 10 October 2011.

[46] Qvortrup, 'The Three Referendums', 95–6.

[47] This level of EU involvement in a national campaign has been heavily criticized: Mary Lou McDonald and Dick Roche, 'Head to Head: Is the Second Referendum on Lisbon an Abuse of Democracy?', *Irish Times* (Dublin, 22 December 2008) 12. However, for a more nuanced interpretation of the EU's response to No votes see Gráinne de Búrca, 'If at First You Don't Succeed: Vote, Vote Again: Analyzing the Second Referendum Phenomenon in EU Treaty Change' (2011) 33 Fordham Int'l LJ 1473, 1478. She points out the difficulty of getting unanimous consent for new treaties (if one country says No the alternative to revisiting the issue in that state is another round of mega-constitutional horse-trading); the fact that a No vote is not an opt-out but in effect a veto affecting every other state which, it might be argued, gives those states an interest in the result; and the possible availability of opt-outs as a via media to accommodate states which wish to hold back from elements of an agreement without killing the agreement itself. The ultimate point for the purposes of this book is not the ethical appropriateness or inappropriateness of this level of EU pressure, but simply to observe how this dynamic, which extends even to such a paradigmatically indigenous process as a referendum, exposes the decreasing autonomy of states and their citizens.

that may not have been taken seriously in broader constitutional processes. But this comparison only goes so far. These processes are not self-contained constitutional struggles taking place only within states, nor are they just about competing visions of sovereignty within one state. One analysis describes the integrationist process of the EU through national referendums as 'dual constitutionalisation', whereby national 'Constitutional Revision' and 'Transnational Constitutional Construction' are taking place concurrently.[48] The two processes—on the one hand individual countries reviewing their national constitutions 'to facilitate intra-state constitutional revision', and on the other member states directly participating 'in the constitutional construction of the EU'—are not separable. Instead,

> the constitutional debates invoked by EU referendums have resulted in continuous multilevel deliberations on the integration process. The three-level political mobilisation shows that constitutional deliberation has involved voters at the citizen level, the incumbent governments at national level, as well as the EU institutions at transnational level.[49]

When we envisage the referendum as part of this broader deliberative process it becomes impossible to set it exclusively within the old-style paradigm of a self-contained demos exercising its popular sovereignty. The referendum in one member state has knock-on consequences for all. One demos is speaking directly, but other actors, from other member states to the institutions of the EU itself, feel entitled to intervene to represent their own constituencies, which arguably include the incipient *people of the EU*.

A number of commentators are trying to find models with which to analyse this new development of constitutionalism going beyond the traditional sovereignty paradigm.[50] And into this mix the referendum appears further to unsettle older understandings of a binary state—supra-state relationship.[51] The people of distinct polities are speaking directly, recalling at least symbolically their vernacular sovereignty. But they do so in processes the substantive outcomes of which belie the viability of constitutional authority as internally complete. The people are speaking—and therefore

---

[48] Shu, 'Referendums and the Political Constitutionalisation of the EU', 440.

[49] ibid 443.

[50] Dieter Grimm, 'The Constitution in the Process of Denationalization' (2005) 12 Constellations 447; James Tully, 'A New Kind of Europe? Democratic Integration in the European Union' (2007) 10 Critical Rev of Int'l Social and Political Philosophy 71; Neil Walker, 'Taking Constitutionalism Beyond the State' (2008) 56 Political Studies 519; Julio Baquero Cruz, 'An Area of Darkness: Three Conceptions of the Relationship Between European Union Law and State Constitutional Law' in Walker, Shaw, and Tierney (eds), *Europe's Constitutional Mosaic*.

[51] Roberts-Thomson, 'EU Treaty Referendums and the European Union'; Thomas Christin and Simon Hug, 'Referendums and Citizen Support for European Integration' (2002) 35 Comparative Political Studies 586.

forming *distinctive* constitutional relationships—not only with the representative institutions of the state but also with those that claim a representational legitimacy at the level of the EU. Taggart touches on the range of constitutional voices operating with this framework. With the Dutch and French referendums of 2005, he says,

> we have in stark relief a vision of a political process that, in resorting to plebiscitary politics, has regularized the possibility of domestic political processes to have a profound impact on European integration. We have different domestic politics creating 'no' votes for very different reasons.[52]

And this interaction of the domestic and the European creates new avenues with which to attempt to control referendum outcomes. First, we have seen the usual attempts by domestic elites to set the agenda and how these can backfire, particularly where national identity is perceived by voters to be at stake. Second, we have seen the attempts by EU actors also to intervene in referendum campaigns, which again is unsurprising, as is the latitude to do so given to them by integrationist domestic elites. But third and perhaps most controversially we have seen the *ex post facto* mobilization of the EU following a No vote which extends even to an unwillingness to accept a referendum outcome. The trajectory here is unpredictable. The enormous power of the EU points in one direction—that national electorates will not be allowed to frustrate closer integration.[53] But with the referendum becoming a more and more utilized tool of constitutional change, further conflicts may well arise which, when vital issues of national identity are at stake, may not be so easily resolved.[54]

---

[52] Taggart, 'Questions of Europe', 21.

[53] A postscript is that the Lisbon Treaty itself attempts to pre-empt a minority of dissenting states from holding up future treaty processes. It contains a provision to the effect that 'if, two years after the signature of a treaty amending the Treaties, four fifths of the Member States have ratified it and one or more Member States have encountered difficulties in proceeding with ratification, the matter shall be referred to the European Council'. Consolidated Version of the Treaty on European Union [2008] OJ C115/13, Art 48(4). However, this is not an end to the unanimous ratification rule. It is difficult to see what the European Council could do in such a situation other than bring pressure on the state or states either to ratify or opt out.

[54] Mendez, Mendez, and Triga describe the 'collusion' by EU elites to ensure member states followed a parliamentary rather than a referendum ratification route for the Lisbon Treaty as a 'heroic coordination effort', but still conclude that 'it is unlikely that this could ever be repeated, especially if the "sleeping giant" of European political contestation has finally awoken'. And, of course, even here the strategy was not entirely successful given the No vote in Ireland. Fernando Mendez, Mario Mendez, and Vasiliki Triga, 'Direct Democracy in the European Union: How Comparative Federalism Can Help Us Understand the Interplay of Direct Democracy and European Integration' (2009) 29 Revista de ciencia política 57, 76. A further potential complication is that the French Constitution has been amended to require a referendum for the ratification of any treaty 'pertaining to the accession of a state to the European Union'. Constitution of France, Art 88(5). This can only be avoided by a three-fifths majority voting in favour of the measure in each House of Parliament. One might anticipate this provision causing difficulty, for example in any move towards the accession of Turkey to the EU.

III. INTERNATIONAL ENGAGEMENT IN THE CREATION OF NEW STATES

External involvement in referendums held by territories moving to statehood since the dissolution of the USSR and SFRY has been pronounced. This has taken place on different levels. First, in the broad context of an international community active both in setting recognition criteria for new states and in promoting democracy we have seen international involvement in the very decision to hold a referendum. We will look at the EU criteria on state recognition which emerged in the early 1990s and in particular at how this was applied to Bosnia-Herzegovina and Kosovo. Second, we find international institutions involved in the very process of referendums. This can be through hands-on engagement in specific referendums, playing a role in helping to frame referendum law, referendum monitoring, and the like; and partly by way of broader processes of norm creation through, for example, the issuing of guidelines particularly through the Council of Europe's Commission for Democracy Through Law (Venice Commission). Here the Montenegro referendum in 2006 will be our case study.

International engagement in the plebiscitary process is of course not new, starting with a high level of involvement by the Great Powers through the nascent League of Nations in the inter-war plebiscites. For example, in relation to the plebiscite on North Schleswig in 1920, the process by which it was conducted, the appropriate boundaries between North and South Schleswig, and the distribution of the franchise were all heavily disputed between Denmark and Germany. The Commission of Belgian and Danish Affairs, under the auspices of the Paris peace process, took the lead in settling the future of the disputed territory. It made the decision of principle that there should indeed be a plebiscite held in North Schleswig.[55] It was also in a position to determine the border for the two plebiscites between North and South; that the working of the plebiscite be overseen by a specially convened International Commission with representatives of the Allied and Associated Great Powers, as well as delegates of the Norwegian and Swedish governments;[56] and that this Commission would have powers of administration and policing in the territory until the final status of the territory was settled.[57] In Chapter 3 we also saw how after the Second World War the United Nations occasionally applied plebiscites in processes of decolonization. Notably, in those cases where a plebiscite

---

[55] Sarah Wambaugh, *Plebiscites Since the World War* (Carnegie Endowment for International Peace 1933) vol I, 59.

[56] ibid vol I, 60.

[57] The provisions it put in place were approved by the League's Central Commission on Territorial Questions.

was used the General Assembly also authorized UN missions to set the question and make determinations as to timing.[58] And before the collapse of the USSR and SFRY, international involvement in elections more generally was reviving: for example, in the transition of Rhodesia-Zimbabwe in 1980 and in El Salvador in 1982.[59] But what is novel in the processes we have seen since 1990, in contrast with the inter-war and decolonization regimes, is the engagement of international actors in referendums which not only alter existing boundaries but lead to the emergence and recognition of entirely new states.

(i) Greek gods and new states: the Badinter process and the dissolution of the Socialist Federal Republic of Yugoslavia

As Croatia and Slovenia declared independence from the SFRY on 25 June 1991 the international community intervened. Realizing the futility of supporting attempts to hold the country together in light of the worsening security situation and overwhelmingly secessionist tendencies of these two republics in particular, the pressing issue rapidly became how to deal with state collapse. The Conference for Yugoslavia was established by the European Community, resulting in a set of guidelines on the recognition of new states.[60] This led also to the creation of the Arbitration Commission of the Conference on Yugoslavia, established by the Council of Ministers of the EEC on 27 August 1991, which was to interpret the application of the Guidelines and more generally give advice to the Conference on Yugoslavia. The Commission had five members, each a Constitutional Court president of one of the EEC Member States, and was chaired by Robert Badinter, the president of the French Constitutional Council. 'The Badinter Commission' issued 15 Opinions on legal questions arising from the collapse of the SFRY, including important Opinions on recognition matters. In Opinion No 7 (Slovenia) the Commission recommended that the European Community recognize the republic of Slovenia as a state. In Opinion No 5 (Croatia) it was more reticent, taking the view that Croatia's independence should not yet be recognized, because the new Croatian constitution had not incorporated the protections for minorities set out as requirements by the European

---

[58] A Rigo Suredi, *The Evolution of the Right of Self-Determination: A Study of United Nations Practice* (AW Sijthoff 1973) 304–6. It also recommended broad organizational powers for the administrative bodies concerned, eg UNGA Res 1350 (XIII) (13 March 1959); UNGA Res 1473 (XIV) (12 December 1959); UNGA Res 1569 (XV) (18 December 1960).

[59] Also Commonwealth observers contributed to the 1980 election in Uganda. Lawrence T Farley, *Plebiscites and Sovereignty: The Crisis of Political Illegitimacy* (Westview Press 1986) 42–6.

[60] Issued on 16 December 1991: European Community Conference on Yugoslavia Arbitration Commission, Declaration on the 'Guidelines on the Recognition of New States in Eastern Europe and the Soviet Union' (1992) 31 ILM 1486 (Guidelines on New States).

168 ∞ *Constitutional Referendums*

Community. This was quickly remedied, at least to the Committee's satisfaction. The President of Croatia, Franjo Tudjman, wrote to Robert Badinter giving assurances that the constitution would be corrected and on this basis European states started to recognize Croatia.

Traditionally state recognition has worked on the basis of formal guidelines laid down by the Montevideo Convention on the Rights and Duties of States of 1933. This is generally taken to set out the standard criteria for statehood in customary international law. These are: a permanent population; a generally well-defined territory; an effective government; and 'capacity to enter into relations with other States', which is usually interpreted as independence from other states.[61] These in themselves define a state: 'The political existence of the state is independent of recognition by the other states.'[62]

What we see emerge from the Guidelines and the Opinions of the Badinter Commission is a considerable development on these criteria, including the emergence of the referendum as a significant stage in the recognition process. The Opinion on Bosnia-Herzegovina (Bosnia) is particularly pertinent. The thickening out of the recognition criteria in the Guidelines included an emphasis upon democracy: 'The Community and its Member States... affirm their readiness to recognize... those new States which... have constituted themselves on a democratic basis.'[63] In Opinion No 4 on Bosnia, the Badinter Commission added flesh to the bones of this criterion, giving the Bosnian government a strong steer towards holding a referendum. The Opinion ended as follows:

> the Arbitration Commission is of the opinion that the will of the peoples of Bosnia-Herzegovina to constitute the SRBH [Socialist Republic of Bosnia and Herzegovina] as a sovereign and independent State cannot be held to have been fully established. This assessment could be reviewed if appropriate guarantees were provided by the Republic applying for recognition, possibly by means of a referendum of all the citizens of the SRBH without distinction, carried out under international supervision.[64]

This interpretation by the Commission seems to acknowledge both the importance of sub-state constituent power in any legitimate move to new statehood and the role of the referendum in validating the expression of that constituent power.[65] More importantly, it hints that the holding of the

---

[61] Montevideo Convention on the Rights and Duties of States (Montevideo, Uruguay, 26 December 1933, 165 LNTS 19) Art 1.

[62] ibid art 3.

[63] Guidelines on New States.

[64] 'European Community Conference on Yugoslavia Arbitration Commission, Opinions on Questions Arising from the Dissolution of Yugoslavia' (1992) 31 ILM 1488, Opinion No 4, para 4.

[65] Roland Rich, 'Recognition of States: The Collapse of Yugoslavia and the Soviet Union' (1993) 4 European J Int'l L 36, 49–50; Richard Caplan, *Europe and the Recognition of New States in Yugoslavia* (OUP 2005).

referendum is a precondition for recognition. And indeed Bosnia did go ahead with the referendum, with the disastrous consequences we discussed in Chapter 3.

In this period, therefore, state recognition moved from being effectivity-based to normativity-based, an ethical as much as, if not more than, a descriptive concern.[66] One consequence of this is that the referendum, while traditionally thought of as a domestically generated vehicle for popular expression, appeared now to take on an unprecedented level of external direction, and as a prerequisite of state recognition, in effect it became an externally imposed condition for the exercise of self-determination.

(ii) Kosovo and the Rambouillet process

Kosovo was left in limbo by the Badinter process since it did not meet another of the EU's recognition criteria—namely that only former 'republics' under the 1974 constitution could apply for recognition as new states. Since it was, in Yugoslav terms, relatively ethnically homogeneous[67] and highly autonomous (as a Socialist Autonomous Province of the Socialist Republic of Serbia), Kosovar nationalists felt aggrieved by this and mobilized an unofficial referendum to express this sense of grievance.[68] This set the scene within which the referendum was to remain an important backdrop to international engagement in Kosovo, which has now in effect moved to full statehood.[69]

---

[66] As Rich puts it:

> It could be argued that the Guidelines make the process of recognition more difficult because they purport to retain the 'normal standards of international practice' while adding a series of new requirements. In fact, however, the new requirements have tended to supplant the previous practice which was largely based on meeting the traditional criteria for statehood.

Rich, 'Recognition of States', 43. He continues:

> In Bosnia and Herzegovina's admission to the UN, the UN Security Council had unanimously recommended this country's membership and the General Assembly had unanimously accepted the recommendation. Yet every newspaper reader in the world knew by that time that not only could Bosnia and Herzegovina not be accurately described as independent, but it could hardly be described as a state.

See also: Allen Buchanan, *Justice, Legitimacy and Self-Determination: Moral Foundations for International Law* (OUP 2007) 6, 261–88; Nicholas Tsagourias, 'International Community, Recognition of States and Political Cloning' in Warbrick and Tierney (eds), *Towards an International Legal Community?: The Sovereignty of States and the Sovereignty of International Law*.

[67] By the 1981 census its two largest groups were Albanians (77.4 per cent) and Serbians (14.9 per cent).

[68] For a damning critique of the selective recognition policy applied to the former Yugoslavia and the argument that it exacerbated conflagrations in the region see Susan L Woodward, *Balkan Tragedy: Chaos and Dissolution after the Cold War* (The Brookings Institution 1995).

[69] Particularly in light of the International Court of Justice Opinion that Kosovo's 2008 unilateral declaration of independence did not violate general international law. *Accordance with International Law of the Unilateral Declaration of Independence in Respect of Kosovo (Request for an Advisory Opinion)* <http://www3.icj-cij.org/docket/files/141/15987.pdf> accessed 18 July 2011. Kosovo has now been widely recognized as a state, including by the vast majority of EU and NATO member states.

Between 1989 and 1992, both Serbia and the SFRY embarked upon a process of constitutional centralization which terminated Kosovan autonomy, a process which in turn led to the emergence of the strong separatist movement within Kosovo.[70] This process began with constitutional changes, eventually entrenched in the Constitution of the Republic of Serbia adopted in 1990. The process extensively centralized many important areas of power, thereby reducing substantially the powers of Kosovo as an Autonomous Province.[71] As the Special Rapporteur of the Commission on Human Rights noted:

> Under its [ie, the 1990 Constitution's] provisions the 'autonomous provinces' retained some authority over the provincial budget, cultural matters, education, health care, use of languages and other matters, but the authority was thenceforth to be exercised only in accordance with decisions made by the Republic. In fact, the new Constitution gave the Republic the right directly to execute its decisions if the provinces failed to do so.[72]

Tim Judah also observed: 'Although legally the province still existed, the changes meant they were no longer autonomous.'[73]

Kosovo opposed these changes strongly, and a defining moment in this campaign of resistance came on 2 July 1990 with a political declaration by the parliament of Kosovo which declared the Autonomous Province to be a republic of the Yugoslav Federation.[74] Shortly thereafter the parliament and government of Kosovo were dissolved by the Republic of Serbia, which in turn led a number of deputies from the Kosovo provincial parliament to issue a declaration of independence; this resulted in the proclamation of the Constitution of the Republic of Kosovo on 7 September 1990 shortly before the adoption of Serbia's new constitution. In September 1991, with war having broken out in Croatia, an unofficial referendum was held in Kosovo to validate this declaration of independence.[75] Backed by the overwhelmingly positive result in the referendum,[76] the Kosovo Albanian leadership

---

[70] Veton Surroi, 'Kosova and the Constitutional Solutions' in Thanos Veremis and Evangelos Kofos (eds), *Kosovo: Avoiding Another Balkan War* (ELIAMEP 1998).

[71] Evangelos Kofos, 'The Two-Headed Albanian Question' in Veremis and Kofos (eds), *Kosovo: Avoiding Another Balkan War* (ELIAMEP 1998) 55.

[72] UNCHR, 'Special Report on Minorities by Special Rapporteur Elisabeth Rehn, Situation of Human Rights in the Territory of the Former Yugoslavia' (1996), UN Doc E/CN.4/1997/8, ch II(c).

[73] Tim Judah, *Kosovo: War and Revenge* (Yale University Press 2000) 56.

[74] Surroi, 'Kosova and the Constitutional Solutions', 150.

[75] The referendum was conducted between 26 and 30 September 1991 and was largely clandestine.

[76] Reportedly, of 1,051,357 eligible voters, 87 per cent participated and 98 per cent voted for an independent Republic of Kosovo. See, International Crisis Group, 'ICG Kosovo Report' (*Refworld*, 10 March 1998) <http://www.unhcr.org/refworld/docid/3ae6a6ec4.html> accessed 18 July 2011; Miranda Vickers, *Between Serb and Albanian: A History of Kosovo* (Columbia University Press 1998) 251–2; Dajena Kumbaro, *The Kosovo Crisis in an International Law Perspective: Self-Determination, Territorial Integrity and*

pressed on with its quest for independence, holding presidential and parliamentary elections for the 'Republic of Kosova' on 24 May 1992.

This referendum was to retain a symbolic importance when the western powers intervened to stop the slide into civil war between 1998 and 1999. Diplomatic intervention from March 1998 onwards had little effect on the ground and in the end the Contact Group of great powers (USA, UK, France, Germany, Italy, and Russia) summoned representatives from the FRY, Serbia, and the Kosovo Albanians to meet at Rambouillet in France by 6 February, 'to begin negotiations with the direct involvement of the Contact Group'.[77] What is remarkable about this final attempt to broker a settlement is that, as talks got underway both sides were presented with what amounted to a virtual fait accompli: a detailed agreement, which included a fully detailed autonomy model for Kosovo, and provision for an international peacekeeping force in the region, which both sides were expected to accept. Furthermore, this was backed up by the threat of NATO military action,[78] directed in particular at the FRY side. As a Washington spokesman put it: 'If the Serbs fail to agree to the... plan and the Kosovar Albanians do... the Serbs will be subject to air strikes.'[79] Judah's laconic summation of the situation was: 'both sides were being told: "Sign or die"'.[80] After weeks of negotiation the Kosovo Albanian side did indeed sign an agreement on 18 March and the FRY's refusal to do so led directly to air strikes commencing on 24 March in Operation Allied Force.

The draft accord provided a programme of detailed autonomy for Kosovo, but only in the short term:

> Three years after the entry into force of this Agreement, an international meeting shall be convened to determine a mechanism for a final settlement for Kosovo, *on the basis of the will of the people*, opinions of relevant authorities, each Party's efforts regarding the implementation of this Agreement, and the Helsinki Final Act, and to undertake a comprehensive assessment of the implementation of this Agreement and to consider proposals by any Party for additional measures.[81]

---

the NATO intervention (Final Report, NATO Office of Information and Press 2001) 39; UNCHR, 'Special Report: Situation of Human Rights in the Territory of the Former Yugoslavia', ch II(c), also confirms that over 90 per cent of those taking part opted for independence.

[77] Contact Group statement, London, 29 January 1999.

[78] 'NATO Warns Both Sides in Kosovo', *Reuters* (28 January 1999) <http://www.newsday.com/news/nato-warns-both-sides-on-kosovo-1.431847> accessed 16 October 2011.

[79] 'Washington Renews Warnings to Serbs over Accepting Kosovo Agreement', *Associated Free Press* (10 February 1999).

[80] Judah, *Kosovo: War and Revenge*, 233.

[81] 'Interim Agreement for Peace and Self-Government In Kosovo', Rambouillet, France, 23 February 1999, Ch 8, Art 1(3). Emphasis added. For a discussion of the Rambouillet process and the agreement see Marc Weller, 'The Rambouillet Conference on Kosovo' (1999) 75 International Affairs 211.

172   *Constitutional Referendums*

For Kosovan nationalists the reference to a final settlement for Kosovo on the basis of the will of the people seemed to open the promise that the referendum of 1991 would at last be acted upon, or that a new referendum would be held, similar to those in Bosnia, Croatia, and Slovenia, as a vehicle towards independent statehood; the ethnic homogeneity of Kosovo, increased by the flight of many Serbs following NATO's intervention, left few in any doubt as to the result of any future referendum.[82] That Kosovo has moved towards seemingly inevitable independence without a recent referendum is, in the context of the overwhelming support for this in Kosovo, unsurprising. But it should not be overlooked that important international actors at Rambouillet in 1999 seemed prepared to offer the prospect of such a referendum even though it would almost certainly have led to the break-up of a sovereign state.[83]

(iii) *Referendum rules and process*

International involvement in the conduct of referendums has taken on a number of forms. International actors have played a role in setting out guidelines for good electoral practice which has extended to detailed guidance on specific elections and referendums. This can also involve sending monitors to oversee a particular election, and the passing of judgment on the democratic credentials of the process. As we will see in due course, all of these components were at work in the Montenegro referendum in 2006.

The Venice Commission of the Council of Europe has been particularly engaged in setting out good practice for referendums. Two documents stand out. First, the *Guidelines for Constitutional Referendums at National Level*[84] were issued in 2001 ('the 2001 Guidelines'). This document sets out prescriptions in a number of areas specifically in the context of constitutional referendums, including: the legal framework; the procedural and substantive validity of texts submitted to a referendum; the franchise; fairness of the vote; funding, advertising, and the media; and quorum rules. A document covering referendums more generally followed. The 'Code of Good Practice on Referendums' ('the 2007 Code') was adopted by the Venice Commission at its 70th plenary session in March 2007.[85] Together these two documents are the

---

[82] Stephen Tierney, 'The Long Intervention in Kosovo: A Self-Determination Imperative?' in James Summers (ed), *The Kosovo Precedent: Implications for Statehood, Self-determination and Minority Rights* (Brill 2012) 249.

[83] It is also notable that since then the international community has also overseen a referendum in South Sudan leading to statehood for this territory.

[84] Venice Commission, *Guidelines for Constitutional Referendums at National Level* (11 July 2001), COE Doc CDL-INF(2001)10.

[85] Venice Commission, 'Code of Good Practice on Referendums' Study No 371/2006 (20 January 2009), COE Doc CDL-AD(2007)008rev.

culmination of a number of interventions which have attempted to set referendum standards across Europe since the 1990s, and testify to the increasing use of referendums in the constitutional practice of new states. In this context it is indeed notable that the first set of guidelines in 2001 came specifically in the context of *constitutional* referendums.

Turning to the 2007 Code, it also contains a set of 'Guidelines on the Holding of Referendums'. These are divided into three sections: Section I concerns 'General Principles: Referendums and Europe's Electoral Heritage' and franchise issues; Section II covers 'Conditions for Implementing these Principles' which concerns other organizational and process matters for the staging of a referendum; and Section III on 'Specific Rules', offers more detailed recommendations on some of these matters and on additional issues such as quorum and the effects of referendums. As such there is considerable crossover with the 2001 Guidelines. A number of the recommendations and guidelines from both documents have been and will be discussed further throughout the book.

It is particularly notable that the 2007 Code also includes recommendations on compliance with international law.[86] This is explained in categorical terms in the 2007 Code's Explanatory Memorandum: 'Irrespective of what national law has to say about the relationship between international and domestic law, texts put to a referendum must not be contrary to international law or to the Council of Europe's statutory principles (democracy, human rights and the rule of law).'[87] In recommendations on 'Observation of the Referendum', the 2007 Code also provides recommendations on the involvement of external actors: 'Both national and international observers should be given the widest possible opportunity to participate in a referendum observation exercise.'[88] The preparedness of the Council of Europe to set out so clearly both the principle of international observation and the recommendation that its own statutory principles should be the basis for the conduct of referendums, was a highly significant backdrop to the intense level of engagement by the Council of Europe and other European institutions in the process leading to the Montenegro referendum of 2006.

IV. MONTENEGRO: A CASE STUDY IN INTERNATIONAL ENGAGEMENT

Montenegro was the last republic to leave the former Yugoslav state and it did so by way of referendum on 21 May 2006. With a turnout of 86.5 per cent, 55.5 per cent voted Yes and 44.5 per cent No to the question: 'Do you want the Republic of Montenegro to be an independent state with a

---

[86] ibid III, 3. [87] ibid para 33. [88] ibid II, 3.2.

full international and legal personality?'[89] Its move to statehood was complete when it joined the UN on 26 June 2006.

This was the last step on a long constitutional journey, with Montenegro finally ending a relationship with Serbia that had passed through various iterations as the SFRY began to collapse in the early 1990s. Ironically this journey began as well as terminated with a referendum. In 1992, at a time of turmoil throughout the federation, a poll was held in Montenegro which resulted in an official result of 96 per cent voting to stay with Yugoslavia.[90] This result remained controversial, with Montenegrin separatists boycotting the poll and insistent that the result was unfair.[91] By the late 1990s, and in particular with Belgrade's attention fixed on trying to resist separatism in Kosovo, and with Serbia becoming increasingly isolated from international public opinion as a consequence, Montenegro was quietly distancing itself from central control, leading to a breakdown in relations with the central government and the creation of a de facto independent government based in Podgorica.

Some measure of constitutional coexistence was however achieved in 2002, through the 'Belgrade Agreement', which created the State Union of Serbia and Montenegro. This realigned the rump state of the former Yugoslavia—by then the Federal Republic of Yugoslavia—along looser, more confederal lines, and led to the Constitutional Charter in 2003 which created a 'State Union', but more significantly gave Montenegro the right to hold a referendum on independence after three years,[92] a provision that contains echoes of Rambouillet.

The periods leading first to the Belgrade Agreement and then to the 2006 referendum are each marked by the considerable influence—some might say control—exercised by international actors. Three aspects of this involvement are particularly notable: the level of detail in which international institutions became involved in addressing the evolving constitutional affairs of Serbia and Montenegro; the extensive role they played in the

---

[89] As translated by Organization for Security and Co-operation in Europe/Office for Democratic Institutions and Human Rights (OSCE/ODIHR), 'Republic of Montenegro—Serbia and Montenegro Referendum, 21 May 2006—Needs Assessment Mission Report, 7–9 March 2006' (Warsaw, 14 March 2006).

[90] On a 66.04 per cent turnout only 3 per cent No votes were recorded.

[91] Srdjan Darmanovic, 'Montenegro: A Miracle in the Balkans' (2007) 18 J Democracy 152, 153.

[92] Upon the expiry of a 3-year period, member states shall have the right to initiate the proceedings for the change in its state status or for breaking away from the state union of Serbia and Montenegro.

The decision on breaking away from the state union of Serbia and Montenegro shall be taken following a referendum.

Constitutional Charter of the State Union of Serbia and Montenegro (2003) Art 60.

planning and organization of the 2006 referendum itself; and the interplay and coordination of roles among such a wide range of international actors in this long-running saga.

Initial involvement was in the context of overall constitutional reform at the turn of the millennium and there does seem to have been a genuine aspiration among international actors to make the 2002 agreement work, particularly in light of the removal of Slobodan Milosevic from power in October 2000. A number of European states, keen to avoid further constitutional disruption in the Balkans, saw this as a new start for Serbia and felt that the union with Montenegro would help provide stability.[93] But by then, as so often in the recent history of the Balkans, the position on the ground rapidly moved beyond the conservative aspirations of outside powers. Although Belgrade wanted the consolidation of a more centralized union, a strong body of opinion within Montenegro was not prepared to relinquish the constitutional powers acquired de facto before 2000 and now wanted either a decentralized federation or independence. With each side so polarized, internal constitutional deliberations failed in 2001 and in this atmosphere the EU became engaged, acting as a broker in the emergence of the Belgrade Agreement and, after a year of difficult negotiations, the ensuing Constitutional Charter.[94]

And even at this stage a referendum was on the table. It was a key goal of the Montenegrin government, as it had been of the Kosovo negotiators at Rambouillet, that any constitutional agreement falling short of independence should be temporary in nature, backed up by the promise of a referendum embedded in the constitutional agreement. Confident of popular support for independence, such a provision would, it was hoped, turn a

---

[93] According to Friis, the international community: 'strongly engaged to support the new-born democracy and the fragile...government in Belgrade. In this context, the attitude of many international actors towards the Montenegrin quest for independence in Montenegro soured.' Karsten Friis, 'The Referendum in Montenegro: The EU's 'Postmodern Diplomacy' (2007) 12 European Foreign Affairs Rev 67, 70. In particular, the EU was keen to avoid a referendum on independence in 2001: International Crisis Group, 'Still Buying Time: Montenegro, Serbia and the European Union' Europe Report No 129 (International Crisis Group, 7 May 2002) 8 <http://www.crisisgroup.org/en/regions/europe/balkans/montenegro/129-still-buying-time-montenegro-serbia-and-the-european-union.aspx> accessed 10 October 2011.

[94] Europe's institutions were central to this. The Belgrade Agreement provided that the EU would be responsible for the implementation of the agreement. Article 3 of the Agreement also set out that a goal of the agreement was the establishment of a common market in order to facilitate its 'integration in European structures, the EU in particular'. The adoption of the Constitutional Charter by 17 September 2002 was also a prerequisite to the Union joining the Council of Europe. Reneo Lukic, 'The Painful Birth of the New State—"Union of Serbia and Montenegro"' (Southeastern Europe: Moving Forward conference, Ottawa, 23–24 January 2003). See also Duško Lopandic and Vojislav Bajic, *Serbia and Montenegro on the Road to the EU* (Friedrich Ebert Stiftung 2003).

transitional union agreement into a one-way path to separation.[95] And indeed Article 60 of the Constitutional Charter has proven to be the key provision of the 2002–03 constitutional process.

The role of international actors intensified by the time of the 2006 referendum, but this role needs to be traced back to the framing of the appropriate referendum law and process. This was itself a long process, pre-dating the constitutional developments of the early 2000s, through low-profile observer and capacity-building roles. The OSCE/ODIHR was an early player, setting out its role in promoting democratic development and observing both the 1997 presidential and the 1998 parliamentary elections. The Montenegrin government felt more secure from Belgrade's influence in light of this international involvement, and after these elections it requested that the OSCE/ODIHR retain an office in Montenegro, which it agreed to do.[96] And so an international infrastructure was already on the ground and in position to advise on the drafting of a new referendum law which was passed by the Montenegrin parliament in 2001.[97] This in turn would be influential in shaping Article 60 of the Constitutional Charter.

Another notable feature of this period, which continued up to 2006, was the coordination by a range of different international actors as they contributed to these developments. As well as the OSCE/ODIHR,[98] the Council of Europe also got involved in 2001, addressing process questions surrounding a possible referendum. For example, the Venice Commission issued a series of reports and opinions on Montenegrin referendum law and practice.[99] Also in the background throughout this period was the EU's high representative for foreign and security policy, Javier Solana. The EU engaged with these constitutional debates under the pretext that the FRY was potentially an EU Common Foreign and Security Policy concern. Although not taking any hands-on role in the detail of Montenegro's referendum law, the intervention of the EU was influential in encouraging

---

[95] Nathalie Tocci, 'EU Intervention in Ethno-political Conflicts: The Cases of Cyprus and Serbia-Montenegro' (2004) 9 European Foreign Affairs Rev 551, 563.

[96] Vesko Garčević, 'Montenegro and the OSCE' in *OSCE Yearbook 2007* (CORE Centre for OSCE Research 2008) 104.

[97] OSCE/ODIHR, 'Assessment of the Referendum Law, Republic of Montenegro, Federal Republic of Yugoslavia' (Warsaw, 6 July 2001).

[98] Which issued a further paper: OSCE/ODIHR, 'Comments on the Draft "Referendum Law on the State Status of the Republic of Montenegro" Federal Republic of Yugoslavia' (Warsaw, 5 November 2001).

[99] Culminating in the Venice Commission, 'Opinion on the Compatibility of the Existing Legislation in Montenegro Concerning the Organisation of Referendums with Applicable International Standards' (19 December 2005), COE Doc CDL-AD(2005)041.

Serbia and Montenegro to reach consensus on the Belgrade Agreement in 2002 and the Constitutional Charter.[100]

With the spectre of a final status referendum in the background, three central issues of potential difficulty were emerging. These would remain crucial to referendum preparations through to 2006. First, there was controversy over the franchise: would eligibility to vote be open to all citizens of the FRY, born in Montenegro but now living in Serbia, or only people who were registered residents of Montenegro? In a territory with such a small population (Montenegro has only some 650,000 residents) this was important, as a few thousand votes could well tip the result of any referendum.[101] How this issue arose in Montenegro has already been discussed in Chapter 3 and so we will not revisit it in detail here. Second, the size of the majority needed for a valid decision to secede became a central issue. We will return to this in Chapter 9 dealing with decision-making, when the Montenegro experience will be compared to other controversial situations where the threshold issue has arisen, such as that in Canada/Quebec. The third controversial question concerned the constitutional status of a referendum and the constitutional impact of its outcome. The constitutionality of a referendum and its legal effect are in ordinary course matters normally decided under the sovereign prerogative of any state, and so the degree to which opinions were offered from outside the FRY in this period from 2001–03 on such a sensitive question is particularly relevant in demonstrating the degree to which the constitution of the FRY and its remaining sub-units had by this time become European public property in the process leading to the 2006 referendum.

At stake was the extent to which the referendum would be a clean break from the existing constitutional order. On the one hand, Article 60 of the Constitutional Charter provided the right of each member state to initiate proceedings to secede from the Union within three years. Furthermore, the constitution of Montenegro contained a provision to the effect that: 'Any change in the state status...shall be decided only by citizens in a referendum.'[102] On the other hand, Article 118 of that constitution also provided: '...The Assembly shall decide on the amendment to the Constitution by a two-thirds majority vote of all representatives.'[103] The Belgrade government

---

[100] Friis, 'The Referendum in Montenegro', 78.

[101] By the census of 2003 the territory has a large number of ethnic Serbs (about one-third of the population) who, together with a minority of ethnic Montenegrins, comprised most of the pro-Union voice. Ethnic Montenegrins made up about 43 per cent of the population and there were other fairly sizeable minorities (mainly Albanians c 5 per cent and Muslims c 11 per cent) among the population.

[102] Constitution of Montenegro, 12 October 1994, Art 2.

[103] Article 119 elaborates on this provision.

and pro-Serbian forces in Montenegro contended that by this latter provision any referendum result, to have constitutional effect, would still require the endorsement of a two-thirds majority in the Montenegrin parliament. The pro-independence bloc countered that the Constitutional Charter of 2003 superseded the provisions of the 1994 constitution and accordingly the referendum would in itself constitute a new constitutional settlement which should be binding on the parliament.

Both the OSCE/ODIHR and the Council of Europe were consulted on this question. The initial approach taken by the OSCE/ODIHR was to attempt to maintain neutrality. It took the view that the constitution was indeed ambiguous, but the Serbian reading seemed to be correct.[104] By now, however, the referendum law of 2001 was being used to support the Montenegrin nationalist position, since it provided: 'The outcome of a referendum shall be binding on the assembly calling the referendum.'[105] The central question then shifted to the constitutionality of this law. In order to avoid being dragged further into such a sensitive question the OSCE/ODIHR in its report suggested that this should be referred to the Constitutional Court of Montenegro.[106] This led to a remarkable decision in which the Constitutional Court held that the citizens of Montenegro have 'original sovereignty' and that the result of a referendum on independence would be binding upon the Parliament.[107]

Nonetheless the issue of the constitutionality of a future referendum and its compatibility with the constitution remained controversial. Both the OSCE/ODIHR and the Council of Europe had managed to maintain some kind of distance from the issue, but as we will see, as Montenegro took its final steps towards independence, international actors were set to intervene again and in this case in a more determinative manner.

(i) The process towards the 2006 referendum

The Charter of 2003 put international involvement on the back-burner and the issue of a referendum itself was now on hold as the three-year clock started to tick. But this was only a temporary lull and the international role

---

[104] OSCE/ODIHR, 'Assessment of the Referendum Law'. The Venice Commission interim report of 2001 agreed in unequivocal terms: 'In [the] case of a positive result, a referendum on independence would have to be confirmed by two-thirds of the Assembly of Montenegro.' Venice Commission, 'Interim Report on the Constitutional Situation of the Federal Republic of Yugoslavia' (26 October 2001), COE Doc CDL-INF (2001)23.

[105] Law on Referendum of the Republic of Montenegro (Serbia and Montenegro) Art 4.

[106] OSCE/ODIHR, 'Assessment of the Referendum Law'.

[107] 'Decision by Constitutional Court of Montenegro 17 March 2002', The Official Gazette of Montenegro No 14/2002.

once again became intense in 2005 as the referendum approached and international bodies became fully engaged in the detailed rules of process for the anticipated referendum. Once again, the Venice Commission was central to the process. Invited to do so by the Parliamentary Assembly of the Council of Europe, in December 2005 the Commission issued another Opinion on the various issues at stake.[108]

Notably its mandate had been to consider specific issues of referendum design and process; it was not asked to comment on the constitutionality of the referendum itself, which had already proven to be so divisive.[109] Nonetheless it did issue a bland statement to the effect that any referendum result 'must be implemented in a manner that maintains constitutionality within Montenegro',[110] an approach similar to its earlier Opinion of 2001. By now, of course, the Constitutional Court had ruled that the referendum would bind the parliamentary assembly, and with no contradiction of this, and a reference to constitutionality, the Venice Commission seemed to accept that this was settled constitutional principle.

Furthermore, the EU was now to prove to be more directive, particularly with the appointment of Miroslav Lajčák as Javier Solana's special envoy to Montenegro in December 2005. Lajčák played a key role not only in increasing and formalizing the influence of the EU but in coordinating, and to a large extent taking over from, the OSCE. A team of experts under his leadership—encompassing also representatives of the Venice Commission, the OSCE/ODIHR, and the OSCE Mission to Serbia and Montenegro—was now in a position to immerse itself in the political and legal detail of the planned referendum, and from the start of 2006 it began to issue advice on these matters.

The central document issued by the Lajčák team: 'Key principles of a democratic referendum process in the republic of Montenegro' was a detailed account of a wide range of matters including legislative regulation of the referendum, the franchise, the threshold, the referendum question itself, and other organizational and funding issues. These ongoing areas of difficulty had so far largely been skirted around by the OSCE/ODIHR and Venice Commission. But now the Lajčák team asked for both sides to set out their views on each of these issues. His team also showed itself prepared to take a strong position on these matters, knowing that it had the weight of

---

[108] Venice Commission, 'Opinion on Montenegro Legislation'.

[109] The Parliamentary Assembly on 27 May 2005 had requested that the Opinion cover 'the compatibility with applicable international standards of the existing legislation in Montenegro concerning the organisation of referendum, with a special focus on the issues of required turnout, majority and the criteria for the eligibility to vote'. Venice Commission, 'Opinion on Montenegro Legislation'.

[110] Venice Commission, 'Opinion on Montenegro Legislation'.

the EU behind it. We see this on the central question of the constitutional effect of a referendum. Lajčák endorsed the view of the Constitutional Court in 2002, stating that the EU would consider the referendum result to be the settled will of the Montenegrin people.[111] In effect the Lajčák team was prepared to take a position on whether the continuing sovereignty of the existing constitution would be displaced by a referendum intervening as a sovereign event, in light of the Constitutional Charter of 2003. There is a strong argument for such a position, and it was the position adopted by the Constitutional Court, but nonetheless it is remarkable that an international agency felt itself entitled to intervene on a matter that is generally taken to be for the exclusive internal determination by sovereign states. It needs to be borne in mind that this interpretation of the status of the referendum was likely to have, and indeed did have, determinative consequences for the very territorial integrity of the state.

This deep involvement led to the Lajčák team providing recommendations on all aspects of the referendum process that were subject to dispute and providing guidelines for negotiations on the details between the two sides. The political influence of the EU team was such that it is difficult to see the policy positions it took as being simply 'recommendations'. As we move to address the legal framework that was established for resolving disagreements we see that the institutional competence which the EU team acquired backed up its political power, with the EU team taking on what was in effect a casting vote on vital process issues.

Several institutions were established to organize and administer the referendum itself: the Republic Referendum Commission (RRC) and two lower level bodies, the Municipal Referendum Commissions and the Polling Boards.[112] Lajčák's team proposed that both pro- and anti-independence blocks should have equal representation on each body. This was an attempt to make both sides negotiate openly without the opportunity to overrule the other. However, it also promised the possibility of stalemate. This would be a particular disadvantage to the pro-independence bloc since the status quo obviously suited the pro-Union grouping. The suggestion of the pro-independence group was that representatives of the international community should be involved in each of the administrative bodies and should

---

[111] As Friis puts it: 'The Milošević era constitution was not considered to be a legitimate impediment to a final resolution to the relationship between Serbia and Montenegro. Thus, in effect, the EU considered the referendum binding upon the parliament.' Friis, 'The Referendum in Montenegro', 83. The OSCE/ODIHR also changed its mind: the two-thirds parliamentary procedure 'should not be necessary if a referendum has already been held'. OSCE/ODIHR, 'Republic of Montenegro, Referendum on State-Status' (Warsaw, 21 May 2006); OSCE/ODIHR, 'Referendum Observation Mission, Final Report' (Warsaw, 4 August 2006) 4.

[112] Law on the Referendum on State-Legal Status of the Republic of Montenegro, Art 9.

have a casting vote in the event of failure to agree. This was not implemented for either the Polling Boards or the Municipal Referendum Commissions, which retained equal representation, but crucially it was decided that the Chairman of the RRC should be appointed by the Assembly 'from amongst the relevant European organisations'.[113] The two blocs appointed ambassador Frantisek Lipka from Slovakia as the chairman of the RRC. His was the ultimate authority which, with a tie-breaking vote, could also determine disputes emerging from the other, lower, bodies. The most potent external involvement, therefore, came at the most important time: in the heart of the referendum campaign in 2006.

It is interesting to observe what this meant in practice, particularly over the crucial issue of the size of majority needed to validate the claim for independence. On this question the Venice Commission Opinion of 2005 to some extent endorsed its own earlier view set out in 2001. It remained formally non-directive, suggesting it was for domestic actors to reach agreement, but it emphasized 'that there are reasons for requiring a level higher than a simple majority of those voting, since this may be necessary to provide legitimacy for the outcome of a referendum'.[114] Interestingly, it concluded:

> As regards the choice between a rule requiring the support of a specific proportion of the total national electorate... and a rule requiring a qualified majority of those who vote..., the Commission would not recommend the latter since that could mean approval of a fundamental change being given on a very low turnout.[115]

As we have noted, this issue will be discussed in detail in Chapter 9, but for now it is interesting to observe how this matter was settled by the Lajčák team in precisely the way recommended against by the Venice Commission. The issue was, of course, controversial and potentially crucial. On the one hand, the pro-independence lobby claimed that 50 per cent plus 1 of those voting should be enough to endorse independence, while the anti-independence lobby insisted that a super-majority should be required for such a momentous step and referred back to the original claim that the 1994 constitution required two-thirds support within parliament for independence. The Lajčák solution was a more explicit recommendation of a super-majority requirement that would require the assent of 55 per cent of the participating voters for independence, and ultimately the EU was crucial in setting this detailed rule.[116]

---

[113] ibid Art 11.

[114] Venice Commission, 'Opinion on Montenegro Legislation', para 36.

[115] ibid para 37.

[116] The OSCE was also important in hinting to the pro-independence bloc that it could withhold its monitoring role if 'European standards' were not followed. This was read to include the 55 per cent

In the end, and somewhat fortuitously, with a Yes vote of 55.5 per cent the threshold proved low enough for independence to be achieved but high enough to mute dissent from anti-independence supporters.[117] But in reality it seems that the political power of the EU was perhaps the main factor in the acceptance by both sides of the threshold requirement and of the referendum outcome. The control of the EU was based on the fact that neither side could afford to reject it. As Friis puts it: 'The EU was capable of promoting the 55 per cent threshold in the referendum since it had the "stick and carrot" power of future membership.'[118] For political reasons this compromise was one which both sides felt they had to accept.[119]

And so when the pro-independence side achieved this threshold the further break-up of the rump state was a fait accompli. The influence of external actors remained crucial in the post-referendum period. We have noted how the Lajčák team declared that the referendum would be in and of itself determinative, notwithstanding any constitutional provisions to the contrary. Treating the referendum as a free-standing expression of constituent power by a discrete Montenegrin demos thus led to quick recognition by many states and the rapid admission of Montenegro to the UN. Even Serbia realized that the status quo was unsustainable and itself recognized the finality of the referendum result independent of any subsequent endorsement by the Montenegrin Parliament by way of the Article 118 procedure.

V. CONCLUSION

This chapter has explored the 'control syndrome' in the context of external influence. The two cases we have looked at—EU integration and new statehood—are at first sight very different. In substantive terms the former involves states relinquishing sovereignty to a supra-state proto-polity, the latter is about small entities claiming the fullness of state sovereignty for

---

threshold rule: 'This amounted to a threat to deprive the referendum of its international legitimacy'. Darmanovic, 'Montenegro: A Miracle in the Balkans', 159 fn 5.

[117] And, of course, the level of external observation was extensive, with more than 3,000 observers from the OSCE, the Council of Europe, and other non-governmental organizations. According to Darmanovic, they 'attested that the contest had been a fair one, conducted in an atmosphere of peace and without significant irregularities'. Darmanovic, 'Montenegro: A Miracle in the Balkans', 157.

[118] Friis, 'The Referendum in Montenegro', 86. Notably in 1999 Montenegro adopted the Deutschmark as its currency, switching to the euro in 2002.

[119] International Crisis Group, 'Montenegro's Referendum' Europe Briefing No 42 (International Crisis Group, 30 May 2006) 2–3 <http://www.crisisgroup.org/en/regions/europe/balkans/montenegro.aspx> accessed 10 October 2011. Even a member of the OSCE, closely involved in the process, noted that in introducing this 'unprecedented' threshold, 'political arguments appear to have prevailed over legal ones'. Garčević, 'Montenegro and the OSCE', 111.

themselves. But a common factor is the extent to which external forces are increasingly engaged in conditioning each context.

In the first case the pressure to secure a pro-integrationist result can be overwhelming, from the political class within the state, from other (often powerful) member states, and from the institutions of the EU itself. This can extend even to a refusal to take No for an answer. Although there are signs of increasing Euroscepticism and that the referendum, when it involves national identity, can be an unpredictable vehicle with which to move forward the polity-building vehicle of the EU, so far the EU's size and strength have been sufficient to see off the occasional expression of dissent. The referendum, it seems, has exposed the uncomfortable fact that the assumptions which exist at elite level within the EU that it is appropriate to try to shape referendum outcomes and overcome retrospectively those popular votes with which they are unhappy, and the use of the referendum by citizens as one of the only meaningful opportunities they have to protest against both the democratic deficiencies they find in the EU and the messianic vision of an integrationist elite, share the same root in that very democratic deficit.[120]

It is also notable how influential international institutions including the EU itself have been in the progress towards statehood of the various territories of the former Yugoslavia. The framing of the referendum as an important step in the recognition of new states, the seeming imposition of a sovereignty referendum as a component of the Rambouillet settlement, the setting of international standards for the conduct of referendums (and the insistence that these trump inconsistent domestic laws), and the detailed hands-on mediation of crucial constitutional conflicts surrounding the referendum in Montenegro, all suggest that any notion of the referendums from Bosnia to Montenegro (and beyond Europe to South Sudan) as simply the reclamation of incipient constituent power by sub-state people must be heavily qualified. The different international actors engaged in Montenegro did make much play of their role as honest brokers and in some ways they did seem keen to take a back seat and to avoid the overt politicization of

---

[120] One scholar who is generally enthusiastic about the EU project and a seeming sceptic of referendums has, in a carefully crafted assessment of the Irish referendums on Europe, observed:

> The various domestic referenda concerning ratification of EU Treaties have provided some of the few occasions for real public engagement and debate on EU matters, countering the normal voter apathy and disinterest in EU affairs that has been such an intractable part of the democratic deficit.

She goes on to cite research to the effect that 'average EU voter turnout has been declining but that the Irish and Dutch referendums produced a much higher turnout than normal'. Gráinne de Búrca, 'If at First You Don't Succeed: Vote, Vote Again: Analyzing the Second Referendum Phenomenon in EU Treaty Change' (2011) 33 Fordham Int'l LJ 1472, 1488.

their roles. For example, the OSCE/ODIHR, when offering a position on the franchise question, sought to base its position on 'international standards, commitments and best practices'.[121] But increasingly it is these very organizations that are setting these standards. And with so much 'soft' political influence at their disposal, for example through the promise of membership of important institutions and with the threat of exclusion from monopolistic trade agreements as a disincentive, overt dictation of detailed rules is arguably unnecessary to achieve the desired compliance with externally framed standards. In light of all of these factors, and the former Yugoslav experience taken as a whole, few features of recent constitutional practice display more clearly the extent to which international normative orders condition state sovereignty than the detailed intervention and fashioning of processes of direct democracy. The referendum is perhaps the key political instrument mapping the pathway to statehood; but it can be a statehood whose very own attributes are increasingly conditioned by the standards set by powerful states.

[121] OSCE/ODIHR, 'Assessment of the Referendum Law'.

7

Participation in Constitutional Referendums

I. INTRODUCTION

If the principles of civic republicanism and the goals of deliberative democracy are to be brought together successfully in a constitutional referendum process, the next key issue is whether citizen participation can be facilitated actively and meaningfully in such an exercise and, more precisely, how this might be achieved. Having addressed the issue of control in a wide range of possible settings in the last three chapters, the problems of aggregative decision-making (the 'deliberation deficit') and the structural hegemony of majoritarian interests (the 'majoritarian danger') remain to be fully considered. My key criterion remains the model of 'civic republican democracy' which stresses the political engagement of the public as an important democratic value. From a deliberative perspective such an active participatory role for citizens must also meet the 'aggregative' and 'majoritarian' criticisms if the referendum as an instrument of direct democratic engagement can also bear normative credibility as an instrument of *deliberative* constitutional authorship. 'Elite deliberative democrats' and 'popular deliberative democrats' agree that deliberation in democratic decision-making is crucial. Turning the decision-making process into a public act and causing decision-makers to exchange reasons can, it is agreed, lead to better and more consensual decision-making. However, this must also be viewed in the context of the civic republican aspiration that ordinary citizens should be encouraged to engage in democratic deliberation where possible; deliberative decision-making whether by citizens or elites leads to better decisions, but it is, specifically, popular involvement that can give these decisions enhanced democratic legitimacy.

The entitlement of people to participate in decisions that affect their lives is now internationally recognized as a value in any democratic process, not only referendums. The leading UN and regional human rights covenants and conventions guarantee the right to participate in the conduct of public affairs[1]

---

[1] Universal Declaration of Human Rights (UDHR), UNGA Res 217A (III) (10 December 1948), UN Doc A/810/71, Art 21(1) (this is not technically a 'convention' but rather a non-binding UNGA declaration);

and ancillary rights that are essential to support political participation, such as access to information,[2] freedom of assembly and association,[3] and freedom of expression.[4] From the perspective of civic republicanism another key argument of this book is that this level of citizen engagement, although of general importance in any political process, is all the more vital at the constitutional level and, in particular, in respect of fundamental constitutional decisions that implicate the very identity of a constitutional people.

In this chapter we will consider the opportunities for deliberation within a constitutional referendum process as they arise in different ways during a series of *stages*, across various *settings*, and in a plurality of *modes*. First, it has been noted that: 'A deliberative model involves citizens at every stage of policy formation, including research and discovery stages.'[5] When we think of a referendum as a series of stages—initiation, issue-framing, and question-setting, and the campaign itself, a number of avenues open up to encourage patterns of deliberation in various ways at these different points, leading, it is hoped, to an overall picture of a referendum that has been infused with deliberative elements from start to finish.

The first (initiation) stage we have largely addressed in Chapters 4 to 6; the decision to hold a referendum is invariably in the hands of elites with varying degrees of constitutional regulation from state to state. There is scope here for elite deliberation, but much will depend upon the political culture of the polity in question. From my civic republican perspective I am principally concerned with the feasibility of popular deliberation in the referendum and therefore will concentrate more on the prospects for deliberative participation at the second and third stages, addressing whether an active role for citizens can be built into these parts of the process in a systematic way.

International Covenant on Civil and Political Rights (ICCPR) (New York, 16 December 1966, 999 UNTS 171) Art 25; American Convention on Human Rights (ACHR) (San José, 22 November 1969, 1144 UNTS 144) Art 23; African Charter on Human and Peoples' Rights (ACHPR) (Nairobi, 27 June 1981, 1520 UNTS 217) Art 13.

[2] ACHPR, Art 9(1).

[3] UDHR, Art 20; European Convention for the Protection of Human Rights and Fundamental Freedoms (ECHR) (Strasbourg, 4 November 1950, 213 UNTS 221) Art 11; ICCPR, Arts 21–2; ACHR, Arts 15–16; ACHPR, Arts 10–11.

[4] UDHR, Art 19; ECHR, Art 10; ICCPR, Art 19; ACHR, Art 13; ACHPR Art 9(2). Specifically in the context of referendums the Venice Commission has asserted:

> Democratic referendums are not possible without respect for human rights, in particular freedom of expression and of the press, freedom of movement inside the country, freedom of assembly and freedom of association for political purposes, including freedom to set up political parties.

European Commission for Democracy Through Law (Venice Commission), *Guidelines for Constitutional Referendums at National Level* (11 July 2001), COE Doc CDL-INF(2001)10, para II.1.

[5] Simone Chambers, 'Deliberative Democratic Theory' (2003) 6 Annual Rev of Political Science 307, 316–17.

The recognition that a referendum is in fact a series of stages—or deliberation opportunities—leads to a distinction between two *settings* for participation. The first is where small groups of citizens 'with some claim to representativeness of the public at large'[6] are brought together to deliberate (what I will call micro-level citizen participation), and the second is where the entire population is encouraged to deliberate (macro-level citizen participation[7]). I will be concerned with both types, considering at which stages of the referendum process each setting might be more appropriate or feasible. How these two settings might work will be the principal focus of the chapter, and to explain them I will address two contrasting case studies in constitutional civic deliberation: the British Columbia Citizens' Assembly on Electoral Reform (BCCA) in 2004, and the Australia Constitutional Convention (ACC), which deliberated on proposals for a new model of head of state and a new constitutional preamble in 1999.

The second (issue-framing and question-setting) stage seems to lend itself more to micro-level deliberation than macro. In Section II I will consider how feasible this is in light of the practical attempts to develop such models within our two case studies, where micro-level processes were used to frame referendum issues to be put to the people. Turning to the third (referendum campaign) stage, it is here we meet the most sceptical voices. There is, not surprisingly, widespread disbelief that mass deliberation is in any society feasible.[8] This extends to a more specific doubt that meaningful, deliberative discussion by millions of citizens is realistic in the heat of a referendum campaign. My key concern in Section III, therefore, is whether there is any way in which a referendum campaign might be turned into a national deliberative moment, facilitating a broad, macro-level participatory process. This again will be examined through our two case studies since in each case the micro-level process led in different ways to attempts to build in deliberative elements also at the macro stage of the referendum campaign itself.

Throughout the chapter, of course, we must also address what in qualitative terms is meant by 'deliberative' participation, given that I am talking about different *modes* of deliberation taking place at different stages and within different settings of the referendum process. Here I will consider the distinction emphasized by Robert Goodin between 'discussion' and

---

[6] Robert E Goodin and John S Dryzek, 'Deliberative Impacts: The Macro-Political Uptake of Mini-publics' (2006) 34 Politics and Society 219, 220.

[7] Goodin and Dryzek define the macro level as 'the larger political system and its need for collective decisions'. Ibid 220. My meaning is narrower, focusing upon the mass of citizens engaged in an act of direct democracy, although appreciating, of course, that this happens in the context of, and is inevitably conditioned by, the broader representative political system.

[8] James D Fearon, 'Deliberation as Discussion' in Jon Elster (ed), *Deliberative Democracy* (CUP 1998) 64.

'consideration' as two distinctive components of deliberation,[9] and his suggestion that the latter may be a feasible goal for nationwide processes of deliberation even where the former is not.

In short, I will ask in this chapter whether, looking at the referendum as a series of three stages, envisaging two theatres for deliberation (micro level and macro level), and appreciating that deliberation can manifest itself through different forms (discussion and consideration/reflection), we might envisage the very possibility of a 'deliberative referendum', in recognition of its full complexity, as a democratic event taking place over time in a series of process phases, among different actors in different fora, and through different modes of public reasoning.

II. MICRO-LEVEL DELIBERATION: ISSUE-FRAMING

Typically, as we have seen, elites will attempt to set the referendum agenda. The process rules, its length, and the question that is set are typically in the keeping of government, albeit subject to parliamentary approval. Although levels of control vary greatly according to constitutional and political context, executives tend to manage the agenda-setting stage of a referendum, and even where there is intense competition among elites, constitutionally guaranteed opportunities for citizens or other deliberative bodies to influence the process are invariably lacking.

Our case studies are useful in that they offer contrasting ways of constructing a micro-level process. The British Columbia model was comprised only of ordinary citizens and has therefore offered political scientists an ideal experiment in evaluating the success of a purely popular deliberative engagement at the agenda-setting stage of referendums. The Australian model, by contrast, was comprised of what we can certainly term elites, but included actors who have not traditionally been engaged in such high-level constitutional deliberation. It involved, therefore, not only a more elite but also an overtly 'representative' (as opposed to randomly selected) model of micro-level deliberation when compared to the BCCA. In Section II(i) I will explain briefly the political and constitutional background to these contrasting models.

I will also address how elements of micro-deliberation were built into the issue-framing stage in both of our case studies. These cases will be elaborated in some detail throughout the section, since it is in this detail that we can see how different these models were from one another, each displaying

---

[9] Robert E Goodin, *Innovating Democracy: Democratic Theory and Practice after the Deliberative Turn* (OUP 2008) 40–2. See also Robert E Goodin, 'When Does Deliberation Begin? Internal Reflection versus Public Discussion in Deliberative Democracy' (2003) 51 Political Studies 627.

contrasting strengths and weaknesses. This will then allow us to evaluate in Section III how these respective micro-models helped inform the macro-deliberation of the respective citizen bodies as a whole in the course of the referendum campaign.

Since we are now witnessing a turn towards micro-level deliberation as a way of informing the issue and question-setting stage in a number of referendums,[10] it is important to begin by asking what the key goals of such a 'micro-level constitutional process' are and how we might seek to evaluate deliberation in such a forum. At the end of Chapter 2 I set out a series of central principles commonly shared by many deliberative democracy theorists, arguing that these are key to meeting the classical critique of the referendum process as fundamentally undeliberative. The micro-level processes contained in both the BCCA and ACC will be explored at length in Section II(ii) against the standards set by these four principles.

(i) Introducing the BCCA and ACC processes

An experiment in introducing micro-level deliberation was undertaken in British Columbia on the subject of electoral reform, a process which resulted in a referendum in 2005.[11] Electoral reform has been the focus of much attention in Canada in recent years. The disjuncture between support for parties on the one hand and success at the ballot box on the other has led to disproportionate results, bringing the first-past-the-post voting model into disrepute. British Columbia (BC) has been affected by this in a particularly dramatic way. For example, the Liberal government of BC which introduced the BCCA had won 77 of the 79 seats in the 2001 provincial election, despite polling only 58 per cent of the vote.

By one argument, citizens can become frustrated if they feel their votes are wasted when voting preferences are not properly reflected in the make-up of the legislature. It is therefore pertinent that in response to this sense of democratic deficit and the potential for popular disenchantment, the government of BC moved towards substantive reform through a process which itself attempted to engage direct citizen participation in the province's deliberations. What is revolutionary about the BC experience is how a randomly selected body of citizens was vested with drawing up the

---

[10] Another example was a citizens' assembly model in Ontario on Electoral Reform very similar to the British Columbia model, which led to a referendum in 2007.

[11] This ended in defeat for a proposal to introduce a single transferable vote (STV) model for provincial elections. A threshold was set: in order to pass, the referendum had to receive 60 per cent of the province-wide popular vote and a simple majority in 60 per cent (48 of 79) of the electoral districts. The measure failed narrowly on the former criterion, with 57.69 per cent of the popular vote in favour. A second referendum held in 2009 on the same issue also failed, this time more decisively.

alternative model of franchise to be put to its fellow citizens in the 2005 referendum. As Warren and Pearse observe, the Assembly represented 'the first time a government has responded to citizen discontents by empowering a citizen body to redesign political institutions so as to address democratic deficits'.[12]

The BCCA was established between 2003 and 2004, deliberating throughout most of 2004. It was composed of a randomly selected group of citizens.[13] The remit of the BCCA was to assess models for electing Members of the Legislative Assembly of BC and to issue a report recommending whether the current model should be retained or another model adopted, this issue to be put to the people of the province in a referendum. The Assembly's work took place in three phases. The BCCA met initially in Vancouver every second weekend for two months to March 2004. This was an educational phase, where the Assembly learned about different models of electoral system with case studies from around the world. This led to a 'preliminary statement'—a form of interim report—to the people of BC. The next two months were taken up with public hearings, this time on rotation across the province, to take the views of diverse groups. In this way an opportunity was given to the broader public to participate and be heard. Following a summer break, the BCCA reconvened for three months from September to November 2004 for a final period of deliberation, ending with a final report issued in December, 2004.

There are a number of structural reasons why the ACC differed so markedly from the BCCA. First, the Australian referendum process of 1999 was both a nationwide rather than sub-national process, and one concerning the sovereign status of the head of state and a constitutional preamble, the former in particular having enormous symbolic as well as substantive significance to the people of the whole country. In addition, a very distinctive constitutional setting, the long and disputed process that led in the end to the use of the referendum, the far greater intensity of partisan disagreement over the head of state issue, and the nature of the pre-referendum deliberation process, all mark out the Australian experience as very different from that in BC.

Starting with the constitutional position, unlike the Canadian constitution, which is silent on the use of referendums, Australia requires a referendum for any constitutional amendment. Under the constitution, a referendum is initiated by the government, which first of all must submit the referendum

---

[12] Mark E Warren and Hilary Pearse, 'Introduction: Democratic Renewal and Deliberative Democracy' in Mark E Warren and Hilary Pearse (eds), *Designing Deliberative Democracy: The British Columbia Citizens' Assembly* (CUP 2008) 7.

[13] Amy Lang, 'But Is It for Real? The British Columbia Citizens' Assembly as a Model of State-Sponsored Citizen Empowerment' (2007) 35 Politics & Society 35, 41; RS Ratner, 'British Columbia's Citizens' Assembly: The Learning Phase' (2004) 27(2) Canadian Parliamentary Rev 20, 22. See generally Warren and Pearse (eds), *Designing Deliberative Democracy*.

proposal to both houses of parliament where this legislative proposal requires to secure an absolute majority of each house.[14] The referendum proposal itself has a double-threshold requirement. To pass, it must win a majority of all voters nationally and majorities of voters in at least four of the six states. The votes from the two territories are only counted in relation to the national result. In the 1999 referendum the first proposal on the ballot would have replaced the Queen and her representative, the governor-general, with a president appointed by two-thirds of Australia's bicameral Commonwealth Parliament, which would have made the appointment in a plenary session of both houses sitting as one body. This proposal was rejected by 55 to 45 per cent of voters. There were majorities against the change in all six states and the Northern Territory, with only the Australian Capital Territory voting in favour. The second proposal on the ballot, to add a preamble to the Constitution, failed even more heavily.[15]

The campaign to make Australia a republic has been on the political agenda for decades but we can trace back the 1999 initiative to events beginning more specifically in 1993 when Paul Keating's Labor government appointed a Republic Advisory Committee to consider what constitutional changes would be required to replace the Queen as head of state.[16] Keating campaigned in the 1996 federal election with the goal of an Australian republic being constituted in time for the centennial celebration of federation in 2001. Labor lost the federal election of 1996 and a coalition of Liberal and National Parties under John Howard continued with the initiative, albeit with less enthusiasm. A Constitution Convention (Election) Bill was introduced to Parliament in 1997, resulting in the Australian People's Constitutional Convention (ACC), which was convened by the government from 2–13 February 1998.[17] Although its mode of composition and process of operation were, as we will see, very different from those of the BCCA, the ACC was nevertheless for Australia a radical constitutional innovation.[18]

---

[14] Australian Constitution, s 128.

[15] 60.7 per cent voting No. John Higley and Rhonda Evans Case, 'Australia: The Politics of Becoming a Republic' (2000) 11(3) J Democracy 136, 136–7.

[16] Australian Republic Advisory Committee, *An Australian Republic: The Options* (Report, Australian Government Publishing Service 1993). There had been earlier organic moves within civil society on the republic issue, as we see in the formation of the Australian Republican Movement (ARM) by academics and other civic figures. The ARM's goal was 'a Head of State who is an Australian citizen, who is appointed by Australians and who represents the independent and sovereign nation of Australia'. Higley and Evans Case, 'Australia: The Politics of Becoming a Republic', 142.

[17] 'Report of the Constitutional Convention', Old Parliament House, 2–13 February 1998 (Commonwealth of Australia 1998) vols I and II ('Report of the Australian Constitutional Convention 1998').

[18] Brian Galligan, 'Amending Constitutions through the Referendum Device' in Matthew Mendelsohn and Andrew Parkin (eds), *Referendum Democracy: Citizens, Elites, and Deliberation in Referendum Campaigns* (Palgrave 2001) 119–23.

Traditionally, deliberation over the framing of constitutional issues has been the preserve of parliament alone and so the institution of a broader deliberative process was both new and controversial.

(ii) Micro-level participation and the principles of deliberative democracy

I will now assess these two processes in light of the four principles of deliberative democracy introduced in Chapter 2: popular participation; public reasoning; equality and parity of esteem; and consent and collective decision-making.

(a) Popular participation

The BCCA and ACC models differ considerably in the respective ways in which they fostered citizen participation, and in this sense they reflect different ideas about how citizen-informed deliberation at the agenda-setting stage ought to be structured. It is one thing to advance a commitment to popular participation as both a way of constraining, and an appropriate complement to, government in its task of setting the referendum agenda; it is another to come up with a micro-model that is suitable for these tasks.

Let us begin then with the key goals of participation from the perspective of civic republican deliberation. These might be summarized as the right of those affected by a decision to have a say in the making of it,[19] and the good that inheres in the politically active citizen. Important elements to consider in our case studies therefore include: how they were composed, the rationale for this model of composition, and the degree of representativeness they might claim in relation to the broader polity. Further specific questions flow from these issues: how will a micro-model be any more legitimate than governmental decision-making? Since those affected by a decision should have a say in it, what, if any, claims to representational authority will such a small group have? By definition, a micro-level process is not inclusive of all citizens. Therefore, is there a danger that a selected or self-selected group will claim a popular democratic legitimacy it simply does not possess? And in any case, is a legislature not itself a model of representative, small-group citizen deliberation—do elected politicians in the legislature not perform this function, backed by the legitimacy of popular endorsement at the ballot box? But as we have seen in the background to the BC process, the initiation of a Citizens Assembly was intended to provide an alternative to the heavily party-dominated politics of the legislature, through its composition by

---

[19] Per Dahl: 'everyone who is affected by the decisions of a government should have the right to participate in that government'. Robert A Dahl, *After the Revolution? Authority in a Good Society* (Yale University Press 1970) 64.

people who are not professional politicians and so are free of party ties and the constraints and inducements of, respectively, the whip or patronage systems. In other words, it was a response to the purported issues of legitimacy that the electoral system had been experiencing in recent times. Given that the BC model was entirely popular in composition, it is useful to assess both this radical populist model of micro-deliberation and the alternative traditional elite–civil society hybrid model used in Australia—which was intended to fit into the normal patterns of representative government rather than overtly supplant them—in light of this legitimacy debate.

The initiative for the BCCA came from the government of BC. The decision to set up the Assembly was effectively taken by the provincial Premier, and by definition in a system with one party controlling the legislature, the government had considerable leeway to design its structure. The degree to which the government kept its distance from the selection, deliberative, and decision-making processes of the Assembly is all the more notable, therefore. Even the model of membership for the BCCA was removed from the government's hands. This task was delegated to Gordon Gibson, a respected former politician, who consulted on the best mode of selection, looking to establish an assembly that would be independent, non-partisan, and yet still representative.[20] It was decided that rather than go with a model of peer selection and in the interest of greater representativeness, the Assembly should be composed of a random group of citizens 'in order to avoid electioneering and politicizing of the Assembly'.[21] Members were thus chosen randomly from the voter role, which also ruled out self-selection by particularly keen citizens. This general principle of randomness was subject to some modification. Gibson had recommended one member from each riding but at the recommendation of the chair of the Committee this was doubled to ensure gender equality, leading to 158 rather than 79 members, supplemented by two members from aboriginal communities to give a total of 160.[22]

The Australian model was very different. The ACC was established by the government which retained considerably more control over the process, including membership. The ACC had 153 delegates (including a Presiding Officer) on a mixed model appointment system. Half the delegates to the convention were popularly elected and the other half were appointed by the

---

[20] Gordon Gibson, 'Report on the Constitution of the Citizens' Assembly on Electoral Reform. Government of British Columbia' (Report, Citizens' Assembly on Electoral Reform 2002) <http://www.citizensassembly.bc.ca/resources/gibson_report.pdf> accessed 10 October 2011.

[21] Ratner, 'British Columbia's Citizens' Assembly', 21.

[22] The term 'near-random' selection may be more appropriate. Warren and Pearse, 'Introduction' in Warren and Pearse (eds), *Designing Deliberative Democracy*, 6.

government.[23] Of those appointed, 40 were members of parliament in the Commonwealth and state parliaments. Among Commonwealth representatives were party leaders as well as backbenchers, while state premiers and opposition leaders in addition to the chief ministers of the Australian Capital Territory and the Northern Territory were also appointed at sub-national level. The remaining 36 were chosen to represent a range of groups across civil society, including former politicians and judges, people from indigenous communities, and religious leaders.[24] The other half were elected through a national non-compulsory postal vote (in Australia voting is, of course, generally compulsory). The government's influence also extended to the appointment of the Presiding Officer. Again, this was a source of dispute in the Senate committee. The opposition was anxious to ensure that this role would not go to a government party member. In the end a respected former politician, Ian Sinclair, was appointed.

Evaluating the composition of these two assemblies it is clear that the BC model marks a high-water mark for relatively unmediated popular power in micro-level decision-making. The fact that citizens were selected at random removed the opportunity open to elites to shape the process by proxy, or for particular constituencies to be over-represented thanks to self-selection. A representative element was built in by selecting two citizens randomly from each riding, and through the achievement of gender balance. Criticisms were still levelled in relation to under-representation of aboriginal peoples and members from visible minorities on the Assembly.[25] It may be

---

[23] 'Report of the Australian Constitutional Convention 1998'.

[24] Bernard Cross, 'The Australian Republic Referendum, 1999' (2007) 78 Political Quarterly 556, 557; John Warhurst, 'From Constitutional Convention to Republic Referendum: A Guide to the Processes, the Issues and the Participants' (Parliamentary Library Research Paper 25 1998–99, Parliament of Australia 1999) 8–9 <http://www.aph.gov.au/library/pubs/rp/1998-99/99rp25.htm> accessed 10 October 2011.

[25] Lang, 'But Is It for Real?', 41. See also Michael Rabinder James, 'Descriptive Representation in the British Columbia Citizens' Assembly' in Warren and Pearse (eds), Designing Deliberative Democracy.
And despite the innovative and radical-selection model deployed, there have also been broader questions about the selection process as a whole. Initially 23,000 random citizens were invited to participate; of these 1,715 said they were interested, of the 964 that came to selection meetings the random selection for the BCCA was made. As Fishkin has pointed out, since those who took part were in effect volunteers, there are question marks as to how representative these people were of broader opinion. James S Fishkin, 'Deliberative Democracy and Constitutions' (2011) 28 Social Philosophy and Policy 242, 256. And data show that members of the BCCA were more likely to be white, older, university-educated and professional 'than the BC population as a whole'. Warren and Pearse, 'Introduction' in Warren and Pearse (eds), Designing Deliberative Democracy, 10. This highlights how difficult it is to achieve true representation at the micro level. Also, one commentator points to the lack of research on this: 'we know that only 7 per cent of the citizens randomly selected to participate in the Assembly ultimately chose to serve as members. But no data were collected on why the other 93 per cent chose not to serve.' JH Snider, 'Designing Deliberative Democracy: The British Columbia Citizens' Assembly' (2008) 4 J Public Deliberation 1. One criticism of such an appointment model is that random selection is not a representative model in the normal sense, which can also create an accountability gap. John Parkinson, Deliberating in the Real World: Problems of Legitimacy in Deliberative Democracy (OUP 2006).

that certain groups are more geographically concentrated than others. In such a case there is possibly an argument for a more proportional mode of representation (particularly in an Assembly debating proportional representation), rather than simply taking two people from each constituency. On the other hand, it might be thought that once random selection is departed from and attempts are made to select people according to identities and interests, then this would change the dynamic of an assembly that intends to bring together a group of random and disinterested citizens, free of the weight of dedicated representation, to debate and deliberate freely as 'a public',[26] and could instead create the risk of interest groups and factions within the assembly itself.

By contrast, appointed members of the ACC were chosen on an overtly representative basis by the government, while the remainder stood for election in a representative capacity. Nonetheless, the way in which the government appointees were selected was not particularly controversial, including as it did a significant number of apolitical or non-aligned members. Also Ian Sinclair was viewed almost universally to have done a good and fair job as Presiding Officer.[27] The only particularly contentious issue was the use of the postal ballot. Some argued that the middle classes and those most motivated by the issue would take part at the expense of less educated voters, thus leading to a distorted convention.[28] On the other hand, it was argued that the Convention should be distinguished from parliament with its compulsory voting requirement and reflect the fact that its powers were merely advisory.[29] In the end, turnout for this vote was 46 per cent.[30] It is also notable that the representation that resulted was very diverse. Two campaign groups which each embraced a broad range of interests, the Australian Republican Movement (ARM) which we met earlier, and Australians for Constitutional Monarchy (ACM) which was also formed in the early 1990s, won most of the votes: the ARM 30.34 per cent and the ACM 22.51 per cent. Warhurst reports that in the election there were 609 candidates, including 80 groups and 176 non-aligned individuals.[31] This left scope for representation for many non-traditional groups, including

---

[26] Iris Marion Young, *Inclusion and Democracy* (OUP 2002) 20.

[27] John Uhr, 'The Constitutional Convention and Deliberative Democracy' (1998) 21 U New South Wales LJ 875.

[28] For some this would mean an assembly loaded with conservative members opposed to changing the constitution. Higley and Evans Case, 'Australia: The Politics of Becoming a Republic', 150.

[29] Australian Senate Legal and Constitutional Legislation Committee, 'Report on the Constitutional Convention (Election) Bill 1997' (Senate, May 1997) 10.

[30] For a discussion of the break-down in voting see Glenn Patmore, 'Choosing the Republic: The Legal and Constitutional Steps in Australia and Canada' (2006) 31 Queen's LJ 770, 775–6.

[31] Warhurst, 'From Constitutional Convention to Republic Referendum', 8.

Women for a Just Republic, the Greens, Bill of Rights, Indigenous Peoples, Voice of Ordinary Fair-Minded Thinking Citizens, and An Open Mind for the Future.[32] These elected members gave the Convention a broader political membership, particularly when coupled with the non-aligned and apolitical appointed members, than one would find in a parliamentary process.

By the measure of popular participation it would seem at first sight that the BCCA is clearly a preferable composition model. But at the same time it is vital to bear in mind that any such process must be assessed against the broader constitutional environment from which it emerges and the issue at stake. It is also important to recall that direct democracy and active citizen participation does not take place in a vacuum but in close symbiosis with institutions of representative democracy; and that a micro-process should properly have a representative element if it is to meet the goal of allowing those affected by a decision to have a say in making it. In light of these factors and in relation to their own specific contexts, both models in different ways have much to commend themselves. In BC the issue to be determined was electoral reform—to improve the representational nature of the votes of ordinary citizens, set against the backdrop of a perceived popular disenchantment with elements of the existing electoral system. In other words, its subject matter was the enhancement of the popular voice, and so this can be presented as one issue where an exclusively popular model of deliberative decision-making was particularly appropriate. By contrast, the Australian model sought to accommodate traditional political alignments while bringing these actors together with non-aligned persons and non-conventional interest groups in a mixed appointment/electoral, conventional elite/unconventional elite model. This reflects the fact that deliberation was taking place on matters of the highest constitutional consequence for the nation as a whole, which also concerned Australia's relations with the UK and the monarch. In addition to being highly sensitive, the matters under consideration presaged potentially highly complex institutional change, fitting a new and possibly presidential head of state model onto an existing parliamentary system.

In light of this, one possible criticism of the BCCA is that it did not account for the need to build a link between popular and elite deliberation. The decision of the BCCA was, of course, final and the alternative model of electoral reform it produced was one which the government was obliged to put to a referendum. However, the recommendation that the BC Assembly came up with was radical when compared to the alternative vote model

---

[32] Patmore, 'Choosing the Republic', 775–6.

favoured by many in the political classes and there is an argument that it was not entirely realistic. The focus of much of the deliberation was on the impact of different systems on groups defined by gender, ethnicity, and culture, and much less on how it would affect political parties and in turn the political system itself, as well as class-based interests around which party systems have tended to evolve. One might well conclude that there is nothing wrong with this. It is for the group to speak to the interests they feel make up the demos. But there are still serious questions to be asked about excluding party interests and voices from an issue that is so central to electoral politics in a representative system.[33] This is, of course, always a risk in a fully popular process. And a deliberative commitment to popular participation in constitutional decision-making is not a commitment to *exclusively* popular models of decision-making. The ACC clearly had a model of composition that attempted to balance civic (if not directly 'popular') and party elite inputs. The ACC model, therefore, reminds us very clearly that popular deliberation in constitutional matters, particularly in constitution-changing rather than polity or constitution-forming moments, must always be seen as part of, and not abstracted from, the deeper current of representative democracy that characterizes the modern polity.

When considering the appropriate composition of a micro-deliberative model with the power to set the issue and perhaps even the question for a referendum, clearly the BCCA model fits with an intuitive sense of maximizing the popular role. But it seems that it is not the only model that serves to enhance the prospect of a more diffuse level of deliberation on the referendum issue, involving directly or indirectly the voices of ordinary people and civil society; and in light of the absence of political parties from the BCCA deliberation there are also strong arguments for a mixed popular/elite model in order better to represent the different interests at stake and to set these in the context of the overarching constitutional and political system of the polity. Since the ACC also reflected some popular element both in its elected dimension and in the presence of non-traditional elites, one might also envisage other variations, involving hybrids of the two models, combining a randomly selected popular element with an elite element which itself includes civil society representation. Of course, this in turn leads to many questions about how the latter component would be selected, the numerical balance between the different popular and elite

---

[33] This has caused commentators to ask whether the final model which might be characterized as 'anti-party' was a result of the exclusion of any party representation from the proceedings: 'there was no consistent presence in the assembly able to counter the negative sentiments about political parties with real personal experience'. Henry Milner, 'Electoral Reform and Deliberative Democracy in British Columbia' (2005) 94 National Civic Rev 3, 8.

groupings, and the mode of decision-making appropriate for such a model. In the end it is for each polity to determine how best to compose a micro-process in framing a referendum issue. But the BCCA model has shown that a popular model can work, while other innovative processes, such as the ACC, suggest that options for integrating the voice of ordinary citizens into such a process are many and varied.

(b) Public reasoning: reflection and discussion

Perhaps the most damaging criticism of referendums from the perspective of deliberative democracy theory is that they foster merely an aggregative model of decision-making ('the deliberation deficit' per Chapter 2). The core value of deliberative democracy, by contrast, is that decision-making should be conditioned by public reason, offering the opportunity for reflection and discussion before people cast their votes. We are therefore now concerned with the *content* of deliberation. How do participants in the micro-process engage: are they well informed; do they learn more about the issue during the deliberation process; are they open to the ideas of others while being resistant to possible 'elite capture' and the excessive influence of 'experts'; and are they in particular prepared to revise their opinions of the issue at stake in light of evidence and debate?

Dryzek makes the important point that in the real world, as opposed to the world of theoretical ideals, a deliberative process should not be over-burdened with prerequisites: 'The only condition for authentic deliberation is...the requirement that communication induce reflection upon preferences in non-coercive fashion.'[34] For him a key value is authenticity. To ensure that participation has the potential to be influential it must be well-intentioned on all sides. Each participant must take part in a spirit of goodwill, with a degree of openness to the persuasive value of other opinions. In this sense we move from the thin notion of participation as simply voting to the thicker idea of *meaningful* participation as discussion that is open to compromise, a search for consensus, and the possible transformation of preferences. Another expression of this idea is to be found in Iris Marion Young's idea of reasonableness as being about disposition not substance,[35] encapsulated in a willingness to listen and engage without judging too quickly.

---

[34] John S Dryzek, *Deliberative Democracy and Beyond: Liberals, Critics and Contestations* (OUP 2000) 1–2. Jane Mansbridge et al, 'The Place of Self-Interest and the Role of Power in Deliberative Democracy' (2010) 18 J Political Philosophy 64, 94, who stress the importance of avoiding coercion.

[35] Young, *Inclusion and Democracy*, 24. Benhabib has taken the view that deliberation means it must be possible to think 'from the standpoint of all involved'. Seyla Benhabib, 'Deliberative Rationality and Models of Democratic Legitimacy' (1994) 1 Constellations 26, 33. It is notable that these writers also embrace non-rational forms of communication, eg Dryzek's conception of deliberation can embrace

Composition of the group is central to this, of course, but so too is process. Careful design of the chairing and participation rules in a micro-process are important, as are educational elements involving expert panellists and informational material.[36] Process models can be designed so as not to favour the most vocal and the best arguers to the 'disadvantage of the inarticulate'.[37]

One of the purported strengths of a micro-process at the agenda-setting stage in a referendum is that it can foster this kind of public reasoning in a way often considered impossible in referendums. The BCCA and ACC again offer insights here. The BCCA is particularly interesting in this context in offering a window through which to consider whether genuine deliberation can be introduced among ordinary citizens within a referendum process. It is also notable for the way in which it fostered deliberation in three distinct phases: an educational phase, a hearings phase, and a decision-making phase, each of which was designed to encourage discussion and reflection.

The educational phase took place between 10 January and 21 March 2004. This involved discussions mediated by staff—often graduate students in political science specializing in electoral politics—and also presentations by a staff member or experts on a particular issue coupled with question-and-answer sessions with experts. Lectures were also delivered by experts including academics, discussing the pros and cons of adversarial versus consensual politics, the differences between majoritarian and proportional representation systems, and the impact of different electoral systems on party politics and government accountability. An account of the process is offered by Ratner, himself a professor of sociology, who attended the hearings and conducted some interview research with participants. According to his study, some in the discussion groups found the lectures difficult. But despite this, with a fairly lengthy educational period and a lot of small-group discussion mediated as it was by informed staff, he concludes that

---

emotional expression and story-telling provided it induces 'reflection upon preferences in non-coercive fashion'. Dryzek, *Deliberative Democracy and Beyond* ibid. Young also stresses the importance of including alternative forms of communication. Young, *Inclusion and Democracy*, 71–6. See also Mansbridge et al, 'The Place of Self-Interest', 67–8.

[36] As Barber argues, 'there is only one route to democracy: education'. Benjamin R Barber, *An Aristocracy of Everyone: The Politics of Education and the Future of America* (OUP 1992) 15. Relatedly he has argued that direct political participation is itself 'a completely successful form of civic education for democracy'. Benjamin R Barber, *Strong Democracy: Participatory Politics for a New Age* (University of California Press 1984) 235–6.

[37] Ian O'Flynn, *Deliberative Democracy and Divided Societies* (Edinburgh University Press 2006) 6; Young, *Inclusion and Democracy*, 37–40. For a discussion on how to reduce the danger of polarization in a deliberative forum by fashioning a process to include moderators, by bringing people together randomly, and by restricting voting see Cass R Sunstein, 'The Law of Group Polarization' (2002) 10 J Political Philosophy 175.

there were 'surprisingly few difficulties that members encountered as they passed through the learning phase of their collective experience'.[38] Another positive feature was the near-perfect attendance of delegates throughout;[39] which offers indirect evidence that members of the BCCA were committed to the process.

It is notable that from the beginning delegates were asked by facilitators in the small groups into which they were divided for discussion, to reflect on the kinds of values that members ought to share and display together. These groups reported back at a plenary session the following values: 'respect, open-mindedness, listening, commitment, inclusivity, positive attitude, integrity, and focus on mandate'. These were then, with slight revision, adopted by the Assembly.[40] At the end of this stage the Assembly was charged with issuing an interim report which was published as an eight-page 'Preliminary Statement to the People of British Columbia', setting out arguments for and against reform and inviting input from citizens. At this point the Assembly was unwilling to commit to a preference for a particular alternative electoral system, but still this document was released so that the citizens of BC who wished to take part in the hearings stage could do so, duly informed as to where the Assembly's deliberations had taken it.

The hearings phase, over a two-month period, broadened things out to include other citizens and groups who could come and speak to the BCCA. Also, a total of 1,603 written public submissions were received.[41] By this point the BCCA seems to have developed a strong non-partisan culture so that members were alert to the presence of interest groups appearing before the Assembly whom they treated with some degree of scepticism. Indeed, it was clear also that a partisan approach by those addressing the Assembly could backfire.[42]

The BCCA continued to deliberate into the autumn with a view to preparing recommendations to deliver to the Attorney General by 15 December 2004. This was the final phase of discussion and reflection. By now the members had narrowed their choice down to mixed-member proportional representation (MMP) and STV. The BCCA met for a further

---

[38] Ratner, 'British Columbia's Citizens' Assembly', 24.

[39] ibid 24.

[40] ibid 23. See also Lawrence LeDuc, 'Electoral Reform and Direct Democracy in Canada: When Citizens Become Involved' (2011) 34 West European Politics 551.

[41] Milner, 'Electoral Reform and Deliberative Democracy', 5.

[42] Lang notes the hostility towards the Green Party, which campaigned so vociferously for a particular model that this approach may in fact have been self-defeating, turning Assembly members against it. Lang, 'But Is It for Real?'; see also Milner, 'Electoral Reform and Deliberative Democracy', 6.

two weekends to set out a preferred design. These were plenary sessions and the discussions were open to the public.

Turning to Australia, the ACC was given the task of addressing three main issues: whether Australia should become a republic; which republic model should be put to the electorate to consider against the status quo; and in what time frame and under which circumstances might any change be considered. This is clearly a remit that combines issues of principle, of substantive detail, and of procedure. Although its deliberations were not binding on the government, its role proved to be very important in informing how the head of state issue would in the end be framed for the referendum.

The process was more heavily influenced by the government than it was in BC. The government retained the power to select the presiding officer and set the agenda of business. Nevertheless, commentators have noted how the Convention, which did have the power to determine its own rules of procedure, developed its own dynamic to some extent, using its power to determine its own rules of procedure to raise a number of issues for itself.[43]

> Much of the debate, and indeed the final Communiqué, strayed beyond [the] narrow confines [set by the government], as a kind of proof that particularly the popularly elected delegates would not be prevented from raising a wider range of issues for constitutional change.[44]

It is also interesting that the period for deliberation was much shorter than that in BC, with the ACC meeting for ten working days, 2–13 February 1998; and nor was there an educational or hearings phase as there was in BC. The former is no surprise, as most of those appointed or elected were generally already experts on the issue. The absence of a hearings phase is perhaps more notable as this meant that ordinary citizens had less opportunity to petition the convention with their own views.

It is difficult to make too many comparisons between processes with such deep differences in composition, remit, and modus operandi but each seem to have displayed considerable strengths from the perspective of civic republican deliberation. The deliberations of the BCCA certainly seem to have been entirely free of party political interference.[45]

Independence is one thing, neutrality another. It is, of course, vital in such a situation that a citizens' assembly is not 'captured' by experts who seek to

---

[43] Uhr, 'The Constitutional Convention and Deliberative Democracy'.

[44] ibid.

[45] Dennis Thompson, 'Who Should Govern Who Governs? The Role of Citizens in Reforming the Electoral System' in Warren and Pearse (eds), *Designing Deliberative Democracy*, concludes that members were generally free to consider options and were not subjected to excessive external influence.

influence the choices that are made. According to Lang: 'the Assembly staff made a point of not divulging their own opinions about electoral systems, even when directly questioned by participants. In interviews, most participants felt that the group had made a decision that was authentically theirs.'[46]

The evidence also suggests that delegates approached the deliberative process in a dedicated way. The principles and values which were set out at the beginning of the BCCA's deliberations seem to reflect the commitments to authenticity and reasonableness which deliberative theorists highlight. It is also important that delegates were provided with information and that they were sceptical—in the eyes of some, too sceptical—of interest groups in the hearings phase. An acquiescent susceptibility to elite influence was certainly avoided. On the other hand, there is clearly a negative dimension to this if a non-partisan culture becomes in effect an anti-interest group and even anti-political party culture. This may be a consequence of a composition model that is so exclusively popular, detaching members from the reality that any electoral system they are proposing to be put to a referendum must be designed for a living political system wherein parties and interest groups engage and compete perfectly legitimately on a day-to-day basis.

Ratner's survey work after the BCCA had concluded its deliberations comprised telephone interviews with 18 members of the Assembly, which is roughly a 10 per cent sample 'reflecting the main characteristics of the CA member profile'. The general impression he got was of people feeling honoured to have been selected who

> came to value the intellectual enrichment and sense of kinship with other members that the experience provided. The decisions that they reached together gave substance to the rhetoric of 'citizen empowerment', and the consensual nature of their decision-making, in what started out as a gathering of virtual strangers, was a testament to the devotion of staff and the unflagging commitment of the delegates.[47]

The exit interviews done by Ratner suggest that members themselves approached the issues in good faith and in addition to being free of coercion, also attempted to overcome self-deception.

---

[46] Lang, 'But Is It for Real?', 53, and at 56 notes: 'Assembly members interviewed felt that the staff did not give away a particular preference for any electoral system or overemphasize particular criteria for evaluating electoral systems.'

[47] Ratner, 'British Columbia's Citizens' Assembly', 25; Blais, Carty, and Fournier, who carried out extensive surveys of BCCA members throughout the process, conclude that the reasoning of the Assembly is reflected in the fact that it made a 'reasonable and intelligent choice'. André Blais, R Kenneth Carty, and Patrick Fournier, 'Do Citizens Assemblies Make Reasoned Choices?' in Warren and Pearse (eds), *Designing Deliberative Democracy*, 144.

The ACC deliberations have been subjected to less detailed scrutiny, but generally the level of debate was received with approval: it was televised and as a result 'it attracted considerable and favourable attention from both the media and the public who were able to watch the proceedings from the visitors' galleries'.[48] The final communiqué of the Convention itself observed the 'wide participation by delegates' in the deliberations of the Convention and while debate was robust it was conducted with 'a strong spirit of civility and compromise'.[49]

(c) Equality and parity of esteem

This principle of deliberative democracy responds to another criticism of referendums, their tendency to override the interests of minorities—'the majoritarian danger'. For deliberative democrats it is vital that those who deliberate enter the forum and participate as equals: 'Participation in such deliberation is governed by the norms of equality and symmetry; all have the same chance to initiate speech acts, to question, interrogate, and to open debate.'[50] In other words, people need to feel they are being taken seriously and are being treated with respect in the deliberative process.

This again links to republican values. For example, the importance of non-domination to both republicans (Iris Marion Young[51]) and deliberative democrats (Dryzek) requires that the complexity of society be taken into account and if necessary that the structure of a deliberation process moves beyond formal equality to take difference seriously in order that all groups in society are able to participate fully and freely and in order that the history of their marginalization is taken fully into account in the design of process models.[52] Dryzek again addresses this in the context of non-coercion which exists where domination through 'manipulation, indoctrination, propaganda, deception, expressions of mere self-interest, threats, and the imposition of ideological conformity are all absent'.[53]

---

[48] Warhurst, 'From Constitutional Convention to Republic Referendum', 9.

[49] Cited by Uhr, 'The Constitutional Convention and Deliberative Democracy'.

[50] Seyla Benhabib, *Democracy and Difference: Contesting the Boundaries of the Political* (Princeton University Press 1996) 70.

[51] We observed in Chapter 2 that non-domination is of course also a key republican value; indeed for Pettit it is *the* central republican virtue. Philip Pettit, *Republicanism: A Theory of Freedom and Government* (OUP 1997).

[52] Melissa S Williams, 'The Uneasy Alliance of Group Representation and Deliberative Democracy' in Will Kymlicka and Wayne Norman (eds), *Citizenship in Diverse Societies* (OUP 2000). Note Sanders, however, who is sceptical of the very possibility of such a model. Lynn M Sanders, 'Against Deliberation' (1997) 25 Political Theory 347.

[53] Dryzek, *Deliberative Democracy and Beyond*, 8. See also Jürgen Habermas, *The Theory of Communicative Action* (Thomas McCarthy tr, Polity Press 1984).

This is one of the more contested areas of deliberative democracy since it finds itself situated within the highly charged environment of identity politics. This in turn leads to debates between those satisfied by formal equality and those who assert that equality must be 'differentiated' (Chapter 3) to account for deep imbalances within society and also the fact that many people see their individuality as mediated through groups to which they belong. In this sense participation must not only be based upon equality in the formal sense, but must also be meaningful in giving diverse and often weak groups an equal chance of affecting the outcome.[54] This principle suggests that when constituting a micro-deliberative process in the framing of a referendum issue, those doing so should be attentive to how this might promote equality, facilitate non-domination or coercion, and include minorities in a meaningful way, so that they are not overwhelmed by the discussion opportunities and voting power of majorities.[55]

In this context the BCCA process will be our focus rather than the ACC, given that the former was composed of ordinary citizens. In the BCCA process equality in terms of gender representation at least was emphasized in the composition phase. Arguments were made for the inclusion of members of specific minority groups, but this served to highlight how difficult it can be to reach consensus on this and in the end specific representation was only extended to aboriginal peoples. The Assembly was not intended to be a meeting of different interest groups. Since any move from random selection can be a minefield in terms of determining the bases of inclusion and exclusion, it may be the case that paying heed to this principle of differentiated equality in such a micro-process is only really appropriate within divided societies such as Bosnia or Northern Ireland, where histories of minority oppression are very real or for particular minorities such as aboriginal peoples who have suffered deep structural historical injustice within otherwise undivided societies such as BC.[56] It is notable, however, that four aboriginal people were chosen based on those who put themselves forward. But this begs further questions about representativeness. Were they being included as 'ordinary citizens'? There does

---

[54] Dryzek, *Deliberative Democracy and Beyond*, 172. He also moots the idea of need for material equality as 'poverty can inhibit communicative capacity'. Young also takes the view that: 'In actually existing democracies there tends to be a reinforcing circle between social and economic inequality and political inequality that enables the powerful to use formally democratic processes to perpetuate injustice or preserve privilege.' Young, *Inclusion and Democracy*, 17.

[55] The dangers of this are drawn by Sanders, 'Against Deliberation', 353–4.

[56] There is also an issue of how accountable voices from civil society can be when taking part in deliberative politics and also the risk that these people will be co-opted by other elites. Christine Bell and Catherine O'Rourke, 'The People's Peace? Peace Agreements, Civil Society, and Participatory Democracy' (2007) 28 Int'l Political Science Rev 293, 294–5.

not seem to have been an attempt to include people on the basis of representation of particular aboriginal interests. There are many native bands in BC and these do not automatically share the same interests or views.

At the deliberation phase of the BCCA process there were efforts to determine the views of other aboriginal people. Interestingly delegates themselves were keen to pursue this issue. Some took the initiative to speak to local aboriginal groups to find out their positions on electoral issues, while staff from the BCCA also offered presentations and invited submissions on their preferences regarding the electoral system. According to one commentator both delegates and staff concluded that: 'Aboriginal groups were not ready to deal with the issue of electoral reform and had higher political priorities', but he concluded: 'Despite the lack of vocalization, aboriginal interests were legitimately on the agenda.'[57] Of course, this final observation does raise a broader question of how important the whole issue of electoral reform was to aboriginal people, for so long excluded from mainstream politics.

Lang analysed participation in this third, deliberation phase. She found that

> comments were distributed by age groups, minority status and region pretty much in proportion to the presence of these groups in the Assembly—for all groups except the oldest age cohort, there was no more than a 4 percentage point difference between that group's share of the assembly and share of total comments.[58]

There was some discrepancy on grounds of gender however, with women offering only 41–2 per cent of the comments made.[59] We might wonder what lay behind this discrepancy and whether it might have been alleviated by more effective chairing. Also we should bear in mind that these bare statistics do not tell us how effective each contribution was; the loudest and longest interventions are not necessarily the best informed or most persuasive. The fact that by region and age contributions to discussions were fairly pro rata also suggests a culture of non-domination.

In general then the BCCA is notable for meeting high standards of non-domination and avoiding coercion. We have noted the absence of governmental control and broader political interference, and also the scope for all to participate, the absence of manipulation or coercion, and genuine, if not perfect, attempts to engage minorities in the issue.

(d) Consent and collective decision-making

This republican value of consent builds upon that of participation; not only should those affected by decisions be able to participate in the making of

---

[57] Lang, 'But Is It for Real?', 19.   [58] ibid 15.   [59] ibid 15.

them, those bound by a decision should, ideally, consent to it. In this way we move to the end of deliberation, from talking to voting. A micro-process which is set the task of framing the referendum issue to be put to the people must in the end reach decisions. This is a consequence of real-world deliberation. Deliberative theorists are alive to this and hope for agreement. Broad consensus is perhaps too much to aim for, but agreement may still be achievable by way of compromise and perhaps even a transformation in preferences. But that is not to dismiss the fact that there can indeed be a significant tension between the openness of a participatory process, and the final outcome of the process. Voting in the end, of course, forecloses deliberation, and it is often seen to be inimical to a deliberative process; we have noted Chambers' idea that deliberative democracy should be talk-centric, not vote-centric. So although a micro-process must end in a decision, and that decision may well need a vote, this decision-making process should be one that builds upon the openness and goodwill generated in the deliberative discussions, and should focus upon reaching agreement through discussion where possible and maintaining the trust and acceptance of those whose preferences are not in the end met.

The BCCA process seems to encapsulate such an approach. A nine-month period of deliberation was clearly focused upon reaching consensus. Thus when it came to a vote on the model which a plurality of members had agreed upon—a vote that would, of course, be determinative—there was resounding support for the proposal of one particular model of voting reform with the STV model being endorsed on 23 October 2004 by 123 to 31 as the best alternative to first past the post.

The ACC process was more contentious, reflecting how controversial the issue was and that the Convention's make-up was largely partisan. Perhaps as a result, voting was more heavily used than in the BCCA. The Convention concluded Yes to the first issue of Australia becoming a republic (89 to 52 with 11 abstentions). There was much debate over the second more specific issue as to which model to follow, and indeed this was the issue on which the referendum would ultimately fail. The Convention favoured an indirect model for selection of the President—so-called 'Bipartisan Appointment' rather than direct election (supported by 73 to 57 with 22 abstentions).[60]

That is not to say the decision was taken in a rancorous way. Although the final model was carried without a majority of delegates, there was agreement to disagree. When it came to deciding whether to recommend

---

[60] There was also agreement on a preamble to be put to the people. Warhurst, 'From Constitutional Convention to Republic Referendum', 10; Patmore, 'Choosing the Republic', 775.

to the Prime Minister and Parliament that this model be put to a referendum, the Convention voted Yes by 133 votes to 17 with two abstentions.[61] Clearly those whose preference had not been successful were still prepared to endorse the outcome of the votes taken: agreement to, if not with, the result of the deliberations, per Bellamy.[62]

But what is also interesting is that the Convention recommended ongoing revision. If the republican system of government were indeed introduced by referendum, the Commonwealth Government should convene a further Constitutional Convention in the next three to five years as a continuing process of constitutional review.[63] One feature for which referendums are often criticized from the perspective of deliberative democracy, especially in the constitutional context, is the way in which they can act to foreclose debate on a major issue. This particular proposal is therefore significant for the way it seeks to avoid finality, emphasizing that in a republican democracy constitutional change should be an ongoing dialogical process and not just one grand-standing event.

The ACC, in contrast to the BCCA, only had power to recommend a model to be put to a referendum, the final decision resting with parliament—it was after all designed to fit within rather than supplant established patterns of representative democracy. Nonetheless, its advice seemed to be politically binding on the government and was treated in this way. The model of head of state which it recommended was the one that was put to the people. But the government—with the Attorney-General taking the lead—was still able to frame the question based on this model, which led to some controversy on the question's wording. This is another important issue from the deliberative perspective. Empowering the micro-group to frame the very referendum question may be problematic both from the perspective of expertise and also for the extent to which this bypasses representative government, perhaps skewing the balance of power too much towards a small group. On the other hand, to leave this matter in the hands of the government can cause a slip between cup and lip allowing the executive to frame the question in a prejudicial way. But as we will see when we return to this issue in Chapter 9, although the Prime

---

[61] 'Report of the Australian Constitutional Convention 1998'.

[62] 'The test of a political process is not so much that it generates outcomes we agree *with* as that it produces outcomes that all can agree *to*, on the grounds that they are legitimate.' Richard Bellamy, *Political Constitutionalism: A Republican Defence of the Constitutionality of Democracy* (CUP 2007) 164. See also Ailsa Henderson, 'Referendums and Losers' Consent: Understanding Risk and Satisfaction with Democracy' (Referendums and Deliberative Democracy workshop, University of Edinburgh, 8 May 2009).

[63] 'Report of the Australian Constitutional Convention 1998'.

Minister in Australia was able to frame the question, in light of the detailed nature of the proposal it arrived at, the publicity this attracted, and the popularity of the ACC process, his room for manoeuvre was tightly circumscribed.

(iii) The proliferation of micro-level deliberative fora

The British Columbia and Australian cases are the best examples of micro-level deliberation being built into large-scale referendum processes. But the use of such fora has proliferated in other contexts in recent years with a number of experiments using different types of small-group citizen deliberation. This has come on the back of renewed academic interest in the subject and the recommendation of different models by academics. The idea of citizens' assemblies was advanced by Benjamin Barber over 25 years ago.[64] Barber, as an early and major figure in the revival of republican interest in popular deliberative democracy, argued that ordinary citizens were capable of and should be encouraged to make 'reasonable political judgements' and that a deliberative forum, bringing ordinary citizens together in an assembly of some kind, would be the place to nourish this.[65] Since then other modifications of this idea have been put forward. We have seen proposals for citizen juries,[66] citizen panels,[67] deliberative polls,[68] and other models of mini-publics[69] which are all variations around this idea.[70]

The claim that small-group deliberation can indeed work to produce decisions that meet the key principles of deliberative democracy hangs upon empirical evidence. In particular, a strong claim for the success of these initiatives would emerge with evidence that they can involve the

---

[64] Barber, *Strong Democracy*, 267–98.

[65] Earlier we find the idea of a small, randomly selected citizen advisory council in Dahl, *After the Revolution?*, 122–3. He called this a 'minipopulus' in Robert A Dahl, *Democracy and Its Critics* (Yale University Press 1989) 340.

[66] Graham Smith and Corinne Wales, 'Citizens' Juries and Deliberative Democracy' (2000) 48 Political Studies 51; Eric Ghosh, 'Deliberative Democracy and the Countermajoritarian Difficulty: Considering Constitutional Juries' (2010) 30 OJLS 327.

[67] John Gastil, *By Popular Demand: Revitalizing Representative Democracy through Deliberative Elections* (University of California Press 2000).

[68] James S Fishkin, *When the People Speak: Deliberative Democracy and Public Consultation* (OUP 2009).

[69] Robert E Goodin and John S Dryzek, 'Making Use of Mini-publics' in Robert E Goodin (ed), *Innovating Democracy: Democratic Theory and Practice after the Deliberative Turn* (OUP 2008) esp 16–19.

[70] For discussion of the wide variety of micro-deliberative models which have been formulated and experiments that have taken place see Robert E Goodin and John S Dryzek, 'Deliberative Impacts' in Shawn Rosenberg (ed), *Deliberation, Participation and Democracy: Can the People Govern?* (Palgrave Macmillan 2007); John S Dryzek, *Foundations and Frontiers of Deliberative Governance* (OUP 2011) 155–76.

changing of minds (transformation of preferences) in line with the principle of public reasoning. A less ambitious but still important goal stemming from the other principles we have addressed (participation, equality, and consent) would be to show that those who take part, and indeed other citizens looking on, feel positive about the process, perhaps even to the point of increasing levels of losers' consent among those whose goals were not achieved by the process; while evidence of the negative effect of these processes by these three criteria would be that they serve to polarize opinion, leaving considerable dissatisfaction with the process in contrast to one carried out by traditional political elites.

There are data measuring positive and negative impacts of the ACC on participants and non-participating citizens.[71] Among matters we have considered is the fact that 133 members of the ACC voted to put the Convention's decision to a referendum, which itself suggests high levels of satisfaction even among losers. We have also seen data such as that offered by Ratner which record positive endorsements by participants of the deliberative qualities of the BCCA. In addition, there is other empirical work carried out by way of experiments which has tested micro-processes more broadly, focusing mainly upon the transformation of preferences. James Fishkin, initially with Robert Luskin and then together with a number of other research teams, has developed the 'deliberative poll' whereby a random sample of people is first polled on a particular issue and then invited to deliberate together. Then a second poll is taken, and the resulting changes of opinion are treated as evidence of the influence of these discussions.[72] The evidence from the polls the Fishkin teams have carried out does indicate that there are high levels of attitude mutation among participants. As Fishkin and Luskin put it: people 'learn from the articulation of interests very different from their own when they speak across social cleavages, class differences and geographical boundaries'.[73] It is, of course, another matter to extrapolate such a small-scale process to a national electoral event. But one interesting project was undertaken in Australia at the time of the referendum in 1999,[74] and the data suggest that among those who participated in

---

[71] David Gow, Clive Bean, and Ian McAllister, *Australian Constitutional Referendum Study, 1999* (Australian Social Science Data Archive 2000).

[72] James S Fishkin and Robert C Luskin, 'Experimenting with a Democratic Ideal: Deliberative Polling and Public Opinion' (2005) 40 Acta Politica 284.

[73] James S Fishkin and Robert C Luskin, 'The Quest for Deliberative Democracy' in Michael Saward (ed), *Democratic Innovation: Deliberation, Representation and Association* (Routledge 2000) 26. See also Gastil, *By Popular Demand*.

[74] Project organized by Issues Deliberation Australia in collaboration with the Research School of Social Sciences at the Australian National University, 1999.

deliberative processes at that time many did indeed change their view of the matter, voting differently from the way in which they had originally intended. As Ackerman and Fishkin report: 'The results showed that deliberation made a big difference. The microcosm of Australia gathered in Canberra for a weekend of deliberations massively increased their support for a republic that was independent of the British Crown.'[75] The percentage saying Yes within this polling group went up from 56 per cent to 73 per cent, a statistic which held up against a control group that did not deliberate in this way.[76]

This is perhaps a window into how different the agenda-setting process might have been if a citizens' assembly in the BCCA style had been tried in Australia. Whether that would have been a good thing depends upon one's views on the respective merits of heavily popular versus more elite-representative models of issue-framing. But one notable feature of the deliberative poll is that it is modelled on a situation where decisions are reached at the end; in other words they are not merely talking shops. O'Flynn observes that the Fishkin research

> has provided considerable evidence showing not just that deliberation can lead to more informed decisions, but that it can also change the way in which people vote. Crucially, the deliberative poll does not prescribe consensus but instead assumes that deliberation will end in voting.[77]

He concludes: 'It suggests that there need be no inherent, unavoidable tension between the requirement of reciprocity and the act of voting.'[78] In all of these features interesting possibilities of building micro-deliberation into a referendum process are opened up.

III. EXTRAPOLATING DELIBERATION TO THE MACRO LEVEL: THE REFERENDUM CAMPAIGN

Although micro-processes such as the BCCA offer the opportunity of engaging ordinary citizens in framing the referendum issue, there remains a democratic gap. It has been asked: 'How can micro deliberation be democratic at all, given that it cannot include even a small number of

---

[75] Bruce Ackerman and James S Fishkin, *Deliberation Day* (Yale University Press 2004) 171.

[76] ibid 171. See also Robert C Luskin et al, 'Information Effects in Referendum Voting: Evidence from the Australian Deliberative Poll' (Annual Meeting of the American Political Science Association, Washington DC, 31 August–3 September 2000).

[77] O'Flynn, *Deliberative Democracy*, 86–7.

[78] ibid 88. However, for a voice sceptical of the value of such small-group deliberation or at least of the extent to which empirical evidence for its value has been conclusively offered see Chambers, 'Deliberative Democratic Theory', 318–20.

those affected, let alone all of them?'[79] And an important issue is representation. Dahl argues that 'The judgments of a minipopulus would "represent" the judgment of the demos... [and] would thus derive their authority from the legitimacy of democracy.'[80] But can we be so sure that this is accurate; as Fishkin has pointed out, 'internal validity' must be complemented by 'external validity'.[81]

A carefully crafted micro-level process, even one with credible representational legitimacy, is not itself an act of demotic constitutional authorship; it can only establish in a fair way the issue and perhaps the process guidelines for the mass exercise in popular deliberation that would constitute such an act. This begs the question: when the question is set and the referendum campaign put in motion, is any level of state-wide, mass popular deliberation also feasible? The very idea that a constitutional referendum can be an act of constitutional authorship by a public acting together hinges on the idea that millions of people can and will deliberate on the question. This is the key issue for civic republican deliberation, particularly in the ambitious attempt to situate it in a referendum process: it is not enough that a small group of citizens participate, the republican commitment is to the widespread participation of the people as a whole, so that the outcome of the deliberation can be seen as genuinely an act of collective decision-making.

However, it is in turning to the prospects for deliberation at the mass level that we encounter new difficulties. Parkinson alerts us to the dangers:

> if we attempt to increase the numbers involved and be more 'democratic', we run the risk of reopening the doors of the forum to manipulation of agendas, to speech-making rather than deliberation; to the attempt to sway an audience, often at the expense of, rather than out of feelings of reciprocity towards, one's interlocutors...; that is, to the pathologies of public debate that drove many to embrace normative deliberative democracy in the first place.[82]

There is also the question of the very possibility of such a process as raised by Walzer: 'Deliberation is not an activity for the demos... 100 million of them, or even 1 million or 100,000, cannot plausibly "reason together".'[83] To

---

[79] John Parkinson 'Beyond "Technique": The Role of Referendums in the Deliberative System' (Referendums and Deliberative Democracy workshop, University of Edinburgh, 8 May 2009); see also John Parkinson, 'Legitimacy Problems in Deliberative Democracy' (2003) 51 Political Studies 180.

[80] Dahl, *Democracy and Its Critics*, 342. But see Mark B Brown, 'Citizen Panels and the Concept of Representation' (2006) 14 J Political Philosophy 203.

[81] Fishkin, 'Deliberative Democracy and Constitutions', 251.

[82] Parkinson, 'Beyond "Technique"'. See also Michael Walzer, 'Deliberation, and What Else?' in Stephen Macedo (ed), *Deliberative Politics: Essays on 'Democracy and Disagreement'* (OUP 1999).

[83] Walzer, 'Deliberation, and What Else?', 68. Dryzek calls this the 'large scale' problem: John S Dryzek, 'Legitimacy and Economy in Deliberative Democracy' (2001) 29 Political Theory 651, 652. See also Colin

some extent it is simply a practical problem: how can one instigate such a process of national deliberation, finding time to do so etc in the course of a referendum campaign? Certainly it is impossible to set the same goals as those for small-group deliberation given the role of the small group in allowing each participant to raise issues and to have those subjected to critical exploration in dialogue with others.

Thus we seemingly have a paradox. To create the conditions for proper deliberative discussion we must sacrifice mass democracy, and to reach the level of inclusion demanded by democracy means surrendering the conditions for proper deliberation. But one place to begin questioning such a negative prognosis is to note a fundamental difference between a macro-process and a micro-process beyond merely the number of participants. A micro-process can be carefully designed and planned in fairly elaborate detail and can therefore be infused self-consciously with normative values either by elites framing the process or by the actors themselves, as we saw at the beginning of the BCCA's deliberations. At the macro level of mass society by contrast, although there is an opportunity to try to foster the conditions for deliberation, the capacity to do so is much less. What is feasible in this context needs to be assessed against the reality of what happens and how voters behave in a referendum campaign largely on their own initiative. As Parkinson explains:

> The macro account... is much more of an attempt to provide a new descriptive theory of democracy, one that accounts better than previous theories for the real processes of opinion formation, claim making and argumentation that go on in democracies, especially theories which focus solely on voting without considering how options come to a vote in the first place.[84]

Our account in this section will focus upon a different mode of deliberation from that assessed at the micro level. In moving from the second (agenda and question-setting) to the third (referendum campaign) stage, and in moving to a new setting (engaging the broader public rather than just a small group), it is appropriate that we also broaden out what is meant by deliberation itself, moving from the intuitive notion of a select group sitting in discussion round a table to a different way of conceptualizing the participation of citizens. It is in this context that we return to Robert Goodin's

---

Farrelly, 'Making Deliberative Democracy a More Practical Political Ideal' (2005) 4 European J Political Theory 200, 201.

[84] Parkinson, 'Beyond "Technique"', 4–5. That is not to suggest there will be no normative underpinning here. Parkinson continues: 'Certainly there is a strong normative current in macro deliberative thinking as well, but no descriptive theory is without normative anchors, no matter how vociferously its advocates pretend otherwise.' But these norms will be generated by organic societal values rather than by any top-down value-setting exercise.

work and in particular his breakdown of the idea of deliberation into two discrete but related components—'discussion' and 'consideration'. It is clearly the former that is taken to be the key component by most deliberative theorists, as we saw in our account of the principle of public reason expressed by Dryzek as 'recurrent communicative interaction'.[85] But for Goodin, deliberative theorists have perhaps placed undue emphasis on discussion when in fact consideration or reflection 'should enjoy pride of place' in accounts of deliberation.[86] What he calls 'internal-reflective deliberation' requires us to call up reasons from stored memory about why we think something. But this need not come only from interpersonal interaction.[87]

The kind of discursive deliberation that can take place within a small group is not possible, at least not in the same way, at the macro level. But still there is the possibility that people can be encouraged to reflect on the issues, to learn more about them, and then to engage in a more attenuated national process of communicative deliberation. If an environment is created whereby those expected to deliberate are provided with information and the time to reflect, then Goodin argues, on the basis of empirical evidence, it is feasible to expect them to deliberate internally. He addresses an Australian case study in deliberation as empirical evidence to support this claim. In this experiment a 'Far North Queensland Citizens' Jury' was established to address policy options for the use of a particular piece of land, the environmental impact of development plans etc. Jurors were polled at different stages of deliberation and addressing the data emerging from this exercise Goodin notes that attitudes shifted more during the 'information' phase than the 'discussion' phase.[88] Even if the final part of this process does not really happen, Goodin points out that consideration is itself a significant aspect of deliberation; since it can lead people to 'considered and settled judgements, not top-of-the-head or knee-jerk reactions'.[89] And such transformative effects may be enhanced if this process causes an individual to reflect internally on the perspective of others.

There are, of course, strong grounds for scepticism here: will people really be 'internally reflective', especially in a referendum campaign? But it is significant that Goodin sees this as a supplement to, rather than substitute for, communication. One reason for optimism in the referendum context is data which suggest that many people make up their minds in the course of a

---

[85] John S Dryzek, *Discursive Democracy* (CUP 1990) 43.
[86] Goodin, *Innovating Democracy*, 41.
[87] ibid 60.
[88] ibid 49–50, and see further discussion at 53 and 58.
[89] Robert E Goodin, *Reflective Democracy* (OUP 2003) 1.

referendum campaign. For example, LeDuc notes that over 50 per cent of voters did so in the course of the Quebec referendum in 1980, and about 30 per cent did so in the 1995 referendum campaign.[90] He notes also that in the course of the three-month referendum campaign in Spain on NATO membership in 1986, the national debate 'was capable of changing the result from almost certain defeat to a dramatic and unexpected victory'.[91] Indeed there is a broader argument that the referendum is in fact in some ways a good forum in which to engage people in important issues: 'Supporters of deliberative and participatory democracy would point out the developmental potential of political participation, and argue that initiatives and referendums encourage public debate on political issues, which increases people's competence.'[92] In this respect the interplay of the micro and macro stages might be fostered by the media. Fishkin reports how a Deliberative Poll held one week before the 1999 referendum in Australia had a lot of media coverage, which coincided with a big rise in support for the republican option.[93]

Nonetheless, there are environmental factors that will condition how successful attempts to induce deeper citizen reflection might be. We have seen that when the issue is one of high constitutional significance large numbers of people can become engaged, as evidenced, for example, by high turnout. On the other hand, this might have the counter-effect of entrenching already fixed views, particularly in divided societies.[94] One issue we

---

[90] Lawrence LeDuc, *The Politics of Direct Democracy: Referendums in Global Perspective* (Broadview Press 2003) 105 fn 12, and 106 fn 16, respectively.

[91] ibid 83. See also Claes H de Vreese, 'Context, Elites, Media and Public Opinion in Referendums: When Campaigns Really Matter' in Claes H de Vreese (ed), *The Dynamics of Referendum Campaigns: An International Perspective* (Palgrave Macmillan 2007) 11. And for discussion of an interesting case study see Goodin, *Innovating Democracy*, 42–55.

[92] Maija Setälä, 'On the Problems of Responsibility and Accountability in Referendums' (2006) 45 European J Political Research 699, 717. We have observed Setälä's general point about a referendum facilitating deliberation. This seems to be an argument for heightened opportunities for deliberation crossing over from elite to popular levels. And one aspect of this is that the very fact of a referendum may make politicians more deliberative as they frame the issue and engage in the campaign, since they will have to 'give public justifications for their policy choices'. Setälä, 'On the Problems of Responsibility', 718.

[93] Although he also observes how by the time of the referendum this effect dropped away and the measure was defeated. James S Fishkin, 'Consulting the Public through Deliberative Polling' (2003) 22 J Policy Analysis and Management 128, 131. Hug is sceptical that existing empirical evidence proves the transformative effect of referendums on citizens. Simon Hug, 'Some Thoughts About Referendums, Representative Democracy, and Separation of Powers' (2009) 20 Constitutional Political Economy 251.

[94] Also, not all political systems have achieved a level of democratic culture that can make the achievement of an elite-fostered model of deliberative democracy realistic. Merkel argues that the circumstances in Eastern Europe in the early 1990s were 'miles away from that kind of conceptual structure of public discourse which lifts the referendum out of manipulative ratification into the higher sphere of "deliberative politics", called for by Jürgen Habermas.' Wolfgang Merkel, 'Institutions and Democratic Consolidation in East Central Europe' (1996) Instituto Juan March de Estudios e Investigationes Estudio/Working Paper 86, 26 <http://www.march.es/ceacs/ingles/publicaciones/

discussed in terms of the participation component of the micro-process was education. The provision of voters with information on the issue at stake is also an important component of the macro-level process. As LeDuc notes: 'The argument that referendums are a superior device for democratic citizen participation depends heavily on the assumption that institutions and rules can be created to guarantee high levels of knowledge and participation.'[95] This recalls the competence and capacity arguments from Chapter 2. Even rejecting elitist notions that people are not competent to take part in political deliberation,[96] we need to heed Setälä's qualification about the time and energy people have to deliberate about political issues.[97] It seems that in order to generate *informed* reflection, education is therefore vital[98] as is providing enough time for this reflection to take place.[99] In fact, it has been argued that direct democracy without education to facilitate deliberation is potentially dangerous.[100] In other words, the opportunity for deliberation alone is not enough if it is not in fact fostered to maximize the quality of that deliberation; people must not only be given the opportunity to engage actively with an issue but also sufficient information with which to make informed choices. A final point to make, of course, is that it is important not to set the bar too high when assessing competent participation in referendums, and in particular that we do not impose higher standards than are expected of citizen engagement in other electoral processes.[101]

---

working/archivos/1996_86.pdf> accessed 11 October 2011. In is in this context that we will return to the specific pressures of decision-making in divided societies in Chapter 9.

[95] LeDuc, *The Politics of Direct Democracy*, 14.

[96] Setälä argues that competence 'may develop due to participation'. Setälä, 'On the Problems of Responsibility', 717.

[97] ibid 717.

[98] Barber, for instance, urges that people be encouraged to 'think publicly'. Barber, *Strong Democracy*, 152.

[99] Lithuania's referendum on constitutional reform in the early 1990s has been criticized inter alia because there were only 12 days available for public discussion of the constitutional draft between parliamentary approval and the referendum itself. Robert Elgie and Jan Zielonka, 'Constitutions and Constitution-Building: A Comparative Perspective' in Jan Zielonka (ed), *Democratic Consolidation in Eastern Europe* (OUP 2001) vol I, 41.

[100] Barber, *Strong Democracy*, 278.

[101] Lupia and Johnston warn us not to conflate information and competence. In the referendum context they say:

> A voter's choice is competent if it is the same choice that she would make given the most accurate available information about its consequences. Would she make the same decision if fully informed about the consequences of her actions? If yes, then her choice is competent.

And their research concludes 'that referendum voters are not as incompetent as commonly portrayed'. Arthur Lupia and Richard Johnston, 'Are Voters to Blame? Voter Competence and Elite Manoeuvres in Referendums' in Mendelsohn and Parkin (eds), *Referendum Democracy*, 191.

Clearly the level of information that can be transmitted at the micro level is significantly higher than at the macro. We saw with the BCCA how lectures were provided and experts were on hand to answer questions. But information can still be offered to the larger body of voters and here ordinary citizens in the micro-process might make useful recommendations based upon how they came to understand the issues.[102] Members of the BCCA, for example, were concerned about how successfully its deliberative processes could be rolled out. Ratner from his interviews reports: 'A prevalent concern was whether the public would be sufficiently enlightened about the issues to vote intelligently on a referendum motion, given that there was no formal budget for public education.'[103] A copy of its report was sent to every household in the province in advance of the May referendum.[104] This is a commonly used model; for example, the Belfast Agreement was also sent to every address in advance of the 1998 Northern Ireland referendum. However, there is an argument that it would be better to offer summarized information that is more digestible for voters, and ensure that the material is in fact informative rather than partisan; in other words 'attempting to improve the quality of information rather than the quantity'.[105] Voters make short cuts, and information should be geared towards allowing them to do so more effectively.[106]

It is notable that for all the energy put into the micro-process of the BCCA, the referendum process was notably less successful in fostering deliberation when the process moved to the referendum campaign.[107] Ian Ward cites one poll carried out the February before the May referendum where 'only half... of British Columbians say they [had] read, seen or heard anything about the British Columbia Citizens' Assembly on Electoral Reform'[108] and shortly before the referendum nearly two-thirds of British Columbians still knew 'very little' (39 per cent) or 'nothing' (25 per cent)

---

[102] See Goodin and Dryzek, 'Deliberative Impacts'. They chart the ways in which mini-publics can impact upon the 'macro' world of politics.

[103] Ratner, 'British Columbia's Citizens' Assembly', 25.

[104] Milner, 'Electoral Reform and Deliberative Democracy', 7.

[105] Lupia and Johnston, 'Are Voters to Blame?', 208.

[106] ibid 208.

[107] Dennis Pilon, 'The 2005 and 2009 Referenda on Voting System Change in British Columbia' (2010) 4 (2–3) Canadian Political Science Rev 73. See also Lang, 'But Is It for Real?'; Goodin and Dryzek, 'Deliberative Impacts'.

[108] Ipsos-Reid, 'BC Public Has A Lot To Learn About BC-STV' (*Ipsos*, 21 February 2005) <http://www.ipsos-na.com/news-polls/pressrelease.aspx?id=2566> accessed 10 October 2011, cited by Ian Ward, 'The British Columbia Citizens' Assembly on Electoral Reform. An Experiment in Political Communication' (Australasian Political Studies Association conference, University of Newcastle, 25–27 September 2006) <http://www.newcastle.edu.au/Resources/Schools/Newcastle%20Business%20School/APSA/PUBPOLICY/Ward-Ian.pdf> accessed 10 October 2011.

about the electoral system being proposed.[109] It seems that in this process and in the similar one in Ontario in 2007,[110] far more energy and resources were expended on the micro-process than in providing information, education, and in fostering deliberation at the macro level.[111] Ward concludes that this suggests

> a troubling disconnection between the public and the Citizen's Assembly. For all the efforts of its members and support staff to publicise its activities and to obtain public input through public hearings and submissions via the internet, significant numbers of British Columbians appear to have been unaware of the Assembly's existence and mission. This is a gap which will need to be closed if indeed citizens' assemblies are to be used in the future to counter the democratic deficit.[112]

Australian law also makes provision for such a distribution of information, traditionally allowing each of two campaign teams to present their view of the issue. Until 1999, for any referendum campaign the government was required to distribute to each household a pamphlet of no longer than 2,000 words, setting out the cases for Yes and No. It also contained a statement of the textual alterations and additions to the Constitution that were being proposed.[113] The cases were prepared by those parliamentarians who voted for the position in question in parliament. George Williams has argued that this model

> demonstrably fails in educating Australians, not only because it came at the very end of the process, when it is almost too late for people to learn about these issues, but because it is such a partisan document with little or no opportunity for separating out the key underlying constitutional material that

---

[109] Ipsos-Reid, 'Two-Thirds Still Know Very Little or Nothing About BC-STV' (*PR Direct*, 30 April 2005) <http://www.ipsos-na.com/news-polls/pressrelease.aspx?id=2665> accessed 25 January 2012, cited by Ward, 'The British Columbia Citizens' Assembly on Electoral Reform'.

[110] Karen Howlett, 'Referendum? Now What Referendum Would That Be?', *Globe and Mail* (Toronto, 24 September 2007) <http://www.theglobeandmail.com/archives/article783471.ece> accessed 10 October 2011; LeDuc, 'Electoral Reform'.

[111] Simeon is critical of both the BC and Ontario processes on this basis. One problem he points to is that a model that excludes the government, parties etc can be undermined by them at the macro stage by a lack of publicity, funding etc. Richard Simeon, 'The Referendum Experience in Canada' (Referendums and Deliberative Democracy workshop, University of Edinburgh, 8 May 2009). LeDuc also comments on the Ontario process: 'The small amount of media coverage that the Citizens' Assembly received over the eight months of its deliberations meant that the public was largely unaware of its existence, or even that a debate on electoral reform had been taking place.' LeDuc, 'Electoral Reform', 556. He cites polling results to justify this conclusion (557) and also observes: 'Voters were poorly informed both because of the one-sided media coverage and an inadequate public information campaign run by Elections: Ontario.' LeDuc, 'Electoral Reform', 560.

[112] Ward, 'The British Columbia Citizens' Assembly on Electoral Reform'.

[113] Referendum (Machinery Provisions) Act 1984, s 11.

people understand. It is unable to do its job of educating Australians satisfactorily.[114]

In consequence, it was argued that voters would be better served by more objective information provided by a neutral body attempting to set out the key facts concerning the issue at stake.[115]

Some modification of this approach was taken in the Referendum Legislation Amendment Bill 1999 in advance of the 1999 referendum. The ACC also became involved, issuing a Communiqué directing the government that prior to the holding of the referendum it 'undertake a public education programme directed to the constitutional and other issues relevant to the referendum'.[116] The amendments to the 1984 Act allowed both the government to spend money on proposed public information activities it had announced in the lead-up to the 1999 referendum (it set aside $20 million to educate voters about the issues), and the Electoral Commission to provide a *neutral* information document to be sent to each voter, as well as to provide for the wider distribution of the Yes/No pamphlets, including publication on the internet (the Electoral Commission was allocated $5 million in order to organize the referendum and to cover the cost of this information campaign).[117] So public money was divided between the provision of a neutral document which addressed the current system of government, the referendum process, and the questions, on the one hand, and two officially constituted Yes and No committees on the other.[118] These were organized by two ten-person teams made up from the Constitutional Convention delegates. The idea was that this campaign, advised by a panel of experts, would take place after the end of the government's public education campaign, in the month before the referendum.[119] We should also note that after 1999 the Senate Legal and Constitutional References Committee Inquiry into an Australian Republic tabled a report which recommended further legislative reform to ensure that in advance of a future referendum on the republic issue a Parliamentary Joint Committee should oversee the preparation and dissemination to voters *solely* of independent information, rather than partisan arguments for the Yes and No

---

[114] Australian Senate Legal and Constitutional References Committee, *The Road to a Republic* (Commonwealth of Australia 2004) (*The Road to the Republic*) para 3.27.

[115] Warhurst, 'From Constitutional Convention to Republic Referendum', 13.

[116] Cited by Uhr, 'The Constitutional Convention and Deliberative Democracy'.

[117] Australian Electoral Commission, 'Yes/No Referendum '99: Your Official Referendum Pamphlet' (Pamphlet, Australian Electoral Commission 1999). The new pamphlet was mailed to all Australian citizens by the Australian Electoral Commission. Patmore, 'Choosing the Republic'.

[118] Higley and Evans Case, 'Australia: The Politics of Becoming a Republic', 136–50.

[119] Warhurst, 'From Constitutional Convention to Republic Referendum', 16.

cases, changes they envisage by further amendment of the Referendum (Machinery Provisions) Act 1984.[120] According to Williams, such changes would 'clearly separate the basic information required by Australians to cast their vote, from the partisan arguments of the Yes and No cases'.[121]

We should also note that in addition to government information, voters will be informed by the campaigning of the two sides (issues of campaign funding, spending, and advertising are, of course, inextricably linked to the information provision issue in a referendum campaign), and through the media, blogs, and other online fora, and that these will be heavily partisan. But the Australian model at least tried to provide some more objective information to counterbalance this. And, of course, spending restrictions etc can complement this as a means of controlling the domination of the campaign by one side. It is, of course, idealistic to expect too much of such a process as a vehicle with which to foster consideration and reflection at the macro level, but an appropriate test from the perspective of whether the constitutional referendum is an acceptable complement to the erstwhile generality of representative democracy would once again seem to be whether the reflection that occurs is any weaker than in an ordinary election.

In general, and realizing that the details will vary from place to place, an effort to give people a fair representation of the issue at stake seems central to the fostering of macro-deliberation. Of the two models tried in Australia, the presentation of their respective positions by the Yes and No sides, or a document issued by a neutral body seeking to explain the issues, the latter seems preferable, or would at least be an important supplement to the former; in either case it is essential also that information is presented in digestible form. It is interesting that when we turn to how Goodin sets out issues that distinguish micro-processes of deliberation such as citizens' juries etc from mass politics[122] it seems that on a number of points it would be possible to extrapolate these to the macro level, for example by helping to focus people on a single issue, by providing time for deliberation, by issuing a background briefing setting out the issues as we saw happen in

---

[120] *The Road to a Republic*, para 8.66.

[121] ibid para 3.28. See also Paul Kildea and George Williams, 'Reworking Australia's Referendum Machinery' (2010) 35 Alternative LJ 22. In a European context it is notable that the Venice Commission has recommended that the authorities in a referendum process must provide objective information by sending the text submitted to a referendum and an explanatory report or balanced campaign material directly to citizens 'sufficiently far in advance of the vote', and 'the explanatory report must give a balanced presentation not only of the viewpoint of the executive and legislative authorities or persons sharing their viewpoint but also of the opposing one'. Venice Commission, 'Code of Good Practice on Referendums', Study No 371/2006 (20 January 2009), COE Doc CDL-AD(2007)008rev, para I, 3.1.

[122] Goodin takes the 'citizens' jury' as a particular example: Goodin, *Innovating Democracy*, 61–2.

Australia,[123] and by encouraging members of the micro group, particularly ordinary citizens, to take part in dissemination processes.[124]

And so we ought not to dismiss the possibility of communication at the macro level. Of course, the meeting conditions of micro-deliberation cannot be replicated, but it is possible to expand what we mean by communication beyond discussion among people in the same room.

Goodin also urges a move beyond the traditional concept of deliberation as one act, envisaging it instead as a number of inter-related events. Standard deliberative democracy accounts postulate a 'unified deliberative agent of a single mind'.[125] But he argues for 'distributed deliberation',[126] with different agents playing different deliberative roles. This analysis of different modes of deliberation leads also to the possibility of different theatres of deliberation. Micro-deliberation encapsulates the traditional idea of small-group deliberation, while macro-deliberation explores what kinds of engagement are feasible at the level of mass society. Goodin suggests that deliberation is possible at both levels if we think of different kinds of deliberation taking place at each level. Discussion in the traditional sense is possible at the micro level; this is clearly not feasible in the same way at the mass, macro level, but here reflection can be fostered.

> In this model of 'distributed deliberation', the component deliberative virtues are on display sequentially, over the course of this staged deliberation involving various component parts, rather than continuously and simultaneously present as they would be in the case of a unitary deliberating actor.[127]

We might think of developing upon the discussion phase of micro-deliberation in two ways as a referendum process moves to a national deliberative stage. One is to try to provide a bridge from the micro to the macro. We see this in the BCCA hearings stage. After the educational phase, we observed that the next two months were taken up with public hearings, 'in order to obtain direct citizen input and reaction to the interim report'.[128] There was a lot of interest in this from the public and it enabled individuals

---

[123] Another example of a campaign of public education was in relation to the referendums held on electoral reform in New Zealand in 1992 and 1993. LeDuc, *The Politics of Direct Democracy*, 64–5.

[124] eg Dryzek and Goodin take a very positive view of how the culture of deliberation extended for members of the BCCA into the macro stage of the referendum campaign: 'most members of the British Columbia Citizens' Assembly participated actively in public debate leading up to the referendum after their formal role had ceased, and they were no longer being paid'. Goodin and Dryzek, 'Deliberative Impacts', 234. Although for difficulties they encountered in entering the broader public space see RS Ratner, 'Communicative Rationality in the Citizens' Assembly and Referendum Processes' in Warren and Pearse (eds), *Designing Deliberative Democracy*.

[125] Goodin, *Innovating Democracy*, 186.

[126] ibid 192–205.   [127] ibid 186.

[128] Ratner, 'British Columbia's Citizens' Assembly', 21.

and groups to enter into dialogue with the Assembly and also to begin a dialogue or multilogue beyond the Assembly.[129]

Another notion conceives of deliberation as discussion (what Dryzek calls 'discursive democracy'[130]) in broader and less spatially confined terms. Instead we might imagine a national discussion taking place through the workings of civil society in various dialogues and multilogues across a range of sites. The reference to interactions through the internet is one new avenue; it also embraces social movements, the media, and semi-formal political interactions. Dryzek takes up this idea in his account of deliberation taking place across traditional boundaries and over time.[131]

This is all very well as a description of how democratic politics works on a day-to-day basis in an open society, but it begs the question about how this level of national deliberation can really be fostered in a referendum process. Much will depend upon how energized people are by the issue and how well they assimilate the information provided. It seems that the length of the referendum campaign will be a crucial factor in allowing the conditions for such a public conversation to take place,[132] and as we saw from LeDuc's work earlier, allowing space for minds to be made up.

And so the question is whether a referendum campaign can in fact help foster a genuinely open and engaging national conversation.[133] There are a number of dynamics to this beyond the top-down provision of information. One is the vernacular generation of civic engagement through which people themselves establish fora for discussion, which can embrace non-conventional modes of political organization through social movements and the like.[134] Dryzek points to the importance of organically generated patterns of deliberation,[135] as does Habermas.[136] There is a role

---

[129] Again, see the extensive public hearings in New Zealand prior to the Royal Commission report on electoral reform in 1986. LeDuc, *The Politics of Direct Democracy*, 63.

[130] Dryzek, *Discursive Democracy*.

[131] Dryzek, *Deliberative Democracy and Beyond*. New technology also promises to revolutionize the opportunities available for communication and deliberation among citizens: Rean van der Merwe and Anthony Meehan, 'Direct Democracy Catalysed by Resident-to-Resident Online Deliberation' (2011) 6847 Lecture Notes in Computer Science 169.

[132] Bruno S Frey, 'Direct Democracy for Transition Countries' (2003) 7 J Institutional Innovation, Development and Transition 42.

[133] An interesting example we will discuss in Chapter 8 is the Scottish Government's 'National Conversation' on Scotland's constitutional future, launched in 2007 and intended to precede a referendum on multiple issues including independent statehood.

[134] John A Hall, 'In Search of Civil Society' in John A Hall (ed), *Civil Society: Theory, History, Comparison* (Polity Press 1995); John Keane, *Civil Society: Old Images, New Visions* (Polity Press 1998).

[135] John Dryzek, *Foundations and Frontiers of Deliberative Governance* (OUP 2011) 31–5.

[136] Jürgen Habermas, *Between Facts and Norms: Contributions to a Discourse Theory of Law and Democracy* (MIT Press 1999) 373–4.

for the media here in offering an environment for internal-reflective deliberation, although the possibility of irresponsible skewing of the issues is a clear danger. But increasingly citizens are able to generate their own multiple interactions on the internet through social networking, blogging etc.[137]

Our account so far suggests that the extension of participation and public reasoning to the macro level is feasible in referendum campaigns under the right conditions, but we also need to address equality and parity of esteem. In a sense, equality is dealt with through the principle of one person one vote. There is an assumption that referendums imply a form of equality and in a strict sense this is true: 'One of the primary appeals of using referendums as a means of democratic decision-making is to...level distinctions that might otherwise divide the community.'[138] People have the right to vote and everyone's vote carries equal weight but potential problems do remain, particularly in the way that campaigns can become heavily distorted by uneven resources available to the two sides.[139]

This leads us to the important question of equality of arms. This is an age-old problem in democracy generally and we can recall John Rawls's call for democracy to be 'set free from the curse of money' through the public financing of campaigns.[140] The issue of material equality is often neglected in accounts of deliberation. As Chambers asks: 'Where have distribution questions gone in all this talk of recognition and the public sphere?'[141] She identifies this as one of the crucial issues for the next phase of deliberative democracy theory.[142] And indeed there is considerable evidence for the pernicious influence of open campaign financing in referendums, particularly in the USA.[143]

---

[137] Van der Merwe and Anthony Meehan, 'Direct Democracy Catalysed'.

[138] Avigail Eisenberg, 'The Medium is the Message: How Referendums Lead Us to Understand Equality' in Mendelsohn and Parkin (eds), *Referendum Democracy*, 163.

[139] 'Referendum outcomes may be less reflective of the popular will than of the amount of campaign spending by competing elites.' James Gray Pope, 'Republican Moments: The Role of Direct Popular Power in the American Constitutional Order' (1990) 139 U Penn L Rev 287, 294.

[140] John Rawls, 'The Idea of Public Reason Revisited' (1997) 64 U Chic L Rev 765, 772. See also Karin Gilland Lutz and Simon Hug (eds), *Financing Referendum Campaigns* (Palgrave Macmillan 2009).

[141] Chambers, 'Deliberative Democratic Theory', 322.

[142] She also notes (Chambers, 'Deliberative Democratic Theory', 322) some who are re-engaging with the question of distribution and poverty, eg James Tully, 'Struggles over Recognition and Distribution' (2000) 7 Constellations 469; Nancy Fraser and Axel Honneth, *Redistribution or Recognition? A Political-Philosophical Exchange* (Verso 2003).

[143] David Broder, *Democracy Derailed: Initiative Campaigns and the Power of Money* (Harcourt 2000); Elizabeth Garrett and Elisabeth R Gerber, 'Money in the Initiative and Referendum Process: Evidence of its Effects and Prospects for Reform' in M Dane Waters (ed), *The Battle over Citizen Lawmaking* (Carolina Academic Press 2001) 73. For all of the efforts to introduce deliberation and provide citizens with objective information in advance of the 1999 referendum in Australia, this process has still been criticized

But once again it seems that legal regulation can play an important role in providing both for public funding of referendum campaigns on an equal basis[144] and in restricting the amount of private finance that can be spent. European standards set out by the Venice Commission require that: 'Equality of opportunity must be guaranteed for the supporters and opponents of the proposal being voted on', which more specifically requires a 'neutral attitude by administrative authorities' with regard to: the referendum campaign; coverage by the media, in particular by the publicly owned media; public funding of the campaign and its actors; billposting and advertising; and the right to demonstrate on public thoroughfares.[145] An elaborate regime that sets out detailed controls is to be found in the UK's Political Parties, Elections and Referendums Act 2000. This provides for the establishment of two official campaigns each of which can apply for the same level of public funding. Beyond this there are tight restrictions on the amount of money that can be donated and spent on the campaign.[146] Of course, this is only part of the problem; the Australian experience shows how the media can present a one-sided view of the issue which is very hard to regulate in a free society. But once again there is no evidence that with adequate regulation this should be a bigger problem for referendums than other electoral processes.

IV. CONCLUSION

In this chapter we have seen how deliberation can be built into a referendum in different ways, through various fora and across a range of stages. The BCCA and ACC experiences are each interesting alternative models for micro-processes—a more radical populist model and a more elite-led model, respectively. But both have displayed very positive features; in their own ways they each show how a micro-process of deliberation can work well in providing legitimacy for the framing of a referendum issue. Also each model set the stage for at least the possibility of fostering a more deliberative

---

for the fact that the pro-republic side massively outspent its opponents and also had 'overwhelming press support'. Cross, 'The Australian Republic Referendum, 1999', 561.

[144] It is, of course, also important to constrain partisan public expenditure. In Ireland the Supreme Court held that the spending of public money to support the government-approved side in constitutional referendums was unconstitutional. *McKenna v An Taoiseach (No 2)* [1995] IESC 11. This led to the Referendum Act 1998.

[145] The 2007 Code goes on to give detailed recommendations on equal media access and balanced coverage in the media of both campaigns (para I, 2.2, b–c). There are also provisions on access to radio and television advertising (para I, 2.2, e–f) and the permissibility of spending restrictions (para I, 2.2, h). Venice Commission, 'Code of Good Practice on Referendums', para I, 2.2.

[146] Political Parties Elections and Referendums Act 2000, Part VII.

environment for a macro-deliberative process in the referendum campaign itself.

Certainly the challenges in engaging the broader public at the macro level in the 'distributed deliberation' that Goodin talks about are significant, but we addressed a number of factors—the rolling out of the micro-process in public hearings; provision of information to voters; the proper management of time for the referendum campaign; engagement of civil society; and regulation of campaign funding and expenditure—which together seem to offer the basis for a genuine national conversation if the public's interest can be stimulated. And indeed it is important also not to abstract the referendum as one event. The building of deliberative processes for a referendum would seem more plausible within a political culture that fosters such processes more broadly for other elections and even beyond.[147] There is indeed a new interest in reviving mass democracy, which we see, for example, in the Ackerman and Fishkin 2002 proposal for a 'National Deliberation Day' in the USA.[148]

And in substantive terms it is also important to note that referendums are part of broader deliberative processes rather than lone standing events. Participation and deliberation do not end constitutional processes. We see this in the French constitution of 1946, which was adopted by a referendum after a deliberative process in which the people were consulted about the prima facie decision to draft a new constitution or reinstate that of the Third Republic. Despite its legitimacy being founded in deliberation and a referendum the constitution of the Fourth Republic fell in 1958 in a bitter process. But the French people had been engaged in this and they remained engaged; the referendum did not foreclose deliberation but seemed to generate it and gave the people a sense of ownership over the constitution. When they became disillusioned with it a grassroots movement mobilized to replace it, and as we have seen the referendum became a fixed feature under the new constitution.

Our ambitions must remain modest:

> The larger point is that distributing deliberative virtues across the different stages of a deliberative process might be 'good enough', if not perhaps ideal,

---

[147] As Goodin observes:

> there is no realistic prospect of deliberative mini-publics systematically supplanting the institutions of representative democracy. There is, however, every hope that deliberative mini-publics can serve as truly invaluable adjuncts to those other familiar features of the democratic process.

Goodin, *Innovating Democracy*, 269.

[148] In 2005 Taiwan also introduced the idea of 'a day of contemplation and deliberation' for citizens prior to a constitutional referendum.

from a deliberative point of view. It is, in any case, probably the most to which we can realistically aspire.[149]

Addressing the referendum as a broad process with a number of stages etc allows for these virtues to be fostered in a number of ways, engaging in a serious practical way with the task of improving the deliberative quality of constitutional referendums, and in doing so facilitating better the direct political participation of citizens in matters of the highest consequence for their polity.

---

[149] Goodin, *Innovating Democracy*, 203.

8

Framing the Substantive Issue in Constitutional Referendums

I. INTRODUCTION

Beyond considerations of process and participation, the credibility of the constitutional referendum from the perspective of republican democracy hangs on the content of the question put to the voters. By the functionalist normativity of constitutional theory, a deliberative process is only part of the story; we need also to explore what a fair question would, in substantive terms, look like. In this chapter we will address the content of a fair question focusing upon the clarity of the question and also the particular difficulties that can arise in framing a referendum within divided societies.

What factors then contribute to the fairness, and hence the legitimacy, of a referendum question? First, deliberation itself depends entirely on clarity: a meaningful exchange of reasons is only possible if people understand, and agree upon the meaning of, the issues at stake. A frequent criticism of referendum processes is that elites use their power to make a question deliberately obscure or ambiguous in order to manipulate the electorate. In Section II we will address clarity and intelligibility as basic requirements for the legitimate expression of constitutional authorship, addressing also attempts by elites to make a question deliberately obscure; difficulties for voters where the consequences of a Yes vote are unclear; and the general problem of engaging citizens in extremely complex constitutional matters.

Second, a referendum might be clear, but is it relevant? Does it represent a meaningful choice between constitutional options which a plurality of people consider important and worth both deliberating over and voting on. In Chapter 2 we distinguished between the issue to be addressed and the question which will put that issue to the people. In certain situations the issue is a complex one that needs some time for reflection and possibly for the building of consensus on how to distil it in a way that is both amenable to a referendum question Yes/No format and yet still capable of speaking to people's real concerns.

There are potential difficulties here for referendums in that such a process may, through strategy or compromise, arrive at a question which may not in fact suit a plurality of people: for example, they are offered two alternatives when the strongest body of opinion favours a third and unasked option. We have explored how this problem arose in Australia in 1999. But a more central concern in this chapter is the particular justice issues that arise in setting constitutional referendums, particularly constitution-framing referendums, within divided societies where any consensus can be extremely difficult to reach. In Section III I will ask whether a question can be formed that will speak to the aspirations of all sides in such a difficult environment. The referendum in Northern Ireland on the Belfast Agreement will be used as a case study, and in this context I will consider whether it is possible to frame a referendum question with sufficient consensus to overcome the majoritarian danger in the pursuit of equality and parity of esteem.

In all of this it will be evident that the substance of the issue and the process by which it is arrived at cannot be rigidly separated. Therefore, in addressing the interconnection between the two I will consider, in light of Chapter 7, whether it is possible to factor in procedural guarantees that make more likely the achievement of a question that is substantially satisfactory to a plurality of voters.

II. CLARITY

Clarity is central to any process of deliberation. If, by the principle of public reasoning, citizen reflection (and where feasible, discussion) are to be meaningful, a prerequisite is that the issues presented to the people are transparent and commonly understood. As Gutmann and Thompson put it: 'A deliberative justification does not even get started if those to whom it is addressed cannot understand its essential content.'[1] We will discuss a number of referendums where the clarity of the question has been an issue, threatening the very legitimacy of the referendum process. There are a number of discrete issues wrapped up in the clarity question which need to be untangled. The first is intelligibility. Is a question unclear because of the way it is framed linguistically, and could it be made more intelligible simply by better syntax? The problem can be the result of a technical deficiency through clumsy grammar or it can stem from deliberate obfuscation used by question-setters seeking to procure a higher (or, as the case may be, lower) level of support among voters for the matter in question. The

---

[1] Amy Gutmann and Dennis Thompson, *Why Deliberative Democracy?* (Princeton University Press 2004) 4.

Venice Commission Code sets out detailed recommendations on clarity: 'The question put to the vote must be clear; it must not be misleading; it must not suggest an answer; electors must be informed of the effects of the referendum; voters must be able to answer the questions asked solely by yes, no or a blank vote.'[2] A second issue is the running of more than one question together, which can serve to obscure the respective levels of support for each one. This again is open to criticism, as an attempt by an elite to push a less popular issue through under cover of a more popular issue. It seems that in general these two problems are avoidable through a suitable process of question design.

A third issue of clarity concerns not so much the framing of the question itself but what the consequences of a Yes vote might be. In other words, the question is unclear because the issue is unclear, and the issue is unclear because of the unpredictable political contingencies that would attend the implementation of a vote for the proposition in question, in particular where there is uncertainty surrounding how political actors will behave following a particular referendum outcome. This third issue relates to a fourth and final matter we will address. A question may seem unclear but this may be due to the nature of the issue being tested. The intricacies of constitutional change are not always easily understood, particularly by citizens who in general pay little heed to such matters. These latter two issues—the inchoate nature of the issue and/or its complexity—raise questions about the very appropriateness of the referendum as a constitutional device. If the outcome is so incommensurable that a voter does not know what is likely to result from an endorsement of the proposition, or the issue is so complicated that even a reasonably well-informed voter is unlikely to understand it, then we must ask, is a referendum at all suitable to determine the issue, at least until the consequences of the vote can be made more clear, where that is possible?

Turning to the first of these issues—controversies that have arisen in the language of question formation—there are many instances of elite actors framing a question with a view to maximizing support either for or against a particular proposition. For example, Mikhail Gorbachev framed a question on maintaining the USSR 'as a renewed federation of sovereign republics' which was carefully designed to be ambiguous.[3] It sought to hold the country together but did so with a nod to the 'sovereignty' of the republics. This was a bid to see off the separatist aspirations of sub-state nationalists by

---

[2] European Commission for Democracy Through Law (Venice Commission), 'Code of Good Practice on Referendums' Study No 371/2006 (20 January 2009), COE Doc CDL-AD(2007)008rev, para I, 3.1.

[3] Stephen White and Ronald J Hill, 'Russia, the Former Soviet Union and Eastern Europe: The Referendum as a Flexible Political Instrument' in Michael Gallagher and Piers Vincenzo Uleri (eds), *The Referendum Experience in Europe* (Macmillan Press 1996) 157.

seeming to accommodate them. And, of course, ambiguous wording can be exacerbated by other process flaws. Here the central government was also vague about how votes would be counted and restrictive of media time for the opposition.[4] Gorbachev's tactic was ultimately unsuccessful. But at the time it was endorsed by voters, even in republics which at the same time (on concurrent questions) or shortly thereafter (in separate referendums), would vote overwhelmingly for independence. This might suggest some degree of misunderstanding among many voters as to what the Gorbachev referendum was seeking to achieve, although it is also possible that voters understood exactly what was going on and many were inclined to vote for any model of reform presented to them.

Turning to Spain's referendum in 1986 on membership of NATO, the wording was again controversial, with some arguing that it was carefully designed to advance the government's agenda: 'Do you think it advisable for Spain to remain in the Atlantic Alliance under the terms set down by the government?' Critics charged that this served to soften the issue at stake, helping to win over wavering voters who would be reassured by the notion that the government was in control of the terms of membership of NATO.[5] Most surveys had predicted a strong No vote, but in the end the Yes side won 57–43.[6]

To take a third example, in Chapter 7 we saw that despite the role of the Australia Constitutional Convention (ACC), the power to set the question remained in the hands of the government in the Australian referendum of 1999. This led to criticism that the government drafted a question which in subtle ways encouraged No voters. One early formulation proposed a simple question asking voters whether they wanted a republic headed by a president. The final version, however, was more detailed, asking whether voters approved:

> A proposed law: 'To alter the Constitution to establish the Commonwealth of Australia as a republic with the Queen and Governor-General being replaced by a President appointed by a two-thirds majority of the members of the Commonwealth Parliament.'

Bernard Cross argues that this formulation—framed by the office of Prime Minister Howard[7]—may have been drawn in a way that would be 'less

---

[4] Henry E Brady and Cynthia S Kaplan, 'Eastern Europe and the Former Soviet Union' in David Butler and Austin Ranney (eds), *Referendums Around the World: The Growing Use of Direct Democracy* (Macmillan Press 1994) 186–9. See also Mark Clarence Walker, *The Strategic Use of Referendums: Power, Legitimacy, and Democracy* (Palgrave Macmillan 2003).

[5] Lawrence LeDuc, *The Politics of Direct Democracy: Referendums in Global Perspective* (Broadview Press 2003) 81.

[6] Anthony Gooch, 'A Surrealistic Referendum: Spain and NATO' (1986) 21 Government and Opposition 300, 300.

[7] The Prime Minister was also instrumental in deciding on a two-question approach—including a question on the preamble issue. John Warhurst, 'From Constitutional Convention to Republic Referendum: A Guide to the Processes, the Issues and the Participants' (Parliamentary Library Research

appealing to wavering voters'. It draws attention to the process of electing a president in parliament rather than directly, which was controversial, and specifically refers to replacing the Queen, which might discourage voters inclined towards republicanism but retaining a personal loyalty to a well-respected monarch. Cross concludes: 'In common with most tests of opinion, as much rode on the precise wording of the question as on the underlying issue.'[8] The question was reluctantly accepted by the Labor opposition to make progress on the issue and in the end, of course, the people voted No.

The Quebec referendum in 1995 also provoked criticism. The question that was put to the electorate was: 'Do you agree that Quebec should become sovereign, after having made a formal offer to Canada for a new Economic and Political Partnership, within the scope of the Bill respecting the future of Quebec and of the agreement on 12 June 1995? YES or NO?'[9] This was a modification of the draft question which had been proposed at the end of 1994, which read: 'Are you in favour of the Act passed by the National Assembly declaring the sovereignty of Quebec? Yes or No?'[10] Inevitably this change led to the charge that the government of Quebec was obscuring the straightforward issue of secession in order to maximize a Yes vote. For its critics the question was too long and too convoluted in its reference to extraneous documents. And indeed there were opinion polls taken after the Quebec referendum which showed that voters had widely varying apprehensions of what the consequences of a Yes outcome would be for Quebec's constitutional status.[11] The narrowness of the result served only to intensify these criticisms.

Related to this point, there is evidence that variations in a question can lead to very different outcomes on substantively the same issue. In polls taken after the Quebec referendum, people were also asked how they would

---

Paper 25 1998–99, Parliament of Australia 1999) 16 <http://www.aph.gov.au/library/pubs/rp/1998-99/99rp25.htm> accessed 10 October 2011. Although the Cabinet was ultimately responsible for the framing of each question, Mr Howard took a keen personal interest in drafting the proposed preamble to the Commonwealth of Australia Constitution Act 1901 and to this end recruited the help of the poet Les Murray. Glenn Patmore, 'Choosing the Republic: The Legal and Constitutional Steps in Australia and Canada' (2006) 31 Queen's LJ 770, 777–8.

[8] Bernard Cross, 'The Australian Republic Referendum, 1999' (2007) 78 Political Quarterly 556, 560.

[9] An Act Respecting the Future of Quebec, Quebec National Assembly, 1st sess, 35th leg Bill 1 (introduced to the National Assembly on 7 September 1995 but not enacted). See Robert A Young, *The Struggle for Quebec: From Referendum to Referendum?* (McGill-Queen's University Press 1999) 24–7; Warren J Newman, *The Quebec Secession Reference: The Rule of Law and the Position of the Attorney General of Canada* (York University Press 1999) 12.

[10] An Act Respecting the Sovereignty of Quebec, Quebec National Assembly, 1st sess, 35th leg (draft Bill introduced to the National Assembly on 7 December 1994 but not enacted) s 17.

[11] Young, *The Struggle for Quebec*, 41–2; Michael Keating, *Nations Against the State—The New Politics of Nationalism in Quebec, Catalonia and Scotland* (2nd edn, Palgrave Macmillan 2001) 98, 101.

vote in a hypothetical future referendum against a range of questions. Words such as 'sovereignty' or 'independence' or 'separation' triggered markedly different responses; for example, some people said they would vote for sovereignty, but when the option was the more unambiguous notion of independence they changed their minds.[12] In Australia similar research was conducted which experimented with different questions on the head of state issue; again, these produced widely varying results.[13] To take another example, this time from the UK, the question posed to voters in the 1975 UK referendum on membership of the Common Market was 'Do you think that the United Kingdom should stay in the European Community (The Common Market)?': 67.2 per cent voted Yes on a 64 per cent turnout. Butler and Kitzinger show just how widely polls swung against a range of different questions.[14] There is also an ongoing debate in the UK concerning how people would vote in any future referendum on the UK's continuing membership of the EU, with very different statistics appearing, depending on the questions asked.[15] In another area, Michael Keating has tracked a number of polls asking people in Scotland their views on independence. He has observed that the 'harder' the question, for example when it refers to independence as a seemingly imminent prospect or when it mentions separation from the UK, support is considerably lower than a softer or more open-ended question such as: 'In a referendum on independence for Scotland how would you vote?'[16] This leads him to conclude that the wording of a polling question—and presumably also a referendum question—is 'critical'.[17] A lack of certainty as to the meaning of a question and the confusion this can cause is a democratic problem in itself. In addition to

---

[12] Stephen Tierney, *Constitutional Law and National Pluralism* (OUP 2004) 316.

[13] Warhurst, 'From Constitutional Convention to Republic Referendum', 15. At 16 Warhurst concludes in reference to any future referendum: 'the wording of the referendum question may ... be crucial to the outcome'.

[14] David Butler and Uwe Kitzinger, *The 1975 Referendum* (Macmillan Press 1976) 246–62.

[15] In 2010 the Angus Reid polling firm asked in a poll: 'If a referendum on whether the United Kingdom should remain a member of the European Union (EU) were held tomorrow, how would you vote?' 48 per cent responded: 'Against the United Kingdom remaining a member of the EU' and 27 per cent in favour of the United Kingdom remaining a member of the EU (35 per cent June 2010). Angus Reid, 'Almost Half of Britons Would Vote to Abandon European Union' (*Angus Reid*, 6 December 2010) <http://www.angus-reid.com/wp-content/uploads/2010/12/2010.12.06_EU_BRI.pdf> accessed 10 October 2011. However, in another poll by Yougov in 2009 only 16 per cent were in favour of withdrawal when the option of a 'looser relationship' (48 per cent in favour) was also offered. Patrick Hennessy, 'Loosen Britain's Ties with European Union, Say Two-thirds of Voters', *The Telegraph* (London, 10 January 2009) <http://www.telegraph.co.uk/news/politics/4214369/Loosen-Britains-ties-with-European-Union-say-two-thirds-of-voters.html> accessed 10 October 2011.

[16] Michael Keating, *The Independence of Scotland: Self-government and the Shifting Politics of Union* (OUP 2009) 72–3.

[17] ibid 73.

this, however, there is also evidence that this kind of confusion can serve to heighten voter alienation.[18]

The second issue is the running of more than one issue together in a referendum question.[19] Like the first issue, this leads to criticisms that elites are using the question to deliver a particular result. Charles de Gaulle was accused by critics of deploying this tactic in three of the four referendums he held during his presidency of France. In 1961, the question asked: 'Do you approve of self-determination and the proposed provisional institutions of Algeria?' This created a political difficulty for the left, who favoured the former but not the latter since it did not provide for direct negotiations with the *Front de Libération Nationale* (FLN), the leading nationalist movement in Algeria.[20] We see a similar tactic in 1962, when voters were asked both if they approved of the Evian agreement with the FLN and the grant of full powers to the president to enforce this;[21] and again in 1969, where proposals for regional reforms were run together with reform of the Senate. One conclusion that might be drawn is that a referendum should only address one single issue if it is to produce a process that can be transparently deliberative and an outcome that is an unequivocal statement of popular will. But this notion of a single issue cannot be construed too narrowly. For example, referendums on independent statehood, on a new constitution, ratifying a peace/constitutional treaty, or on accession to (or significant constitutional development of) an international organization, often involve a range of different issues packaged together as one. Citizens voting for such a constitution or peace treaty may have to weigh provisions with which they agree against those which they oppose. Nonetheless, this presentation of a constitutional package to the voters which results from a process of constitutional negotiation and agreement on a larger issue—constitutional authorship, peace-making etc—is conceptually distinguishable from a situation where two different (perhaps even incompatible) and separable issues are run together as a ploy by an elite to secure endorsement for the less popular on the coat-tails of the more popular.

The two potential problems we have considered so far are largely surmountable by process design and by legal regulation. On the former

---

[18] Bowler and Donavan cite a poll from California that found that one of the most frequently cited complaints by voters in relation to referendum propositions was confusing wording. Shawn Bowler and Todd Donovan, *Demanding Choices: Opinion, Voting, and Direct Democracy* (University of Michigan Press 1998).

[19] Again, the Venice Commission is highly critical of such manoeuvring, calling inter alia for unity of form and unity of content in the text submitted to referendum: Venice Commission, 'Code of Good Practice on Referendums', para III, 2.

[20] Vernon Bogdanor, 'Western Europe' in Butler and Ranney (eds), *Referendums Around the World*, 57.

[21] Laurence Morel, 'France: Towards a Less Controversial Use of the Referendum' in Gallagher and Uleri (eds), *The Referendum Experience in Europe*, 73.

point we have seen how agenda-setting can be removed entirely from the hands of elites, as in the British Columbia Citizens' Assembly (BCCA) process. In Australia in 1999, although the government was left with some leeway in drafting the question, this was quite tightly delimited by the outcome of the ACC, which set out in detail the substance of the model to be put to the people. Criticisms as to the language of the question should be tempered by the fact that the government, which opposed any move to a republic, did have to put this issue to the people and was left with comparatively little room to manoeuvre over the question's composition; this is in stark contrast to processes such as the Gorbachev referendum in 1991, which was not regulated by any such democratic agenda-setting process.

Law can also be used to regulate questions. The UK's Political Parties, Elections and Referendums Act 2000 provides for independent oversight of the question to be asked. When a Bill is introduced into Parliament which provides for the holding of a referendum and specifies the wording of the referendum question, the independent Electoral Commission is required to consider that wording and publish a statement of any views it has as to the intelligibility of the question. This is to be done as soon as practicable after the introduction of the Bill so that Parliament may take into account the Commission's views during the passage of the Bill. If the wording is to be set out in secondary legislation the Secretary of State concerned must consult the Commission on the intelligibility of the referendum question before the draft statutory instrument is laid before Parliament. The Commission's remit also extends to assessing any statement preceding the question on the ballot paper of the referendum—that is, a preamble and the like—with this to be read together with the question for an overall assessment of intelligibility.[22] In this way, an attempt to elide two discrete issues, for example, could be identified and declared to be, in the eyes of the Commission, illegitimate. The role of the Commission, having considered the wording of the referendum question, is to 'publish a statement of any views of the Commission as to [its] intelligibility'.[23] Other ways to assess intelligibility include the use of sample polls to help them determine how well understood the question is by the general public.[24] But at the same time this system is designed to leave to Parliament any final decision on the

---

[22] Political Parties, Elections and Referendums Act 2000, s 104(6).

[23] The Commission has interpreted its remit to include suggesting 'alternative drafting or to offer suggestions on how a particular question and its preamble might be reframed'. Electoral Commission, 'Referendum on the UK Parliamentary Voting System: Report of Views of the Electoral Commission on the Proposed Referendum Question' (Report, Electoral Commission 2010) para 1.21.

[24] This is done by the UK Electoral Commission by 'undertaking public opinion research through focus groups and in-depth interviews' and by 'writing to interested parties (including the main political parties)

wording of the question, in recognition that this is fundamentally a political decision.[25] It is conceivable that this model of regulation could also be made stronger, by empowering such a body either to reject a question with the option of a judicial appeal, or itself to seek judicial review in advance of any referendum.

Inevitably perhaps in such a politicized environment even an attempt to regulate by law the setting of referendum questions can itself be a source of dispute as it has been in Canada. Following the Secession Reference in which the Supreme Court expressed the view that the rest of Canada would be constitutionally obliged to negotiate the secession of Quebec in the event that a 'clear' majority voted in favour of this on a 'clear' question, important issues left begging were—what is a clear question and how would its clarity be determined?[26] The federal Parliament followed up by passing the Clarity Act which provides that, within 30 days after the government of a province officially releases the question that it intends to submit to its voters in a referendum 'relating to the proposed secession of the province from Canada', the House of Commons 'will consider the question and, by resolution, set out its determination on whether the question is clear'.[27] In considering the clarity of a referendum question, the House of Commons is to consider whether the question would result 'in a clear expression of the will of the population of a province on whether the province should cease to be part of Canada and become an independent state'.[28] It is notable that section 1 is not concerned simply with the 'clarity' of the question. It seems to constrain the constitutional options which can be presented to the people of a province in a sovereignty referendum: a clear expression of the will of the population of a province that the province cease to be part of Canada could not result from

---

and would be campaigners to seek their views'. 2010 Electoral Commission Report on Proposed Referendum Question, para 1.12.

[25] eg the Commission's role does not extend to a broader examination of the substantive context of the referendum. It noted that the Bill to introduce the alternative voting system in advance of the 2011 referendum provided that this introduction was conditional on legislation being approved by Parliament to reduce the number of MPs, by redrawing parliamentary constituency boundaries; in other words, to some extent the running together of two reasonably distinct issues. However, the Commission did not address this linkage, since the issue did not in its view 'impact on the intelligibility of the proposed referendum question'. 2010 Electoral Commission Report on Proposed Referendum Question, paras 2.12 and 2.13.

[26] *Reference re Secession of Quebec* [1998] 2 SCR 217.

[27] Bill C-20, 2nd sess, 36th Parliament, 48 Eliz II, 1999 (as passed by the House of Commons, 15 March 2000) (Clarity Act 2000) s 1(1).

[28] Clarity Act 2000, s 1(3).

(a) a referendum question that merely focuses on a mandate to negotiate without soliciting a direct expression of the will of the population of that province on whether the province should cease to be part of Canada; or
(b) a referendum question that envisages other possibilities in addition to the secession of the province from Canada, such as economic or political arrangements with Canada, that obscure a direct expression of the will of the population of that province on whether the province should cease to be part of Canada.[29]

However, the Quebec Referendum Act provides that the National Assembly of Quebec has exclusive authority to adopt the text of a question which is to be the subject of a referendum.[30] This is supported by Bill 99, which confirms that the Quebec people, 'acting through its own political institutions, shall determine alone the mode of exercise of its right to choose the political regime and legal status of Québec'.[31]

These reactions served only to widen the dispute over control of a referendum question and to the competence of authorities to determine its clarity, an outcome that seems to enhance rather than pre-empt the prospect for future legal dispute if Quebec moves again towards a sovereignty referendum. In Scotland, in relation to the referendum initiative aborted in 2010, there was a proposal by the Scottish Government to establish a Scottish Referendum Commission to oversee the referendum whose members would be 'nominated by, and accountable to, the Scottish Parliament' and which would be 'with limited exceptions,... completely independent of the Scottish Parliament and Government' in the conduct of its affairs.[32]

The intention was that the Scottish Commission would be modelled on the UK Electoral Commission.[33] The Government also made clear that the process of the referendum would be based upon the UK Political Parties, Elections and Referendums Act 2000.[34] Therefore, it seems that for the Scottish Government the issue was not about trying to engineer substantially different rules or procedures from those used at the UK level, but about bringing control of the process within the devolved Scottish system. The Scottish Referendum Commission's functions would have included

---

[29] Clarity Act 2000, s 1(4). See Patrick J Monahan, 'Doing the Rules: An Assessment of the Federal Clarity Act in Light of the Quebec Secession Reference' (2000) 135 CD Howe Institute Commentary 1.

[30] Special Version of the Election Act for the Holding of a Referendum, Referendum Act RSQ, c C-64.1, updated 2001, Title I, Ch III, s 8.

[31] An Act respecting the exercise of the fundamental rights and prerogatives of the Québec people and the Québec State, Quebec National Assembly, 1st sess, 36th leg Bill 99 (assented to 13 December 2000) s 3.

[32] *Scotland's Future: Draft Referendum (Scotland) Bill Consultation Paper* (The Scottish Government 2010) paras 3.3–3.5.

[33] ibid para 3.4.   [34] ibid para 3.1.

publishing guidance for voters, Counting Officers, and permitted participants on financing and spending, and observing the conduct of the referendum at polling stations etc.[35] It remains to be seen whether this proposal will revive in a new proposal for a referendum on independence.

Our third scenario is where clarity issues arise not so much from the wording of the question but from the uncertain intentions of political actors or a broadly unpredictable political environment that will result from the referendum. The Quebec referendum of 1995 again serves as a good example. As the rancorous post-referendum litigation and legislation suggests, the referendum itself was held in a heavily contested environment which served to muddy the waters for voters. A certain tension existed within the Yes camp, which was a coalition of Quebec nationalist parties whose aspirations for a 'sovereign' Quebec could be situated at various points along a federalist–independentist axis.[36] What approach this coalition would take to negotiations with the federal government and the other provinces following a Yes vote was not clear, nor was it evident how each party would react in the event of failure on the part of the rest of Canada to enter such negotiations.[37] Political contestation also made things difficult for voters. Those intending to vote Yes and expecting that a Yes outcome would lead to a sovereign Quebec were faced with statements by the federal government that they would not negotiate the break-up of the country. The government was also hostile to the very idea of a partnership of sovereign states, suggesting that Quebec could vote only for secession—and a complete break from Canada—as an alternative to status quo federalism (a position later formalized in the Clarity Act).[38] Prime Minister Jean Chrétien, for example, rejected the question that was being asked and argued it should be replaced with a 'clearer' question such as 'Do you want to separate from Canada, yes or no?'[39] This is very different from the considerably more nuanced question that was put to the people and which proposed a partnership with the rest of Canada. The reaction of the federal government is

---

[35] ibid para 3.6.

[36] The *Action démocratique du Québec* leaned more towards a renewed partnership with the rest of Canada, while the *Parti Québécois*, to a greater extent than the more centrist coalition partner, the federal *Bloc Québécois*, aspired towards independent statehood for Quebec. Since the referendum was fought on the issue of sovereignty and partnership, different parties in the Yes campaign could emphasize either component according to their preference.

[37] Legislation did provide that negotiations must conclude by October 1996 'unless the National Assembly decides otherwise . . .'. Bill 1, s 26. This left uncertainty, since it would be for the National Assembly to conclude if negotiations proved 'fruitless', and the coalition parties may have disagreed over whether this stage had been reached and what should follow. Young, *The Struggle for Quebec*, 92, 113.

[38] ibid 26.

[39] *Montreal Gazette* (Montreal, 8 December 1994).

perhaps not surprising. If a territory votes for sovereignty it cannot necessarily expect the rest of the state to agree to a new type of quasi-confederal arrangement, the model of which is offered by the secessionist entity. The point here, however, is not to defend or critique each of these rival positions, but simply to highlight that the significant challenge voters face in a referendum on complex levels of constitutional change becomes all the greater, and arguably unmanageable, when they cannot safely predict what the implications of a particular referendum result will be.

Such uncertainty can arise from a range of situations where the political situation is volatile. The would-be secessionist group may be attempting to frame a question that will meet the test of constitutionality, leave open the prospect or a re-worked federal or confederal arrangement, or appease the international community upon which it will depend for future recognition. We see all three factors at work in the 1991 referendum in Croatia, where the question was:

> Do you want the Republic of Croatia to be a sovereign and independent State that guarantees cultural autonomy and all civil rights to Serbs and members of all other nations in Croatia, which could enter into an alliance of sovereign states with other republics (in accordance with the proposal for the solution of the crisis of the SFRY proposed by the Republic of Croatia and the Republic of Slovenia)?[40]

Complex political dynamics can also make a seemingly straightforward question in fact quite complicated and potentially ambiguous. For example, the question asked in Slovenia in 1990 was: 'Should the Republic of Slovenia become an autonomous and independent state?' Yes/No. This seems a simple question on secession but in fact, according to Ciril Ribicic, a constitutional law scholar involved in the 1990 process, this question was designed to mask significant disagreement between reformists and secessionists by joining

> those forces that were in favour of independence of Slovenia with the others who aimed at a greater level of autonomy for Slovenia, without excluding the possibility of a confederal union of sovereign independent states that would be created in the territory of former Yugoslavia.[41]

The situation in the collapsing Yugoslavia was admittedly very difficult, with the threat of war facing both Croatia and Slovenia, but as a broader

---

[40] Sinisa Rodin, 'Croatia' in Andreas Auer and Michael Bützer (eds), *Direct Democracy: The Eastern and Central European Experience* (Ashgate 2001) 37–8.

[41] Ciril Ribicic, 'Slovenian Experiences in the Preparation and Administration of Referendum and Gaining Independence' in Sanja Elezovic (ed), *Legal Aspects for Referendum in Montenegro in the Context of International Law and Practice* (Foundation Open Society Institute-Representative Office Montenegro 2005) 95.

issue, and from the perspective of popular deliberative democracy, it must be asked in light of the Canada/Quebec scenario: is it fair of either side to put voters in such a position? Another issue is that even where the intention of the organizers is fairly clear, it is also important to consider how likely it is that following a Yes vote the outcome envisaged by the referendum will in fact be achievable. The issue of decision-making cannot be divorced from that of issue-framing, highlighting once again how each component of a constitutional referendum relates to each other component from the perspective of deliberative democracy. Given the potential in cases like this for high levels of uncertainty, in the next chapter we will return to this matter, asking what scope there is to clarify matters further prior to the referendum or even if there is an argument for a second referendum in situations that anticipate potentially fractious negotiations pursuant to a Yes vote.

A fourth issue is complexity. The question offered in Quebec was criticized as obtuse in referring to 'sovereignty and partnership'. It was also criticized for making reference to two extraneous documents: a Bill setting out the process which Quebec would follow consequent to a Yes vote, and an agreement between the main parties in the Yes campaign reached in June 1995, thereby expecting detailed knowledge of both on the part of the voter. But such a reference to documents is not uncommon in a referendum on a constitutional package. The Canadian federal government used it for the Charlottetown Accord, where the question was: 'Do you agree that the Constitution of Canada should be renewed on the basis of the agreement reached on 28 August 1992?'[42] The referendum on Scottish devolution in 1979 asked: 'Do you want the provisions of the Scotland Act 1978 to be put into effect?', and in the 1998 Northern Ireland referendum over the Belfast Agreement, the issue put to the people was: 'Do you support the agreement reached in the multi-party talks on Northern Ireland and set out in Command Paper 3883?' It is also the case that in each of these situations the issue at stake was a complex one. This was certainly so in Quebec, where the nationalist proposal for a model of economic and political partnership between two 'sovereign entities' seemed to stretch the boundaries of the traditional concept of statehood. It is no surprise, and arguably essential, that its detail be elaborated in an extraneous document. We might also say the same of the Belfast Agreement, with its three strands building towards a novel and intricate model of power-sharing government. It is important then not to confuse the complexity of constitutional process with either the lack of clarity that emerges from poor question construction, or the uncertainty that can stem from disagreements among political actors. I have

---

[42] See Richard Johnston et al (eds), *The Challenge of Direct Democracy: The 1992 Canadian Referendum* (McGill-Queen's University Press 1996).

argued that the first of these latter two concerns is arguably remediable by regulation while the second is dependent upon relations between political actors with the possibility of a second referendum at the end of a difficult negotiation process. Instead, the issue of complexity raises a more fundamental concern: are some matters simply too complicated to be put to the voters in a referendum?

Civic republicans would tend instinctively to baulk at such an objection. It is a republican commitment that the people should be entitled to participate meaningfully in processes of constitutional authorship. To conclude that they are incapable of doing so because the matter is too difficult for them smacks of elitism. But lack of understanding of the issue in a referendum is an important concern that should not be dismissed because of an idealistic commitment to the good of an informed public. We saw in Chapter 6 the recurrent complaint in the French and Dutch referendums on the draft Constitutional Treaty that voters felt they did not understand the issues clearly, although we also observed that voters reported additional, well-informed, reasons for voting No. However, should lack of knowledge not be confronted rather than accepted? Arguably there are ways to surmount this difficulty in the way the referendum process is structured. In Chapter 7 we addressed how microprocesses can be used to help frame both the issue and the question. It would seem that such a setting, particularly one involving ordinary citizens, can lead to a referendum question that is intelligible to citizens. Also, in this situation the provision of information attempting to set out in a neutral way what the key issues are, and the provision of time for deliberation at the macro stage, can be helpful in unravelling the complexity of the issue. Certainly, when the package of constitutional changes is set out in a detailed document it is perhaps unrealistic to expect people to read this and fully understand it, even if it is sent to every household as the Belfast Agreement was. But it can also be argued that a referendum might help make an obscure issue better understood. It has been suggested that the Denmark referendum on the Maastricht Treaty meant that an arcane piece of draftsmanship which had obscured the depth of its real impact on national sovereignty ('designed to conceal divergent interests and shade ambiguities' as LeDuc puts it) was exposed to real democratic analysis. Danish electoral laws required the draft Treaty to be set out in a comprehensible way and summarized in a campaign pamphlet sent to every home introducing the real implications of the Treaty not only to Danes but to a wider European audience.[43] We have also explored how a model of providing neutral and succinct information to voters has been evolving within Australian legislation; such efforts seem to be crucial to the fostering of an

---

[43] LeDuc, *The Politics of Direct Democracy*, 84.

environment within which citizens can reflect and discuss on the basis of accurate and relatively disinterested information.

One recent initiative was the Scottish Government's 'National Conversation', a public consultation exercise established in 2007 by the minority Scottish National Party (SNP) government. This addressed future constitutional options for Scotland, including changes to the powers of the Scottish Parliament and the possibility of Scottish independence. The latter is the clear policy preference of the SNP. The National Conversation began with the White Paper, 'Choosing Scotland's Future', and a website which solicited the views of the general public on Scotland's constitutional options. It involved local events in the form of town hall meetings, with ministers, members of local communities, and other interest groups attending. The Scottish Government's official figures suggest that some 15,000 people were involved in the National Conversation process, including 5,300 people attending events, many events held round the country, participation in blogs, and 500,000 website visits.[44] Two commentators have noted that much of the discussion at town hall-type meetings concerned policy rather than the constitutional future.[45] It is also the case that no independent data exist tracking citizen perceptions of the National Conversation process or of any changes in participants' views of the constitutional issue following this exercise. One of the achievements of the National Conversation was arguably in forcing a response from the other parties, leading to the Commission on Scottish Devolution (Calman Commission) which recommended the devolution of further powers, resulting in the Scotland Bill 2010. On the other hand, since this Commission was set up by the Scottish Parliament as a rival process, and given the degree of rivalry between the nationalist and unionist parties, the overall picture has been described by one commentator at an early stage of both these initiatives as 'disjointed'.[46] But it is notable that the referendum proposal in 2010 clearly reflected both processes, containing as it did two separate questions. The first was on enhanced autonomy (per Calman); the second on independence. In the event of a No vote on the second question, then the results of the first would be relevant. But if a majority voted Yes on the second, then the first question would have been rendered redundant. It is also interesting that this model gives people more

---

[44] Scottish Government, *Your Scotland, Your Voice: A National Conversation* (The Scottish Government 2009). See also Malcolm Harvey and Peter Lynch, 'From National Conversation to Independence Referendum?: The SNP Government and the Politics of Independence' (Political Studies Association conference, Edinburgh, 29 March–1 April 2010) <http://www.psa.ac.uk/journals/pdf/5/2010/1041_870.pdf> accessed 10 October 2011.

[45] Harvey and Lynch, 'From National Conversation to Independence Referendum?'.

[46] Alan Trench, 'Introduction: The Second Phase of Devolution' in Alan Trench (ed), *The State of the Nations 2008* (Imprint Academic 2008) 14.

than a simple binary, one of the criticisms of many referendums. People who want more devolution than the present model offers could vote for this while also voting against independence on the second question.

Processes of deliberation and the delivery of literature clearly will not engage the uninterested voter, and indeed many citizens will not fully understand the implications of difficult constitutional issues. But this is a broader problem of democracy in general, and few would argue that people should be denied access to representative elections on the basis of ignorance or that representative democracy is delegitimized by the ignorance of elected officials. In light of our discussion in Chapter 2, to exclude people from decision-making processes on the basis of their purported incompetence might serve only to further alienate people from constitutional politics, exacerbating rather than solving the problem of disaffection and consequent civic disengagement. The education and engagement of citizens will always be a difficult challenge, but republican democracy is not a search for the ideal; rather it can only be an ongoing process of improving democratic processes and democratic legitimacy by, where possible, stimulating citizen interest and participation in the decision-making process.

III. HOW MEANINGFUL IS THE QUESTION? TOWARDS DELIBERATIVE PLURALISM IN DIVIDED SOCIETIES

We have seen that a number of difficulties can attend framing a referendum issue in any constitutional setting. It is important to turn now to the particular case of divided societies because these raise particularly acute problems for referendum democracy, problems which have largely gone unaddressed within existing research on referendums. We must confront first the broader challenge as to whether a popular deliberative process is at all possible in such a fractious environment before considering how such a process might be fostered in such a way that it might lead to a referendum process agreed to by all sides with a question accepted across communities.

One argument for the use of referendums in processes of constitutional change discussed in Chapter 1 is the implications they can have for the constitutional articulation of the very identity of the demos. As such, of course, an act of constitutional authorship and the issue of sovereignty which it implicates can be the site of particularly intense levels of contestation. Peter Russell describes such processes as mega-constitutional politics[47]

---

[47] eg politics that go beyond 'disputing the merits of specific constitutional proposals and addresses the very nature of the political community on which the constitution is based... the identity and fundamental principles of the body politic'. Peter H Russell, *Constitutional Odyssey: Can Canadians Become a Sovereign People?* (2nd edn, Toronto University Press 1993) 75.

and refers to the tensions they can generate: 'Precisely because of the fundamental nature of the issues in dispute—their tendency to touch citizens' sense of identity and self-worth—mega constitutional politics is exceptionally emotional and intense.'[48] In Chapter 2 we observed that the intensity of the issue might enhance the readiness of citizens to participate. But the other side of that coin is that they might do so with already fixed, and passionately held, opinions, possibly precluding the very possibility of open and conciliatory deliberation. It is inevitably the case that attempts to use the referendum in a deliberative way can be particularly fraught when the constitutional issue is deeply contested, making open and genuine interchanges of public reason more difficult to facilitate. Even in Canada, where inter-ethnic relations are generally very good, and in a nationally cohesive society like Australia, national referendum campaigns became fractious in 1992 and 1999 respectively, even after elite-level agreement on the entire issue was reached through some form of elite-led deliberation in the former case and on the issue to be put to the people by a process of micro-level deliberation held at arm's length from normal party politics in the latter.

But the difficulty in generating open and authentic public reasoning leads us to another problem with referendums in such an environment: the danger that majority decision-making in referendums can threaten the interests of minorities. This threat is all the more pressing for divided societies. There is no settled definition of such a society. The classic account given by Lijphart distinguishes culturally homogeneous political communities from plural societies.[49] Choudhry builds upon this definition by suggesting that a divided society is not merely one which is ethnically, linguistically, religiously, or culturally diverse but one where these differences are politically salient:

> that is, they are persistent markers of political identity and bases for political mobilization. Ethnocultural diversity translates into political fragmentation. In a divided society, political claims are refracted through the lens of ethnic identity, and political conflict is synonymous with conflict among ethnocultural groups.[50]

We have seen how in both Northern Ireland in 1973 and Bosnia-Herzegovina in 1992 a referendum served to fragment further already deeply troubled societies. Another example of an inflammatory referendum is that held in

---

[48] ibid 75.

[49] Arend Lijphart, *Democracy in Plural Societies: A Comparative Exploration* (Yale University Press 1977) 71–4.

[50] Sujit Choudhry, 'Building Comparative Politics and Comparative Constitutional Law: Constitutional Design in Divided Societies' in Sujit Choudhry (ed), *Constitutional Design for Divided Societies: Integration or Accommodation* (OUP 2008) 3.

Belgium in 1950 on the retention of the monarchy. A majority voted to keep the king, but since this majority was composed mainly of citizens from the Flemish region, there was rioting by Walloons and in consequence the king abdicated in favour of his son. The referendum brought to the surface latent tensions between the two communities, intensifying an already controversial issue in the heat of a winner-takes-all poll. It is perhaps no surprise that the 1950 vote remains the only national referendum ever held in Belgium.

Indeed, the most fundamental issue when the prospect of a referendum arises in a divided society is not who should control such a process, what should the question be etc, but rather, should a referendum be held at all, and is it possible in an atmosphere of such division to generate deliberation that is meaningful in light of the principles of participation, public reasoning, and equality with parity of esteem? We will now address what deliberative theorists have to say in general about deliberation in situations of deep division, before turning to the specific question of whether a referendum can possibly fit into an attempt to foster such a process.

A number of theorists, who have been called 'agonists' or 'radical difference democrats', are very sceptical of the idea of deliberation at all in divided societies, and for some in any society, given the impossibility of meaningful deliberation across identities.[51] Indeed some question the very notion of shared public reason, seeing deliberation

> in terms of the erasure of identity, a form of communication stuck in neutral that does not recognize difference... Those asserting identities for their part may feel insulted by the very idea that questions going to their core be deliberated. What they want is instead 'cathartic' communication that unifies the group and demands respect from others.[52]

At the level of high constitutional politics this critique, if valid, has the potential to pose a particularly significant problem. I have argued that the importance of identity might help stimulate constitutional deliberation, yet for agonists, it is precisely identity—set within the context of 'deep difference'—that should not, and perhaps cannot, be deliberated over with others. And this applies not just in what are traditionally seen as divided societies, but in modern and otherwise ostensibly cohesive polities where agonists argue that deliberation is impossible across (for them) irreconcilable cleavages such as gender, race, and ethnicity.[53]

---

[51] Chantal Mouffe, 'Deliberative Democracy or Agonistic Pluralism?' (1999) 66 Social Research 745; Chantal Mouffe, *The Democratic Paradox* (Verso 2000).

[52] John S Dryzek, 'Deliberative Democracy in Divided Societies: Alternatives to Agonism and Analgesia' (2005) 33 Political Theory 218, 220.

[53] Bonnie Honig, *Political Theory and the Displacement of Politics* (Cornell University Press 1993).

Such a radical position represents for many republican critics an empirically false position that seems to be infused by the psychology of despair. If taken seriously it would preclude meaningful social discourse among citizens across the normal identity markers that are a feature of any society.[54] But even deliberative democrats with a republican commitment to the feasibility of popular participation within a diverse community, such as Dryzek, recognize that deep-seated antagonisms within divided societies do pose a considerable epistemic challenge to republican deliberation. And indeed it is the case that the very possibility of cross-community deliberation in divided societies is a surprisingly underexplored area. Ian O'Flynn, who has written the first monograph that directly addresses the subject, observes that 'deliberative theorists have been extremely slow to respond to these challenges' given the proliferation of ethnic conflicts worldwide.[55] But in the new wave of deliberative theory that addresses in a more hands-on way the reality of social complexity, we do find such engagement. Dryzek introduces the idea of 'discursive democracy', which by 'partially decoupling the deliberative and decisional moments of democracy' he argues, 'can handle deep differences'[56] and allow deliberative theory to address genuinely divided societies beset by political conflict across ethnocultural groups. Although deliberation in these situations is possible, there are certain important conditions for its success. In a divided society: 'communication is required to be first, capable of inducing reflection; second, noncoercive; and third, capable of linking the particular experience of an individual or group with some more general point or principle'.[57]

But how can it achieve these things? There are two issues at stake. The first is how meaningful deliberation—capable of inducing reflection—might be fostered when the issue of identity is at stake, as it can be so contentious and emotional. A second is how a majority can be induced to deliberate in a referendum scenario (in particular non-coercively and alive to general points of principle) when it can achieve victory in the referendum. This second issue—the majoritarian disincentive—will be addressed in the next chapter. For now we will address the a priori issue of the very possibility of deliberation

---

[54] O'Flynn is sceptical of the agonistic focus upon 'narrative' which is used to encapsulate the particularity of different human experiences, which for some cannot be understood across these particularities. Ian O'Flynn, *Deliberative Democracy and Divided Societies* (Edinburgh University Press 2006) 10–11.

[55] ibid 3. For exceptions see Jorge M Valadez, *Deliberative Democracy, Political Legitimacy, and Self-Determination in Multicultural Societies* (Westview Press 2001); Michael Rabinder James, *Deliberative Democracy and the Plural Polity* (University Press of Kansas 2004).

[56] Dryzek, 'Deliberative Democracy in Divided Societies', 220. See also John S Dryzek, *Deliberative Global Politics: Discourse and Democracy in a Divided World* (Polity Press 2006).

[57] Dryzek, 'Deliberative Democracy in Divided Societies', 224.

in a divided context. At stake here is how to frame an issue which all sides would agree needs to be deliberated upon in a cross-community way, and with which they would be willing to engage on this basis.

It is incontestable that identity and, in particular, its political salience can be a considerable impediment to deliberation in divided societies.[58] Hirschman talked about identity issues as raising an 'either/or' rather than a 'more or less' dichotomy.[59] In other words, these disputes are inherently binary and hence not open to compromise; there can only be winners and losers. This envisages different groups inhabiting hermetically sealed identity structures. And in this context the possibility that people will be open to reaching agreement across identity divides and even to revising their positions is indeed unlikely if their views are driven entirely be pre-fixed, identity-based positions.[60] Dryzek, however, does believe that deliberation is possible across identity divides. The key for him, as we have noted, is to stretch the time for deliberation, removing it as far as possible from the constant fixation with decision-making. For one thing, this allows some breathing space. It sees reflection as a 'diffuse process, taking effect over time. With time, the degree of activation of concern on particular issues can change.'[61] Given his claim that communication must be capable of inducing reflection and be non-coercive, he is very sceptical of the role of elections in attempts to foster deliberation, given how electoral processes can be manipulated by different sides.[62] This echoes Chambers' call, which we met earlier, for talking to supersede voting as the central currency of deliberative democracy.

While Dryzek contends that deliberation in a divided society may be possible under the conditions he lays out, he also acknowledges that it is not easy. Although critical of agonism for its pessimistic prognosis, he is also aware that the assumption of many liberals that a one-size-fits-all model of

---

[58] James Tully, 'Diversity's Gambit Declined' in Curtis Cook (ed), *Constitutional Predicament: Canada after the Referendum of 1992* (McGill-Queen's University Press 1994).

[59] Albert O Hirschman, 'Social Conflicts as Pillars of Democratic Market Society' (1994) 22 Political Theory 203, 214.

[60] As Leydet puts it:

> This apparent disjunction is explained in a number of ways. To begin with, much is made of the difficulty of reaching a sound compromise when the conflict concerns not the distribution of social products but issues of identity and recognition that go to the very heart of what the country 'is' or should become. When the constitution is asked to address such questions, discussions become highly intense and emotional; constituencies are mobilized, and the give and take of compromise becomes all the more difficult. When an agreement is achieved, chances are it will look like a betrayal of the principles prized by the various constituencies.

Dominique Leydet, 'Compromise and Public Debate in Processes of Constitutional Reform: the Canadian Case' (2004) 43 Social Science Information 233, 235.

[61] Dryzek, 'Deliberative Democracy in Divided Societies', 229.

[62] Dryzek, *Deliberative Global Politics*, 62.

Rawlsian public reason can be applied to any situation, no matter how troubled inter-communal relations are, is misplaced. An example of the over-generalized approach to deliberation which he criticizes is Gutmann and Thompson's model of deliberation which assumes the feasibility of reasonableness by all parties to deliberation in most situations. But for Dryzek 'mutual acceptance of reasonableness is exactly what is lacking in divided societies'.[63]

But one way to confront this is to introduce an important distinction concerning the content of deliberation. People can adopt a reasonable attitude in the sense that they share a desire to reach agreement. But that does not mean that they communicate in the same way or that we can hold expectations that the content of their communications will follow a commonly shared attitude. For example, Iris Marion Young was a difference democrat who avoided the extreme dissonance of the agonists. She believed in the possibility of a common form of reasonableness across identity divides, provided that this was open to expression through alternative communicative forms which did not create hierarchies among these.[64] People with different identities can, for Dryzek and Young, deliberate together—indeed, they will seek to do so in order not to be excluded from important decision-making processes—but in doing so they want to have their distinctiveness recognized and respected. In other words, deliberation must steer clear of what Lindahl calls the Scylla of 'exclusion' and the Charybdis of 'assimilation'.[65]

What emerges from this advocacy of a more nuanced discourse that attends to rather than overlooks the importance of different identities is the possibility of what we might call 'deliberative pluralism'. This would remain compatible with republicanism's need for a base level of societal unity; in other words, a republicanism that depends upon an (albeit thin) civic commonality within a polity, but which takes full account of the need to recognize, include, and respect distinctive identities in the modes of interaction by groups within that civic setting.

---

[63] Dryzek, 'Deliberative Democracy in Divided Societies', 219.

[64] Iris Marion Young, *Inclusion and Democracy* (OUP 2002) 71–6. O'Flynn is sympathetic, but only to a point: 'deliberative democracy must make room for alternative forms of political expression and engagement' but in the end 'the appeal to general political principles cannot ultimately be avoided'. Narratives are inevitably particular and as such

> they cannot provide a common reference point to which citizens can appeal in order to build composite compromises... public policy cannot be based on stories. What is more, narrative may itself be a source of unjust exclusion, since, in the hands of manipulative ethnic elites, it can be used as a means of enforcing internal conformity.

O'Flynn, *Deliberative Democracy*, 11.

[65] Hans Lindahl, 'Recognition as Domination: Constitutionalism, Reciprocity and the Problem of Singularity' in Neil Walker, Jo Shaw, and Stephen Tierney (eds), *Europe's Constitutional Mosaic* (Hart Publishing 2011) 225.

Such an aspiration seeks to retrieve not only societal commonality but also popular participation from the potentially agonistic turn to identity politics. One assumption which often arises is that deliberation across a divided society can only really be conducted at the elite level. But this returns us to one of the key arguments for direct democracy with which we ended Section II of this chapter, namely that ordinary people may feel particularly disenfranchised by constitutional processes that exclude them, especially when compromises are made that seem to harm vital interests, central to their identities. As Leydet puts it:

> there exists an unavoidable disjunction between the kind of compromise agreement that can come out of complex intergovernmental negotiations and the type of outcome that a majority of citizens might be made to support. Any agreement produced by formal talks can be assumed to have involved significant logrolling and be made of various mutually dependent sets of compromises. Such a composite agreement, it is argued, has but little chance to stand the test of public debate and attract sufficient popular support to ensure ratification.[66]

In other words, compromise agreements can find their unpopularity exacerbated by a process that seems democratically defective. When a referendum enters the process at the end, a frustrated people will finally have the chance to speak, and in doing so they may well veto the agreement as, in Leydet's example, the peoples of Quebec and the rest of Canada each did in relation to the draft Charlottetown Accord in 1992.

Such an assumption that only elite deliberation is feasible belies the civic republican commitment to popular deliberation. And so we are left with a difficult question: in an attempt to reconcile both popular participation and deliberative pluralism, can popular deliberation, perhaps mediated by broader institutions of civil society across the lines of a divided society, ever be possible? In other words, can ordinary people, where their identities are at stake, really engage in intense processes that are capable of inducing reflection, are non-coercive, and are capable of linking particular experiences to points of broader principle?

As a starting point it is imperative to note that direct democracy and indeed popular deliberation cannot occur in a vacuum. Both are part of a broader system of elite-led representative government rather than divorced from it. And so in the context of divided societies in particular, the agenda-setting role of elites is crucial, as we will see in our case study—Northern Ireland. Inter-party/inter-ethnic group negotiations (which may also be intergovernmental in a multi-level democracy) are almost certainly needed

---

[66] Leydet, 'Compromise and Public Debate', 235.

to begin to frame constitutional issues in divided societies which might then be deliberated on. But this does not necessarily mean that there is no scope for popular participation at any stage from the beginning of the deliberation process through to the final decision. We have seen how a referendum can act as an incendiary device in a divided society, but as we look to the Belfast Agreement process we will also ask whether a referendum can, alternatively, act as a forum for macro-level deliberation, becoming yet another building block in constructing the possibility of a cross-communal 'public'.

The two models of micro-deliberation that we addressed in Chapter 7 might provide alternative bases from which such forms of engagement in more divided societies can begin. On the one hand, some version of the more populist BCCA convention could perhaps be adapted to reflect the demotic composition of a divided society based upon parity between the different communities involved. But if it seems that, more realistically, a prominent role for elites is needed to kick-start constitutional communication across a divided polity, then the ACC model is perhaps more applicable than that used in British Columbia, offering as it did a central role for elites, while extending membership to include non-traditional elites and also offering space for other voices from broader civil society in the process—including possibly more moderate voices that often miss out on electoral representation in a polarized community.[67] There is also a strong argument for some form of power-sharing representation so that majority hegemony is not simply reinforced in such a micro setting. One innovation of the Belfast Agreement is the establishment of the Civic Forum for Northern Ireland, which coexists alongside the elected Assembly.[68] This is a consultative body made up of representatives from organizations detached from the party political system[69] and designed to represent the interests of business, trade union, and voluntary sectors (seats are allocated to various groupings),[70] and to provide a means of engagement with policy-makers. This, of course, resulted from rather than led to the settlement, but it is itself an interesting model that seeks to foster cross-community civic engagement.

---

[67] Indeed, there is also the difficult reality that in attempting to produce agreement in a divided society, the notion of civil society might have to be extended to include paramilitaries or their political wings. Christine Bell and Catherine O'Rourke, 'The People's Peace? Peace Agreements, Civil Society, and Participatory Democracy' (2007) 28 Int'l Political Science Rev 293, 294.

[68] Agreement between the Government of the United Kingdom of Great Britain and Northern Ireland and the Government of Ireland (Belfast, 10 April 1998, 2000 UKTS 50) (Belfast Agreement or Good Friday Agreement) Strand 1, para 34 and given legal status by the Northern Ireland Act 1998 (NI Act 1998) s 56.

[69] John McGarry and Brendan O'Leary, *The Northern Ireland Conflict: Consociational Engagements* (OUP 2004).

[70] Cathal McCall and Arthur Williamson, 'Governance and Democracy in Northern Ireland: The Role of the Community and Voluntary Sector after the Agreement' (2001) 14 Governance: An International Journal of Policy and Administration 363.

However, in the last chapter we discussed how republican deliberation warns against small-group micro-deliberation being seen as a substitute for macro-level engagement of the broader people. It is as important, if not more so, in divided societies that the public as a whole is not cut off from such a micro-level agenda-setting deliberation, given that levels of political disaffection can already be high. One advantage of the BCCA model, even if its radically popular membership would be unsuitable for a deeply divided society, was the openness of its process, allowing ordinary people to engage through attending hearings, offering submissions, and following ongoing deliberations through the media. We have noted Goodin's idea that at the macro level this is how we should envisage deliberation, not just as physical communication between individuals which at the level of mass society can only be limited, but also through broader reflections on debates and discussions taking place at micro level. If the process is sufficiently open, and long enough in duration to engage people meaningfully in debates, an environment can be created within which people are offered the necessary information and space to reflect before the referendum moves to the macro-level vote.

(i) The Belfast Agreement: a study in deliberative pluralism?

One of the important features of the peace process in Northern Ireland is the intervention of a range of voices in addition to traditional government and party elites. From this we can attempt to assess in retrospect how deliberative the 1998 referendum was, and whether the combination of traditional elite, civil society, and in some sense also popular, processes which the Belfast Agreement involved, offers us at least one instance where the referendum has played a generally successful role in the resolution of an entrenched conflict.

In particular, having addressed the problems of the 1973 referendum, it is interesting to contrast this with the later process. In 1998, 71 per cent of those voting in the North said Yes to the Belfast Agreement. This agreement was a devolution process, bringing constitutional change to Northern Ireland, but at the same time it was also a peace pact, ending the use of violence by the province's main paramilitary organizations and attempting to provide the constitutional structures that would deliver a lasting peace. Importantly, the agreement also concerned itself with identity. The devolution agreement is a consociational one,[71] resulting in a power-sharing Northern Ireland Legislative Assembly and Executive, a North/South (island of Ireland)

---

[71] John McGarry and Brendan O'Leary, 'Consociational Theory, Northern Ireland's Conflict, and its Agreement. Part 1: What Consociationalists Can Learn from Northern Ireland' (2006) 41 Government and Opposition 43.

Ministerial Council, a British–Irish Council, and the 'consultative' Civic Forum. As part of this it also contains detailed protection for Northern Ireland's cultural diversity, including veto rights, encapsulated in cross-community decision-making within governmental institutions and individually focused minority rights, centred upon the idea of equality.[72]

Although the different sides came to the table with categorical positions on the sovereignty question—unionists for continued union with the UK, republicans, and in a less categorical way, other nationalists, for a re-united Ireland—the dynamics of deliberation moved to the detail and a series of compromises became possible through log-rolling or what Richard Bellamy and Martin Hollis call 'bartering'.[73] By such a process, as we saw with the Belfast Agreement, it also becomes possible to frame these compromises within the broader policy positions with which participants began the process. After the Belfast Agreement, each side could conclude that its agenda had in large measure been achieved. For unionists, the Union was preserved and the Republic of Ireland would remove its overt constitutional claim to Northern Ireland; for nationalists, power-sharing was established, a role for the Republic of Ireland in Northern Ireland's affairs was guaranteed, and the constitutional commitment by the UK to the possibility of a future referendum on Irish unity was embodied in law. This process of elite bargaining, therefore, set up a referendum where the people could take cues from elites for endorsement of the agreement.

But in a remarkable innovation, elites also took cues from the people. Colin Irwin has charted how political polling was used throughout the Belfast process to inform the different parties to the negotiations. Eight surveys of public opinion were conducted on issues central to the Northern Ireland peace process between April 1996 and May 2000 and for seven of these polls the party negotiators were involved in drafting and agreeing the questions.[74] This involved 'in-depth interviews with party negotiators, the testing of their proposals by public opinion survey and the publication of the results of these polls in the popular press', making the process transparent, engaging elites and ordinary citizens in a genuine dialogue, and allowing 'politicians on both sides of the conflict to map out areas of compromise and common ground without

---

[72] NI Act 1998, s 75. Shane O'Neill, 'Mutual Recognition and the Accommodation of National Diversity: Constitutional Justice in Northern Ireland' in Alain-G Gagnon and James Tully (eds), *Multinational Democracies* (CUP 2001) 233; Christopher McCrudden, 'Mainstreaming Equality in the Governance of Northern Ireland' (1999) 22 Fordham Int'l LJ 1696.

[73] By this they mean that because groups often have different priorities, they will make concessions on issues of lower priority in order to make gains on more important matters. Richard Bellamy and Martin Hollis, 'Consensus, Neutrality and Compromise' in Richard Bellamy and Martin Hollis (eds), *Pluralism and Liberal Neutrality* (Frank Cass 1999).

[74] Colin Irwin, *The People's Peace Process in Northern Ireland* (Palgrave Macmillan 2002) 11.

running the danger of getting too far ahead of their supporters'.[75] In many ways this helped to overcome one of the big problems of elite negotiation in divided societies, namely the need to carry along the communities which elites represent. There is a danger that interaction with other elites will prompt compromise that the rest of the community will not accept. But by use of these polls elites were able to see how far their communities were in fact willing to go, and also which measures they would accept as part of an overall package, even if they did not agree with a particular compromise on its own.

In addition, there were other constituencies which intervened in the deliberations. An innovative feature is the role of the Republic of Ireland and of international actors as a backdrop to the negotiations. The Republic fed into the referendum endorsement model itself. While one referendum was held in Northern Ireland asking for approval or rejection of the Agreement, on the same day a second referendum was held south of the border on the issue of amending the Irish constitution, a core concern of Ulster Unionists, who objected to Articles 2 and 3 of the 1937 constitution and the claim therein that the national territory of Ireland consisted of the whole island of Ireland. The outcome of each referendum in a sense depended upon the other (the British–Irish Agreement between the British and Irish governments for the implementation of the Belfast Agreement required the two governments to notify each other in writing of the completion of the requirements for the entry into force of the Belfast Agreement).[76] In short, constitutional change for Northern Ireland—and therefore for the UK—was tied interdependently to constitutional decisions in a second state.[77] This nuances the idea of elite control, since in addition to indigenous elites within Northern Ireland, we also see the involvement of the British and Irish governments as partly internal and partly external to the process.[78] But we also saw a role for foreign power-brokers, particularly the US President,[79] and also international weapons inspectors.[80]

---

[75] ibid 1.   [76] Belfast Agreement, Art 4(2).

[77] 'It is...an interesting feature of the Belfast Agreement that although the rest of the UK did not vote on the Agreement, Irish citizens did, and that the result of this Irish referendum and the implementation of the Belfast Agreement were dependent upon one another.' See Geoff Gilbert, 'The Northern Ireland Peace Agreement, Minority Rights and Self-Determination' (1998) 47 ICLQ 943, 950.

[78] It has even been argued that the Belfast Agreement is 'laced with elements of co-sovereignty'. McGarry and O'Leary, *The Northern Ireland Conflict*, 280.

[79] Michael Cox, 'The War that Came in from the Cold: Clinton and the Irish Question' (1999) 16 World Policy J 59; GT Dempsey, 'The American Role in the Northern Ireland Peace Process' (1999) 14 Irish Political Studies 104.

[80] An Independent International Commission on Decommissioning was established. See McGarry and O'Leary, *The Northern Ireland Conflict*, 225, 282.

In addition, we should not ignore how, even at the level of elite negotiation, non-traditional elites and broader civil society played a role.[81] The Belfast process went beyond traditional elites to include paramilitary organizations which, through their political organs, could claim to speak for some of the most entrenched positions in the polity. The advantage of this engagement was that these organizations in turn played a crucial role in 'selling the agreement'. But there were also green shoots of new movements starting to evolve, which aspired to transcend the traditional communal divisions, such as the Women's Coalition.[82] It was on this basis that many hoped the new Civic Forum would continue the work of allowing particularly non-traditional voices to build inter-communal ties. As Birrell and Williamson comment: 'The Civic Forum represents an innovation in democratic practice because it has the potential to broaden and deepen discourse and deliberation on many issues that will affect the people of the region.'[83]

In the end, with broader level elite agreement secured, the great democratic dilemma of using a referendum in a divided society was confronted, and it might be argued that this process met with considerable success; the referendum proposal achieved the strong endorsement of both communities in Northern Ireland together with an overwhelming Yes vote in the related referendum in the Irish Republic.[84] It is therefore useful to reflect on how these referendums, in particular that in Northern Ireland, overcame the identity challenge.

We have discussed how, by even the most optimistic civic republican analysis, a constitutional referendum faces considerable, and in some cases perhaps insurmountable, challenges, in a divided society, since a constitutional referendum implies a pre-existing demos, the absence of which is precisely the dilemma of the divided society. How then did 'a people' engage in constitutional authorship when so many on either side of the divide in Northern Ireland do not consider themselves to constitute, with those on the other side of the polity, one joint collective author?

---

[81] Indeed, the role of civil society throughout the Troubles was extensive if often forgotten; and by the late 1990s a culture of broader community engagement at the grassroots level already existed. It has been estimated that some 5,000 voluntary and community associations were active in Northern Ireland at this time. Derek Birrell and Arthur Williamson, 'The Voluntary–Community Sector and Political Development in Northern Ireland, Since 1972' (2001) 12 Voluntas: Int'l J Voluntary and Nonprofit Organizations 205, 212. According to Birrell and Williamson these bodies were important: 'in community empowerment, in filling the demographic deficit, and in peace building, reconciliation, and cross-border work' (217).

[82] Which won two seats in the first Northern Ireland Assembly elections in 1998.

[83] Birrell and Williamson, 'The Voluntary–Community Sector', 214. See also J Woods, 'The Civic Forum' in Robin Wilson (ed), *Agreeing to Disagree: A Guide to The Northern Ireland Assembly* (The Stationery Office 2001).

[84] 94.4 per cent voted Yes to amending the Irish constitution on a 55.6 per cent turnout.

In a sense this issue was in fact sidestepped. Perhaps the Belfast Agreement's main contribution to the deliberative construction of referendum processes is to show the feasibility of transcending the thick republican prerequisite of a common demotic identity in a process of constitution-making, and in doing so demonstrating that a referendum can also be used in one territorial space in an innovative way that need not call upon an instantiation of one national voice. The substance of the Belfast Agreement goes a long way to explaining why people from both communities were able to go into a polling station and vote for the same thing. In the first place the outcome of the elite/micro-level deliberation process did not impose one idea of justice, one final constitutional settlement, or a one-size-fits-all constitutional identity for the different communities of Northern Ireland. The process of compromise meant that the settlement was not a clear victory for one side or another. A Yes vote could be promoted by elites on both sides arguing plausibly that their respective community would be gaining from a constitutional agreement that was not a zero-sum game.

Of course, one objection might be that the Belfast Agreement was not in fact an instance of republican deliberation at all, but the suspension of any republican aspiration in recognition of irreconcilable difference. The principal outcome of the Belfast Agreement is, of course, power-sharing institutional arrangements. From a republican perspective this seems to be inherently problematic. By one reading of the process we might say there was no exchange of reasons or attempt to see the other side; the two sides in effect agreed to disagree, taking the territory no closer to building the kind of cross-communal ties that would build towards a joint commitment to sharing the same polity. Is this really a successful republican deliberation if all that happened was that two communities agreed on a pact to live and let live without any attempt at broader society-building? But such an interpretation seems to be rather a caricature of what was in fact agreed and how it was agreed, ignoring the fact that at some level people were inspired with a common spirit to reach an agreement, and then to make it work. For some no doubt the Belfast process at both micro-elite and macro-popular levels was entirely pragmatic and agonistic, and for a few, rejectionism and violence are still the drugs of choice.[85] But there is in the breadth of the agreement, the extent to which paramilitary organizations bought into it, the way in which ordinary people engaged with it, and the nascent cross-community institutions that have resulted from it, surely enough to suggest the green shoots of 'deliberative pluralism'. Space was created to induce

---

[85] Martin McGuinness, a leading Irish Republican and now Deputy First Minister of Northern Ireland, has famously labelled refusenik Republicans 'conflict junkies'. Henry McDonald, 'Martin McGuinness condemns Real IRA's Derry bomb', *The Guardian* (London, 5 October 2010).

reflection—the Agreement was made over a long and difficult period in which elites needed constantly to engage with their own constituents both to gauge how far they were prepared to go and to try to take their constituents with them. This process was, second, non-coercive; if it had not been it would surely have collapsed at the referendum vote if not before, with unionists in particular in a position to veto the whole Agreement. But also we see the third of Dryzek's criteria in the linking of particular experiences of individuals and groups to more general experiences. At the time of the Agreement it seems that there was a genuine exchange across identities, for example, with both sides explaining the sense of loss and hurt they had suffered from the decades of violence and fear.[86] But as always with Northern Ireland any note of optimism needs to be tempered by the painful legacy of the past. While there has been a process of dialogue, at the same time this has inevitably been fractious, and arguably it has not been helped by selective enquiries into particular incidents but without any community-wide truth and reconciliation process.

The Civic Forum, bolstered by the formal status it acquired through the Agreement, is a sign of how it was intended that Northern Ireland would build upon this engagement and in some sense move beyond consociation, at least at the civic level. This is very much a long game. The constitutional machinations have continued to leave bitterness, up to the recent dispute over the devolution of policing and justice, an agreement on which was only reached between the main parties in Northern Ireland in February 2010. But from a situation of deep division any road forward is necessarily a difficult one. In this sense we need to see the deliberative referendum as a process and not just a one-off event, and this prolongation of civic engagement is a key issue for deliberative democracy theory. The referendum sprang from deliberation; but the Agreement it endorsed aspires also to foster it.

What lessons then can we learn from how the referendum was applied here successfully, particularly when contrasted with that of 1973? First, the people from both sides and their elites engaged, often tentatively at first, and with suspicions and antagonisms very present. But crucially the holding of a referendum was not set in stone as negotiations began. It emerged as part of the agreement itself, rather than as a pre-set resource that one dominant community could cling to, refusing to make compromises, because the prospect of total victory through a referendum was guaranteed. In short, the referendum was the outcome of deliberation, not its inevitable, and possibly frustrating, end point.

---

[86] Colin Irwin, *The People's Peace Process in Northern Ireland* (Palgrave Macmillan 2002).

Second, with discussions that were very open-ended the role of deliberation became the art of the possible, and here we see it at its most pragmatic. An illuminating account of the transformative potential of deliberation, while not expecting the highest level of agreement—consensus—is offered by Dryzek: 'In a pluralistic world, consensus is unattainable, unnecessary, and undesirable. More feasible and attractive are workable agreements in which participants agree on a course of action, but for different reasons.'[87] In a similar way, for Iris Marion Young the outcome of political discussion and decision-making is not some thick, general conception of justice, 'but rather a *particular judgement* about what actions and policies *this* collective should adopt to address these circumstances'.[88] It is about agreeing to policies on the ground, rather than expecting any a priori consensus on the principles that might inform such policies; we can each agree to X even if our motivations are our own.[89] The Belfast Agreement was arrived at in very much this way. And indeed this is one of the features of deliberation; it 'may throw up ways of dealing with conflicts that otherwise might not come to the fore'.[90]

Third, the people were able to deliberate on this agreement and then to vote without being asked to surrender their differing senses of self. The agreement and hence the referendum question respected different identities and left certain polarizing issues in abeyance, in particular the ultimate sovereignty question. The provision on possible reunification of Ireland was kicked into the distance; the prospect of a border poll in Northern Ireland on this issue was held out,[91] but no definite timeline was set for this.[92] Similarly, national and ethnic identities were respected through elaborate provisions on cross-community decision-making and a stronger and judicially enforceable commitment to equality. And so the referendum concerned a fundamental constitutional agreement but one that did not try to force agreement where it did not exist or settle identity issues that could not be concluded. And unlike 1973 it did not promise uncompromising victory to a particular position, but rather represented an agreed mode of coexistence for the different groups.

But what of the charge that the referendum cannot be seen to have intervened here as part of a process of republican deliberation because no such process took place—it was in effect a consociational referendum? This

---

[87] John S Dryzek, *Deliberative Democracy and Beyond: Liberals, Critics and Contestations* (OUP 2000) 170.

[88] Young, *Inclusion and Democracy*, 28–9.   [89] ibid 29.

[90] Ian Shapiro, 'Optimal Deliberation?' (2002) 10 J Political Philosophy 196, 199.

[91] NI Act 1998, s 1 and Sch 1.

[92] The Act provides that the Secretary of State shall hold a poll 'if at any time it appears likely to him that a majority of those voting would express a wish that Northern Ireland should cease to be part of the United Kingdom and form part of a united Ireland'. NI Act 1998, Sch 1, para 2.

seems to be a limited and oversimplified account that misses how the deliberation process and the referendum itself played a 'public-building' role. The Agreement could not and did not entirely reconcile deep identity cleavages, but although the Agreement was ultimately consociational, the referendum itself can be seen as a public act commonly engaged in by all, and notably with a very high turnout (81 per cent). For the referendum result to have been accepted by both sides, and for its outcome to have survived very considerable challenges in the years since, it seems that it must have taken on the role of a collective project that in some measure transcended the demotic divide. People from both sides voted knowing that they were agreeing to, and hence recognizing the legitimacy of, every other person having an equal determining role in ratifying, or indeed rejecting, the Agreement, regardless of whether that person was a member of their primary community or not. This required the people involved accepting some minimal level of societal interconnection to make such a collective expression feasible. And what is more, the referendum was not conducted on a consociational basis, requiring a double majority—one from each community. People voted as individuals and their votes were collated on an individual basis alone.

In some sense the very act of engaging in such a referendum on the basis of one person, one vote implies mutual recognition. Honneth would trace this back even further, arguing that conflict itself is the first step to recognizing the other:

> if the social meaning of the conflict can only be adequately understood by ascribing to both parties knowledge of their dependence on the other, then the antagonized subjects cannot be conceived as isolated beings acting only egocentrically. Rather, in their own action orientation, both subjects have already positively taken the other into account, before they become engaged in hostilities. Both must, in fact, already have accepted the other in advance as a partner to interaction upon whom they are willing to allow their own activity to be dependent.[93]

As Lindahl explains: 'this struggle takes place against the background of *a more fundamental mutual reciprocity that the parties must already have acknowledged*, even if only implicitly, if they are at all to engage in a struggle the stake of which is reaching mutual recognition'.[94] And so when discussions begin on the basis of resolving such a conflict, that is, when any process of deliberation is undertaken across divided societies, each side coming to the table does so in implicit recognition of the other.

---

[93] Axel Honneth, *The Struggle for Recognition: The Moral Grammar of Social Conflicts* (Joel Anderson tr, Polity Press 1995) 45.

[94] Lindahl, 'Recognition as Domination', 212.

But how can we describe this process of mutual recognition in the Belfast referendum as deliberative when it clearly falls short of an agreement that all share the same demos?[95] It did not transcend the fact that the two groups have fundamentally different national identities, that unionists are intent on preserving Northern Ireland's position within the UK state, nor that nationalists aspire to Irish unity in the future. The latter point in particular demonstrates that the referendum did not represent any acceptance by Irish nationalists of Northern Ireland as a nation or even a people. Iris Marion Young offers a more modest concept than nation in her idea of 'the public': 'formed from the interaction of democratic citizens and their motivation to reach some decision'.[96] The key it seems is to see such a referendum—which after all ratified an agreement that itself left the sovereignty issue deliberately unfinished—not as a demotic act of a nation or a people, but rather of different communities who agree to act as a common 'public' for the purpose of one constitutional moment. And so the referendum, while certainly not having a nation-building role, arguably did in this case have a 'public-building' role.[97] In this way, the referendum intervened to give the people from these different traditions the chance to deliberate upon this process and in the end vote as joint constitutional authors for or against the model of constitutional coexistence, based as it was upon compromise and open-ended as it was in its future trajectory, worked out in the Agreement. And one subtle shift is that the Agreement instantiated mutual recognition in political rather than cultural terms; power-sharing within the Agreement is between Nationalists and Unionists, not Catholics and Protestants.[98] With this instantiation of political identities these constitutional authors came together as a contingent public rather than a unified demos, but come together they did.[99] As an act of constitutional authorship the constitutive referendum confronts constitutional authors with the relationship they now share in

---

[95] O'Flynn goes so far as to say a shared identity is essential to move from conflict to democracy. This is necessary or there 'will be nothing to hold citizens together or to make them feel that they are engaged in a common political enterprise'. O'Flynn, *Deliberative Democracy*, 5.

[96] Young, *Inclusion and Democracy*, 20.

[97] And in Young's idea of 'the public' we can perhaps also find a way to reconcile civic republicanism, which is traditionally hostile to pluralism, as an obstruction to communal solidarity, with the notion that common civic ends can be developed within the context of difference, perhaps even deep difference. Notably Irwin notes from the political polling stage that many people, while opposed to individual elements being proposed, 'were willing to accept them as part of an overall agreed settlement.' Irwin, *The People's Peace Process* 20. And there had been indications that people would support such a package in a referendum (19).

[98] McGarry and O'Leary, *The Northern Ireland Conflict*, 284. In this way it may be that political identities can be reshaped and alliances reframed while culture distinctiveness remains in place.

[99] Again, there is strong evidence that the people sought the chance to vote. Polls showed that only 12 per cent wanted to leave the process entirely to politicians, whereas a plurality of opinion thought a referendum should be used either to 'advance', 'advise', or 'endorse' the talks. Irwin, *The People's*

community with their co-authors. The act of authorship here was the conclusion of a chapter in the ill-starred history of Northern Ireland, but not the concluding chapter. The public agreed to accept constitutional progress in Northern Ireland to be a continuing journey, perhaps open to some level of completion or at least further development through a subsequent referendum on Irish unity, but it was now agreed by the vast majority that this journey would be undertaken by one public engaged in political contestation (and embracing the other publics of the Republic of Ireland and wider UK) and agreeing together to use the political path in overwhelming rejection of political violence. This was the common commitment of the public, a goal that united a very broad plurality in a shared vision of a peaceful—albeit deeply disputed—constitutional future.

And so a final but crucial point of distinction, it seems, is that between the outcome of consociational agreements and the mode of their creation. The result of the Belfast Agreement was undoubtedly a power-sharing one, but that does not mean that constitutional deliberations engaged at either micro or macro levels to bring the Agreement about were entirely consociational. A process of deliberation once begun can build links that previously looked unthinkable.[100] Lijphart famously argued that consociationalism is the only workable type of democracy for deeply divided societies.[101] But Dryzek challenges this: 'ethnic hatreds are the product of symbolic politics in particular political circumstances. As such, they are learned, and so can be unlearned or transformed, though that can be an uphill task.'[102] However, even if it seems that the process of the Belfast Agreement for a number of actors went beyond mere log-rolling of entrenched and polarized interests towards an attempt to understand the other's point of view, some argue that the substance of the Agreement is so heavily consociational that it now works against the building of further cross-communal links.[103] But the process itself and the referendum it resulted in do at some level demonstrate the potential for popular republican expression within a divided society by a

---

Peace Process, 152–3. Irwin (162) also notes one poll which asked, 'Do you want to be given the opportunity to vote on the terms of a settlement in a referendum?': 94 per cent said Yes.

[100] Indeed, as O'Flynn puts it: 'It is difficult to see... how such a... relationship could ever emerge or develop in the absence of deliberation.' O'Flynn, *Deliberative Democracy*, 5.

[101] Arend Lijphart, 'Prospects for Power Sharing in the New South Africa' in Andrew Reynolds (ed), *Election '94 South Africa: An Analysis of the Results, Campaign and Future Prospects* (St Martin's Press 1994), 222.

[102] Dryzek, 'Deliberative Democracy in Divided Societies', 222. See also Stuart Kaufman, *Modern Hatreds: The Symbolic Politics of Ethnic War* (Cornell University Press 2001); Valadez, *Deliberative Democracy, Political Legitimacy, and Self-Determination*, 36–8.

[103] Rupert Taylor, 'Consociation or Social Transformation' in John McGarry (ed), *Northern Ireland and the Divided World* (OUP 2001).

public prepared to deliberate across borders, and even the possibility that the referendum might be a suitable vehicle through which such a society might express its joint, albeit thin, sense of cross-demotic commonality.

IV. CONCLUSION

In some sense the theme of this chapter has been possibility. We began by addressing four potential problems in framing the substance of a referendum issue, but we also identified how each of these might be overcome. The first two clarity issues seem surmountable if political actors work in good faith, and through proper legal regulation where this is unrealistic. The third we will return to in the next chapter addressing the possibility of clarifying the referendum issue in negotiation before the referendum takes place. The fourth—that some issues are too complex to put to the people— returns us to Chapter 2 and the notion that one's views of referendums will be largely informed by broader ideological dispositions towards the purpose of democracy and the potential of citizens.

But the issue of substantive fairness which must be confronted when framing the issue, and in due course the question to be put to the people, raises particular difficulties in divided polities. For those sceptical of the idea that detailed and intricate constitutional issues can be put before the people in a referendum, and for those who are understandably wary of the dangers of direct democracy in such a fractured climate, the second part of the chapter will hopefully provide some kind of answer. There we saw how citizens in Northern Ireland confronted an enormously complex constitutional settlement, engaged with it, and came together to ratify it. And they did so despite deep cleavages that divided them. The deliberative engagement of a society in matters of high constitutional consequence does require that faith be put in the capacity and willingness of citizens to engage, but the Belfast Agreement shows that this is possible. It seems that we can reasonably conclude that in a divided society a referendum can play a successful role at the end of a deliberative process that combines crucial roles for elites and the people. The former, in their representative capacity, came together to frame the Agreement, reminding us that direct democracy never takes place in a vacuum but is integrally connected to the broader generality of representative democratic process that both shapes and results from constitutive popular decision-making. But perhaps the crucial element of legitimation in Northern Ireland was letting the people have a direct voice. This served the practical purpose of preventing rejectionist elites from undermining the deal by claiming it lacked popular support. But more importantly it allowed the people, or indeed the peoples, to take ownership of a settlement and in doing so establish the institutional basis for ongoing popular engagement.

9

Referendums and Constitutional Decision-Making

I. INTRODUCTION

Republicans hold that the engagement of popular deliberation in democratic decision-making, where this is feasible and meaningful, is a political good. We have examined the extent to which constitutional referendums can and do meet this deliberation challenge. But there is one major issue still to be addressed: ultimately it is decision-making that distinguishes deliberative democracy from mere deliberation;[1] as Elster puts it: 'One can discuss only for so long, and then one has to make a decision, even if strong differences of opinion should remain.'[2] In this chapter we will address the fact that the goal of constitutional politics is, in the end, political action, and that constitutional referendums must therefore be assessed not only in light of deliberative process criteria but also by the measure of good or bad decision-making. We have seen the scepticism certain deliberative theorists have for decision-making, at least where the democratic process goes straight to the decision without scope for serious deliberation. But since for democratic practitioners the arrival at decisions is unavoidable, it is important that referendums are not criticized simply because they bring finality to a particular issue for a particular period of time. The same decision taken in another way, for example through representative actors, might well have the same effect. The question for this chapter, therefore, is not to determine whether constitutional decision-making is a good or bad thing, nor whether the referendum is the best possible means of making constitutional decisions, but rather whether the difficulties in arriving at a properly deliberative decision by way of a referendum mean that in the end the referendum is not

---

[1] Simone Chambers, 'Deliberative Democratic Theory' (2003) 6 Annual Rev of Political Science 307.

[2] Jon Elster, 'The Market and the Forum: Three Varieties of Political Theory' in Jon Elster and Aanund Hylland (eds), *Foundations of Social Choice Theory* (CUP 1986) 115.

a democratically legitimate decision-making device in processes of constitutional creation and amendment.

Thus far we have addressed process design that embraces deliberation and, where possible, the active engagement of citizens in these deliberative processes, noting the importance of inclusion. But one of the imperfections of democracy in practice is that its outcomes will inevitably better suit some citizens than others. It is here therefore that the democratic credibility of the well-designed referendum will be put to perhaps its sternest test. We have addressed how the referendum can be split into different stages, and how micro and macro elements of popular participation can be combined to help foster deliberation in a referendum process from the initiation stage through to the final result. In this chapter we are concerned with the end of the macro stage—the referendum vote itself and its aftermath. The build-up to the referendum may engage the public, citizens may be involved in helping to set the issue and even the question to be asked, educational material may be distributed to try to encourage macro-level deliberation, fair campaign funding and expenditure rules may be in place, but in the end a final decision must be taken by way of a vote. It is therefore important to address the different ways in which constitutional rules can shape this final stage of the process, assessing these for their democratic credentials, particularly in light of the three democratic objections to referendums we have used throughout.

To begin it is useful, as a final point of context-setting, to recall in principle how it is that the decision-making power of the referendum provides, for its supporters, much of its appeal and, for its detractors, much of its threat. From a republican perspective there are at least three intuitively attractive features of referendums as decision-making mechanisms. First is their simplicity. They condense an issue into, typically, one question which can be answered Yes or No in a straightforward act of popular expression. They offer a solution to a difficult issue, and they seem to suggest that this solution can be easily reached. By addressing the complexity of the referendum and its symbiotic relationship to broader representative structures we have contested such an assumption in this book, but it remains for advocates of referendums a point of compelling symbolic value. A second purported benefit of the referendum is its democratic legitimacy. To a civic republican seeking to maximize the engagement of the people in democratic decision-making the referendum is an obvious device. But this links to a third virtue: completion. A referendum promises to settle a matter, at least for the time being, to the satisfaction of both winning and losing sides. A referendum's finality hinges, of course, on a number of factors, not least the constitution, which determines whether a referendum result is binding or not. But in Chapter 4 we discussed the political as well as the legal weight a referendum carries. The fact that the people have been invoked to speak can indeed give a referendum a particular level of completion, which is perhaps lacking in the other decision-making processes of representative democracy. In other words, even if the constitution allows for this result to be overridden by the legislature, politically that would be very difficult to do. And even though a particular referendum result could be revised by way of a later referendum, elites purporting to organize such a vote shortly after the first would doubtless face the charge that they were trying to subvert the settled will of the people. Referendums allow for conflict but this is set within a time frame: there follows a vote in which a solution results that is agreed to, if not with, by the losing side; a solution that will have lasting constitutional credibility.

But it is precisely these three characteristics which for critics of referendums, particularly from the perspective of deliberative democracy, represent dangers not virtues. The notion of a straightforward solution merely serves to underestimate the complexities of modern democracy and the interlinked and mutually dependent nature of decision-making over a range of areas. Unscrupulous elites can hijack the referendum with simplistic campaign slogans, appealing to populist sentiments which ignore the complexity of the issues involved. In such a process another danger is that the people, long excluded from what they envisage as an undemocratic process of elite bargaining, may rebel not so much on the substance of the issue but against the process which has preceded it. It may be argued that this is precisely what happened to the Charlottetown Accord in Canada.[3] The legitimacy point has also been attacked, as we saw in addressing 'the control syndrome', 'the deliberation deficit', and 'the majoritarian danger'. And the purported virtue of finality is challenged by a number of deliberative democrats who argue that this can in fact undermine the very promise of deliberation because for the losing side it closes debate prematurely and irrevocably. One of the key markers of deliberative democracy is that dialogue is not foreclosed, and while decisions need to be taken, constitutional democracy should so far as possible be an ongoing process of exchange.[4] For deliberative democrats a referendum can reify one particular decision among many, giving it an almost metaphysical level of purported legitimacy that serves to deny the possibility of ongoing political engagement within society over its merits and the prospect of its revision. This is ironic, since one of the republican arguments for referendums is that they

---

[3] Richard Johnston et al, *The Challenge of Direct Democracy: The 1992 Canadian Referendum* (McGill-Queen's University Press 1996) 11–12; Ian Peach, 'The Death of Deference: The Implications of the Defeat of the Meech Lake and Charlottetown Accords for Executive Federalism in Canada' in Stephen Tierney (ed), *Multiculturalism and the Canadian Constitution* (UBC Press 2007).

[4] Robert E Goodin, *Innovating Democracy: Democratic Theory and Practice after the Deliberative Turn* (OUP 2008) 2.

free a democratic people from the conservative constraints of constitutional entrenchment. And so if the direct popular engagement of the people at the moment of constitutional decision-making is considered itself to offer legitimacy for entrenchment then this perhaps offers merely a new setting for the constituent power/constitutional form paradox; that is, the constituent power manifest in an exercise of direct democracy can become a particularly strong validation of the constitutional form that results from it.

But in addressing these concerns we should also note that deliberative democrats must remain alive to the fact that in democratic practice decisions need to be made. Indeed, for these theorists one of the goals of good deliberation is to help legitimize such decisions. Gutmann and Thompson, two of the leading writers on the normative theory of deliberative democracy are unequivocal on this point. For them a key characteristic of deliberative democracy is:

> producing a decision that is binding for some period of time. In this respect the deliberative process is not like a talk show or an academic seminar. The participants do not argue for argument's sake; they do not argue even for truth's own sake ... They intend their discussion to influence a decision the government will make, or a process that will affect how future decisions are made.[5]

For Gutmann and Thompson deliberation performs two functions. One is the constructive role that we have addressed whereby deliberation helps solve political or moral disagreements. The second, however, is a coercive role—what we might call 'democratically permissible coercion', in that deliberation can help provide legitimacy for decisions that are not unanimous.[6] Democratically permissible coercion is, of course, a difficult issue for democracy in general, and does not arise simply in the referendum context. Democracy is in part about making decisions, decisions which will inevitably better suit some than others; the existence of losers is a reality of any system. And as such the referendum cannot be evaluated against a different standard than representative democracy.

And decision-making in referendums of course means vote-taking. It is one of the curious features of deliberative democratic theory that we do not find a great deal of discussion on the subject of decision-making through voting. Indeed, O'Flynn has recently argued that 'it almost beggars belief' that so little has been done to address the relationship between deliberation,

---

[5] Amy Gutmann and Dennis Thompson, *Why Deliberative Democracy?* (Princeton University Press 2004) 7.

[6] Amy Gutmann and Dennis Thompson, *Democracy and Disagreement* (Harvard University Press 1996). See also Emily Hauptmann, 'Deliberation = Legitimacy = Democracy' (1999) 27 Political Theory 857, 863; Michael Saward, 'Enacting Democracy' (2003) 51 Political Studies 161; Jane Mansbridge et al, 'The Place of Self-Interest and the Role of Power in Deliberative Democracy' (2010) 18 J Political Philosophy 64, 65 fn 2.

particularly the concept of reciprocity as a principle of public reasoning, and voting.[7] But this is not a universal omission. Although we have observed the scepticism of deliberative democrats with voting, others are inclined to see signs of virtue in necessity. For example, Ackerman offers three defences of voting from a republican perspective: it is a form of participation that makes only a limited demand of the citizen; it is strategically important to the system as a whole; and, third, it is something citizens do together.[8] Deliberative theorists of 'the new wave', who now address the practical implications of deliberative theory, seem to appreciate more clearly that voting must be included in any meaningful account. Iris Marion Young, as an early contributor to the practicalities of deliberation, noted that both aggregative and deliberative models have things in common, including the notion that 'voting is the means of making decisions when consensus is not possible or too costly to achieve'.[9] Robert Goodin is another recent contributor to address the need for voting. He observes that mini-publics cannot claim 'electoral representation' nor 'statistical representativeness', and so we should end deliberation by voting 'given that conversations can be arbitrarily path dependent'.[10] He addresses the view that contentious issues are best not talked about, but concludes, '[a]wkward topics must sometimes be confronted and resolved, one way or another, politically'.[11] Hence, 'the time for deliberation must at some point end and a decision (however provisionally) be settled upon'.[12]

In this chapter we will address how deliberative theorists face up to the moment of decision, viewing it as an inevitable part of the imperfect and difficult business of democracy. Decisions do need to be taken, voting can be central to this process, and so the task is to find ways of achieving vote-based decisions that will imbue this process with a 'more complex and richer interpretation' (per Chambers[13]), in the ultimate quest for deliberation, than might otherwise be the case.

But, of course, from the perspective of republican deliberative democracy there are a number of concerns with the final moment of decision-making

---

[7] Ian O'Flynn, *Deliberative Democracy and Divided Societies* (Edinburgh University Press 2006) 86.

[8] Bruce Ackerman, *We the People: Foundations* (Harvard University Press 1991) 238–9.

[9] Iris Marion Young, *Inclusion and Democracy* (OUP 2002) 18.

[10] Goodin, *Innovating Democracy*, 4.

[11] ibid 65. Pettit also addresses this in his notion of 'contestatory democracy'. Philip Pettit, *Republicanism: A Theory of Freedom and Government* (OUP 1997) 277–8.

[12] Goodin, *Innovating Democracy*, 65. See also Ian Shapiro, 'Optimal Deliberation?' (2002) 10 J Political Philosophy 196, and Przeworski, who observes 'deliberative theorists... wish away the vulgar fact that under democracy deliberation ends in voting'. Adam Przeworski 'Deliberation and Ideological Domination' in Jon Elster (ed), *Deliberative Democracy* (CUP 1998) 141.

[13] Chambers, 'Deliberative Democratic Theory', 308.

that are specific to the referendum. We will return to the problem raised in the last chapter of the referendum result which is inchoate, in the sense that its implications are unclear to voters. In such a situation the referendum can leave considerable discretion to elites to act pursuant to the referendum result in ways unforeseen or indeed unforeseeable by many voters. One example we will consider is referendums on sovereignty or independence for sub-state territories. A referendum on independence may seem like a straightforward issue but in fact it is often merely the beginning of a complex process of negotiation between centre and sub-state governments. One possibility is that no referendum should be held until final negotiations have taken place. But in many cases a referendum is essential in encouraging the central authorities to negotiate in the first place. Another possibility is two referendums, one to mandate political actors to enter negotiations and another to ratify or reject the outcome of negotiations. I will address arguments for and against such an option in Section II.

Second, the very finality of a major constitutional decision raises again the spectre of majoritarian danger. If an unfair decision is taken which is itself irreversible, the damage done to the interests of minorities can be particularly egregious. Iris Marion Young offers the interesting insight that it is the very prospect of a decision made through agreement that induces people to participate in deliberation at all:

> While actually reaching consensus is thus not a requirement of deliberation reason, participants in discussion must be *aiming* to reach agreement to enter the discussion at all. Only if the participants believe that some kind of agreement among them is possible in principle can they in good faith trust one another to listen and aim to persuade one another.[14]

Jane Mansbridge echoes the point made by Gutmann and Thompson about the coercive element in democracy: 'democracies must have their coercive as well as their deliberation moments'.[15] But she does so with an important caveat. For such coercion to be justified, it must be shown that the process of public deliberation was 'equally open to all'[16] in order for it to be considered legitimate even to losers. This brings us back to the idea of differentiated equality in the context of pluralist societies. One danger of simple majority decision-making is that it can overlook the existence of distinct groups within society, particularly the reality of national pluralism. In this context, in Section III we will address the use of threshold or quorum

---

[14] Young, *Inclusion and Democracy*, 24.
[15] Jane Mansbridge, 'Using Power/Fighting Power: The Polity' in Seyla Benhabib (ed), *Democracy and Difference: Contesting the Boundaries of the Political* (Princeton University Press 1996) 46.
[16] ibid.

rules which require particular levels of turnout or support for a referendum outcome to pass, and in doing so we will address divided societies as a special case.

II. ONE REFERENDUM OR TWO? WIDENING THE SPACE FOR PUBLIC REASONING

A number of deliberative theorists emphasize the importance of avoiding closure to political debate. Clearly when we are talking about decision-making then some kind of end point is implied. But one way in which these concerns can be accommodated is by seeking to prevent *premature* foreclosure of deliberation. For in certain types of deliberation a referendum can intervene seemingly in a finalizing way, when in fact the issue itself remains unsettled, and hence the referendum decision uncertain as to its effect.

The case study we will use is the referendum that authorizes a government to enter into negotiations to bring about constitutional change. Let us take two examples: a central government being authorized by referendum to negotiate an international treaty, and a sub-state government being authorized to negotiate 'sovereignty' or secession. In each case the elite in question may well feel itself empowered to reach an agreement claiming the referendum as the endorsement for this, even though voters in the referendum merely authorized negotiations and cannot necessarily foresee the outcome of these. And indeed the result might be an agreement very different from the one that voters believed they were mandating, perhaps leaving citizens feeling excluded from and disenfranchised by the final result. Another consequence of ending citizen participation prematurely is that, with no further control over the ongoing negotiations and the outcomes of these discussions, citizens may switch off and cease to deliberate about these important developments, potentially reducing any sense of authorship they will feel in respect of potentially momentous changes to the system of government.

The democratic deficit here does not necessarily imply bad faith on the part of elites. Even if negotiators embark on negotiations with the best intentions and attentive to what they take to be the wishes of the voters, the outcome of negotiations is by definition unforeseeable. This is particularly so when the actors vested with the power to negotiate are in a weak position. For example, a national government mandated to negotiate an international treaty setting conditions for entry or reformed membership of an international organization, enters a process which will be influenced and shaped by many (and often more powerful) states as well as the institutions of the international organization itself. Similarly, a sub-state elite seeking to negotiate secession may well come up against the impediment of a strong central government, one with no obligation under international law or domestic constitutional law to agree to secession, and indeed facing strong political pressure either to refuse to agree or to drive a hard bargain.

In these situations, no matter how deliberative the referendum has been in terms of an inclusive and carefully planned participatory process, one that has fostered discussion and reflection at micro and macro levels, and one that has attempted to be as pluralistic and accommodating of minority interests as possible, all of these efforts to give the people authorship over important constitutional change might be undone by a back-room negotiation process involving the horse-trading of interests.

In light of this, is there an argument from the perspective of deliberative democracy for a second referendum to ratify or reject the outcome of the negotiations? If an issue is of such importance that from the perspective of republican democracy the people have a prima facie claim to authorize negotiations, then it might seem that this authorship entitlement should extend to validating or rejecting the outcome of these negotiations too, at least when the eventual outcome reached is one that was not clearly anticipated at the time of the referendum vote itself.

Where the referendum is not a mandate to negotiate because the detail of the constitutional package is broadly agreed before the referendum, the implementation process subsequent to the referendum is quite straightforward. We see this, for example, after the devolution referendums in the UK in 1997 and 1998. Taking the referendum on Scottish devolution in 1997 as an example, the people were asked if they were in favour of a Scottish Parliament and a limited tax-varying power for that Parliament. The model of devolution was set out in a White Paper published before the referendum. Following a Yes vote in the referendum, this was enacted into law in a way that was faithful to the vast bulk of the White Paper's provisions. In this sense it can fairly be said that the Scottish people got the model of devolution for which they had voted. A second referendum here on the terms of the Scotland Act would have been absurd and consequently no political actors called for it.

But this should be distinguished from 'mandate referendums' where the consequences of a Yes vote are less clear. In 1980 the Quebec government held a referendum on sovereignty. The referendum asked voters to give the Quebec government a mandate to negotiate 'sovereignty-association' with Canada. In other words, the referendum envisaged independent statehood coupled with a continued economic and political association with the rest of the country. A commitment was given in the very question to the effect that the outcome of the negotiations with the rest of Canada, following a Yes vote in the first referendum, would need to be ratified by a second referendum in Quebec.[17] This never took place, as the first referendum was unsuccessful.

By contrast, the Quebec referendum process in 1995, which also envisaged a similar association through negotiation scenario—in effect independent statehood for Quebec coupled with a partnership agreement with Canada—did not explicitly anticipate a second referendum. As we observed in Chapter 5, the hostility towards Quebec sovereignty within the federal government and the other provinces, not to mention among certain aboriginal communities within Quebec itself,[18] suggests that if a Yes vote had been secured, and if the rest of the country had been persuaded to enter into negotiations, a hard bargain might well have been driven. It could be argued that a second referendum in Quebec would have been important in legitimizing the final settlement.[19]

Again, the scenario that would have followed the referendum that was planned but then postponed by the Scottish National Party government in 2010 was unclear. As we saw in Chapter 8, the proposed referendum contained two separate questions. A Yes vote on the second question would have been taken to authorize negotiations towards independence.[20] The UK government would most likely have been willing to negotiate independence but it may well not have agreed to the model of sovereignty set out in the White Paper which anticipates some form of 'monarchical and social union'.[21] This again begs the question. Would the Scottish Government then have attempted to make a declaration of independence or would

---

[17] The question in the referendum actually made reference to this:

> The Government of Quebec has made public its proposal to negotiate a new agreement with the rest of Canada, based on the equality of nations; this agreement would enable Quebec to acquire the exclusive power to make its laws, levy its taxes and establish relations abroad—in other words, sovereignty—and at the same time to maintain with Canada an economic association including a common currency; any change in political status resulting from these negotiations will only be implemented with popular approval through another referendum; on these terms, do you give the Government of Quebec the mandate to negotiate the proposed agreement between Quebec and Canada?

[18] An interesting postscript is that there was a second referendum in 1995 called by the aboriginal peoples in the province. They argued that their constitutional relationship was primarily with the Crown through the federal government, and that on this basis they had a discrete right to a determinative say on the issue of Quebec secession.

[19] The prospect that the federal government and other provinces would refuse to negotiate or would put strenuous hurdles in Quebec's path seems to have been anticipated by Quebec nationalists, who wrote into the enabling legislation provision for a unilateral declaration of independence in the event that negotiations remained unsuccessful after one year.

[20] *Scotland's Future: Draft Referendum (Scotland) Bill Consultation Paper* (The Scottish Government 2010) 17–19, paras 1.33–1.40.

[21] Michael Keating, *The Independence of Scotland: Self-government and the Shifting Politics of Union* (OUP 2009) 130.

they have accepted a different but agreed model of government with the UK government? The White Paper provided that: 'While the referendum will have no legal effect on the Union, the Scottish Government would expect the UK and Scottish Parliaments and the respective Governments to listen to the views of the Scottish people and act on them.'[22] This implies negotiation. And: 'Following the necessary negotiations between the Scottish and UK Governments, it would then be for the Scottish and UK Parliaments to act on the expressed will of the Scottish people... in line with the position set out in paragraph 1.32.'[23] A second referendum was clearly not anticipated by the Scottish Government,[24] a position that has been confirmed since the 2011 Scottish parliamentary elections.[25] Although it has been suggested that constitutionally such a referendum would be appropriate and even that it should be authorized by Westminster,[26] this would seem to be a very high-risk strategy for the central government that could well serve only to intensify nationalist sentiment in Scotland. But where negotiations will lead in the event of a Yes vote on some model of independence remains unclear and the difficult issue does remain that the negotiations might produce a result that was not anticipated by many people voting Yes in the referendum.[27]

A different scenario from the mandate referendum is using the first referendum to narrow down people's preferences. One interesting precedent is the Dominion of Newfoundland, where two referendums were held in 1948. On 3 June the voters were offered three options. These were: a return to dominion status based upon 'responsible government', union with the Canadian Confederation, or the status quo, termed 'Commission of Government'. The first option gained 44.6 per cent support, the second 41.1 per cent, and the third 14.3 per cent. The first two options were then offered in a second referendum, with the confederation option winning by 52.3 per cent to 47.7 per cent.

---

[22] *Scotland's Future*, para 1.32.

[23] ibid para 1.40.   [24] ibid para 1.37.

[25] Brian Currie and Michael Settle, 'Moore Blasted by SNP on Second Referendum Plan', *The Herald* (Glasgow, 7 June 2011) <http://www.heraldscotland.com/news/politics/moore-blasted-by-snp-on-second-referendum-plan-1.1105507> accessed 20 October 2011.

[26] Jo E Murkens, Peter Jones, and Michael Keating, *Scottish Independence: A Practical Guide* (Edinburgh University Press 2002) 39–40.

[27] Polls show there can be very different understandings of 'independence', with some anticipating traditional independent statehood and others that Anglo-Scottish relations will be more confederal in nature, involving a common army, currency etc. Keating, *The Independence of Scotland*, 76–7.

In certain situations it would seem that a second referendum would help facilitate further deliberation. People would be encouraged to continue to reflect upon and discuss the ongoing negotiation process (thus reducing the prospect of precipitate foreclosure of debate that is in many ways the antithesis of an open process of public reasoning), knowing that they will have the ultimate say in ratifying or rejecting the outcome of this. An additional benefit in a second referendum might be that elite negotiators will be induced to approach the negotiations in a more transparent, deliberative, and even conciliatory way, knowing that they will ultimately have to justify the agreement reached to the people in the macro-level deliberation of the referendum campaign and ultimately at the ballot box.[28] The principle of an issue-framing referendum might be extended to other situations where constitutional deliberations take place on particularly complex or highly disputed issues. The first referendum could serve the task of generating the initial views of the public on an issue that requires further elaboration or even of clarifying what issues people would like to see put to them in the final referendum. An 'issue-framing' referendum, might also serve an information-giving or educational purpose for citizens and in this way help to generate further deliberation. This has been suggested in the context of the Australian head of state issue. Following the defeat of the republican proposal in 1999, the Australian Republican Movement in evidence to the Senate's Legal and Constitutional References Committee recommended three framing plebiscites to be followed by a final referendum. The first would ask whether Australia should become a republic, the second would ask Australians their preferred model, and a third would ask them to choose the title of the head of state. A fully elected Convention would then draft the model to be put to the Australian people in a referendum.[29] In a difficult situation where the issue is complex, the options many, the views of the public unclear, or the possible implications of a Yes vote in an initial referendum uncertain there are, it seems, significant arguments from the perspective of popular deliberation for two polls. But there are practical problems here and the expense of two referendums should not be underestimated. In addition, particularly in the sub-state context there is the

---

[28] The Charlottetown referendum is perceived to show the danger in not doing so. Here ordinary people were not generally involved and when the deal was put to them in a referendum it was summarily rejected.

[29] When the Senate Legal and Constitutional References Committee Inquiry into an Australian Republic tabled its report it recommended two framing plebiscites. The first would be a non-binding plebiscite asking Australians whether they want Australia to become a republic with an Australian head of state. The second would be another non-binding plebiscite, where Australians would choose their preferred model for a republic from a range of options. Australian Senate Legal and Constitutional References Committee, *The Road to a Republic* (Commonwealth of Australia 2004) para 8.28.

considerable danger that the prospect of a second referendum would allow the central state to drive a hard bargain, perhaps imposing terms which they expect would be rejected by voters.

III. THRESHOLD FOR ENDORSEMENT: EQUALITY VS MAJORITARIANISM

One of the key criticisms we have addressed in the book is the propensity of referendums to become the weapon of choice for a majority seeking to assert, and in so doing legitimize the expression of, its will over that of minorities. I have argued that in accordance with the principle of equality and parity of esteem, a referendum process to be properly deliberative must give minorities a meaningful voice. This is a difficult and for many a counterintuitive possibility in a referendum process. For all the efforts to build consensus throughout a constitution-making procedure it is, in the end, at the moment of decision-making that the interests of minorities can fall prey to the simple force of numbers that compose the majority will. A referendum comes down to a vote and a majority knows that at this point it can get its way, leading to what I have called the 'majoritarian disincentive' to deliberation.

This leads us to arguments for counter-majoritarian devices to be included in referendums, requiring a model of support for a particular proposition in some way greater or at least different from a simple majority of those voting. We should distinguish two arguments. One is that a high level of consensus should be secured for constitutional change because of the importance of the issues involved in higher order lawmaking. This is in some sense a subset of the broader argument that super-majorities should be required to endorse constitutional change of any kind, whether this is done by representatives or by the direct decision of citizens in a referendum.[30] In other words, setting a threshold ensures a broad level of consensus, which is important for constitutional change in any polity, whether particularly pluralist in composition or not. A different although related argument is that a super-majority is required specifically to protect particular minorities, and therefore the consent of these specific minorities should be part of any legitimate consensus on the issue at hand. The second argument envisions the polity as multinational or multi-societal and contends that the consent of each community is essential to legitimize certain constitutional decisions. In the course of this section I will argue that from the perspective of civic republicanism the latter justification, which might be crucial in divided societies, has for that reason more to

---

[30] For a discussion see David Dyzenhaus, 'The Rule of Law as the Rule of Liberal Principle' in Arthur Ripstein (ed), *Ronald Dworkin* (CUP 2007) esp 70–1, 73–4.

commend it than the former. In addressing these arguments I will consider various situations where threshold rules have been used and I will also make reference to evolving international standards in this area.

To begin, let us distinguish three models whereby a threshold rule might be applied in a referendum decision. The first and by far the most common quorum model requires the participation of a certain percentage of the registered electorate or voting population. This is very common in Europe, where a number of constitutions, particularly in Central and East European states, set such a turnout threshold for the referendum to be valid,[31] while Estonia, Slovenia, and Albania are unusual in having referendum laws with no quorum requirement. States that require at least 50 per cent of eligible voters to turn out for the referendum to be valid include Poland, Slovakia, Slovenia, Latvia, Hungary, Romania, Italy, Portugal, and Sweden.[32] A variation on this model is a requirement that a particular percentage of eligible voters must actually vote for the measure for it to be approved. The 2003 Hungarian constitution, for example, set a 25 per cent threshold,[33] while in Denmark a referendum to amend the constitution can only be valid if the issue, as well as gaining a majority of those voting, is also supported by 40 per cent of the eligible electorate.[34] Moldova was until recently an exceptional case. Its referendum code set a threshold of 60 per cent of all voters on the voter registry until this was reduced to one-third in 2010.[35]

A second type of threshold rule requires a double majority. This typically arises in a federal state such as Australia, which requires a national majority and majorities in four of the six states to approve a proposed constitutional amendment. When one considers that out of 44 amendments proposed since 1906, 36 have failed it might be thought that this creates gridlock. But as LeDuc argues, on closer inspection 'only a few constitutional proposals have failed solely because of this double-majority requirement'.[36] Galligan

---

[31] See Georg Brunner, 'Direct vs Representative Democracy' in Andreas Auer and Michael Bützer (eds), *Direct Democracy: The Eastern and Central European Experience* (Ashgate 2001) 222; See also Bruno S Frey, 'Direct Democracy for Transition Countries' (2003) 7 J Institutional Innovation 42.

[32] Carlos Flores Juberias, 'Some Legal (and Political) Considerations about the Legal Framework for Referendum in Montenegro, in the Light of European Experiences and Standards' in Sanja Elezovic (ed), *Legal Aspects for Referendum in Montenegro in the Context of International Law and Practice* (Foundation Open Society Institute-Representative Office Montenegro 2005) 63.

[33] Constitution of the Republic of Hungary, Art 28C(6).

[34] Constitution of Denmark, s 88. The 40 per cent rule was also used for referendums on devolution in Scotland and Wales in 1979: Scotland Act 1978, s 85(2); Wales Act 1978, s 80(2).

[35] Pavel Cabacenco, 'Moldova, On the Threshold of Change' (*Election Guide Digest*, 1 September 2010) <http://digest.electionguide.org/2010/09/01/cabacenco-moldova-on-the-threshold-of-change-2/> accessed 10 October 2011.

[36] Lawrence LeDuc, *The Politics of Direct Democracy: Referendums in Global Perspective* (Broadview Press 2003) 69.

also rejects the stasis argument and says that the trend in Australia has been for voters to reject 'self-serving'[37] attempts by central government to enhance its powers. Another example is Switzerland, which has a double majority requirement for constitutional referendums involving international treaties and constitutional amendments. Such a referendum must receive a majority of all the votes cast, and a majority in more than half of the country's cantons.[38] One can find the requirement of double majority even *within* a federal sub-state. For example, the referendums in British Columbia on electoral reform in 2005 and 2009 required 60 per cent approval across the province together with 50 per cent approval in at least 60 per cent of ridings. In neither case was this threshold reached.

One interesting scenario is synchronized, and mutually dependent, referendums held in two places at once. As we saw in Chapter 8, the Belfast Agreement needed majorities in referendums held in both Northern Ireland and the Republic of Ireland to take effect. One referendum was held in Northern Ireland asking for approval or rejection of the Agreement; on the same day a second referendum was held in the Republic of Ireland on the issue of amending the Irish constitution. It is one of the unique features of the Belfast Agreement that we see constitutional change for Northern Ireland, and by extension for the wider UK, being tied so closely to constitutional decisions in a second state.[39]

A number of these examples are significant in showing that the specificity of the demos, or demoi, is being taken into account. For example, the rationale of the Swiss case is to prevent the German-speaking majority of the population from enacting legislation 'which impairs the rights of the minorities'.[40] The Irish case illustrates that the interested actors extend beyond Northern Ireland itself. The UK as a whole would indirectly assent to the Agreement through the passage of legislation such as the Northern Ireland Act by the UK Parliament. But the link between Irish nationalists in Northern Ireland and the Republic of Ireland, and the historical claim of Ireland to sovereignty over the North were also recognized in the fact of the Irish referendum and more crucially in the very dependence of the Agreement upon its outcome.

---

[37] Brian Galligan, 'Amending Constitutions through the Referendum Device' in Matthew Mendelsohn and Andrew Parkin (eds), *Referendum Democracy: Citizens, Elites and Deliberation in Referendum Campaigns* (Palgrave 2001) 119.

[38] Constitution of Switzerland 1999, Art 142.

[39] Geoff Gilbert, 'The Northern Ireland Peace Agreement, Minority Rights and Self-Determination' (1998) 47 ICLQ 943, 950.

[40] Matt Qvortrup, *A Comparative Study of Referendums: Government by the People* (Manchester University Press 2005) 15.

The third and in some ways most obvious model is to set a number of votes higher than 50 per cent plus 1 of those who turn out for the measure to pass (this is different from the first scenario, since it focuses on turnout rather than voter registration). Going back to the ratification of the state constitutions in the new American federation, Massachusetts and New Hampshire both set thresholds of two-thirds of those citizens voting to ratify their constitutions.[41] However, modern examples of such a requirement are surprisingly rare and tend to be focused upon the most fundamental issue of territorial integrity. For example, the constitution of St Kitts and Nevis provides for the possibility of the secession of Nevis but one requirement is that the measure is approved in a referendum on Nevis by not less than two-thirds of all the votes validly cast.[42] Lithuania's constitution also seeks to preserve the independence of the country by providing that this independence 'may only be altered by referendum if not less than 3/4 of the citizens of Lithuania with the electoral right vote in favour thereof'. In other words, this is a citizen threshold that by definition brings with it a supermajority threshold for those who turn out.[43]

The issue of such a threshold arose in Canada after the Quebec referendum of 1995. We have seen how the Supreme Court of Canada opined that Quebec's partners in confederation would be required to negotiate the secession of Quebec in the event of a 'clear majority' voting for such an option in a future referendum; and how this resulted in both federal legislation seeking to replicate this requirement and a legislative response by Quebec.

This issue arose also in the Montenegro referendum in 2006, and in doing so involved a number of international organizations which were engaged in helping draft the rules for that referendum. We have observed that a 55 per cent threshold was set under the heavy influence of the EU Special Envoy.[44] Montenegro's referendum law already stipulated that a referendum would be valid only if turnout was greater than 50 per cent of eligible voters. This, in addition to a 55 per cent rule, was endorsed by the EU.[45]

---

[41] Dennis C Mueller, *Constitutional Democracy* (OUP 1996) 180.

[42] Constitution of St Kitts and Nevis, s 113(2)(b).

[43] Constitution of the Republic of Lithuania, Art 148.

[44] Organization for Security and Co-operation in Europe/Office for Democratic Institutions and Human Rights (OSCE/ODIHR), 'Statement of Preliminary Findings and Conclusions—Referendum on State-Status, Republic of Montenegro (Serbia and Montenegro)—International Referendum Observation Mission, 21 May 2006' (Podgorica, 22 May 2006) 3; see also OSCE/ODIHR, 'Republic of Montenegro—Serbia and Montenegro Referendum, 21 May 2006—Needs Assessment Mission Report, 7–9 March 2006' (Warsaw, 14 March 2006) 5–6.

[45] International Crisis Group, 'Montenegro's Referendum' Europe Briefing No 42 (International Crisis Group, 30 May 2006) 2–3 <http://www.crisisgroup.org/en/regions/europe/balkans/montenegro.aspx> accessed 10 October 2011.

(i) A case for thresholds?

One argument for a threshold in a referendum is that requiring higher levels of agreement can encourage the building of broader consensus before an agreement is reached, which may in turn require participants to be more deliberative in their dealings with others. The analogy to juries which require unanimity or near unanimity is sometimes drawn.[46] One factor that should be taken into account in this context, however, is that we have set out in the preceding two chapters various procedural devices that might be used to help build deliberation and agreement, allowing the myriad of voices in society to have a chance to be heard and to influence decision-making. If a process is made to be as deliberative as possible up to the point of the referendum vote, then it might be argued that there is less reason for the referendum not to be settled by simple majority. It is also intuitively undemocratic that group A who want X are required to demonstrate greater support than group B who want Y.

Returning to the two possible justifications for a threshold requirement which we set out at the beginning, it is interesting that while many constitutions do have super-majority voting requirements for constitutional change, this usually applies only to representative institutions or territorial subdivisions of the state; it is very rare for such a requirement to be set for referendums. In other words, although turnout thresholds which require that a certain percentage of the electorate must participate to validate the referendum are common, in terms of the actual vote itself 50 per cent plus 1 remains overwhelmingly the most frequently used method. Indeed, in many systems where a hybrid requirement for constitutional change is in place—that is, needing the approval of both the legislature and the people—we see a super-majority requirement within parliament which is then followed by a referendum which merely needs 50 per cent of those who vote to support the measure (with or without a turnout threshold, as the case may be).

This suggests that while institutions are expected to build consensus in order to amend the constitution, when the people are mobilized to speak the principle of simple majoritarianism is generally accepted. This is perhaps because such a referendum is seen as some instantiation of a revived constituent power, and in this light it is perhaps considered illegitimate to prevent the popular will from prevailing by the most instinctively obvious majority.

It is also possible to see considerable objections to a threshold. In the first place, the setting of super-majorities in any form of constitutional amendment process can seem to be somewhat arbitrary. What will the threshold

---

[46] Chambers, 'Deliberative Democratic Theory', 318.

be—two-thirds? Three-quarters? And why such a number? We see the difficulty in the open-ended 'clear majority' signal offered by the Supreme Court of Canada, which it then failed to clarify. The 55 per cent rule in Montenegro again was, as we will discuss later, largely arbitrary and in many ways a political fix. This is arguably just as problematic when setting turnout thresholds. As Kobach observes:

> there is nothing magical about the number 50 when it comes to defining legitimate participation levels... if 50 per cent participate, then 25 per cent of the population, plus one, can decide the issue. And there is certainly nothing magical about 25 per cent. The minimum level of participation cannot be set objectively at any particular number.[47]

There is also the danger of stasis with constitutions very difficult to change. We see this in the USA without the explicit need for a referendum in the constitutional amendment process, and at least potentially in Australia discussed earlier.

Michael Gallagher offers an interesting critique of the turnout threshold rule which is, as we have seen, very common across Europe. He points to the referendum in Italy in April 1999, where over 90 per cent voted to change the electoral system but the turnout was just below the required 50 per cent of eligible voters. One way to look at such a result is that the measure is defeated not because of lack of support but because not enough opposed it.[48] Another example is a referendum in Denmark in 1939 on reforming the upper house. At that time a threshold rule required that 45 per cent of the electorate vote Yes to approve the measure: 92 per cent of those voting did so but, given a low turnout, that amounted to only 44.5 per cent of the electorate.[49] We can also see how a particular threshold can be set for strategic rather than principled reasons by turning again to Montenegro, where there was for a time also a serious risk of a boycott of the 2006 referendum by unionists.[50] The referendum law of 2001 had a turnout requirement of 50 per cent of eligible voters and a serious risk was that those opposed to independence would boycott on the assumption that the

---

[47] Kris W Kobach, 'Lessons Learned in the Participation Game' in Auer and Bützer (eds), *Direct Democracy*, 293. In opposing approval quorums, the Venice Commission also points to the potential political risks that can arise 'if the draft is adopted by a simple majority lower than the necessary threshold'. European Commission for Democracy Through Law (Venice Commission), 'Code of Good Practice on Referendums' Study No 371/2006 (20 January 2009), COE Doc CDL-AD(2007)008rev, para III.7 and Explanatory Memorandum, para 52.

[48] Michael Gallagher, 'Popular Sovereignty and Referendums' in Auer and Bützer (eds), *Direct Democracy*, 233.

[49] Vernon Bogdanor, 'Western Europe' in David Butler and Austin Ranney (eds), *Referendums Around the World: The Growing Use of Direct Democracy* (Macmillan Press 1994) 44–5.

[50] International Crisis Group, 'Montenegro's Referendum', 2–3.

pro-vote would not secure the necessary turnout threshold.[51] In the end, this turnout rule was retained along with the 55 per cent voting threshold.[52] We must therefore also see the intervention of the EU and the 55 per cent rule as part of a strategy that would make a Yes vote achievable for Montenegro separatists, but would also give the No side sufficient confidence to vote.

In statistical terms, the lower the turnout in such a scenario, the higher the majority needs to be supporting the measure: for example, with a requirement that 50 per cent of eligible voters must vote Yes to approve a measure, a 75 per cent turnout would need 66.7 per cent to vote Yes, and on a 65 per cent turnout a 76.9 per cent Yes vote would be required. As de Vreese observes, some actors may 'aim simply to demobilize voters'.[53] In countries with particular problems with voter turnout this can be a considerable weapon for political parties and, more generally, Uleri observes the role of parties 'is almost always crucial to ensure that the voter forum required by the Constitution be reached'.[54] Certainly if a threshold rule, by making a boycott a strategically sensible option, actively discourages participation, then its value must be carefully questioned, particularly from the perspective of deliberative democracy.

It is also important to note that a threshold requirement, no matter what general arguments can be offered in its defence, can in particular referendums be introduced for strategic and unprincipled reasons. Political calculations were at least partly responsible for the 40 per cent turnout rule for the 1979 devolution referendums in Scotland and Wales. At issue here was an internal dispute within the Labour Party. Qvortrup discusses how it was clear to opponents of devolution in the Labour Party that if devolution Bills were defeated the government would fall in the course of the 1978–79 parliament. Therefore their aim was to do damage to the Bills without

---

[51] The boycott risk seems to be a principal reason why the Venice Commission is opposed to a turnout quorum. In the 2007 Code it argues that such a rule 'assimilates voters who abstain to those who vote No'. Venice Commission, 'Code of Good Practice on Referendums', para III.7 and Explanatory Memorandum, para 51: 'Encouraging either abstention or the imposition of a minority viewpoint is not healthy for democracy'. Although notably this position has not always been consistently held: Venice Commission, 'Opinion on the Compatibility of the Existing Legislation in Montenegro Concerning the Organisation of Referendums with Applicable International Standards' (19 December 2005), COE Doc CDL-AD(2005)041, para 37, discussed in Chapter 6.

[52] OSCE/ODIHR, 'Republic of Montenegro, Referendum on State-Status' (Warsaw, 21 May 2006); OSCE/ODIHR, 'Referendum Observation Mission, Final Report' (Warsaw, 4 August 2006) 5.

[53] Claes H de Vreese, 'Context, Elites, Media and Public Opinion in Referendums: When Campaigns Really Matter' in Claes H de Vreese (ed), *The Dynamics of Referendum Campaigns: An International Perspective* (Palgrave Macmillan 2007) 10. See also Kobach, 'Lessons Learned in the Participation Game'.

[54] Piers Vincenzo Uleri, 'On Referendum Voting in Italy: YES, NO or non-vote? How Italian Parties Learned to Control Referendums' (2002) 41 European J Political Research 863, 880. In relation to Denmark with its 40 per cent requirement Svensson also observes how large parties can destroy such initiatives by being passive (Uleri, 881).

preventing their passage and it was in this regard that they proposed the amendment which required the support of at least 40 per cent of eligible voters.[55] Again if we turn to Montenegro, the reason for the 55 per cent rule in 2006 was the interplay of demographics (two fairly evenly matched communities in terms of size) and polling support for independence, that seemed to hover around the 50 per cent mark.[56] In this context the voting threshold of 55 per cent, effectively imposed by the EU, was a risky strategy. If the result had been a Yes vote for independence between 50 and 55 per cent, both sides could have felt the right to claim victory.[57] In the end the formula worked; a vote in favour of 55.5 per cent was enough to meet the threshold requirement and hence to produce a result that was sufficiently clear to both sides.

IV. DEEPLY DIVIDED SOCIETIES: MAJORITARIAN DISINCENTIVES AND CONSOCIATIONAL REFERENDUMS?

The Montenegro case brings us back to the second justification for thresholds—the minority groups/divided society consideration. One is reminded of de Tocqueville's comment: 'I regard as impious and detestable the maxim which states that in matters of government the majority of a people has a right to do whatever it pleases. Yet I place the origin of all powers in the will of the majority. Am I contradicting myself?'[58] With this conundrum in mind, it might be possible to make a specific case for some model of threshold designed to take account of the societal specificities of, in particular, a plurinational society. In other words, while accepting the general principle of majoritarianism for referendums that have otherwise been designed according to the principles of deliberative democracy, an exception may be justified in the case of divided or plurinational states.[59]

Of course, the referendum is something of a paradox for the divided society, as we discussed in Chapter 8. There we noted the common assumption that elite accommodation is the only viable way of arriving at constitutional solutions for divided societies, but on the other hand from a republican perspective constitutional change requires the sustenance of popular legitimacy. But since popular

---

[55] Qvortrup, *A Comparative Study of Referendums* (2002), 112–13.

[56] 'Opinion polls over several years had usually shown the pro-independence side with a small lead but not an absolute majority.' International Crisis Group, 'Montenegro's Referendum', 2–3.

[57] ibid 6.

[58] Alexis de Tocqueville, *Democracy in America* (Harvey Mansfield and Delba Winthrop eds and trs, University of Chicago Press 2000) T 2, c 7.

[59] Of course, the term 'plurinational state' is not co-terminous with that of divided society. But some of the same issues concerning the need for cross-community inclusion apply in both situations, leading to similar arguments for multiple majorities in referendums to protect a plurality of (and in particular, minority) interests.

legitimacy is so often assumed to be represented by a simple majority in a referendum, we are once again confronted with the particular pathology of referendums if such a model of majoritarianism in divided societies is used perversely to cement existing hegemonic relationships.

To take account of the fact that the state is in effect a 'union-state', comprising a number of nations, there is potentially an argument that in a referendum on a fundamental issue then double (or multiple, depending on the number of nations) majorities ought to be achieved. The uni-national but federal state of Australia goes some way towards such a model, of course, in that as well as the support of a national majority of voters a majority of states needs to approve any referendum proposal. The plurinational model would go beyond this in requiring unanimous approval by its constituent units. The closest model to this seems to be that of Switzerland, with its provision for the consent of all cantons for constitutional amendments. This is, of course, an onerous requirement, but the demands of sub-state nations for equality in the process of constitutional change needs a changing mindset as to the purpose of the constitution in a plurinational state,[60] and the degree of inter-communal agreement needed to secure this in a legitimate way. An analogy might well be made with treaty-making at the international level, or at the level of the EU, where the unanimity of member states is required. If it is unrealistic to expect the unanimous agreement of a number of national societies to every constitutional change, one compromise might be to declare a number of fundamental issues that would need such a requirement, leaving a qualified majority for other matters. And this could be supplemented with a requirement that in relation to matters affecting a particular territory or society, the consent of that group would be specifically required.[61]

We should also recall the danger in not taking account of national pluralism in the staging of referendums in Northern Ireland in 1973, Bosnia in 1992, and in the referendum on the return of King Leopold to Belgium in 1950. Where referendums are applied in this way as the democratic weapon of choice by dominant majorities then the issue of boycott emerges again. We have noted the boycott by nationalists of the 1973 referendum in Northern Ireland, while the prevalence of impercipience as the SFRY collapsed is observed by Emerson: 'In Bosnia, the Serbs abstained. In Serbia, the Kosovars abstained. In Kosovo, the Serbs abstained. While in Macedonia, both the Albanians and the Serbs abstained.'[62] But in some sense the risk

---

[60] Stephen Tierney, *Constitutional Law and National Pluralism* (OUP 2004) 13–17.

[61] eg the Constitution of Australia, s 128 provides that the federal representation of any state cannot be diminished without the consent of that state's voters in a referendum.

[62] Peter J Emerson, *Defining Democracy: Decisions, Elections and Good Governance* (The De Borda Institute 2002) 6.

here is the opposite of that we noted earlier in relation to turnout thresholds. In those cases it was the *existence* of a threshold requirement that could provoke a boycott, allowing a minority to defeat the measure. However, in a divided society it might well be the very *absence* of special threshold arrangements that can have the same effect; here the minority refuses to take part because a pro-hegemonic result is a fait accompli.

Deliberative democracy theory becomes important here not only in embracing the pluralism of the people, but in anterior processes of defining the people in the first place. As Emerson puts it: 'no "people" should be able to determine itself on the basis of only a majority of itself. Instead, all concerned should come to a verbal or votal consensus, both internally within the proposed new borders, and externally with their future neighbours.'[63] We have addressed in Chapter 3 how a crucial first stage in any constitutional referendum is defining the demos. In situations of conflict, hostility, or simply different constitutional aspirations, these differences must also be acknowledged before engaging in attempts to develop the constitution.

We also argued in Chapter 8 that the goal of deliberation across boundaries should not be surrendered too quickly. In ideal terms the aim of deliberative democracy is to reach consensus among different groups. This was shown to be realistic in the case of Northern Ireland, where some degree of inter-communal deliberation was feasible even in a deeply divided environment. But we need to recall Iris Marion Young's insight that it is the very prospect of a decision made through agreement and without the inevitability of majority imposition that induces such people to participate in deliberation at all.[64] And in this context the goal should be finding agreements that are workable for all sides in a divided society. But with the prospect of a winner-takes-all decision at the end there is always a danger that a hegemonic majority can triumph. Just as a referendum cannot build a demos where none exists—and may in fact polarize it; it is also the case, as Bogdanor has said, that a referendum cannot create consensus where none exists.[65]

We must therefore be alive to this danger even after a process which has done everything possible to foster deliberation. One option, of course, is to conclude that the referendum is not a helpful device for constitutional fundamentals in deeply divided societies. But since from a republican perspective constitutional decision-making needs the seal of popular approval, perhaps this conclusion should not be reached too hastily.

---

[63] ibid 30.

[64] Young, *Inclusion and Democracy*, 24.

[65] Vernon Bogdanor, *The People and the Party System: The Referendum and Electoral Reform in British Politics* (CUP 1981) 144; Bogdanor, 'Western Europe', 45.

There seem to be two conditions that either alone or together allow the possibility that the referendum can be useful and legitimate even in plurinational and divided contexts. One is for a constitutional package to be agreed before a referendum takes place, with the referendum an act of public and indeed cross-community ratification—or indeed rejection—of the agreement. As we have noted, the use of a referendum was not set in stone at the start of the peace talks in Northern Ireland. It was only as the Agreement unfolded and was seen to have strong cross-community support, as well as support in the Republic of Ireland and the wider UK, that the idea of the referendum crystallized. In other words, it was clear that it could be a unifying rather than divisive measure, showing that ordinary citizens from both communities could come together to support the same constitutional package. It was a 'workable agreement', but one that resulted from cross-community deliberation. In other words, in a divided society initial cross-community agreement must be secured on the very question of holding the referendum if there is any realistic prospect of broad acceptance of the result.

A second possible device with which to counter majoritarian hegemony in this situation is some kind of 'consociational referendum' arrangement. This type of referendum does not presuppose, as a referendum generally does, prior agreement as to the boundaries of a unified demos, but in fact results from agreement as to the lack of such a reality. An interesting feature of the Northern Ireland referendum is that there was no express requirement that a majority from both communities was needed to approve the Agreement. Although it put in place a carefully crafted consociational arrangement that would thereafter need cross-community consensus in important governmental institutions, no such consensus was expressly needed to ratify the Agreement itself. It can, of course, be persuasively argued that the support of so many elites, paving the way for the referendum suggested that cross-community consent would be secured, but this was by no means certain. For example, the influential Democratic Unionist Party dissented from the Agreement. Nonetheless, polls have shown that a majority of both communities did vote Yes, but whereas the nationalists did so by an overwhelming majority, the unionist support was more muted.[66] And we might ask, what would have happened if a majority of unionists had in fact voted No, but the Agreement was still approved by a simple majority overall; could Northern Ireland have found itself in a reverse of the 1973 situation?

---

[66] Researchers at the University of Ulster estimated that 96 or 97 per cent of Catholics/Nationalists voted Yes but only between 51 and 53 per cent of Protestants/Unionists. 'Results of the Referenda in Northern Ireland and Republic of Ireland, Friday 22 May 1998' (CAIN, May 1998) <http://cain.ulst.ac.uk/issues/politics/election/ref1998.htm> accessed 10 October 2011.

It would seem that a consociational referendum in such a situation would protect against this risk. Each voter when registering could be registered as a member of a particular community. And when votes are counted, the support of each community could then be determined. This is, perhaps surprisingly, envisaged by international standard-setters. The Venice Commission Code of 2007 concludes that special rules providing for an exception to the normal proportionality-based vote-counting rules in the case of a referendum concerning the situation of national minorities 'do not, in principle, run counter to equal suffrage'. More specifically, the Commission explains that in referendums on self-government 'for a territory with a relatively high concentration of a minority population: a *double majority* of electors within that territory and throughout the country may be required'.[67]

One advantage of such a requirement is that no referendum would be held until it was clear that such support was likely. In other words, it is an indirect way of making sure the negotiation process towards a new constitutional arrangement is properly consensual by providing a minority(ies) with a de facto veto. This is in effect how the Swiss system works, and the result of this has been that the German-speaking majority of the population has had to build consensus across the country for the passage of referendums, which in this way ensures that it cannot override minority prerogatives.[68] When we reflect on the experience in Bosnia, it seems that if there was any sense whatsoever in holding a referendum in 1992, only by such a model, requiring the consent of the three national communities, could any degree of consensus and any prospect for successful state-building, have been achieved.

V. CONCLUSION

The moment of decision-making is difficult for democratic theorists in general, and has proven to be a particular concern in the referendum context. We have seen two particular challenges in this chapter: the potential for indeterminacy on the one hand and the risk of exclusion and crude majoritarianism on the other. The first of these issues can be addressed in some situations by properly working through the issue to be put to the people in full detail before the referendum, so that voters are offered a coherent and meaningful choice. This relates back to our account of clarity in Chapter 8. But it is not always possible for the referendum to be so clear where it anticipates a negotiation process. In such a scenario it may be useful

---

[67] Venice Commission, 'Code of Good Practice on Referendums', Explanatory Memorandum, para 11 (emphasis added).

[68] Qvortrup, *A Comparative Study of Referendums* (2002), 15.

to have a second referendum following negotiations, which also allows for deliberation to be prolonged and for people to participate right through the process, but there can be very strong political reasons not to do so, particularly where the prospect of a second referendum can offer an incentive to dominant negotiators to make the final package unattractive to voters. In terms of political realities much will depend on the relative strength of the two sides involved; and at the level of normative justice much will hang on the extent to which the powerful side is in a position to use the second referendum, not for deliberative purposes, but to strengthen its own negotiating position.

The inclusion point has in many ways been dealt with in previous chapters. But it does remain a crucial issue at the point of decision-making. As we saw, voting thresholds above 50 per cent are very rare, the 2006 Montenegro referendum being a recent exception. Turnout thresholds are more common and there may be stronger justification from a deliberative perspective for such a rule than for a voting threshold. It might be argued that both types of threshold seek to maximize support for a particular proposition, ensuring its legitimacy among a larger number of voters. But a second justification that applies only to the turnout rule is that a key goal of deliberative democracy is to mobilize citizen engagement so that constitutional change can lay claim to the authorship of as many people as possible. If a threshold of, say, 50 per cent of voters cannot be motivated to vote or prefers not to as a mode of dissent, then this might suggest that there are flaws in the deliberative process leading to the referendum in the first place, and that the issue then is to work on the deliberative aspects of the process of constitutional change leading up to the referendum.[69] But there are also strong arguments against these. As we have seen, there can be a disincentive to vote in some cases since in effect a non-vote is equivalent to a No vote, and this can, rather than enhance participation as intended by such a rule, perhaps discourage people from voting at all. Anything that reduces the incentive to participate immediately raises concerns from a deliberative perspective. It might also be argued that as a generality there may be less republican justification for any kind of super-majority or threshold rule in situations where the referendum process is otherwise carefully crafted to meet the demands of deliberative democracy theory, since the intuitively obvious model of decision-making in a healthy democracy is 50 per cent plus 1.

---

[69] However, it should also be observed that there are states where electoral turnout is regularly below 50 per cent and in such a scenario it is rarely argued that electoral legitimacy is fatally impaired; again, referendums should not be evaluated by a higher standard than is set for representative democracy.

Finally, however, we addressed the difficult case of deeply divided societies where issues of exclusion and majoritarianism are most problematic. It seems that in many cases the referendum is simply not suited to such a scenario, specifically where no agreement on an overall constitutional settlement can be reached in advance of any referendum. But it is also the case that constitutional innovations such as consociationalism can be successful in conflict resolution. We saw in respect of the Belfast Agreement how a consociational agreement was endorsed, in the end successfully, by a referendum. There was no formal requirement of cross-community support for the agreement in the referendum, but such a scenario is certainly foreseeable in recognition that the constitutional moment is bringing together different demoi rather than one national people. If this is a way to bring different communities together in an act of voting, and for each to accept the outcome and perhaps even feel a sense of ownership over it, then it is a possibility that should be taken seriously in developing constitutional agreements in divided societies.

10

Constitutional Referendums: The Deliberative Challenge

I. INTRODUCTION

This book has assessed constitutional referendums against the normative framework of deliberative civic republicanism with its commitment both to the good of an active citizenry playing a direct role in making fundamental constitutional decisions on its own behalf, and to a model of popular deliberative decision-making that views public reasoning as essential to the instantiation of meaningful citizen participation. Deliberation within this framework therefore performs the instrumental task of facilitating the republican self-government of citizens in processes of constitution-making and changing. The primary claim of the deliberative democrat is that the more deliberative a decision-making process, the more legitimate the decision it reaches; the overriding concern for the civic republican is that this process of deliberation must itself fully engage ordinary citizens for the decision to be properly democratic.

The principal question with which I began the book was whether constitutional referendums can play a defensible or even a useful role in constitutional authorship, or whether they are so problematic in democratic terms that the referendum should be excluded altogether from constitutional decision-making. In conclusion the evidence examined throughout the book suggests that, at least in undivided societies, the referendum can be a successful constitutional instrument provided adequate legal regulation serves to promote and protect a deliberative environment within which citizen participation can be fostered. In Section II I will explain how this conclusion has been reached by way of a series of steps taken throughout the book. I will then attempt to summarize in Section III some of the key elements by which the republican deliberative credentials of referendums might be tested. And in Section IV I will conclude with some general comments about the ongoing democratic challenges which the referendum poses for contemporary constitutional politics.

II. CONSTITUTIONAL DELIBERATION: LOCATING THE REFERENDUM

In Chapter 2 I addressed three main objections to the use of referendums—'the elite control syndrome', the 'deliberation deficit', and the 'majoritarian danger'—observing how each of these raises difficult questions for the efficacy of representative as well as direct models of democracy. Although it is important to bear in mind that one's attitude to referendums is likely to be shaped by one's ideological approach to the meaning and purpose of democracy, and that opposition to referendums can be the consequence of an elite-focused approach to politics and a resulting discomfort with popular democracy, the three main objections to referendums do nevertheless pose considerable challenges for those who would defend referendums on the basis that they promote deeper citizen engagement. In addressing these objections, I enquired whether they might be partly overcome by legal regulation and adequate design of the referendum process.

Focusing upon how constitutions actually operate, my approach has been one of 'functional normativity'; a model of constitutional ethics, rather than morality. Normative presuppositions are inherent within any exercise of constitutionalist analysis, but at the same time the constitutional theorist's role, while alive to this normative dimension, must remain grounded in functional possibility and the suitability of constitutional prescription to the political environment the constitution is modelled to serve. Constitutional theory must engage with the real world of political practice, and in particular any normative turn must, to be meaningful, address feasible improvements in actual constitutional institutions and processes.

As a study of constitutional practice, I addressed in Chapter 4 how referendum processes are in fact controlled. The simple notion that referendums are elite-controlled and pro-hegemonic was challenged. First, I argued for an expanded notion of 'control', setting out three distinct but related contextual factors that must condition how we think about this issue: legal regulation of referendums, political power, and political behaviour. The exercise of elite control takes place within this complex matrix and does not therefore live up to the common caricature that the actor who triggers a referendum process can in effect determine the result. I provided evidence that government actors, seeking to use a referendum to advance a particular policy position, can be faced by an array of complicating political factors which combine with legal regulation to dilute their power; it is in fact the operation of, and potential for, detailed legal regulation of referendums that are, respectively, often overlooked or underestimated in a number of existing accounts by political scientists. In light of this a key premise of the book has been that a reframing from a theoretical perspective of how direct democracy interacts with representative democracy is badly needed, and it is hoped that this attempt to provide such a framework may help inform future work in political science. Particularly in constitutional referendums, it seems that hegemonic attempts to control referendum outcomes can be susceptible to legal as well as political impediments. This means that instead of a general conclusion that elites do or do not control referendums, we need to take account of the details of each referendum process and the complexity of the constitutional environment in which it operates. Clearly the threat of elite manipulation remains a serious obstacle to meaningful democratic deliberation in many referendum processes.

In Chapters 5 and 6 I addressed the issue of control in wider context. The former demonstrated in particular how the referendum exposes the ongoing tension between the commitment of modern democracy to popular sovereignty and the conditioning of that commitment by positive constitutionalism. This tension can come to the surface when elite actors call upon the authority of the people, voiced through a referendum, either to override established amendment processes or to make claims to the legitimacy of self-determination aspirations of sub-state peoples within plurinational states. The latter example in particular is illustrative of how the line between the constitution-changing and the constitution-framing referendum can be a fine one. The referendum can in fact be the motor that moves a process which begins within the confines of a particular constitutional order to the point where it supplants that order and replaces it with a new constitutional regime based upon the legitimacy of popular consent expressed in that referendum.

The transformative potential of the referendum can also stem from the fact that an explicit identification of 'the people' cannot be avoided, particularly since a referendum must fully articulate the boundaries of the demos by way of both territorial demarcation and franchise rules. This is particularly the case in constitutive referendums which carry the promise of constitution-formation and which do so often with the symbolic validation of a particular people. In Chapter 3 I discussed how this process of demotic boundary-drawing can often be highly problematic; if there is a sense that the referendum does not speak to the demotic reality of the territory, the referendum itself can become a source of intense dispute between communities, destabilizing further an already tense constitutional environment.

But the referendum not only challenges some of the complacent assumptions about relations of sovereignty *within* the state. In Chapter 6 we saw how in a globalizing normative environment direct democracy also intervenes awkwardly in processes that can unsettle the *external* dimension of state sovereignty. The role of international actors in influencing referendum processes concerning statehood or supranational integration highlights that the prospect of elite control and pro-hegemonic disposition in referendums is increasingly an issue of *outside* as well as *inside* elite influence. Indeed, whereas problems of democratic deficit can to some extent be remedied inside the state by legal controls and the design of deliberative elements within the referendum process, the encroaching external pressures upon referendum democracy are not so easily regulated or democratized. Since these pressures condition the very reality of referendum democracy as acts of 'self-determination, the referendum in this sense offers a neat vignette of how external normative sites can operate in a broad range of ways—from norm-setting, to process formation, to political influence—in constricting the constitutional autonomy of discrete polities today.

In Chapter 7 we turned to how, at least *within* polities, deliberative democracy can be deployed to counter not only the control syndrome but also the deliberation deficit and the majoritarian danger by building deliberative processes into the referendum. With a focus on participation, we examined how both the opportunity for and the quality of participation might be fostered. This led us to consider the prospects for deliberation within a referendum over a range of stages of the referendum process, across various settings, and in a number of ways. In particular, the prospects for deliberation in both micro- and macro-level settings, and how these might in practice be combined in a referendum process, were addressed. And so too was the notion that 'deliberation' is itself multifaceted, allowing for different processes—internal reflection by the citizen as well as discussion and engagement with others—in light of the full diversity of modes of expression and interaction within the polity. The experiences of British Columbia in 2004 and Australia in 1999 offer interesting case studies by showing how, in very different ways, various elements of deliberation can be built into the framing of the referendum issue, the setting of the question, and in facilitating linkages from the micro-level agenda-setting stage to the macro-level referendum campaign. It is this final task which has in practice posed the sternest challenge.

Process issues are only part of the deliberative challenge posed to referendum democracy and in Chapter 8 we turned to matters of substance. The manipulation of referendum questions by elites is an issue that provokes a great deal of criticism from those who question the deliberative potential of direct democracy. Again, I discussed how law can intervene to regulate this. But I also observed how, in order to foster proper deliberation, the issue must be one which people believe needs to be addressed.[1] This is a

---

[1] Although criticized for the lack of publicity it received, perhaps the most obvious conclusion to draw from the lack of support for the alternative vote electoral system proposal put to the UK public in May 2011 is that people were not particularly interested in the issue and did not detect a problem they felt strongly needed to be fixed. On a turnout of 42.2 per cent, 68 per cent voted No, meaning only 13.4 per cent of registered voters in the end supported the proposal.

particular issue for deeply divided societies and one of the main criticisms of referendums both from the perspective of the deliberation deficit and, more particularly the majoritarian danger, is that deliberative referendums in such a setting are simply not possible, and indeed direct democracy can threaten such stability and justice as exists within these polities. However, the referendum on the Belfast Agreement in Northern Ireland, perhaps counter-intuitively, was in the end a remarkable example of how a referendum can work successfully in a post-conflict situation.

The Northern Ireland scenario, considered further in Section III, does illustrate that if referendums are to be relevant to the pluralistic and often troubled societies of today's world, then more imaginative attempts must be made to fit them within constitutional decision-making processes. In Chapter 9 I considered ways in which the referendum might, for example, be envisaged as part of a longer process of constitution-framing, rather than simply as a quick and irrevocable act. I will now attempt to bring these findings together in offering a tentative model of a deliberative republican referendum.

III. TOWARDS A DELIBERATIVE REPUBLICAN REFERENDUM

In Chapter 2 I set out four principles from the perspective of both civic republicanism and deliberative democracy, which were then used throughout the book to inform how a model of constitutional referendum might be constructed which could overcome the important criticisms the referendum has faced. These principles are popular participation, public reasoning, equality and parity of esteem, and consent and collective decision-making. In light of these we can frame the key characteristics which are central to a deliberative constitutional referendum.

(i) Regulating the trigger power

The first issue in constructing such a referendum is to meet the elite control objection. To some extent the force of this objection is in any case weakened when we analyse the dispersed political power and complex patterns of political behaviour which combine to constrain the capacity of particular elites. But nonetheless there are avenues open to elites, varying from constitution to constitution and referendum to referendum, to activate the referendum for strategic political purposes, and in this context the role of the constitution and of secondary law in regulating referendum practice can, from a republican perspective, be crucial.

Within a written constitution explicit provision for the use of referendums can be made. This can either provide for an automatic trigger or leave elements of discretion to political institutions. In the latter case the constitution can make clear which actors have the power to decide, and can disperse this power, for example giving the initiation power to the executive but requiring parliamentary consent. The constitution can also set thresholds for consent; the default is 50 per cent plus 1 support within the legislature, but a requirement of broader consent can be established where, for example, the assent of two chambers is needed, or where the support of a higher percentage than 50 per cent plus 1 within each chamber is required. The precise structure is a matter for each constitutional system to determine but some type of mixed model of executive/legislative consent is preferable from a deliberative perspective, requiring the building of consensus across institutions.

Even in situations where the constitution does not provide detailed regulation of the referendum process or, as in the UK, where constitutional regulation of the referendum is lacking, ordinary legislation can also be useful in setting, or providing more detail for, such trigger rules. Of course, ordinary legislation is typically open to change more easily than constitutional rules, but such a model can work effectively. We see this in the UK, where the government has the power to propose a referendum but in practice needs parliamentary consent to hold one; the Northern Ireland Act 1998 and the European Union Act 2011 each make a referendum mandatory in certain circumstances. The use of ordinary legislation to provide further details for the referendum process is also useful in moderating the capacity of one elite actor to manipulate the vote and I will return to the utility of detailed law at different points in this chapter. Finally, such constitutional and/or legislative regulation also introduces the possibility of judicial review of the trigger decision, particularly where one institution asserts that its role has been overridden (as we saw in France in 1962). The effectiveness of such regulation will, of course, depend upon the political culture within a state and upon the independence of the judiciary. Within an unhealthy democracy legal regulation of referendums as of any other constitutional process might well be ineffectual, but in a properly functioning democracy, a combination of constitutional and ordinary legislation spreading the referendum trigger power across institutions can do much to undermine the force of the elite control objection, serving to facilitate the meaningful participation of citizens.

(ii) Framing the substantive issue in a deliberative way

There is no one ideal model of a deliberative republican referendum process. As with the trigger power, the detail of what is appropriate for a particular state will in some respects vary from case to case. But having examined how different forms of deliberative participation might be fostered across a series of stages and settings we can offer a number of prescriptions from a republican deliberative perspective that are of general application.

(a) Building a micro-process
At the *issue- and question-framing stage* we looked at how micro-processes might be used to introduce some element of citizen participation. The use of citizens' assemblies and constitutional conventions from the radically popular British Columbia Citizens' Assembly (BCCA) to the more mixed civil society model of the Australia Constitutional Convention (ACC) have their own strengths and weaknesses, but overall are in different ways each positive initiatives in encouraging broader participation in constitutional decision-making beyond traditional narrow governmental elites; and in doing so providing another tonic to the elite control syndrome. In addition, there is also evidence that these micro-processes can enhance the quality of deliberation, which is, of course, the central rationale behind the principle of public reason. One criticism of the BCCA model was that by completely excluding the voices of regular elites such as political parties, the model of constitutional reform which was eventually offered in the referendum question was unsuitable to the constitutional context of the province. The ACC model, by contrast, was a hybrid of traditional elite and civil society voices, linking these together for the purpose of high constitutional change. One promising possibility is to experiment with combinations of these two models in order to retain the realism of the ACC, recognizing that referendums are part of a representative system of government rather than detached from it and that the influence of representative politicians in constitutional change is important, while complementing this with the voices of ordinary citizens. Of course, any degree of popular involvement will raise the issue of how representative such citizens can be. But the BCCA managed to avoid much controversy on this score through what was in effect random selection.

(b) Facilitating 'micro' popular deliberation
Beyond process, the substance of the issue to be put to the people is also crucial in assessing the republican deliberative credentials of the constitutional referendum. A similar principle applies to that of the trigger power, namely that to modify the risk of excessive power resting in the hands of a particular elite (in particular an executive actor), this power should be dispersed among a number of actors. This might be done by requiring that a draft question set by the executive needs to be approved by the legislature. Again, engaging a micro group in framing the question per the

BCCA, or, as did the ACC, offering detailed recommendations on the issue to be put to the people, can serve to condition tightly the discretion open to the government in setting the question. The BCCA model perhaps goes too far the other way, in excluding the important voices of representative political institutions. But on the other hand, the ACC model has been criticized for coming up with a model which, being the result of a compromise between different pro-republican voices, in the end suited very few people. These are clearly important concerns and reflect that the appropriate way to manage this either by involving a plurality of voices at the elite level, or by introducing popular or civil society opinion into issue and question-setting, must be left to the actors on the ground in any particular system to work out based upon their own constitutional traditions and by taking account of the subject matter of the referendum. Arguably the heavily popular model of the BCCA was suitable, given that the issue was about a change in how people in fact vote for their representatives, whereas the Australian scenario which involved a matter of the highest constitutional consequence with complex knock-on implications for many other aspects of the constitution required the technical expertise and political experience of politicians in conjunction with other members of civil society.

Finally there is an important role to be played by an electoral commission in reviewing the question for intelligibility and perhaps even for relevance, assessed against the terms of enabling legislation or the deliberations of a body such as the ACC. The UK's Political Parties, Elections and Referendums Act 2000 (s 104) is an example of legislation providing for such a role. There may well be a final role for the courts to take a view on these matters. This can involve judges in matters of high politics and they should, of course, be aware of their own limited constitutional role, but in cases where the executive is riding roughshod over legislative constraints, thus undermining the deliberative processes either within parliament or within a citizens' assembly/constitutional convention, the courts might well be entitled to adjudicate to ensure that the setting of referendum questions is not abused.

(iii) The referendum campaign: a deliberative environment?

But issue- and question-framing is only part of the process. Maximizing the participation of the broader citizenry at the *campaign stage* leading to the referendum vote is, of course, also crucial from the perspective of civic republicanism. Here public education is vital. Particularly where a proposal is technical or involves a general constitutional document or treaty which most people are unlikely to read, then the supply of a summarized, objective account of the issues by a neutral electoral commission is essential in laying the ground for informed deliberation by citizens, reflection as well as communication being an important vehicle for reasoning. Second, regulation must be deployed to exert funding and expenditure controls. Legislative models exist; for example, the Political Parties, Elections and Referendums Act 2000 offers very detailed rules on these issues.[2] This legislation is not exempt from criticism—in fact it may be deemed over-elaborate in its coverage—but as a model it is certainly a useful framework for helping ordinary citizens engage in a deliberative way, relatively free from the distortions threatened by wealthy vested interests. Again, an efficient electoral commission will be vital to administer and regulate such a system, and the use of subordinate legislation can provide further detailed rules from referendum to referendum as needs be. A third and more difficult issue is media coverage. In some situations the media may be very one-sided. Although international standards exist to attempt to regulate this,[3] such a model is not easy to design, since it comes up against other rights such as private property and freedom of expression, which can make attempted regulation somewhat controversial. It must be observed, however, that where one side is promoted far more than the other, the very possibility of a properly deliberative process involving the informed participation of the population must be called into question.

Another issue is the linkage of the micro to the macro levels of deliberation. I noted that the British Columbia process was criticized for a failure to extend the successful BCCA process into a broader province-wide conversation in the lead-up to the referendum. To some extent the subject matter of the referendum will be a factor here. As we saw in relation to the UK's alternative vote referendum, it can be difficult to mobilize popular interest in such an issue. However, there was to some extent a failure in both of these processes to publicize the referendum and to explain the issues at stake. The lesson particularly from the BC referendum (and that of Ontario which conducted a similar process) is that a failure to invest in public education and publicity leading into the macro-level stage may render redundant the commitment to citizen engagement at the earlier stage. Another possibility is to involve members from the micro group in such publicity efforts, explaining to their fellow citizens why they, with no vested interest in the issue, found it to be important. There is no guarantee that this will mobilize popular interest, but it seems worthwhile to experiment with

---

[2] We have explored the crucial role of electoral commissions in providing an adequate regulatory environment more generally, taking the UK model as an example. Such regulatory regimes are now being increasingly encouraged at the international level to help facilitate a properly democratic referendum process. European Commission for Democracy Through Law (Venice Commission), 'Code of Good Practice on Referendums' Study No 371/2006 (20 January 2009), COE Doc CDL-AD(2007) 008rev, para II, 3.1.

[3] ibid para I, 2.2.

such attempts to connect the two processes; unless the broader public can be engaged and encouraged to deliberate and to vote, the instantiation of popular micro-level deliberation will in large part be an opportunity missed.

Also important is providing sufficient time for citizens to reflect and where possible communicate on the issues, allowing for meaningful deliberation. Again, law can be used to set timescales for a campaign, for example setting minimum and maximum periods between initiation of the issue and the vote itself, or even a fixed date for a referendum, for example three months after the question is approved by parliament or enabling legislation is passed. In general the setting of such a period by law is important and has the added benefit of restricting elite power to vary the date to suit opinion polls.

(iv) Towards deliberative decision-making

Another issue we addressed was the use of various models of quora for approval of a referendum proposition. Interestingly, international practice and international recommendations through the Venice Commission tend not to favour the imposition of a super-majority threshold in relation to those who vote. And this seems to be correct. There is no good reason from a republican perspective, which respects the will of the people, to move beyond the principle of simple majority if other aspects of the process are already adequately deliberative. In any case there seems no obviously principled alternative to simple majority, since any threshold requirement will be arbitrary to some extent.

An alternative model is the use of turnout thresholds. These are more common and they do seem to be more defensible from the perspective of maximizing participation than do voter thresholds. It can be argued from a republican deliberative perspective that if an issue is important to people, then they should evidence this by voting. That said, there are also strong objections from the principle of participation against such a threshold. For one thing it rewards impercipience, making a non-vote equivalent to a No vote. For this reason, as explained in Chapter 9, I do not recommend this model of threshold either. If the process is properly deliberative it should be discovered at the trigger and issue- and question-framing stages, whether the matter is one that is in fact suitable to put to a referendum and whether it is likely to be seen as sufficiently important by the people. Also, if the question is fairly framed, and sufficient educative material and publicity provided, then the grounds are laid for deliberative reflection and discussion among citizens. Beyond this, republican respect for the competence of citizens suggests that the matter should then be left to a majority of those motivated to vote (the specific case of divided societies will be returned to in Section III(vi)(b)).

(v) Ongoing deliberation after the referendum: process not event

In aspiring to a 'deliberative environment', deliberation throughout and indeed *beyond* the referendum campaign is crucial, linking popular and elite deliberation. In many cases, the referendum process does not necessarily end with the vote, particularly where the referendum envisages post-referendum negotiations, the drafting of a constitution, legislation, or a treaty or agreement. And here again it is important that the people should be kept involved through ongoing processes of public education and engagement as these negotiations etc take place, since these have in effect been enabled by the people and they should continue to be seen as the masters of the process.

One option in such a situation is a second referendum. This will in most cases be impracticable. Referendums are expensive to organize and there is little sense in staging another one on a similar issue shortly after the initial referendum. Also there is a significant risk of citizen fatigue. The aim of the constitutional referendum is to stimulate citizen engagement and popular interest in the issue, but there is only so much time and interest people are willing to devote to constitutional affairs; extending the process into a second referendum could be counterproductive if citizens lose interest and switch off.

One hard case is where the referendum envisages negotiations, particularly involving actors who are reluctant to accept the implications of the referendum. Here a final constitutional agreement may be considerably different from that envisaged by many citizens, and it might be argued that a second referendum is appropriate in such a scenario. On the other hand, there is also a risk that the recalcitrant side in negotiations can use the prospect of a second referendum to drive a hard bargain. It would seem unfair that a dominant elite can use what should be a deliberative and democratic device in effect to act undeliberatively and, arguably, undemocratically. It might be said that where the referendum question and result is clear, then the model should be implemented in line with this, and political actors should engage in good faith to give effect to the clearly expressed preferences of the voters. And if both sides do negotiate in good faith on the clearly intended consequences of the referendum, then arguably a second referendum is not necessary (a possible exception in the case of divided societies is returned to in Section III(vi)(b)). One option is to remove the question from the hands of the negotiators, empowering a constitutional court to rule on whether a second referendum is required where in its view the outcome of the post-referendum process does not reflect the outcome of the referendum itself.

(vi) Three exceptional cases

I will now turn to three exceptional cases where setting out a model for a deliberative republican constitutional referendum raises particular issues.

(a) The constitutive referendum

In Chapter 1 I introduced the particular category of 'constitutive referendums'; that is, those constitutional processes that are of such fundamental significance that they in fact lead to a new state or a new constitutional order. This category highlights the transformative power of the referendum, marking it out as a constitutional mechanism like no other for the way in which it can bring forward the people in a real moment of popular sovereignty, fulfilling the latent promise of democracy. Although I have defended the use of the constitutional referendum in general, the republican commitment to the engagement of the people in constitution-making is cast in even sharper relief when a matter of such vital importance is at stake, and one which can in fact take on an identity-forming role, helping to shape the very collective constitutional personality of a people. But there are important conditions that need to be fulfilled. One is the a priori question of determining the borders of 'the demos' both in territorial and in franchise terms, as we saw in Chapter 3. This highlights that the referendum is first and foremost a *process* of constitutional change; a process that, for its success, depends upon the fulfilment of anterior substantive conditions. For the process to be legitimate the drawing of boundaries around those engaged by it must first itself be legitimate. We have learned this lesson in the costs incurred from failing to do so. A referendum cannot solve demotic disputes, but it can certainly exacerbate them. From this we must draw a broader conclusion. The referendum as a decision-making device can only be as successful as the constitutional structure into which it fits.

(b) Towards deliberative pluralism: the particular issues for divided societies

Throughout the book I have alighted on the particularly thorny issue of referendums in divided societies. It is the case that public reasoning, where participants communicate with one another in an engaged way, open to changes of opinion, can be immensely challenging where deep antipathy or resentment characterizes the relationships between groups. The 'majoritarian danger' also looms large, since the referendum seems to offer a dominant group the opportunity to secure its ends. In general, therefore, the model of the referendum seems fraught with difficulty in this context and we saw cases such as Northern Ireland in 1973 and Bosnia in 1992 where the referendum was little short of a disaster for inter-communal relations.

We have, however, observed that by contrast the Belfast Agreement process was relatively successful. The Northern Ireland experience suggests that a referendum is most likely to work in such an environment, to the satisfaction of a plurality of citizens across divides, if it comes at the *end*, and in ratification of, a worked out agreement. In this way the referendum might be envisaged as part of a longer process of constitution-framing, rather than simply as a quick and irrevocable act. Alternatively it might be useful in beginning a process which then leads to elite, or a combination of elite and popularly based, negotiation or reflection. In other words, the referendum cannot create consent across demotic borders; the hard work of securing this consent must be built before any referendum can be feasible.

But if the goal of constitutional lawyers is the resolution of conflict and the building of post-conflict constitutional structures, the active engagement of the people in shaping their own future, and hopefully in entering into deliberation across divides, must be an aspiration. Northern Ireland has shown that the referendum can perhaps be part of the solution if it gives the different sides of a divide the sense of ownership over, and indeed responsibility for, the success of the agreement worked out through a process I have called 'deliberative pluralism'. In particular, the people of the whole society come together to vote for the agreement as a joint public act. This seems crucial if moves are to be made, if not to overcome divisions then at least to build institutions that can manage them and provide for constitutional coexistence despite these divisions.

There are also particular considerations to take into account at the moment of decision-making. Although I have in general not recommended the use of super-majority quora on the basis either of turnout or voting, there needs to be more flexibility when we think about the variety of models of consent-giving that are available for divided societies, including the use of quorum rules to ensure broad levels of support for the measure and to counterbalance the majoritarian danger.

In particular there may be a strong case for a some kind of 'consociational referendum' arrangement, requiring the support of a majority in each national society for the measure to pass. This was not adopted in Northern Ireland, but data do seem to show that a majority of both communities voted for the Agreement. As we reflect on the post-referendum life of Northern Ireland the consent of both communities has been central to the ongoing, albeit not untroubled, success of the Belfast Agreement. In this respect the importance of a legitimate founding constitutional moment, recognized as such by both sides, cannot be underestimated. Again, while I have also not recommended that in general a second referendum is necessary there may be an argument for an issue-framing referendum to encourage (or empower) elites to begin the process of cross-communal engagement. A second referendum could then be used at the end of the process to provide the further cross-communal endorsement of the outcome. In a sense in Northern Ireland we saw the 'second' referendum in this sense rather than the 'first'.

But at the same time we certainly should not be deluded by this one story of relative success. The challenges to bring divided communities meaningfully together in one demotic moment will in other cases be even more fraught, and in some cases it will be thought better not even to attempt it. But the Belfast process suggests that with imagination and the proper mechanisms to emphasize inclusion and limit the threat of majority domination these challenges are not necessarily insurmountable. The referendum showed itself to be an effective vehicle for deliberative pluralism: the definition of a thick, common demotic identity was avoided, and instead the referendum allowed a thinner constitutional public to leave other identities to one side and come together as voters to endorse a jointly agreed upon political solution. Just as the 1973 process showed how an illegitimate referendum can exacerbate disputes over national identity, the 1998 process illustrated that, perhaps paradoxically, a constitutional referendum can also help defuse the divisive issue of national identity by providing the breathing space of a constitutional *modus vivendi* that a majority on both sides could sign up to, at least for the time being.

(c) International influence

A theme that has surfaced repeatedly is the paradox of the referendum reviving as an instantiation of popular sovereignty at the same time as territorial polities become less self-contained and self-determining than ever. The referendum has acted as an intriguing case study into how international influence on state constitutions is growing, and demonstrates vividly that despite the promise of democratic empowerment the referendum cannot compensate for the decline of the state and the shift to supranational constitutional sites. We have seen the growing influence of international organizations and powerful states on processes leading to statehood for sub-state territories, setting the rules for how referendums are conducted and even what level of support is needed to bring about international recognition. In other words the referendum, while apparently highlighting the resilience of popular constitutional competence, in fact can simply provide powerful actors with a process through which to shape the scope for, and conditions of, membership of the club of states for select sub-state peoples; a process also achieved through the promotion of normative standards, particularly by the Venice Commission in Europe, for how a referendum ought to be conducted.

Another area we addressed was the use of referendums in processes of European integration. Here we saw how powerful elites within the European Union have found the referendum to be an irritant in their empire-building schemes, and have reacted first with shock when people vote against treaties and then with attempts to circumvent these rejections. But the trajectory of domestic constitutional developments within EU member states suggests that the referendum will continue to be used, and with so many countries now committed to the referendum within their constitutions, their application in future treaty processes can only proliferate. In light of the serious democratic failings of the EU the referendum has become an important instrument of accountability. It can provide citizens with a voice, perhaps the only meaningful one they will have in such processes. A deliberative republican referendum, properly designed to engage ordinary citizens in open and meaningful participation, can also serve to put into sharp relief the democratic deficit and lack of transparency in constitution-making processes within the EU and in doing so may help force democratic reform upon its institutions and decision-making processes.

IV. THE AGE OF THE REFERENDUM?

In the wider context this study alerts us to the evolving relationship between direct and representative democracy within the contemporary polity, the importance of instantiating deliberation more broadly within constitutional processes, and the specificity of 'constitutional' referendums and the challenges involved in and benefits resulting from engaging citizens in this way. I will offer a final reflection on each of these issues.

What has certainly not been argued for in this book is the replacement of representative democracy with direct democracy; nor do I suggest any preference for the latter over the former. There are overwhelming arguments that for the vast majority of lawmaking decisions within a polity only representative institutions can adequately address issues in their full context, take account of intensities of preferences, and bring diverse interests together in coherent policy packages. Nor would I argue that referendums should replace representative institutions in constitutional amendment processes. Instead, it seems that the referendum, properly structured, can encourage the fuller engagement of citizens and civil society in democratic processes *within* the broader functioning of representative democracy. Therefore, it is important that we situate constitutional referendums as *part of*, and not *apart from*, representative democracy. And indeed in practice this is how things work. Elites will always have a role, whether in initiating the process, setting the agenda, framing the question, formulating the process rules, or implementing any decision taken. A vital elite task remains even in processes that introduce radically popular elements like that in British Columbia—ironically the micro-process did not translate to the macro level, largely because of an elite failure to engage the broader public. And so representative democracy and direct democracy are never either/or options. The issue is whether some element of direct democracy might appropriately be located within the broader workings of representative government, and if so when and how.

A broader aim of this book has been to highlight more generally the centrality of popular deliberation to a healthy democracy. It is important to encourage popular engagement with politics throughout the political and lawmaking processes; this goal should not be reserved only for occasional referendum moments. In addition, in recognizing the interplay of elite and popular elements in contemporary democracy, we must not lose sight of the importance also of improving deliberative processes among representatives, providing sites of interconnection and mutual reinforcement of deliberative decision-making. And this is vital also in those elements of the referendum process that are performed by elites, so that the fostering of deliberation by citizens is complemented by more reflective and reasoned engagement by elites; the green shoots of such a process were arguably seen in the relationship between the ACC and the subsequent referendum campaign in Australia in 1999; while the polling process throughout the Belfast Agreement negotiations offers an interesting template for how to feed popular opinion into ongoing elite deliberation.

This book has focused upon 'constitutional referendums'. It seems that it is in the specific context of exercises of constitutional authorship by a people that the referendum can perform a particularly useful deliberative role. Constitutional issues do not fit easily within the normal ideological structures of party politics which have been built to reflect socio-economic cleavages. There are a number of major issues, such as territorial questions of autonomy, sovereignty, and the transfer of national powers to the EU, that can cut across these class-based lines and hence party differences. And indeed the referendum can offer a safety valve to the party system, helping to avoid damaging splits. Referendums at this level may also be justified on the basis of the importance of the issues at stake and, in particular, the potential of major constitutional questions to impact upon the very constitutional identity of a people.

That is not to say there is a clear line as to which issues should be put to a referendum and which not, as can be seen from the recent deliberations of the UK House of Lords Constitution Committee, which held an inquiry on the use of referendums in the UK. The Committee sought to categorize 'fundamental constitutional issues' upon which referendums might be held and observed the considerable 'difficulties in defining' such a term.[4] Although conceding that each decision must be left to Parliament on a case-by-case basis, it did suggest that the following proposals would fall within this definition:

> To abolish the Monarchy;
> To leave the European Union;
> For any of the nations of the UK to secede from the Union;
> To abolish either House of Parliament;
> To change the electoral system for the House of Commons;
> To adopt a written constitution; and
> To change the UK's system of currency.[5]

The Committee remained sceptical of referendums (as a parliamentary body that is scarcely surprising), but it did recognize all the same that the level of demand for referendums is growing and that the question of defining which changes are so fundamental as to require a referendum does need to be addressed.

We have surveyed a broad and expanding engagement of direct democracy by modern democracies, with some states reserving this device only for the most fundamental constitution-framing issues while others, increasingly, turn to the referendum to effect a wide range of constitutional amendments. The background to this variation from state to state is complex, depending upon existing constitutional structures, constitutional history, political culture, and the expectations of citizens. It is this last component which is particularly central to my conclusion that constitutional referendums can be a positive resource with which to engage citizens in high constitutional politics, provided the process is formulated and conducted in a deliberative way.

It is time to reassess the negative stereotypes that have in many ways come to characterize the debate surrounding referendums. There are, of course, challenges in overcoming the various democratic risks that referendum democracy brings with it. But it is also the case that election campaigns in general have deliberative problems given that they can be partisan, subject to elite deception, and vulnerable to distortion through private expenditure and media influence. The failings of the representative model do not lead critics to suggest non-democratic alternatives. Instead the obvious response is to find ways better to regulate elections and make them more deliberative. It is therefore important that the debate about

---

[4] HL Select Committee on the Constitution, *Referendums in the United Kingdom* (HL 2009–10) Chapter 6 Conclusion, para 206.

[5] ibid Chapter 7 Summary of Recommendations, para 210. It added: 'This is not a definitive list of fundamental constitutional issues, nor is it intended to be' (para 210).

the democratic shortcomings in the referendum context be set against the broader malaise of contemporary democracy, and that referendums not be singled out as the straw man for democracy's wider infirmity. It is also important that the argument against referendums does not result simply from a broader discomfort with popular engagement in constitutional matters. In this book I have tried to offer remedies for recurrent problems in the referendum process and I have also argued that citizens have greater capacity and competence to make important constitutional decisions than is often conceded by the critics of referendums. Otherwise it might also be asked why, if voters are so incompetent or venal, they should be better able to hold politicians accountable in elections than to make decisions on particular issues.

Indeed there is considerable evidence that popular deliberation can be most enthusiastically engaged at important constitutional moments. We have seen many referendum processes which have captured the popular imagination, the emergence of new democracies in Eastern Europe, the decolonization process of East Timor, the emergent statehood of Montenegro and South Sudan, the devolution of government to Scotland, and the movement towards peace in Northern Ireland. If this enthusiasm can be facilitated by infusing the referendum process with the principles and practices of deliberative democracy, then there is evidence from Australia and British Columbia, as well as from Northern Ireland, that it can take on the role of a deliberative forum, and one in which the people can come together to reflect upon and indeed author a settlement for their own collective government. It might well be that in this context the referendum can help fill the gap between the growing interest of people in politics—'cognitive mobilization'—and their aspirations for a greater role in, and heightened control over, decision-making on the one hand, and on the other hand the tapering away of traditional patterns of political participation such as party membership and voting, and weakening chains of responsibility binding political actors to those others who make 'public' decisions at arm's length from political accountability. Curiously this disillusionment on the part of many citizens, and the growing sense that control is being lost, has occurred at a high point of democratization around the world. Democratic government is ever more pervasive but paradoxically its form and effect seem to be thinner and less meaningful in light of its subordination to other power structures. And it is in this context that we see calls to return authenticity to democracy, restoring the real for the symbolic through a fully engaged citizenry.

Of course, the referendum alone cannot fill such a gap. And it is also essential to remain alive to the very real democratic dangers that can attend undeliberative and exploitative plebiscites. A vital democratic political culture is the essential background for a democratic referendum, but this is also true for any legitimate electoral process. However, there is also evidence that the use of referendums leads to heightened citizen satisfaction with democracy in countries that use them. And it might be that, particularly for constitution-framing exercises but also in constitution-changing processes, within a referendum process the first steps to the broader engagement of citizens in important issues of politics might be taken, the institutional setting for public engagement in both micro and macro venues established, the culture of participation nurtured, and the implications of popular decision-making realized. The referendum in this sense is perhaps best characterized not as an end in itself but as a mechanism by which deliberative civic engagement in the contours of democratic life might be re-instantiated within politics. It is now no longer enough to ask *whether or not* the referendum can play a democratically defensible role in an exercise of constitutional authorship by a people. The constitutional referendum is a fixed and growing feature of constitutional politics. Rather, the task for the constitutional scholar today is to engage with *how* deliberative democracy might be fostered within constitutional referendums. It has been the aim of this book to advance this debate.

Appendix: Referendums from 1898–2011 cited in the book

Place	Date	Subject	Turnout %	Result %
Algeria	1 July 1962	Independent statehood	73.8	Approved: 69.5
Anguilla	11 July 1967	Independent statehood	33.1	Approved: 99.9
Armenia	21 September 1991	Independent statehood	95	Approved: 99.2
Australia	6 November 1999	(1) Republic	95.1	(1) Not approved: 54.9
		(2) Constitutional preamble		(2) Not approved: 60.7
Austria	10 April 1938	*Anschluss*—Annexation to Germany	99.7 (claimed by government)	Approved: 99.7 (claimed by government)
Austria	12 June 1994	EU membership	82.3	Approved: 66.6
Azerbaijan	10 December 1991	Independent statehood	95.3	Approved: 99.8
Belarus	24 November 1996	Adoption of the revised 1994 Constitution, including consolidation of presidential powers	84.1	Approved: 70.5
Belgium	12 March 1950	Retention of the monarchy		Approved: 57.7
Bosnia-Herzegovina	9–10 November 1991	Referendum in the Serb-inhabited regions of B-H on maintaining status within Yugoslavia		Approved: 95.3
Bosnia-Herzegovina	29 February–1 March 1992	Independent statehood	63.4	Approved: 99
Burma	10 May 2008	Constitution	99 (claimed by government)	Approved: 92.4 (claimed by government)
Cambodia	3 October 1945	Independent statehood	80.3	Approved: 100
Canada	29 September 1898	Prohibition	44	Approved: 51.3

(*Continued*)

Appendix: Referendums from 1898–2011 cited in the book

Place	Date	Subject	Turnout %	Result %
Canada	27 April 1942	Conscription	71.3	Approved: 64.5
Canada	26 October 1992	Draft Charlottetown Accord	71.8	Not approved: 55
Canada, British Columbia	15 March 2002	First Nations treaty negotiations principles	33	All eight principles approved by over 80%
Canada, British Columbia	17 May 2005	Electoral reform	58.2	Not approved: 57.69 voted in favour but 60% required
Canada, British Columbia	12 May 2009	Electoral reform	51	Not approved: 60.9
Canada, Ontario	10 October 2007	Electoral reform	52.6	Not approved: 63
Canada, New Brunswick	14 May 2001	Lottery gaming	44	Approved: 53.1
Canada, Newfoundland	3 June 1948	(1) Return to dominion status (2) Confederation (3) Status quo	88	Option approval (1) 44.5 (2) 41.1 (3) 14.3
Canada, Newfoundland	22 July 1948	(1) Return to dominion status (2) Confederation	85	(1) 47.7 (2) 52.3
Canada, Quebec	29 September 1898	Prohibition	44 (overall in Canada)	Not approved: 81.2
Canada, Quebec	10 April 1919	Legalized sale of alcohol		Approved: 78.6
Canada, Quebec	20 May 1980	Sovereignty association	85.6	Not approved: 59.6
Canada, Quebec	26 October 1992	Charlottetown Accord	82.8	Not approved: 55.4
Canada, Quebec	30 October 1995	Sovereignty and partnership	94	Not approved: 50.6
Chile	11 September 1980	Constitutional approval	93	Approved: 69
Chile	30 July 1989	Constitutional reforms	85	Approved: 91
Comoras	22 December 1974	Independent statehood	93.3	Approved: 94.6
Croatia (Krajina region)	19 August 1990	Union with the Serbian region of Bosnia	Voting limited to ethnic Serbs	Approved: 99.7 (unrecognized)
Croatia	19 May 1991	Independent statehood	80	Approved: 93.2

Appendix: Referendums from 1898–2011 cited in the book 307

Place	Date	Subject	Turnout %	Result %
Czech Republic	13–14 June 2003	EU membership	55.2	Approved: 77.3
Denmark	23 May 1939	Reforming the upper house	44.5	Not approved: 90 voted for reform but this did not meet turnout threshold (45)
Denmark	2 October 1972	EEC membership	90.1	Approved: 63.4
Denmark	26 February 1986	Single European Act	75.4	Approved: 56.2
Denmark	2 June 1992	Maastricht Treaty	82.9	Not approved: 50.7
Denmark	18 May 1993	Edinburgh Agreement	85.5	Approved: 56.8
Denmark	28 May 1998	Amsterdam Treaty	76.2	Approved: 55.1
Denmark	28 September 2000	Economic and Monetary Union	87.8	Not approved: 46.9
East Timor	30 August 1999	Independence	95	Approved: 78.5
Egypt	26 March 2007	Constitutional reforms	27.1	Approved: 75.9
Eritrea	23–25 April 1993	Independence from Ethiopia	93.9	Approved: 99.8
Estonia	3 March 1991	Independence from the USSR	83	Approved: 78
Estonia	28 June 1992	(1) Draft constitution (2) Russian-speaking participation in elections	66.7	(1) Approved: 91.3 (2) Not approved: 53
Estonia	14 September 2003	EU membership	63	Approved: 67
Finland	16 October 1994	EU membership	70.8	Approved: 56.9
France	21 October 1945	Draft constitution and interim powers for the new Assembly	79.8	Approved: 96
France	5 May 1946	Constitution of the Fourth Republic	80	Not approved: 53
France	13 October 1946	Constitution of the Fourth Republic	66.4	Approved: 53.2
France	28 September 1958	Constitution of the Fifth Republic	79.8	Approved: 82.6
France	8 January 1961	Self-determination for Algeria	73.8	Approved: 75
France	8 April 1962	Self-determination for Algeria—Évian Accords	75.3	Approved: 90.8

(Continued)

308 ∞ *Appendix: Referendums from 1898–2011 cited in the book*

Place	Date	Subject	Turnout %	Result %
France	28 October 1962	Direct election of the president	77	Approved: 62.3
France	27 April 1969	Powers of the Senate and regional devolution	80.1	Not approved: 52.4
France	6 November 1988	Matignon Accords—self-determination for New Caledonia	37	Approved: 80
France	20 September 1992	Maastricht Treaty	69.7	Approved: 51.1
France	29 May 2005	Lisbon Treaty	69	Rejected: 54.8
Germany	12 November 1933	Withdraw from the Geneva Disarmament Conference and the League of Nations	96	Approved: 95 (government statistics)
Germany	19 August 1934	Confirm Hitler as Fuhrer	95	Approved: 90 (government statistics)
Germany	29 March 1936	Confirm German occupation of the Rhineland in violation of the Treaty of Versailles	99	Approved: 98.8 (government statistics)
Germany	10 April 1938	Ratify annexation of Austria Cross-ref to Austria	99	Approved: 99 (government statistics)
Ireland	10 May 1972	EEC membership	70.3	Approved: 83.1
Ireland	26 May 1987	Single European Act	44	Approved: 70
Ireland	18 June 1992	Maastricht Treaty	57.3	Approved: 69.1
Ireland	22 May 1998	Treaty of Amsterdam (18th constitutional amendment)	56.3	Approved: 61.7
		Amend constitution in light of Belfast Agreement (19th constitutional amendment)	55.6	Approved 94.4
Ireland	7 June 2001	Treaty of Nice	34.8	Not approved: 53.9
Ireland	19 October 2002	Amended Treaty of Nice	49.5	Approved: 62.9
Ireland	12 June 2008	Treaty of Lisbon	53.1	Not approved: 53.4
Ireland	2 October 2009	Treaty of Lisbon	58	Approved: 67.1
Italy	24 March 1929	Election of Chamber of Deputies and Senate	91	Approved: 98.3

Appendix: Referendums from 1898–2011 cited in the book 309

Place	Date	Subject	Turnout %	Result %
		with single party list for the National Fascist Party		
Italy	25 March 1934	Single party rule by the National Fascist Party	96.2	Approved: 99.8
Italy	9 June 1991	Preference voting	62.5	Supported abrogation: 95.6
Italy	18 April 1999	Change to the electoral system	49.7	Approved: 91 (failed as 50% threshold not met)
Kazakhstan	17 March 1991	Sovereignty within a new USSR Union	88.2	Approved: 95.6
Kyrgyzstan (Kirghizia)	17 March 1991	Sovereignty within a new USSR Union	96.4	Approved: 94.5
Kosovo	26–30 September 1991 (unofficial)	Validate earlier declaration of independence	87	Approved: 98 (result issued by de facto Kosovar leadership)
Latvia	3 March 1991	Independence from the USSR	88	Approved: 75
Latvia	3 October 1998	Repeal the 1998 citizenship law	73	For repeal: 45 Against repeal: 53
Latvia	20 September 2003	EU membership	72.5	Approved: 74.9
Lithuania	8 February 1991	Independence from the USSR	84.7	Approved: 93.2
Luxembourg	10 July 2005	Lisbon Treaty	88	Approved: 57
Montenegro	1 March 1992	Remain part of Yugoslavia	66	Approved: 96
Montenegro	21 May 2006	Independence	86.5	Approved: 55.5
Netherlands	1 June 2005	Lisbon Treaty	63.3	Not approved: 61.5
New Caledonia	28 September 1958	Constitution of the Fifth Republic		Approved: 82.6
New Caledonia	13 September 1987	Matignon–Oudinot Accords—maintain dependence on France	58.6	Approved: 98.3
New Caledonia	8 November 1998	Noumea Accord	74	Approved: 72
Norway	28 November 1994	EU membership	89	Not approved: 47.8
Poland	30 June 1946	Three questions: (1) Abolish the senate	90.1	(1) Approved: 68 (official) Not approved: 73 (actual)

(Continued)

Place	Date	Subject	Turnout %	Result %
		(2) Constitutional consolidation		(2) Approved: 77 (official) Not approved: 58 (actual)
		(3) Consolidate western border		(3) Approved: 91 (official) Approved: 67 (actual) *Actual results published in 1989 following fall of Communist government*
Poland	29 November 1987	Economic/political reform	67	<50 on both questions
Romania	23 November 1986	Reduce army	100	Approved: 100 (official results)
Russian Federation	12 December 1993	New constitution	58.4	Approved: 54.8
Samoa (then-Western Samoa)	9 May 1961	Independent statehood		Approved
Slovenia	23 December 1990	Independent statehood	93.2	Approved: 95.7
Slovenia	23 March 2003	(1) EU membership (2) NATO membership	60.2	(1) Approved: 89.6 (2) Approved: 66
South Africa	17 March 1992	Support efforts to end apartheid	85	Approved: 68.7
South Sudan	9–15 January 2011	Independence	97.6	Approved: 99
Spain	12 March 1986	NATO membership	59	Approved: 53
Spain	20 February 2005	Lisbon Treaty	42	Approved: 77
Sweden	13 November 1994	EU membership	83	Approved: 52
Turkmenistan	26 October 1991	Independent statehood	97.4	Approved: 94.1
Ukraine	17 March 1991	(1) New USSR Union Treaty (2) Union based on 1990 Sovereignty Declaration	83.5	(1) Approved: 71.5 (2) Approved: 80
Ukraine	1 December 1991	Independence	84.2	Approved: 90.3

Appendix: Referendums from 1898–2011 cited in the book   311

Place	Date	Subject	Turnout %	Result %
Union of Soviet Socialist Republics	17 March 1991	Renewed federation	75.1	Approved: 69.9
United Kingdom	5 June 1975	Continued EC membership	64.5	Approved: 67.2
United Kingdom	5 May 2011	Electoral system: alternative vote	42.2	Not approved: 67.9
United Kingdom, England (North East)	4 November 2004	North East England regional assembly	47.8	Not approved: 78
United Kingdom, Northern Ireland	8 March 1973	Remain in UK	58.1	Approved: 98.9
United Kingdom, Northern Ireland	22 May 1998	Belfast Agreement	81.1	Approved: 71.1
United Kingdom, London	7 May 1998	Devolution of powers	34.6	Approved: 72
United Kingdom, Scotland	1 March 1979	Devolution of powers	33	Approved: 52 (did not meet 40% turnout threshold)
United Kingdom, Scotland	11 September 1997	(1) Creation of a Scottish Parliament (2) Devolution of limited tax-varying powers	60.4	(1) Approved: 74.3 (2) Approved: 63.5
United Kingdom, Wales	1 March 1979	Creation of a Welsh Assembly	58.8	Not approved: 79.7
United Kingdom, Wales	September 1997	Creation of a Welsh Assembly	50.1	Approved: 50.3
United Kingdom, Wales	3 March 2011	Devolution of further powers to the Welsh Assembly	35.4	Approved: 63.5
(British) Cameroons	November 1959	(1) Integrate with Nigeria (2) Postpone decision	87.9	(1) Votes for union: 27.8 (2) Votes to postpone: 62.3
(British) Cameroons	21 February 1960	Constitutional reform	75.5	Approved: 60.3

(Continued)

312 ◦ *Appendix: Referendums from 1898–2011 cited in the book*

Place	Date	Subject	Turnout %	Result %
(British) Cameroons	11 February 1961	(1) Integration into Cameroon (2) Integration into Nigeria		Northern Cameroons (1) Approved: 40 (2) Approved: 60 Southern Cameroons (1) Approved: 70.5 (2) Approved: 29.5
(British) Togoland	9 May 1956	To merge with the Gold Coast		Approved: 63.4
USA, Massachusetts	1778	Ratify state constitution		Approved
USA, New Hampshire	1792	Ratify state constitution		Approved
Uzbekistan	29 December 1991	Independent statehood		Approved: 98
Paris Peace/League of Nations processes				
Allenstein	11 July 1920	Territory to be part of Germany, not Poland	87	Approved: 98
Klagenfurt	10 October 1920	Territory to be part of Austria not Yugoslavia	96	Approved: 59
Marienwerder	11 July 1920	Territory to be part of Germany, not Poland	87	Approved: 98
Schleswig Northern Territory	10 February 1920	Territory to be part of Denmark		Approved: 74.9
Schleswig Southern Territory	14 March 1920	Territory to be part of Germany		Approved: 80.2
Sopron	17 December 1921	Territory to be part of Hungary, not Austria	89.5	Approved: 65
Upper Silesia	20 March 1921	Territory to be part of Germany, not Poland	97.5	Approved: 60
Saarland	13 January 1935	Territory to be part of Germany, not France	98	Approved: 90.7

Bibliography

'Chirac accelerates EU referendum after gains for no camp', *EU Business.com* (18 February 2005) <http://www.eubusiness.com/europe/france/050218132610.w1ahja90/> accessed 14 July 2011.

'Constitutional Watch' (1996) 4 East European Constitutional Rev 5.

'Deeper Look at Poll Illuminates Complex Reasons for Result', *Irish Times* (Dublin, 14 June 2008).

'Nisga'a Treaty Must go to Referendum', *Vancouver Courier* (Vancouver, 26 August 1998).

'Results of the Referenda in Northern Ireland and Republic of Ireland, Friday 22 May 1998' (CAIN, May 1998) <http://cain.ulst.ac.uk/issues/politics/election/ref1998.htm> accessed 25 July 2011.

'Stuart Wheeler loses High Court challenge to the EU Lisbon Treaty', *The Times* (London, 26 June 2008) <http://www.timesonline.co.uk/tol/news/uk/article4214748.ece> accessed 14 July 2011.

'Voting referendum question "too hard", says watchdog', BBC (30 September 2010) <http://www.bbc.co.uk/news/uk-politics-11442445> accessed 14 July 2011.

Ackerman B, 'Transformative Appointments' (1988) 101 Harvard L Rev 1164.

—— *We the People: Foundations* (Harvard University Press 1991).

—— *We the People: Transformations* (Harvard University Press 1998).

—— and Fishkin JS, *Deliberation Day* (Yale University Press 2004).

Aldrich R and Connell J (eds), *France's Overseas Frontier* (Cambridge University Press 1982).

Altman D, *Direct Democracy Worldwide* (Cambridge University Press 2011).

Amar AR, 'Popular Sovereignty and Constitutional Amendment' in S Levinson (ed), *Responding to Imperfection: The Theory and Practice of Constitutional Amendment* (Princeton University Press 1995).

Ambrosius L, 'Dilemmas of National Self-Determination: Woodrow Wilson's Legacy' in C Baecher and C Fink (eds), *The Establishment of European Frontiers after the Two World Wars* (Lang 1987).

Arato A, 'Dilemmas Arising from the Power to Create Constitutions in Eastern Europe' (1993) 14 Cardozo L Rev 661.

Arendt H, *On Revolution* (Penguin 1977).

Aristotle, *Politics* (Benjamin Jowett tr, Modern Library 1943).

Ascherson N, *The Struggle for Poland* (Michael Joseph 1987).

Auer A and Bützer D (eds), *Direct Democracy: The Eastern and Central European Experience* (Ashgate 2001).

Auers D, Ruus J, and Krupavicius A, 'Financing Referendums and Initiatives in the Baltic States' in K Gilland Lutz and S Hug (eds), *Financing Referendum Campaigns* (Palgrave Macmillan 2009).

Barber BR, *Strong Democracy: Participatory Politics for a New Age* (University of California Press 1984).

—— *An Aristocracy of Everyone: The Politics of Education and the Future of America* (Oxford University Press 1992).

Barrett G, 'Building a Swiss Chalet in an Irish Legal Landscape? Referendums on European Union Treaties in Ireland and the Impact of Supreme Court Jurisprudence' (2009) 5 European Constitutional L Rev 32.

Bayefsky A (ed), *Self-Determination in International Law: Quebec and Lessons Learned* (Kluwer Law International 2000).

Bean C, 'Political Personalities and Voting in the 1999 Australian Constitutional Referendum' (2002) 14 Int'l J Public Opinion Research 459.

Bell C and O'Rourke C, 'The People's Peace? Peace Agreements, Civil Society, and Participatory Democracy' (2007) 28 Int'l Political Science Rev 293.

Bell, Jr DA, 'The Referendum: Democracy's Barrier to Racial Equality' (1978–79) 54 Washington L Rev 1.

Bellamy R, *Liberalism and Pluralism: Towards a Politics of Compromise* (Routledge 1999).

—— *Political Constitutionalism: A Republican Defence of the Constitutionality of Democracy* (Cambridge University Press 2007).

—— and Hollis M, 'Consensus, Neutrality and Compromise' in R Bellamy and M Hollis (eds), *Pluralism and Liberal Neutrality* (Frank Cass 1999).

Benedetto G and Hix S, 'The Rejected, the Ejected, and the Dejected: Explaining Government Rebels in the 2001–2005 British House of Commons' (2007) 40 Comparative Political Studies 755.

Benhabib S, 'Deliberative Rationality and Models of Democratic Legitimacy' (1994) 1 Constellations 26.

—— *Democracy and Difference: Contesting the Boundaries of the Political* (Princeton University Press 1996).

—— 'Toward a Deliberative Model of Democratic Legitimacy' in S Benhabib (ed), *Democracy and Difference: Contesting the Boundaries of the Political* (Princeton University Press 1996).

Beran H, 'Who Should be Entitled to Vote in Self-Determination Referenda?' in M Warner and R Crisp (eds), *Terrorism, Protest and Power* (Edward Elgar 1990).

Berman A, 'The Noumea Accords: Emancipation or Colonial Harness?' (2001) 36 Texas Int'l LJ 277.

Berstein S, *The Republic of de Gaulle 1958–1969* (Cambridge University Press 1993).

Besson S, *The Morality of Conflict: Reasonable Disagreement and the Law* (Hart Publishing 2005).

Bethlehem D and Weller M, *The Yugoslav Crisis in International Law* (Cambridge University Press 1997).

Binzer Hobolt S, 'How Parties Affect Vote Choice in European Integration Referendums' (2006) 12 Party Politics 623.
—— 'Campaign Financing in Danish Referendums' in K Gilland Lutz and S Hug (eds), *Financing Referendum Campaigns* (Palgrave Macmillan 2009).
—— *Europe in Question: Referendums on European Integration* (Oxford University Press 2009).
Birrell D and Williamson A, 'The Voluntary–Community Sector and Political Development in Northern Ireland, Since 1972' (2001) 12 Voluntas: Int'l J Voluntary and Nonprofit Organizations 205.
Blais A, Carty RK, and Fournier P, 'Do Citizens Assemblies Make Reasoned Choices?' in ME Warren and H Pearse (eds), *Designing Deliberative Democracy: The British Columbia Citizens' Assembly* (Cambridge University Press 2008).
Bluche F, *Le Bonapartisme. Aux origines de la droite autoritaire (1800–1850)* (NEL 1980).
Bogdanor V, *The People and the Party System: The Referendum and Electoral Reform in British Politics* (Cambridge University Press 1981).
—— 'Western Europe' in D Butler and A Ranney (eds), *Referendums Around the World: The Growing Use of Direct Democracy* (Macmillan Press 1994).
Bohman J, *Public Deliberation: Pluralism, Complexity, and Democracy* (MIT Press 1996).
—— 'The Coming of Age of Deliberative Democracy' (1998) 6 J Political Philosophy 400.
—— 'International Regimes and Democratic Governance: Political Equality and Influence in Global Institutions' (1999) 75 International Affairs 499.
Borrows J, 'Tracking Trajectories: Aboriginal Governance as an Aboriginal Right' (2005) 38 UBC L Rev 285.
Bourke R, 'Enlightenment, Revolution and Democracy' (2008) 15 Constellations 10.
Bowler S and Donovan T, *Demanding Choices: Opinion, Voting, and Direct Democracy* (University of Michigan Press 1998).
——, ——, and Tolbert CJ (eds), *Citizens as Legislators: Direct Democracy in the United States* (Ohio State University Press 1998).
Boyer P, *The People's Mandate: Referendums and a More Democratic Canada* (Dundurn Press 1991).
Brady HE and Kaplan CS, 'Eastern Europe and the Former Soviet Union' in D Butler and A Ranney (eds), *Referendums Around the World: The Growing Use of Direct Democracy* (Macmillan Press 1994).
Broder D, *Democracy Derailed: Initiative Campaigns and the Power of Money* (Harcourt 2000).
Brown MB, 'Citizen Panels and the Concept of Representation' (2006) 14 J Political Philosophy 203.
Brubaker R, *Nationalism Reframed: Nationhood and the National Question in the New Europe* (Cambridge University Press 1996).
Brunner G, 'Direct vs Representative Democracy' in A Auer and M Bützer (eds), *Direct Democracy: The Eastern and Central European Experience* (Ashgate 2001).
Buchanan A, *Justice, Legitimacy and Self-Determination: Moral Foundations for International Law* (Oxford University Press 2007).
Budge I, *The New Challenge of Direct Democracy* (Polity Press 1996).

Budge I, 'Political Parties in Direct Democracy' in M Mendelsohn and A Parkin (eds), *Referendum Democracy: Citizens, Elites, and Deliberation in Referendum Campaigns* (Palgrave 2001).

Bukey EB, *Hitler's Austria: Popular Sentiment in the Nazi Era, 1938–1945* (University of North Carolina Press 2000).

Bungs D, 'Latvia' (1992) 1(27) Radio Free Europe/Radio Liberty Research Report.

Butler D, 'Summing Up' in D Butler and A Ranney (eds), *Referendums: A Comparative Study of Practice and Theory* (American Enterprise Institute for Public Policy Research 1978).

—— 'Conclusion' in D Butler and A Ranney (eds), *Referendums Around the World: The Growing Use of Direct Democracy* (Macmillan Press 1994).

—— 'Theory' in D Butler and A Ranney (eds), *Referendums Around the World: The Growing Use of Direct Democracy* (Macmillan Press 1994).

—— and Kitzinger U, *The 1975 Referendum* (Macmillan Press 1976).

—— and Ranney A (eds), *Referendums: A Comparative Study of Practice and Theory* (American Enterprise Institute for Public Policy Research 1978).

—— and —— (eds), *Referendums Around the World: The Growing Use of Direct Democracy* (Macmillan Press 1994).

Cabacenco P, 'Moldova, On the Threshold of Change' (*Election Guide Digest*, 1 September 2010) <http://digest.electionguide.org/2010/09/01/cabacenco-moldova-on-the-threshold-of-change-2/> accessed 24 July 2011.

Canovan M, 'The People, the Masses, and the Mobilization of Power: The Paradox of Hannah Arendt's "Populism"' (2002) 69 Social Research 403.

—— 'Populism for Political Theorists?' (2004) 9 J Political Ideologies 241.

Caplan R, *Europe and the Recognition of New States in Yugoslavia* (Oxford University Press 2005).

Carcassone G, 'France (1958): The Fifth Republic after Thirty Years' in V Bogdanor (ed), *Constitutions in Democratic Politics* (Gower 1988).

Cassese A, *Self-Determination of Peoples: A Legal Reappraisal* (Hersch Lauterpacht Memorial Lectures, Cambridge University Press 1999).

Chambers S, 'Constitutional Referendums and Democratic Deliberation' in M Mendelsohn and A Parkin (eds), *Referendum Democracy: Citizens, Elites, and Deliberation in Referendum Campaigns* (Palgrave 2001).

—— 'Deliberative Democratic Theory' (2003) 6 Annual Rev of Political Science 307.

—— 'Democracy, Popular Sovereignty, and Constitutional Legitimacy' (2004) 11 Constellations 153.

—— 'Rhetoric and the Public Sphere: Has Deliberative Democracy Abandoned Mass Democracy?' (2009) 37 Political Theory 323.

Chappell DA, 'The Noumea Accord: Decolonization without Independence in New Caledonia?' (1999) 72 Pacific Affairs 373.

Choudhry S, 'Building Comparative Politics and Comparative Constitutional Law: Constitutional Design in Divided Societies' in S Choudhry (ed), *Constitutional Design for Divided Societies: Integration or Accommodation* (Oxford University Press 2008).

—— and Howse R, 'Constitutional Theory and the Quebec Secession Reference' (2000) 13 Canadian J Law and Jurisprudence 143.
Christin T and Hug S, 'Referendums and Citizen Support for European Integration' (2002) 35 Comparative Political Studies 586.
Cobban A, *The Nation State and National Self-Determination* (2nd edn, Collins 1969).
Cohen J, 'Deliberation and Democratic Legitimacy' in J Bohman and W Rehg (eds), *Deliberative Democracy: Essays on Reason and Politics* (MIT Press 1997).
—— and Sabel C, 'Directly-Deliberative Polyarchy' (2001) 3 European LJ 313.
Connolly WE, *Pluralism* (Duke University Press 2005).
Cowley P and Stuart M, 'Parliament' in A Seldon and D Kavanagh (eds), *The Blair Effect 2001–2005* (Cambridge University Press 2005).
Cox M, 'The War that Came in from the Cold: Clinton and the Irish Question' (1999) 16 World Policy J 59.
Craig P, 'Constitutions, Constitutionalism, and the European Union' (2001) 7(2) European LJ 125.
—— *Administrative Law* (5th edn, Sweet & Maxwell 2003).
Craig SC, Kreppel A, and Kane JG, 'Public Opinion and Support for Direct Democracy: A Grassroots Perspective' in M Mendelsohn and A Parkin (eds), *Referendum Democracy: Citizens, Elites, and Deliberation in Referendum Campaigns* (Palgrave 2001).
Crawford J, *The Creation of States in International Law* (Oxford University Press 1979).
Crenson MA and Ginsberg B, *Downsizing Democracy: How America Sidelined Its Citizens and Privatized Its Public* (Johns Hopkins University Press 2002).
Crick B, *In Defence of Politics* (5th edn, Continuum 2000).
Cronin T, *Direct Democracy: The Politics of Initiative, Referendum and Recall* (Harvard University Press 1989).
Cross B, 'The Australian Republic Referendum, 1999' (2007) 78 Political Quarterly 556.
Cruz JB, 'An Area of Darkness: Three Conceptions of the Relationship Between European Union Law and State Constitutional Law' in N Walker, J Shaw, and S Tierney (eds), *Europe's Constitutional Mosaic* (Hart Publishing 2011).
Currie B and Settle M, 'Moore Blasted by SNP on Second Referendum Plan', *The Herald* (Glasgow, 7 June 2011) <http://www.heraldscotland.com/news/politics/moore-blasted-by-snp-on-second-referendum-plan-1.1105507> accessed 20 October.
Dahl RA, *After the Revolution? Authority in a Good Society* (Yale University Press 1970).
—— *Democracy and Its Critics* (Yale University Press 1989).
Daintith T and Page A, *The Executive in the Constitution: Structure, Autonomy, and Internal Control* (Oxford University Press 1999).
Dalton RJ, *Citizen Politics in Western Democracies: Public Opinion and Political Parties in the US, UK, Germany and France* (2nd edn, Chatham House 1996).
—— *Citizen Politics: Public Opinion and Political Parties in Advanced Industrial Democracies* (3rd edn, Chatham House 2002).
—— 'Citizenship Norms and the Expansion of Political Participation' (2006) 56 Political Studies 76.
Darmanovic S, 'Montenegro: A Miracle in the Balkans' (2007) 18 J Democracy 152.

de Búrca G, 'If at First You Don't Succeed: Vote, Vote Again: Analyzing the Second Referendum Phenomenon in EU Treaty Change' (2011) 33 Fordham Int'l LJ 1472.

de Spinoza B, *A Theologico-Political Treatise* (RHM Elwes tr, Dover 1951).

de Tocqueville A, *Democracy in America* (Harvey Mansfield and Delba Winthrop eds and trs, University of Chicago Press 2000).

de Vreese CH, 'Context, Elites, Media and Public Opinion in Referendums: When Campaigns Really Matter' in CH de Vreese (ed), *The Dynamics of Referendum Campaigns: An International Perspective* (Palgrave Macmillan 2007).

—— and Semetko HA, 'News Matters: Influences on the Vote in the Danish 2000 Euro Referendum Campaign' (2004) 43 European J Political Research 699.

Dempsey GT, 'The American Role in the Northern Ireland Peace Process' (1999) 14 Irish Political Studies 104.

Denver D, 'Voting in the 1997 Scottish and Welsh Devolution Referendums: Information, Interests and Opinions' (2002) 41 European J Political Research 827.

Dicey AV, 'Ought the Referendum to be Introduced into England?' (1890) 57 Contemporary Rev 489.

Downs WM, 'Election Report—Denmark's Referendum on the Euro: The Mouse that Roared...Again' (2001) 24 West European Politics 222.

Dreifelds J, *Latvia in Transition* (Cambridge University Press 1997).

Dryzek JS, *Discursive Democracy* (Cambridge University Press 1990).

—— *Deliberative Democracy and Beyond: Liberals, Critics and Contestations* (Oxford University Press 2000).

—— 'Legitimacy and Economy in Deliberative Democracy' (2001) 29 Political Theory 651.

—— 'Deliberative Democracy in Divided Societies: Alternatives to Agonism and Analgesia' (2005) 33 Political Theory 218.

—— *Deliberative Global Politics: Discourse and Democracy in a Divided World* (Polity Press 2006).

—— *Foundations and Frontiers of Deliberative Governance* (Oxford University Press 2011).

—— and Dunleavy P, *Theories of the Democratic State* (Palgrave Macmillan 2009).

—— with Niemeyer S, *Foundations and Frontiers of Deliberative Governance* (Oxford University Press 2010).

Dugard J, *Recognition and the United Nations* (Grotius Publications 1987).

Dunn J, *Setting the People Free: The Story of Democracy* (Atlantic Books 2005).

Dworkin R, *Is Democracy Possible Here? Principles for a New Political Debate* (Princeton University Press 2008).

Dyzenhaus D, 'The Rule of Law as the Rule of Liberal Principle' in A Ripstein (ed), *Ronald Dworkin* (Cambridge University Press 2007).

Effing R, van Hillegersberg J, and Huibers T, 'Social Media and Political Participation: Are Facebook, Twitter and YouTube Democratizing Our Political Systems?' (2011) 6847 Lecture Notes in Computer Science 25.

Eisenberg A, 'Presentation to the Select Standing Committee on Aboriginal Affairs for the BCCLA' in *Proceedings of the Select Standing Committee on Aboriginal Affairs Victoria, BC* (2 November 2001).

—— 'The Medium is the Message: How Referenda Lead Us to Understand Equality for Minorities' in M Mendelsohn and A Parkin (eds), *Referendum Democracy: Citizens, Elites, and Deliberation in Referendum Campaigns* (Palgrave 2001).

—— 'When (if ever) Are Referendums on Minority Rights Fair?' in D Laycock (ed), *Representation and Democratic Theory* (UBC Press 2004).

Electoral Commission, 'Referendum on the UK Parliamentary Voting System: Report of Views of the Electoral Commission on the Proposed Referendum Question' (Electoral Commission 2010).

Elgie R and Zielonka J, 'Constitutions and Constitution-Building: A Comparative Perspective' in J Zielonka (ed), *Democratic Consolidation in Eastern Europe* (Oxford University Press 2001) vol I.

Elkin SL, 'Thinking Constitutionally: The Problem of Deliberative Democracy' (2004) 21 Social Philosophy and Policy 39.

Elster J, 'The Market and the Forum: Three Varieties of Political Theory' in J Elster and A Hylland (eds), *Foundations of Social Choice Theory* (Cambridge University Press 1986).

—— 'Introduction' in J Elster and R Slagstad (eds), *Constitutionalism and Democracy* (Cambridge University Press 1988).

—— 'Constitutional Bootstrapping in Paris and Philadelphia' (1992–93) 14 Cardozo LJ 549.

Emerson PJ, *Defining Democracy: Decisions, Elections and Good Governance* (The De Borda Institute 2002).

Erikson EO, *Understanding Habermas: Communicative Action and Deliberative Democracy* (Continuum 2003).

Farley LT, *Plebiscites and Sovereignty: The Crisis of Political Illegitimacy* (Westview Press 1986).

Farrell DM and Schmitt-Beck R (eds), *Do Political Campaigns Matter? Campaign Effects in Elections and Referendums* (Routledge 2002).

Farrelly C, 'Making Deliberative Democracy a More Practical Political Ideal' (2005) 4 European J Political Theory 200.

Fearon JD, 'Deliberation as Discussion' in J Elster (ed), *Deliberative Democracy* (Cambridge University Press 1998).

Featherstone D, *Resistance, Space and Political Identities: The Making of Counter-Global Networks* (Wiley-Blackwell 2008).

Fishkin JS, 'Consulting the Public through Deliberative Polling' (2003) 22 J Policy Analysis and Management 128.

—— *When the People Speak: Deliberative Democracy and Public Consultation* (Oxford University Press 2009).

—— 'Deliberative Democracy and Constitutions' (2011) 28 Social Philosophy and Policy 242.

—— and Luskin RC, 'The Quest for Deliberative Democracy in M Saward (ed), *Democratic Innovation: Deliberation, Representation and Association* (Routledge 2000).

—— and —— 'Experimenting with a Democratic Ideal: Deliberative Polling and Opinion' (2005) 40 Acta Politica 284.

Flickinger R and Studlar D, 'Exploring Declining Turnout in Western European Elections' (1992) 15 West European Politics 1.
Flinders M, *Delegated Governance and the British State: Walking without Order* (Oxford University Press 2008).
Flinders M, *Democratic Drift: Majoritarian Modification and Democratic Anomie in the United Kingdom* (Oxford University Press 2009).
Foster C, *British Government in Crisis* (Hart Publishing 2005).
Franklin M, Marsh M, and McLaren L, 'Uncorking the Bottle: Popular Opposition to European Unification in the Wake of Maastricht' (1994) 32 J Common Market Studies 455.
Fraser N and Honneth A, *Redistribution or Recognition? A Political–Philosophical Exchange* (Verso 2003).
Frey BS, 'Direct Democracy for Transition Countries' (2003) 7 J Institutional Innovation, Development and Transition 42.
Friis K, 'The Referendum in Montenegro: The EU's 'Postmodern Diplomacy'' (2007) 12 European Foreign Affairs Rev 67.
Gallagher M, 'Popular Sovereignty and Referendums' in A Auer and M Bützer (eds), *Direct Democracy: The Eastern and Central European Experience* (Ashgate 2001).
—— and Uleri PV (eds), *The Referendum Experience in Europe* (Macmillan Press 1996).
Galligan B, 'Amending Constitutions through the Referendum Device' in M Mendelsohn and A Parkin (eds), *Referendum Democracy: Citizens, Elites, and Deliberation in Referendum Campaigns* (Palgrave 2001).
Garčević V, 'Montenegro and the OSCE' in *OSCE Yearbook 2007* (CORE Centre for OSCE Research 2008).
Garrett E and Gerber ER, 'Money in the Initiative and Referendum Process: Evidence of its Effects and Prospects for Reform' in MD Waters (ed), *The Battle over Citizen Lawmaking* (Carolina Academic Press 2001).
Garry J, Marsh M, and Sinnott R, '"Second-Order" versus "Issue-Voting" Effects in EU Referendums: Evidence from the Irish Nice Treaty Referendums' (2005) 6 European Union Politics 201.
Gastil J, *By Popular Demand: Revitalizing Representative Democracy through Deliberative Elections* (University of California Press 2000).
Gay O, 'Referendums: Recent Developments' (1999) House of Commons Library Research Paper 99/30 <http://main.hop.lbi.co.uk/documents/commons/lib/research/rp99/rp99-030.pdf> accessed 13 July 2011.
Gerber ER, 'Does the Popular Vote Destroy Civil Rights?' (1996) 42 Am J Political Science 1342.
—— 'Legislative Response to the Threat of Popular Initiatives' (1996) 40 Am J Political Science 99.
—— *The Populist Paradox: Interest Group Influence and the Promise of Direct Legislation* (Princeton University Press 1999).
Ghaleigh NS, 'Sledgehammers and Nuts?: Regulating Referendums in the UK' in K Gilland Lutz and S Hug (eds), *Financing Referendum Campaigns* (Palgrave Macmillan 2009).

Ghosh E, 'Deliberative Democracy and the Countermajoritarian Difficulty: Considering Constitutional Juries' (2010) 30 OJLS 327.

Gibson G, 'Report on the Constitution of the Citizens' Assembly on Electoral Reform. Government of British Columbia' (Report, Citizens' Assembly on Electoral Reform 2002) <http://www.citizensassembly.bc.ca/resources/gibson_report.pdf> accessed 23 July 2011.

Giddens A, *The Third Way: The Renewal of Social Democracy* (Polity Press 1998).

Gilbert G, 'The Northern Ireland Peace Agreement, Minority Rights and Self-Determination' (1998) 47 ICLQ 943.

Gill S, *Power and Resistance in the New World Order* (Palgrave Macmillan 2003).

Gilland Lutz K and Hug S (eds), *Financing Referendum Campaigns* (Palgrave Macmillan 2009).

Gleason G, 'The Federal Formula and the Collapse of the USSR' (1992) 22(3) Publius 141.

Glencross A and Trechsel A, 'First or Second Order Referendums? Understanding the Votes on the EU Constitutional Treaty in Four EU Member States' (2011) 34(4) West European Politics 755.

Goetz AM and Jenkins R, *Reinventing Accountability: Making Democracy Work for Human Development* (Palgrave Macmillan 2005).

Gooch A, 'A Surrealistic Referendum: Spain and NATO' (1986) 21 Government and Opposition 300.

Goodin RE, *Reflective Democracy* (Oxford University Press 2003).

—— 'When Does Deliberation Begin? Internal Reflection versus Public Discussion in Deliberative Democracy' (2003) 51 Political Studies 627.

—— *Innovating Democracy: Democratic Theory and Practice after the Deliberative Turn* (Oxford University Press 2008).

—— and Dryzek JS, 'Deliberative Impacts: The Macro-Political Uptake of Mini-publics' (2006) 34 Politics and Society 219.

—— and —— 'Deliberative Impacts' in S Rosenberg (ed), *Deliberation, Participation and Democracy: Can the People Govern?* (Palgrave Macmillan 2007).

—— and —— 'Making Use of Mini-publics' in RE Goodin, *Innovating Democracy: Democratic Theory and Practice after the Deliberative Turn* (Oxford University Press 2008).

Gow D, Bean C, and McAllister I, *Australian Constitutional Referendum Study, 1999* (Australian Social Science Data Archive 2000).

Gray M and Caul M, 'Declining Voter Turnout in Advanced Industrial Democracies' (2000) 33 Comparative Political Studies 1091.

Grimm D, 'The Constitution in the Process of Denationalization' (2005) 12 Constellations 447.

Guidry JA, Kennedy MD, and Zald MN (eds), *Globalizations and Social Movements: Culture, Power and the Transnational Public Sphere* (University of Michigan Press 2000).

Gunn PF, 'Initiatives and Referendums: Direct Democracy and Minority Interests' (1981) 22 Urban Law Annual 135.

Gutmann A and Thompson D, *Democracy and Disagreement* (Harvard University Press 1996).

Gutmann A and Thompson D, *Why Deliberative Democracy?* (Princeton University Press 2004).

Habermas J, *Legitimation Crisis* (Thomas McCarthy tr, Beacon Press 1975).

—— *The Theory of Communicative Action* (Thomas McCarthy tr, Polity Press 1984).

—— *Moral Consciousness and Communicative Action* (MIT Press 1990).

—— 'Struggles for Recognition in the Democratic Constitutional State' in Amy Gutmann (ed), *Multiculturalism: Examining the Politics of Recognition* (Princeton University Press 1994).

—— *Between Facts and Norms: Contributions to a Discourse Theory of Law and Democracy* (MIT Press 1999).

—— 'Constitutional Democracy: A Paradoxical Union of Contradictory Principles?' (2001) 29 Political Theory 766.

Habermas J and Pensky M, *The Postnational Constellation: Political Essays* (Polity Press 2001).

Hall JA, 'In Search of Civil Society' in JA Hall (ed), *Civil Society: Theory, History, Comparison* (Polity Press 1995).

Hamon F, *Le Référendum: Étude Comparative* (Librairie générale de droit et de jurisprudence 1995).

—— 'The Financing of Referendum Campaigns in France' in K Gilland Lutz and S Hug (eds), *Financing Referendum Campaigns* (Palgrave Macmillan 2009).

Hansard Society, *The Challenge for Parliament: Making Government Accountable* (Hansard Society 2001).

Hardt M and Negri A, *Multitude: War and Democracy in the Age of Empire* (Penguin Press 2004).

Hart HLA, *The Concept of Law* (Clarendon Press 1961).

Hartley A, *Gaullism: The Rise and Fall of a Political Movement* (Routledge & Kegan Paul 1972).

Hartz-Karp J and Briand MK, 'Institutionalizing Deliberative Democracy' (2009) 9 J Public Affairs 125.

Harvey M and Lynch P, 'From National Conversation to Independence Referendum?: The SNP Government and the Politics of Independence' (Political Studies Association Conference, Edinburgh, 29 March–1 April 2010) <http://www.psa.ac.uk/journals/pdf/5/2010/1041_870.pdf> accessed 24 July 2011.

Haskell J, *Direct Democracy or Representative Government? Dispelling the Populist Myth* (Westview Press 2001).

Hauptmann E, 'Deliberation = Legitimacy = Democracy' (1999) 27 Political Theory 857.

Henderson A, 'Referendums and Losers' Consent: Understanding Risk and Satisfaction with Democracy' (Referendums and Deliberative Democracy workshop, University of Edinburgh, 8 May 2009).

Hennessy P, 'Loosen Britain's Ties with European Union, Say Two-thirds of Voters', *The Telegraph* (London, 10 January 2009) <http://www.telegraph.co.uk/news/politics/4214369/Loosen-Britains-ties-with-European-Union-say-two-thirds-of-voters.html> accessed 24 July 2011.

Hewart L, *The New Despotism* (Ernest Benn Ltd 1929).

Higley J and Evans Case R, 'Australia: The Politics of Becoming a Republic' (2000) 11(3) J Democracy 136.

—— and McAllister I, 'Elite Division and Voter Confusion: Australia's Republic Referendum in 1991' (2002) 41 European J Political Research 845.

Hirschman AO, 'Social Conflicts as Pillars of Democratic Market Society' (1994) 22 Political Theory 203.

Hogg PW, *Constitutional Law of Canada* (2nd edn, Carswell 1997).

Holloway J, *Change the World Without Taking Power* (Pluto Press 2005).

Holmes S, 'Two Concepts of Legitimacy: France After the Revolution' (1982) 10 Political Theory 165.

Honig B, *Political Theory and the Displacement of Politics* (Cornell University Press 1993).

Honneth A, *The Struggle for Recognition: The Moral Grammar of Social Conflicts* (Joel Anderson tr, Polity Press 1995).

Howlett K, 'Referendum? Now What Referendum Would That Be?, *Globe and Mail* (Toronto, 24 September 2007) <http://www.theglobeandmail.com/archives/article783471.ece> accessed 23 July 2011.

Hug S, *Voices of Europe: Citizens, Referendums, and European Integration* (Rowman & Littlefield 2002).

—— 'Some Thoughts About Referendums, Representative Democracy, and Separation of Powers' (2009) 20 Constitutional Political Economy 251.

—— and Sciarini P, 'Referendums on European Integration' (2000) 33 Comparative Political Studies 3.

—— and Tsebelis G, 'Veto Players and Referendums Around the World' (2002) 14 J Theoretical Politics October 465.

Hutchinson AC and Colon-Rios J, 'What's Democracy Got To Do With It? A Critique of Liberal Constitutionalism' (2007) 3(5) CLPE Research Paper 29/2007 <http://ssrn.com/abstractid=1017305> accessed 11 July 2011.

Inglehart R, *The Silent Revolution: Changing Values and Political Styles Among Western Publics* (Princeton University Press 1977).

International Crisis Group, 'ICG Kosovo Report' (*Refworld*, 10 March 1998) <http://www.unhcr.org/refworld/docid/3ae6a6ec4.html> accessed 18 July 2011.

—— 'Still Buying Time: Montenegro, Serbia and the European Union' Europe Report No 129 (*International Crisis Group*, 7 May 2002) <http://www.crisisgroup.org/en/regions/europe/balkans/montenegro/129-still-buying-time-montenegro-serbia-and-the-european-union.aspx> accessed 18 July 2011.

—— 'Montenegro's Referendum' Europe Briefing No 42 (International Crisis Group, 30 May 2006) <http://www.crisisgroup.org/en/regions/europe/balkans/montenegro.aspx> accessed 18 July 2011.

Irwin C, *The People's Peace Process in Northern Ireland* (Palgrave Macmillan 2002).

Jackson RH and Zacher MW, 'The Territorial Covenant: International Society and the Stabilisation of Boundaries' (1997) University of British Columbia Institute of Internal Relations Working Paper No 15 <http://www.ligi.ubc.ca/sites/liu/files/Publications/webwp15.pdf> accessed 13 July 2011.

Jahn D and Storsved A-S, 'Legitimacy through Referendum? The Nearly Successful Domino-Strategy of the EU-Referendums in Austria, Finland, Sweden and Norway' (1995) 18 West European Politics 18.

James MR, *Deliberative Democracy and the Plural Polity* (University Press of Kansas 2004).

James MR, 'Descriptive Representation in the British Columbia Citizens' Assembly' in ME Warren and H Pearse (eds), *Designing Deliberative Democracy: The British Columbia Citizens' Assembly* (Cambridge University Press 2008).

Jaume L, 'Constituent Power in France: The Revolution and Its Consequences' in M Loughlin and N Walker (eds), *The Paradox of Constitutionalism* (Oxford University Press 2007).

Jenkins R and Mendelsohn M, 'The News Media and Referendums' in M Mendelsohn and A Parkin (eds), *Referendum Democracy: Citizens, Elites, and Deliberation in Referendum Campaigns* (Palgrave 2001).

Jennings I, *The Approach to Self-Government* (Cambridge University Press 1956).

Jenssen AT, Pesonen P, and Gilljam M, *To Join or Not to Join: Three Nordic Referendums* (Scandinavian University Press 1998).

Jerome B and Vaillant NG, 'The French Rejection of the European Constitution: An Empirical Analysis' (2005) 21 European J Political Economy 1085.

Johansson P, 'Putting Peace to the Vote: Displaced Persons and a Future Referendum on Nagorno-Karabakh' (2009) 28 Refugee Survey Quarterly 122.

Johnston R, 'Regulating Campaign Finance in Canadian Referendums and Initiatives' in K Gilland Lutz and S Hug (eds), *Financing Referendum Campaigns* (Palgrave Macmillan 2009).

——, Blais A, Gidengil E, and Nevitte N, *The Challenge of Direct Democracy: The 1992 Canadian Referendum* (McGill-Queen's University Press 1996).

Jordan G and Maloney WA, *The Protest Business: Mobilizing Campaign Groups* (Manchester University Press 1997).

—— and —— *Democracy and Interest Groups: Enhancing Participation?* (Palgrave Macmillan 2007).

Juberias CF, 'Some Legal (and Political) Considerations about the Legal Framework for Referendum in Montenegro, in the Light of European Experiences and Standards' in S Elezovic (ed), *Legal Aspects for Referendum in Montenegro in the Context of International Law and Practice* (Foundation Open Society Institute-Representative Office Montenegro 2005).

Judah T, *Kosovo: War and Revenge* (Yale University Press 2000).

Kalyvas A, 'Popular Sovereignty, Democracy and Constituent Power' (2005) 12 Constellations 223.

Kaufman S, *Modern Hatreds: The Symbolic Politics of Ethnic War* (Cornell University Press 2001).

Keane J, *Civil Society: Old Images, New Visions* (Polity Press 1998).

Keating M, *Nations Against the State—The New Politics of Nationalism in Quebec, Catalonia and Scotland* (2nd edn, Palgrave Macmillan 2001).

—— *The Independence of Scotland: Self-government and the Shifting Politics of Union* (Oxford University Press 2009).

Kelsen H, *The Pure Theory of Law* (2nd edn, M Knight tr, University of California Press 1967).

Keohane RO, 'Global Governance and Democratic Accountability' in D Held and M Koenig-Archibugi (eds), *Taming Globalization: Frontiers of Governance* (Polity Press/Blackwell 2003).

Kildea P and Williams G, 'Reworking Australia's Referendum Machinery' (2010) 35 Alternative LJ 22.

Kinder D and Sears DO, 'Public Opinion and Political Action' in G Lindzey and E Aronson (eds), *The Handbook of Social Psychology* (3rd edn, Random House 1985) vol 2.

Knop K *Diversity and Self-Determination in International Law* (Cambridge University Press 2002).

Kobach K, *The Referendum: Direct Democracy in Switzerland* (Dartmouth Publishing 1993).

—— 'Lessons Learned in the Participation Game' in A Auer and M Bützer (eds), *Direct Democracy: The Eastern and Central European Experience* (Ashgate 2001).

Koenig-Archibugi M, 'Transnational Corporations and Public Accountability' (2004) 39(2) Government and Opposition 1.

Kofos E, 'The Two-Headed Albanian Question' in T Veremis and E Kofos (eds), *Kosovo: Avoiding Another Balkan War* (ELIAMEP 1998).

Koskenniemi M, 'National Self-Determination Today: Problems of Legal Theory and Practice' (1994) 43 ICLQ 241.

Kriesi H, *Citoyenneté et démocratie directe* (Seismo 1993).

Kumbaro D, *The Kosovo Crisis in an International Law Perspective: Self-Determination, Territorial Integrity and the NATO Intervention* (Final Report, NATO Office of Information and Press 2001).

Kymlicka W, *Multicultural Citizenship* (Oxford University Press 1995).

Lang A, 'But Is It for Real? The British Columbia Citizens' Assembly as a Model of State-Sponsored Citizen Empowerment' (2007) 35 Politics & Society 35.

Lansing R, *The Peace Negotiations. A Personal Narrative* (Constable and Company 1921).

Laponce JA, 'National Self-Determination and Referendums: The Case for Territorial Revisionism' (2001) 7(2) Nationalism and Ethnic Politics 33.

—— 'Turning Votes into Territories: Boundary Referendums in Theory and Practice' (2004) 23 Political Geography 169.

LeDuc L, 'Opinion Change and Voting Behaviour in Referendums' (2002) European J Political Research 711.

—— *The Politics of Direct Democracy: Referendums in Global Perspective* (Broadview Press 2003).

—— 'Electoral Reform and Direct Democracy in Canada: When Citizens Become Involved' (2011) 34 West European Politics 551.

Leib EJ, *Deliberative Democracy in America: A Proposal for a Popular Branch of Government* (Penn State University Press 2004).

Levinson S, *Our Undemocratic Constitution: Where the Constitution Goes Wrong (and How We the People Can Correct It)* (Oxford University Press 2006).

Leydet D, 'Compromise and Public Debate in Processes of Constitutional Reform: The Canadian Case' (2004) 43 Social Science Information 233.

Lijphart A, *Democracy in Plural Societies: A Comparative Exploration* (Yale University Press 1977).

Lijphart A, *Democracies: Patterns of Majoritarian and Consensus Government in Twenty-One Countries* (Yale University Press 1984).

—— 'Prospects for Power Sharing in the New South Africa' in A Reynolds (ed), *Election '94 South Africa: An Analysis of the Results, Campaign and Future Prospects* (St Martin's 1994).

Lindahl H, 'Constituent Power and Reflexive Identity: Towards an Ontology of Collective Selfhood' in M Loughlin and N Walker (eds), *The Paradox of Constitutionalism* (Oxford University Press 2007).

—— 'Recognition as Domination: Constitutionalism, Reciprocity and the Problem of Singularity' in N Walker, J Shaw, and S Tierney (eds), *Europe's Constitutional Mosaic* (Hart Publishing 2011).

Lopandic D and Bajic V, *Serbia and Montenegro on the Road to the EU* (Friedrich Ebert Stiftung 2003).

Loughlin M, *The Idea of Public Law* (Oxford University Press 2003).

—— 'Constitutional Theory: A 25th Anniversary Essay' (2005) 25 OJLS 183.

—— 'Towards a Republican Revival?' (2006) 26 OJLS 425.

—— *Foundations of Public Law* (Oxford University Press 2010).

—— and Walker N (eds), *The Paradox of Constitutionalism* (Oxford University Press 2007).

Lukashuk A, 'Constitutionalism in Belarus: A False Start' in J Zielonka (ed), *Democratic Consolidation in Eastern Europe* (Oxford University Press 2001) vol I.

Lukic R, 'The Painful Birth of the New State—"Union of Serbia and Montenegro"' (Southeastern Europe: Moving Forward conference, Ottawa, 23–24 January 2003).

Lupia A and Johnston R, 'Are Voters to Blame? Voter Competence and Elite Manoeuvres in Referendums' in M Mendelsohn and A Parkin (eds), *Referendum Democracy: Citizens, Elites, and Deliberation in Referendum Campaigns* (Palgrave 2001).

Luskin RC, Fishkin JS, McAllister I, Higley J, and Ryan P, 'Information Effects in Referendum Voting: Evidence from the Australian Deliberative Poll' (Annual Meeting of the American Political Science Association, Washington DC, 31 August–3 September 2000).

Lyons M, *Napoleon Bonaparte and the Legacy of the French Revolution* (Macmillan Press 1994).

Mack Smith D, *Italy: A Modern History* (University of Michigan Press 1969).

Maclellan N, 'Voters Say Yes to Noumea Accords', *Islands Business* (Suva, December 1998).

—— 'From Eloi to Europe: Interactions with the Ballot Box in New Caledonia' (2005) 43 Commonwealth & Comparative Politics 394.

Madison J, 'No 10: The Union as a Safeguard against Domestic Faction and Insurrection (continued)', *The Federalist Papers* (New York, 18 January 1788) no 10.

—— 'No 40: On the Powers of the Convention to Form a Mixed Government Examined and Sustained', *The Federalist Papers* (New York, 18 January 1788) no 40.

Mahony H, 'France Warns Ireland on EU Treaty "No" vote', *EUObserver.com* (10 June 2008) <http://euobserver.com/9/26299/?rk=1> accessed 25 July 2011.

Mair R, 'Nisga'a Treaty Must Go to Referendum', *Vancouver Courier* (Vancouver, 26 August 1998) 9.

Mansbridge J, 'Using Power/Fighting Power: The Polity' in S Benhabib (ed), *Democracy and Difference: Contesting the Boundaries of the Political* (Princeton University Press 1996).

—— Bohman J, Chambers S, Estlund D, Føllesdal A, Fung A, Lafont C, Manin B, and Martí JL, 'The Place of Self-Interest and the Role of Power in Deliberative Democracy' (2010) 18 J Political Philosophy 64.

Marquis P, 'Referendums in Canada: The Effect of Populist Decision-Making on Representative Democracy' (Government of Canada, Political and Social Affairs Division 1993).

Marrani D, 'Principle of Indivisibility of the French Republic and the People's Right to Self-Determination: The "New Caledonia Test"' (2006) 2 J Academic Legal Studies 16.

Marshall J, 'Membership of UK Political Parties' (House of Commons Library paper, 17 August 2009) <http://www.parliament.uk/documents/commons/lib/research/briefings/snsg-05125.pdf> accessed 12 July 2011.

Marthaler S, 'The French Referendum on Ratification of the Constitutional Treaty', Referendum Briefing Paper No 12, European Parties Elections and Referendums Network, 29 May 2005.

Matsusaka JG and McCarty NM, 'Political Resource Allocation: Benefits and Costs of Voter Initiatives' (2001) 17 J Law, Economics and Organization 413.

Mattern J, *The Employment of the Plebiscite in the Determination of Sovereignty* (Johns Hopkins University Press 1920).

Mayall J, *Nationalism and International Society* (Cambridge University Press 1990).

McCall C and Williamson A, 'Governance and Democracy in Northern Ireland: The Role of the Community and Voluntary Sector after the Agreement' (2001) 14 Governance: Int'l J of Policy and Administration 363.

McCrudden C, 'Mainstreaming Equality in the Governance of Northern Ireland' (1999) 22 Fordham Int'l LJ 1696.

McDonald H, 'Martin McGuinness Condemns Real IRA's Derry Bomb', *The Guardian* (London, 5 October 2010).

McDonald ML and Roche D, 'Head to Head: Is the Second Referendum on Lisbon an Abuse of Democracy?', *Irish Times* (Dublin, 22 December 2008).

McEvoy K and Morison J, 'Beyond the "Constitutional Moment": Law, Transition and Peacemaking in Northern Ireland' (2003) 26 Fordham Int'l LJ 960.

McGann A, *The Logic of Democracy: Reconciling Equality, Deliberation, and Minority Protection* (University of Michigan Press 2006).

McGarry J and O'Leary B, *The Northern Ireland Conflict: Consociational Engagements* (Oxford University Press 2004).

—— and —— 'Consociational Theory, Northern Ireland's Conflict, and its Agreement. Part 1: What Consociationalists Can Learn from Northern Ireland' (2006) 41 Government and Opposition 43.

Mendelsohn M and Cutler F, 'The Effects of Referenda on Democratic Citizens: Information, Politicization, Efficacy and Tolerance' (2000) 30 British J Political Science 669–98.

—— and Parkin A, 'Introduction: Referendum Democracy' in M Mendelsohn and A Parkin (eds), *Referendum Democracy: Citizens, Elites, and Deliberation in Referendum Campaigns* (Palgrave 2001).

—— and —— (eds), *Referendum Democracy: Citizens, Elites, and Deliberation in Referendum Campaigns* (Palgrave 2001).

Mendes CH, 'Deliberative Performance of Constitutional Courts', PhD thesis (University of Edinburgh 2011).

Mendez F, Mendez M, and Triga V, 'Direct Democracy in the European Union: How Comparative Federalism can Help us Understand the Interplay of Direct Democracy and European Integration' (2009) 29 Revista de ciencia política 57.

Merkel W, 'Institutions and Democratic Consolidation in East Central Europe' (1996) Instituto Juan March de Estudios e Investigationes Estudio/Working Paper 86 <http://www.march.es/ceacs/ingles/publicaciones/working/archivos/1996_86.pdf> accessed 23 July 2011.

van der Merwe R and Meehan A, 'Direct Democracy Catalysed by Resident-to-Resident Online Deliberation' (2011) 6847 Lecture Notes in Computer Science 169.

Mill JS, *Considerations on Representative Government* ([1862] Prometheus Books 1991).

Miller D, 'Deliberative Democracy and Social Choice' in D Held (ed), *Prospects for Democracy* (Stanford University Press 1993).

—— *Citizenship and National Identity* (Polity Press 2000).

Milner H, 'Electoral Reform and Deliberative Democracy in British Columbia' (2005) 94 National Civic Rev 3.

Mittelman JH, *The Globalization Syndrome: Transformation and Resistance* (Princeton University Press 2000).

Monahan PJ, 'Doing the Rules: An Assessment of the Federal Clarity Act in Light of the Quebec Secession Reference' (2000) 135 CD Howe Institute Commentary 1.

Moore M, *Ethics of Nationalism* (Oxford University Press 2001).

Morel L, 'France: Towards a Less Controversial Use of the Referendum' in M Gallagher and PV Uleri (eds), *The Referendum Experience in Europe* (Macmillan Press 1996).

—— 'The Rise of Government-Initiated Referendums in Consolidated Democracies' in M Mendelsohn and A Parkin (eds), *Referendum Democracy: Citizens, Elites, and Deliberation in Referendum Campaigns* (Palgrave 2001).

Mouffe C, 'Deliberative Democracy or Agonistic Pluralism?' (1999) 66 Social Research 745.

—— *The Democratic Paradox* (Verso 2000).

Mueller DC, *Constitutional Democracy* (Oxford University Press 1996).

Mueller J, 'Democracy and Ralph's Pretty Good Grocery: Elections, Equality, and the Minimal Human Being' (1992) 36 Am J Political Science 983.

Muiznieks NR, 'The Influence of the Baltic Popular Movements on the Process of Soviet Disintegration' (1995) 47 Europe–Asia Studies 3.

Murkens JE, Jones P, and Keating M, *Scottish Independence: A Practical Guide* (Edinburgh University Press 2002).

Neustadt RE, *Presidential Power and the Modern President: The Politics of Leadership* (Macmillan Press 1960).

Nevitte N, *The Decline of Deference: Canadian Value Change in Cross-National Perspective* (University of Toronto Press 1996).

Newman WJ, *The Quebec Secession Reference: The Rule of Law and the Position of the Attorney General of Canada* (York University Press 1999).

Nino CS, *The Constitution of Deliberative Democracy* (Yale University Press 1996).

Nørgaard O and Johannsen L with Skak M and Hauge Sørensen, *The Baltic States after Independence* (Edward Elgar 1996).

O'Brennan J, 'Ireland says No (Again): The 12 June 2008 Referendum on the Lisbon Treaty' (2009) 62 Parliamentary Affairs 258.

O'Flynn I, *Deliberative Democracy and Divided Societies* (Edinburgh University Press 2006).

O'Neill S, 'Mutual Recognition and the Accommodation of National Diversity: Constitutional Justice in Northern Ireland' in AG Gagnon and J Tully (eds), *Multinational Democracies* (Cambridge University Press 2001).

Oklopcic Z, 'Populus Interruptus: Self-Determination, Independence of Kosovo and the Vocabulary of Peoplehood' (2009) 22 Leiden J Int'l L 677.

—— 'The Migrating Spirit of the Secession Reference in Southeastern Europe' (2011) 24 Canadian J Law and Jurisprudence 347.

Organization for Security and Co-operation in Europe/Office for Democratic Institutions and Human Rights (OSCE/ODIHR), 'Assessment of the Referendum Law, Republic of Montenegro, Federal Republic of Yugoslavia' (Warsaw, 6 July 2001).

—— 'Comments on the Draft "Referendum Law on the State Status of the Republic of Montenegro" Federal Republic of Yugoslavia' (Warsaw, 5 November 2001).

—— 'Republic of Montenegro—Serbia and Montenegro Referendum, 21 May 2006—Needs Assessment Mission Report, 7–9 March 2006' (Warsaw, 14 March 2006).

—— 'Republic of Montenegro, Referendum on State-Status' (Warsaw, 21 May 2006).

—— 'Statement of Preliminary Findings and Conclusions—Referendum on State-Status, Republic of Montenegro (Serbia and Montenegro)—International Referendum Observation Mission, 21 May 2006' (Podgorica, 22 May 2006).

—— 'Referendum Observation Mission, Final Report' (Warsaw, 4 August 2006).

Parekh B, 'Defining National Identity' in E Mortimer with R Fine (eds), *People, Nation and State: The Meaning of Ethnicity and Nationalism* (IB Tauris 1999).

Parkinson J, 'Legitimacy Problems in Deliberative Democracy' (2003) 51 Political Studies 180.

—— *Deliberating in the Real World: Problems of Legitimacy in Deliberative Democracy* (Oxford University Press 2006).

—— 'Beyond "Technique": The Role of Referendums in the Deliberative System' (Referendums and Deliberative Democracy workshop, University of Edinburgh, 8 May 2009).

Patmore G, 'Choosing the Republic: The Legal and Constitutional Steps in Australia and Canada' (2006) 31 Queen's LJ 770.

Peach I, 'The Death of Deference: The Implications of the Defeat of the Meech Lake and Charlottetown Accords for Executive Federalism in Canada' in S Tierney (ed), *Multiculturalism and the Canadian Constitution* (UBC Press 2007).

Pericles' Funeral Oration: Thucydides (c 460/455–c 399 BC), Peloponnesian War, Book 2.34–46.
Petithomme M, 'Awakening the Sleeping Giant? The Displacement of the Partisan Cleavage and Change in Government-Opposition Dynamics in EU Referendums' (2011) 12 Perspectives on European Politics and Society 89.
Pettai V, 'Estonia: Positive and Negative Institutional Engineering' in J Zielonka (ed), *Democratic Consolidation in Eastern Europe* (Oxford University Press 2001) vol I.
Pettit P, *Republicanism: A Theory of Freedom and Government* (Oxford University Press 1997).
Pilon D, 'The 2005 and 2009 Referenda on Voting System Change in British Columbia' (2010) 4(2–3) Canadian Political Science Rev 73.
Pocock JGA, *The Machiavellian Moment: Florentine Political Thought and the Atlantic Republican Tradition* (Princeton University Press 1975).
Polborn MK and Willmann G, 'Referendum Timing' (2004) SSRN Working Paper No 527548 <http://ssrn.com/abstract=527548> accessed 14 July 2011.
Pope JG, 'Republican Moments: The Role of Direct Popular Power in the American Constitutional Order' (1990) 139 U Penn L Rev 287.
Posner RA, *Law, Pragmatism, and Democracy* (Harvard University Press 2003).
Price L, *Where Power Lies: Prime Ministers v The Media* (Simon & Schuster 2010).
Przeworski A, 'Deliberation and Ideological Domination' in J Elster (ed), *Deliberative Democracy* (Cambridge University Press 1998).
Puddington A, 'Estonia' in Freedom House, *Freedom in the World: The Annual Survey of Political Rights and Civil Liberties* (Rowman & Littlefield 2007).
Quesnel J and Winn C, 'The Nisga'a Treaty. Self Government and Good Governance: The Jury Is Still Out' (2011) Frontier Centre for Public Policy Series No 108.
Qvortrup Matt, 'Are Referendums Controlled and Pro-hegemonic?' (2000) 48 Political Studies 821.
—— *A Comparative Study of Referendums: Government by the People* (2nd edn, Manchester University Press 2005).
—— 'The Three Referendums on the European Constitution Treaty 2005' (2006) 77 Political Quarterly 89.
—— 'Rebels without a Cause? The Irish Referendum on the Lisbon Treaty' (2009) 80 Political Quarterly 59.
Rahe PA, *Republics Ancient and Modern: Classical Republicanism and the American Revolution* (University of North Carolina Press 1992).
Ratner RS, 'British Columbia's Citizens' Assembly: The Learning Phase' (2004) 27(2) Canadian Parliamentary Rev 20.
—— 'Communicative Rationality in the Citizens' Assembly and Referendum Processes' in ME Warren and H Pearse (eds), *Designing Deliberative Democracy: The British Columbia Citizens' Assembly* (Cambridge University Press 2008).
Rawls J, *A Theory of Justice* (Harvard University Press 1971).
—— *Political Liberalism* (Columbia University Press 1993).
—— *Political Liberalism* (2nd edn, Columbia University Press 1996).
—— 'The Idea of Public Reason Revisited' (1997) 64 U Chic L Rev 765.
—— *The Law of Peoples* (Harvard University Press 1999).

—— *Political Liberalism* (expanded edn, Columbia University Press, 2005).
Redmond R, *The Right Wing of France: From 1815 to de Gaulle* (James M Laux tr, University of Philadelphia Press 1968).
Reif K and Schmitt H, 'Nine Second-Order National Elections: A Conceptual Framework for the Analysis of European Election Results' (1980) 8 European J Political Research 3.
Renwick A, 'The Role of Non-Elite Forces in Hungary's Negotiated Revolution' in A Bozoki (ed), *The Roundtable Talks of 1989: The Genesis of Hungarian Democracy* (Central European University Press 2002).
Requejo F, 'Democratic Legitimacy and National Pluralism' in F Requejo (ed), *Democracy and National Pluralism* (Routledge 2001).
—— 'Liberal Democracy's Timber is Still Too Straight: The Case of Political Models for Coexistence in Composite States' in N Walker, J Shaw, and S Tierney (eds), *Europe's Constitutional Mosaic* (Hart Publishing 2011).
—— and Sanjaume Calvet M, 'Secession and Liberal Democracy: The Case of the Basque Country' (2009) Universitat Pompeu Fabra Political Theory Working Paper No 7 <http://www.recercat.net/bitstream/2072/43036/1/GRTPwp7.pdf> accessed 21 October 2011.
Ribicic C, 'Slovenian Experiences in the Preparation and Administration of Referendum and Gaining Independence' in S Elezovic (ed), *Legal Aspects for Referendum in Montenegro in the Context of International Law and Practice* (Foundation Open Society Institute-Representative Office Montenegro 2005).
Rich R, 'Recognition of States: The Collapse of Yugoslavia and the Soviet Union' (1993) 4 European J Int'l L 36.
Richard A and Pabst B, 'Evaluation of the French Referendum on the EU Constitution' (*Democracy International*, May 2005) <http://www.democracy-international.org/fileadmin/di/pdf/monitoring/di-francc.pdf>.
Richter M, 'Toward a Concept of Political Illegitimacy: Bonapartist Dictatorship and Democratic Legitimacy' (1982) 10 Political Theory 185.
Rigo Suredi A, *The Evolution of the Right of Self-Determination: A Study of United Nations Practice* (AW Sijthoff 1973).
Roberts-Thomson P, 'EU Treaty Referendums and the European Union' (2001) 23 J European Integration 105.
Rodin S, 'Croatia' in A Auer and M Bützer (eds), *Direct Democracy: The Eastern and Central European Experience* (Ashgate 2001).
Romney P, *Getting it Wrong: How Canadians Forgot Their Past and Imperilled Confederation* (Toronto University Press 1999).
Rosenberg S (ed), *Deliberation, Participation and Democracy: Can the People Govern?* (Palgrave Macmillan 2007).
Rosenfeld M, *The Identity of the Constitutional Subject: Selfhood, Citizenship, Culture and Community* (Routledge 2010).
Rourke JT, Hiskes RP, and Zirakzadeh CE, *Direct Democracy and International Politics: Deciding International Issues Through Referendums* (Lynne Rienner Publishers 1992).

Rousseau J-J, *The Social Contract and Discourses*, Book III (GDH Cole tr, Everyman 1973).

Rowbottom J, *Democracy Distorted: Wealth, Influence and Democratic Politics* (Cambridge University Press 2010).

Rudalevige A, *The New Imperial Presidency: Renewing Presidential Power after Watergate* (University of Michigan Press 2005).

Rudrakumaran V, 'The "Requirement" of Plebiscite in Territorial Rapprochement' (1989) 12 Houston J Int'l L 23.

Ruin O, 'Sweden: The Referendum as an Instrument for Defusing Political Issues' in M Gallagher and PV Uleri (eds), *The Referendum Experience in Europe* (Macmillan Press 1996).

Rumley D, 'The French Geopolitical Project in New Caledonia' in D Rumley, VL Forbes, and C Griffin (eds), *Australia's Arc of Instability: The Political and Cultural Dynamics of Regional Security* (Springer 2006).

Russell PH, *Constitutional Odyssey: Can Canadians Become a Sovereign People?* (2nd edn, Toronto University Press 1993).

Ruus J, 'Estonia' in A Auer and M Bützer (eds), *Direct Democracy: The Eastern and Central European Experience* (Ashgate 2001).

Sanders LM, 'Against Deliberation' (1997) 25 Political Theory 347.

Sartori G, *The Theory of Democracy Revisited* (Chatham House 1987).

Saward M, 'Enacting Democracy' (2003) 51 Political Studies 161.

Schneider G and Weitsman PA, 'The Punishment Trap: Integration Referendums as Popularity Contests' (1996) 28 Comparative Political Studies 582.

Schuck ART and de Vreese CH, 'The Dutch No to the EU Constitution: Assessing the Role of EU Skepticism and the Campaign' (2008) 18 J Elections, Public Opinion & Parties 101.

Scottish Government, *Your Scotland, Your Voice: A National Conversation* (The Scottish Government 2009).

—— *Scotland's Future: Draft Referendum (Scotland) Bill Consultation Paper* (The Scottish Government 2010).

Setälä M, *Referendums and Democratic Government. Normative Theory and the Analysis of Institutions* (Macmillan Press 1999).

—— 'On the Problems of Responsibility and Accountability in Referendums' (2006) 45 European J Political Research 699.

Shapiro I, 'Optimal Deliberation?' (2002) 10 J Political Philosophy 196.

Shennan A, *De Gaulle* (Longman 1993).

Shu M, 'Referendums and the Political Constitutionalisation of the EU' (2008) 14 European LJ 423.

Silber L and Little A, *The Death of Yugoslavia* (BBC 1996).

Simeon R, 'The Referendum Experience in Canada' (Referendums and Deliberative Democracy workshop, University of Edinburgh, 8 May 2009).

Simpson A (ed), *Referendums: Constitutional and Political Perspectives* (Victoria University of Wellington 1992).

Simpson G, *Great Powers and Outlaw States: Unequal Sovereigns in the International Legal Order* (Cambridge Studies in International and Comparative Law, Cambridge University Press 2004).

Sinnott R, 'Cleavages, Parties and Referendums: Relationships between Representative and Direct Democracy in the Republic of Ireland' (2002) 41 European J Political Research 811.

—— 'Attitudes and Behaviour of the Irish Electorate in the Referendum on the Treaty of Nice' (2003) University College Dublin Working Papers <http://www.ucd.ie/dempart/workingpapers/nice2.pdf> accessed 18 July 2011.

Skocpol T, *Diminished Democracy: From Membership to Management in American Civic Life* (University of Oklahoma Press 2003).

Smith DA, *Tax Crusaders and the Politics of Direct Democracy* (Routledge 1998).

Smith G, 'The Functional Properties of the Referendum' (1976) 4 European J Political Research 1.

—— and Wales C, 'Citizens' Juries and Deliberative Democracy' (2000) 48 Political Studies 51.

Snider JH, 'Designing Deliberative Democracy: The British Columbia Citizens' Assembly' (2008) 4 J Public Deliberation 1.

Sprudzs A, 'Rebuilding Democracy in Latvia: Overcoming a Dual Legacy' in J Zielonka (ed), *Democratic Consolidation in Eastern Europe* (Oxford University Press 2001).

Staar F, 'Elections in Communist Poland' (1958) 2 Midwest J Political Science 200.

Steininger R, *Austria, Germany, and the Cold War: From the Anschluss to the State Treaty* (Bergahn Books 2008).

Stone A, *The Birth of Judicial Politics in France: The Constitutional Council in Comparative Perspective* (Oxford University Press 1992).

Stratmann T, 'Is Spending More Potent For or Against a Proposition? Evidence From Ballot Measures' (2006) 50 Am J Political Science 788.

—— 'Campaign Spending and Ballot Measures' in K Gilland Lutz and S Hug (eds), *Financing Referendum Campaigns* (Palgrave Macmillan 2009).

—— 'The Role of Money in Ballot Initiatives' in K Gilland Lutz and S Hug (eds), *Financing Referendum Campaigns* (Palgrave Macmillan 2009).

Sudbery I, 'Bridging the Legitimacy Gap in the EU: Can Civil Society Help to Bring the Union Closer to Its Citizens?' (2003) 26 Collegium 75.

Sunstein CR, 'Beyond the Republican Revival' (1988) 97 Yale LJ 1539.

—— 'The Law of Group Polarization' (2002) 10 J Political Philosophy 175.

Surroi V, 'Kosova and the Constitutional Solutions' in T Veremis and E Kofos (eds), *Kosovo: Avoiding Another Balkan War* (ELIAMEP 1998).

Suski M, *Bringing in the People: A Comparison of Constitutional Forms and Practices of the Referendum* (Kluwer 1993).

Svensson P, 'Denmark, The Referendum as Minority Protection' in M Gallagher and PV Uleri (eds), *The Referendum Experience in Europe* (Macmillan Press 1996).

—— 'Five Danish Referendums on the European Community and European Union: A Critical Assessment of the Franklin Thesis' (2002) 41 European J Political Research 733.

Szczerbiak A and Taggart PA (eds), *EU Enlargement and Referendums* (Routledge 2005).

Szporluk R, *Russia, Ukraine, and the Breakup of the Soviet Union* (Hoover Institution Press 2000).

Taggart P, 'Questions of Europe—The Domestic Politics of the 2005 French and Dutch Referendums and their Challenge for the Study of European Integration' (2006) 44 J Common Market Studies Annual Rev 7.

Tancredi A, 'A Normative "Due Process" in the Creation of States through Secession' in MG Kohen (ed), *Secession: International Law Perspectives* (Cambridge University Press 2006).

Taylor R, 'Consociation or Social Transformation' in J McGarry (ed), *Northern Ireland and the Divided World* (Oxford University Press 2001).

Thompson D, 'Who Should Govern Who Governs? The Role of Citizens in Reforming the Electoral System' in ME Warren and H Pearse (eds), *Designing Deliberative Democracy: The British Columbia Citizens' Assembly* (Cambridge University Press 2008).

Tierney S, *Constitutional Law and National Pluralism* (Oxford University Press 2004).

—— 'The Constitutional Accommodation of National Minorities in the UK and Canada: Judicial Approaches to Diversity' in A-G Gagnon, M Guibernau, and F Rocher (eds), *Conditions of Diversity in Multinational Democracies* (Institute for Research on Public Policy 2004).

—— 'Reframing Sovereignty: Sub-State National Societies and Contemporary Challenges to the Nation-State' (2005) 54 ICLQ 161.

—— 'Crystallising Dominance: Majority Nationalism, Constitutionalism and the Courts' in A Gagnon, A Lecours, and G Nootens (eds), *Dominant Nationalisms* (University of Montreal Press 2008).

—— 'Constitutional Referendums: A Theoretical Enquiry' (2009) 72 Modern L Rev 360.

—— 'The Long Intervention in Kosovo: A Self-determination Imperative?' in J Summers (ed), *The Kosovo Precedent: Implications for Statehood, Self-determination and Minority Rights* (Brill 2011).

Tocci N, 'EU Intervention in Ethno-political Conflicts: The Cases of Cyprus and Serbia-Montenegro' (2004) 9 European Foreign Affairs Rev 551.

Tomkins A, *The Constitution After Scott: Government Unwrapped* (Clarendon Press 1998).

—— 'What is Parliament For?' in N Bamforth and P Leyland (eds), *Public Law in a Multi-Layered Constitution* (Hart Publishing 2003).

—— *Our Republican Constitution* (Hart Publishing 2005).

Topf R, 'Electoral Participation' in H Klingemann and D Fuchs (eds), *Citizens and the State* (Oxford University Press 1995).

Tracy K, *Challenges of Ordinary Democracy: A Case Study in Deliberation and Dissent* (Penn State University Press 2010).

Traynor I and Watt N, 'Lisbon Treaty: Pressure on Ireland for Second Vote', *The Guardian* (London, 19 June 2008) <http://www.guardian.co.uk/world/2008/jun/19/lisbon.ireland> accessed 21 October 2011.

Trechsel AH and Sciarini P, 'Direct Democracy in Switzerland: Do Elites Matter?' (1998) 33 European J Political Research 99.

Trench A, 'Introduction: The Second Phase of Devolution' in A Trench (ed), *The State of the Nations 2008* (Imprint Academic 2008).

Troitsky N, '20 Years Without the Soviet Union', *Baltic Review* (Vilnius, 27 March 2011) <http://baltic-review.com/2011/03/20-years-without-the-soviet-union/> accessed 21 October 2011.

Tsagourias N, 'International Community, Recognition of States and Political Cloning' in C Warbrick and S Tierney (eds), *Towards an International Legal Community?: The Sovereignty of States and the Sovereignty of International Law* (British Institute of International and Comparative Law 2006).

Tully J, 'Diversity's Gambit Declined' in C Cook (ed), *Constitutional Predicament: Canada after the Referendum of 1992* (McGill-Queen's University Press 1994).

—— *Strange Multiplicity: Constitutionalism in an Age of Diversity* (Cambridge University Press 1995).

—— 'Struggles over Recognition and Distribution' (2000) 7 Constellations 469.

—— 'A New Kind of Europe? Democratic Integration in the European Union' (2007) 10 Critical Rev of Int'l Social and Political Philosophy 71.

—— *Democracy and Civic Freedom, Volume I of Public Philosophy in a New Key* (Cambridge University Press 2008).

Uhr J, 'The Constitutional Convention and Deliberative Democracy' (1998) 21 U New South Wales LJ 875.

Uleri PV, 'Introduction' in M Gallagher and PV Uleri (eds), *The Referendum Experience in Europe* (Macmillan Press 1996).

—— 'On Referendum Voting in Italy: YES, NO or Non-vote? How Italian Parties Learned to Control Referendums' (2002) 41 European J Political Research 863.

UNCHR, 'Special Report on Minorities by Special Rapporteur Elisabeth Rehn, Situation of Human Rights in the Territory of the Former Yugoslavia' (1996), UN Doc E/CN.4/1997/8.

Unger RM, *What Should Legal Analysis Become?* (Verso 1996).

Valadez JM, *Deliberative Democracy, Political Legitimacy, and Self-Determination in Multicultural Societies* (Westview Press 2001).

van der Eijk C and Franklin M, 'Potential for Contestation on European Matters at National Elections in Europe' in G Marks and M Steenbergen (eds), *European Integration and Political Conflict* (Cambridge University Press 2004).

Venice Commission (European Commission for Democracy Through Law), *Guidelines for Constitutional Referendums at National Level* (11 July 2001), COE Doc CDL-INF(2001)10.

—— 'Interim Report on the Constitutional Situation of the Federal Republic of Yugoslavia' (26 October 2001), COE Doc CDL-INF(2001)23.

—— 'Opinion on the Compatibility of the Existing Legislation in Montenegro Concerning the Organisation of Referendums with Applicable International Standards' (19 December 2005), COE Doc CDL-AD(2005)041.

—— 'Code of Good Practice on Referendums' Study No 371/2006 (20 January 2009), COE Doc CDL-AD(2007)008rev.

Vickers M, *Between Serb and Albanian: A History of Kosovo* (Columbia University Press 1998).

Walker MC, *The Strategic Use of Referendums: Power, Legitimacy, and Democracy* (Palgrave Macmillan 2003).

Walker N, 'Taking Constitutionalism Beyond the State' (2008) 56 Political Studies 519.

Walker N, 'Out of Place and Out of Time: Law's Fading Co-ordinates' (2010) 14 Edinburgh L Rev 13.

—— Shaw J, and Tierney S (eds), *Europe's Constitutional Mosaic* (Hart Publishing 2011).

Walzer M, 'Deliberation, and What Else?' in S Macedo (ed), *Deliberative Politics: Essays on 'Democracy and Disagreement'* (Oxford University Press 1999).

—— 'Equality and Civil Society' in W Kymlicka and S Chambers (eds), *Alternative Conceptions of Civil Society* (Princeton University Press 2002).

—— *Politics and Passion: Toward a More Egalitarian Liberalism* (Yale University Press 2004).

Wambaugh S, *A Monograph on Plebiscites: With a Collection of Official Documents* (Oxford University Press 1920).

—— *Plebiscites Since the World War* (Carnegie Endowment for International Peace 1933).

Warbrick C and Tierney S (eds), *Towards an International Legal Community?: The Sovereignty of States and the Sovereignty of International Law* (British Institute of International and Comparative Law 2006).

Ward I, 'The British Columbia Citizens' Assembly on Electoral Reform. An Experiment in Political Communication' (Australasian Political Studies Association conference, University of Newcastle, 25–27 September 2006) <http://www.newcastle.edu.au/Resources/Schools/Newcastle%20Business%20School/APSA/PUBPOLICY/Ward-Ian.pdf> accessed 23 July 2011.

Warhurst J, 'From Constitutional Convention to Republic Referendum: A Guide to the Processes, the Issues and the Participants' (1998–99) Parliament of Australia, Parliamentary Library Research Paper 25 <http://www.aph.gov.au/library/pubs/rp/1998-99/99rp25.htm> accessed 22 July 2011.

Warren ME and Pearse H (eds), *Designing Deliberative Democracy: The British Columbia Citizens' Assembly* (Cambridge University Press 2008).

—— and —— 'Introduction: Democratic Renewal and Deliberative Democracy' in ME Warren and H Pearse (eds), *Designing Deliberative Democracy: The British Columbia Citizens' Assembly* (Cambridge University Press 2008).

Waterfield B, 'EU Intervention in Irish Referendum "Unlawful"', *The Telegraph* (London, 29 September 2009) <http://www.telegraph.co.uk/news/worldnews/europe/eu/6239933/EU-intervention-in-Irish-referendum-unlawful.html> accessed 10 October 2011.

—— 'EU Steps Up Pressure on Ireland to Hold Second Lisbon Treaty Referendum', *The Telegraph* (London, 10 October 2008) <http://www.telegraph.co.uk/news/newstopics/eureferendum/3173967/EU-steps-up-pressure-on-Ireland-to-hold-second-Lisbon-Treaty-referendum.html> accessed 10 October 2011.

Weill R, 'Dicey was not Diceyan' (2003) 62 CLJ 474.

Weller M, 'The Rambouillet Conference on Kosovo' (1999) 75 Int'l Affairs 211.

White S, *Communism and its Collapse* (Routledge 2001).

—— and Hill RJ, 'Russia, the Former Soviet Union and Eastern Europe: The Referendum as a Flexible Political Instrument' in M Gallagher and PV Uleri (eds), *The Referendum Experience in Europe* (Macmillan Press 1996).

Williams MS, 'The Uneasy Alliance of Group Representation and Deliberative Democracy' in W Kymlicka and W Norman (eds), *Citizenship in Diverse Societies* (Oxford University Press 2000).

Woodhouse D, 'Individual Ministerial Responsibility and a "Dash of Principle"' in D Butler, V Bogdanor, and R Simmons (eds), *The Law, Politics and the Constitution: Essays in Honour of Geoffrey Marshall* (Oxford University Press 1999).

Woods J, 'The Civic Forum' in R Wilson (ed), *Agreeing to Disagree: A Guide to The Northern Ireland Assembly* (The Stationery Office 2001).

Woodward SL, *Balkan Tragedy: Chaos and Dissolution after the Cold War* (The Brookings Institution 1995).

Wright V, 'France' in D Butler and A Ranney (eds), *Referendums: A Comparative Study of Practice and Theory* (American Institute for Public Policy Research 1978).

Young IM, *Inclusion and Democracy* (Oxford University Press 2000).

—— 'Activist Challenges to Deliberative Democracy' in JS Fishkin and P Laslett (eds), *Debating Deliberation Democracy* (Blackwell 2003).

Young RA, *The Struggle for Quebec: From Referendum to Referendum?* (McGill-Queen's University Press 1999).

Zaller J, 'The Statistical Power of Election Studies to Detect Media Exposure Effects in Political Campaigns' (2002) 21 Electoral Studies 297.

Zielonka J (ed), *Democratic Consolidation in Eastern Europe* (Oxford University Press 2001) vol I.

Ziller J, 'French Overseas: New Caledonia and French Polynesia in the Framework of Asymmetrical Federalism and Shared Sovereignty' in J Oliveira and P Cardinal (eds), *One Country, Two Systems, Three Legal Orders—Perspectives of Evolution* (Springer 2009).

Zurcher AJ, 'The Hitler Referenda' (1935) 29 Am Political Science Rev 91.

Index

Australia 108, 270–1
   1999 referendum 121, 122, 210–25
   Australia Constitutional Convention (ACC) 111, 188–210, 233 *see also* Question

Badinter Commission 167–9 *see also* International institutions and referendums
Basque Country 74
Belarus 101
Belgium
   1950 referendum 242–3, 279
Bonapartism 100–3 *see also* Elite Control
Bosnia-Herzegovina
   1992 referendum 7, 72–3, 75, 96, 168–9, 242
British Columbia
   2005 referendum 111, 210–25
   Citizens' Assembly on Electoral Reform (BCCA) 187–210, 233
   Nisga'a Agreement 83

Canada 59, 140–1, 234–7, 238
   1992 Charlottetown referendum 115, 141, 238, 262 *see also* British Columbia, Newfoundland, Ontario, Quebec
Clarity, *see* Question
Consent
   principle of 54–6 *see also* Decision-making
Constituent power 11–15
Constitutional referendums, *see* Referendums
Constitutional theory 2–6
Croatia 73, 167–8
   1991 referendum 71, 237
Council of Europe, *see* Venice Commission

De Gaulle, Charles, *see* France
Decision-making
   referendums and 260–84, 294
   two referendums 266–71 *see also* Thresholds
Decolonization referendums 64–6
Deliberation deficit
   referendums and 27–39

Deliberative democracy 4–5, 42–56, 188–225, 291–4
   deliberative polling 203–10
   distributed deliberation 220
   macro-level deliberation 210–23, 292–4 *see also* Australia, British Columbia
   micro-level deliberation 188–210, 248, 291–2 *see also* Australia, British Columbia
   modes of deliberation 187–8
   popular 192–8, 208–10
   principles of 56–7 *see also* Decision-making, Divided Societies, Equality, Participation, Public Reasoning
Democracy 8–11, 19–21
   direct 11–15
   popular 21, 31–9
   representative 22–57 *see also* Deliberative democracy
Demos, *see* People
Denmark 106
   referendums on EC/EU 7–8, 108–9, 118, 122, 126, 156–7, 161, 239
Divided Societies
   potential for deliberation in 248–59
   referendums in 241–59, 296–8
   thresholds and the consociational referendum 278–82 *see also* Bosnia-Herzegovina, Northern Ireland

East Timor
   1999 referendum 7, 66, 74, 78
Elite Control, *see* Bonapartism, European Union, International institutions and referendums, Referendums, constitutional framework, Referendums, political factors and
Equality
   principle of 52–4
   and Australia (ACC) and British Columbia (BCAA) 203–8
Eritrea
   1993 referendum 78
Estonia 80–1 *see also* Franchise

Index

European Union 15, 154–65
  accession 113
  draft constitutional treaty, *see* France, Ireland, Netherlands
  influencing the referendum process 161–65, 298–9
  Lisbon treaty, *see* Ireland

France 121–22
  2005 referendum on EU draft Constitutional Treaty 10, 158–60, 162–3 *see also* New Caledonia
  nineteenth century plebiscites 62, 100
  referendums under President de Gaulle 114, 131–7, 151, 232
Franchise 59–60, 75–84
  boundaries and restrictions 75–84
  Estonia and Latvia and 80–2
  Montenegro and 78
  New Caledonia and 91–5
  North Schleswig and 78–9
  United Kingdom 76–8
Functional normativity 2–3, 286
Funding and Expenditure 114–16

Germany
  referendums from 1933–1938 101
Globalization 9–10

Habermas, Jurgen 49–50, 53, 139, 151

Initiatives 106–7
International institutions and referendums 166–84, 298–9 *see also* European Union, Venice Commission
International law
  self-determination 61–6 *see also* League of Nations plebiscibes, Venice Commission
Ireland 106, 108
  1998 referendum on Belfast Agreement 251
  referendums on EC/EU 108–9, 157, 158–9, 160–2
Iraq
  2005 referendum 1, 78
Italy 106
  unification plebiscites 62
  referendums under Mussolini 101

Kosovo
  unofficial referendums 170–1
  Rambouillet Accord 169–72

Latvia 81–2 *see also* Franchise
League of Nations plebiscites 62–4, 78–9, 166
Liberalism 20–1
Lijphart, Arend 23, 98, 109, 116, 242, 258

Majority decision-making
  dangers of 39–42
Media coverage 123–4
Montenegro
  2006 referendum 1, 7, 78, 114
  international influence 173–82 *see also* Franchise, Thresholds, Venice Commission

Nationalism and referendums 137–52 *see also* Quebec, Scotland
Netherlands
  2005 referendum on EU draft Constitutional Treaty 7, 158–60
New Caledonia 60, 84–97
  constitutional status 84–6
  referendums and 87–95 *see also* Franchise
Newfoundland
  1948 referendum 269
New Zealand 106
Northern Ireland 114
  1973 referendum 73–4, 96, 242
  1998 referendum on Belfast Agreement 53–4, 238
  deliberative process in 248–59, 281
Norway
  1905 referendum 62

Ontario
  2007 referendum 140–1, 217

Parity of esteem, *see* Equality
Participation 46–7, 185–225
  Australia (ACC) and British Columbia (BCAA) 192–8
  in politics 27–39
  international standards 185–6
  popular 192–8
  principle of 45–7
  public information 214–20 *see also* Divided Societies, Northern Ireland, Referendums
People, The 14, 58–97 *see also* Franchise
Plebiscites, *see* League of Nations plebiscibes
Poland
  1946 referendum 101
Political Parties, Elections and Referendums (UK) Act 2000 108, 233–4
Public reasoning
  principle of 47–52
  and Australia (ACC) and British Columbia (BCAA) 198–203

Quebec 107, 140–5
  1980 referendum 141–2, 267–8
  1995 referendum 123–4, 141–5, 268
  and Secession Reference 143–5, 151–2, 274
  and timing 112 *see also* Question

Question
　clarity 227–41
　　Australia 1999 referendum 229–30, 231
　　Quebec 1995 referendum and Secession Reference 230–1, 234–8
　　UK 1975 referendum on EC membership 231
　　complexity 238–41
　　control of 110–11
　　substance 241–59, 290–2 *see also* Divided Societies

Rawls, John 48–50, 53, 222
Referendums
　constitutional 11–15, 36
　constitutional framework 104–16, 131–7, 289–90
　constitutive 14, 296
　elite control 23–7, 98–128
　history 61–6
　international norm-setting, *see* Venice Commission
　motives of political actors 125–7
　participation 46–7
　political factors and 116–25
　stages of 51–2, 186–7
　timing 111–14 *see also* Decision-making, Equality, Franchise, Funding and Expenditure, Nationalism and referendums, Question, Sovereignty, Thresholds
Representative democracy, *see* Democracy
　strengths and weaknesses 22–57
Republican theory 3–4
　civic/popular republicanism 14–15, 31–9, 45–56, 239
　and deliberation 42–56
　elite 22–57
Romania
　1986 referendum 101
Russia 112, 118

Scotland 140, 145–50
　1979 referendum 126–7, 277–8
　1997 referendum 113, 267
　independence and 145–50, 231, 235–6, 240–1, 268–9
Self-determination, *see* International law
Slovenia
　1991 referendum 71, 237
South Africa
　1992 referendum 82
South Sudan
　2011 referendum 1, 7

Sovereignty
　and referendums 129–52, 163–5
　command and constituent variations 11–15
　constitutional and extra-constitutional referendums 130–7
　external 153–84 *see also* France, Quebec, Scotland
Spain 105
　1986 referendum 229 *see also* Basque Country
Statehood
　referendums and creation of new states 61–75 *see also* International institutions and referendums, Nationalism and referendums
Sweden 112–13

Thresholds 271–8
　Montenegro and 274, 276–8, 283
　Venice Commission recommendations 276, 283 *see also* Divided Societies

United Kingdom 59
　1975 referendum on EC membership 108–9, 115–16, 126, 231
　2011 referendum on AV voting system 145 *see also* Northern Ireland, Question, Scotland, Wales
　constitution 25–6, 300–1
　European Union Act 2011 107–8
USA 30, 106–07, 114–15, 274
USSR 7, 59
　referendums in the republics 67–71
　state-wide referendum 1991 67–9, 228–9

Venice Commission of the Council of Europe
　and international norm-setting 172–3, 228, 276
　and Montenegro 173–82
　see also Thresholds

Wales
　1979 referendum 126–7, 277–8
　1997 referendum 113, 115
　2011 referendum 7
Western Sahara 65–6, 82–3

Young, Iris Marion 34, 53, 255, 257, 264
Yugoslavia, Socialist Federal Republic of 7, 59, 71–3, 167–72, 279–80 *see also* Badinter Commission, Bosnia-Herzegovina, Croatia, International institutions and referendums, Kosovo, Slovenia, Statehood